# C++ Components
# and Algorithms

A comprehensive reference for designing and implementing algorithms in C++

# C++ Components
# and Algorithms

A comprehensive reference for designing and implementing algorithms in C++

Scott Robert Ladd

M&T BOOKS

M&T Books
A Division of M&T Publishing, Inc.
411 Borel Avenue
San Mateo, CA 94402

**Limits of Liability and Disclaimer of Warranty**
The Author and Publisher of this book have used their best efforts in preparing the book and the programs contained in it. These efforts include the development, research, and testing of the theories and programs to determine their effectiveness.

The Author and Publisher make no warranty of any kind, expressed or implied, with regard to these programs or the documentation contained in this book. The Author and Publisher shall not be liable in any event for incidental or consequential damages in connection with, or arising out of, the furnishing, performance, or use of these programs.

**Library of Congress Cataloging-in-Publication Data**

Ladd, Scott.
C++ Components and Algorithms / Scott Robert Ladd.
    p.   cm.
Includes bibliographical references and index.
ISBN 1-55851-227-6
1. C++ (Computer program language)  I. Title.
QA76.73.C153L3   1992
005. 13'3- -dc20                    92-12487
                                             CIP

**Project Editor:** Christine de Chutkowski

**Trademarks:**
All products, names, and services are trademarks or registered trademarks of their respective companies.

**Cover Design:** Lauren Smith Design

   95 94  93  92        4  3  2  1

# Dedication

*This book is dedicated to my wife Maria,*
*who has been a constant source of inspiration, humor, and sanity.*
*Lord knows I need more of the latter.*

# Contents

**xiv**

## PART IV: APPENDICES

# Why This Book is for You

This book is about implementing algorithms and components in C++. It includes more than 15,000 lines of source code, implementing the following tools:

- A complete class library for BTree-indexed files, including insertion, deletion, and searching! No other C or C++ book on the market has as thorough an explanation of this complex but important subject.

- A complete class library for indexing files via hash tables.

- A discussion of persistent objects, with class libraries, implementing sequential files, random-access files, in-memory hash tables, and dynamic binary trees.

- A powerful library of numeric array classes, which support sorting, statistics, and scientific calculations.

- A comprehensive, extended dynamic string handling class.

- More classes: Random number generation, error reporting, and range-checking.

To get the most out of this book, you should understand the basic mechanics of C++, have written some C++ programs, and be interested in examining C++'s use in developing powerful applications. You should have Microsoft C/C++ 7.0 or Borland C++ 3.0 to fully use the code in this book.

# Introduction

Denver, Colorado, is home to the world's sixth largest bookstore, the Tattered Cover. The computer books are on the second floor; they span 50 feet of 10-foot-high shelving. At last count, there were more than fifty books on these shelves with "C++" in their title — two of these carry my byline.

When I began considering another book project, several questions arose. How do I create a book that's different from all the others? How do I avoid repeating what I've already said in my own books? What hasn't been covered? Why should someone spend their hard-earned money for this book?

I buy lots of books. Almost four thousand of them reside on shelves, floors, and tables in my home. The most useful books in my office are those that contain algorithms, code fragments, and information on techniques for optimizing a programming language. So, after some careful consideration, I decided to write a book describing how to use the powerful features of C++ in creating program components and implementing algorithms.

In *C++ Components and Algorithms,* I assume that you are familiar with the rudiments of C++ programming. This is not a tutorial on C++ programming. Stroustrup, Lippman, and others (including myself) have provided more than enough tutorial material on C++. For the purposes of this book, I assume that you know what a virtual function is, what a class definition looks like, and how overloading is done.

The thrust of this book is, as its title states, components and algorithms, implemented in C++, that use the features of C++ to best advantage. Implementing a sorting function or a file library in C++ is (and should be) different from implementing those tools in C (or Pascal, or FORTRAN, or. . .). I think a book (or two, or three. . .) specifically about algorithms in C++ is needed, and that's why I wrote one.

In this book, I implement classes for error handling, strings, arrays, and file handling. Along the way, I discuss algorithms for random-number generation, sorting, basic statistical analysis, tree structures, and file organization.

A note about compilers: At the time of this writing, all of the code in this book compiles and executes correctly with the following C++ compilers for MS-DOS:

> Borland C++, Version 3.0
> Microsoft C/C++, Version 7.0

In the past, I've had trouble with working code ceasing to compile when a vendor comes out with a new compiler version. C++ is still a growing, evolving language and it should be treated with caution. I hope that the vendors mentioned will keep backward compatibility in mind when working on new versions.

Making the code compatible with both compilers meant that I had to accept some limits. For example, neither of the compilers listed above supports exception handlers; therefore, this book implements my own error-handling scheme. And, while Borland C++ provides some support for templates (parameterized types), Microsoft does not. Therefore, I don't use templates in this book.

I hope that this book provides you with food for thought and code for programs. Good luck!

Scott Robert Ladd
Colorado Springs, Colorado
March 1992

# PART I

# Groundwork

# CHAPTER 1

# A C++ Philosophy

*Axioms in philosophy are not axioms until they are proved upon our pulses: we read fine things but never feel them to the full until we have gone the same steps as the author.*

John Keats (1795-1821), Letter to J.H. Reynolds, May 3, 1818

I'll begin this book by describing my philosophy of C++ and object-oriented programming. Including opinions in any technical discussion can be risky for the author, particularly if those opinions vary from the accepted norm. In my case, I've developed some strong feelings about C++, and this influences how I write my code. Understanding my thoughts about C++ will help you to understand the rest of this book.

My goal isn't to lay down a set of absolute laws; instead, I'd like to make you think about how you develop C++ programs. Don't take what I'm about to say as gospel truth; rather, view it as my perspective on how C++ has (and has not) worked for me.

## 1.1 From Functions to Objects

While programmers may quibble about whose language is best, few practical differences exist between the major function-oriented programming languages. I can move from BASIC to C to FORTRAN to Pascal without difficulty; an *if* statement is an *if* statement, and a function is a function regardless of the language I'm using. When I design a function-oriented program, I don't think in terms of a specific language, because the individual syntaxes and capabilities are generally equivalent.

Programming in an object-oriented language is different from programming in a function-oriented one. Object-oriented programs should be structurally different from function-oriented programs. Whereas a function-oriented program is organized around the actions being performed, a well-designed object-oriented program is arranged according to the objects being manipulated. This is a shift in perspective that causes trouble for programmers steeped in a function-oriented approach to programming.

I've heard it often: *C++ is C with object-oriented extensions*. That's a comforting (but simplistic) statement that gives the impression that moving from C to C++ requires only the gradual addition of C++ features to C programs. The promise is that the use of object-oriented techniques will result in faster, smaller, easier-to-maintain programs. It sure sounds wonderful, doesn't it?

Don't believe everything you hear. C++ programming is more than C programming with a few new keywords. It is possible to write object-oriented programs in C; a programmer can also develop function-oriented applications in C++. The difference between function- and object-oriented programming is that the programmer must switch from designing programs based on actions to designing programs around data types and their interactions. You'll find yourself in trouble if you don't understand the difference in point of view.

In the end, one of these things may happen to the programmer trying to learn C++:

> The programmer gives up, surrendering to frustration caused by the complexities of C++. What can be done with C++ that can't be done with C? the programmer will ask. I've seen this syndrome occur in many C advocates, who tried to use C++ without making the shift from actions to objects in their programming philosophy.

> Finding the new C++ features irresistible, the programmer sets forth to create wonderful and incomprehensible programs. Inline functions, operator overloading, and local declarations proliferate, but very few practical classes appear.

> After reading a dozen books, fighting with C++, and alienating friends and family, the programmer is illuminated by an understanding of object-oriented programming.

Your approach to C++ will determine which of the three scenarios applies to you. If you expect C++ to automatically hand you object-oriented benefits, you'll become disillusioned. Thinking of C++ as a set of new toys for the C programmer will result in your using some C++ features without truly understanding their applications. However, if you're willing to be patient, to open your mind to the possibilities, and to change the way in which you've built programs in the past, you are on the road to success with C++.

## 1.2 Terminology

A unique terminology lends prestige to a new discipline by making it obscure and mystical. Perfectly good words may exist to describe something, but the new philosophy requires new words to distinguish it from the past. (Unfortunately, fancy new terminology can cloud our understanding.)

Let's begin by examining a simple code fragment:

```
double a, b, c, s;

    b = 1.0;
    c = 2.0;
    a = b + c;
    s = sqrt(a);
```

The *double* data type provides an abstraction representing a floating-point number. A programmer doesn't need to know anything about the format of floating-point data types to use a *double*. The compiler takes care of the details involved in working with *doubles*, making the programmer's job easier.

The use of abstractions doesn't end with data types. The *sqrt* function is a functional abstraction, and it provides a "black box" for determining the square root of a floating-point value. Most programmers don't know how to obtain the square root of a floating-point value; they rely upon *sqrt* to do the task for them.

C++ allows programmers to create new abstractions. A *class* defines an interface to a set of related program components. Through the interface (in this case, public functions), you can interact with the abstraction without being involved in its internal

7

workings. As with using *double* and *sqrt* to handle floating-point numbers more easily, your classes should be designed to simplify the use of the abstraction.

The keyword *double* identifies an abstraction. When you declare a *double* in your program, you are creating an *object* that has the characteristics associated with it being a double. The term *object* is literal; it means "a thing that has identifiable properties." When you create a *double* object, you know from experience exactly what that object can do.

Intrinsic data types such as *double* and *int* are built into C++; they are always available and their properties are predefined and unchangeable. A programmer uses classes to create new abstractions in C++; the abstractions you create with classes will have the properties you define. Unlike intrinsic types, you can extend the types defined by classes.

Don't be limited to thinking of classes and objects only in terms of data types. For example, Pascal allows a programmer to define several related functions within an outer-shell function. The shell provides a single entry point for a process, and the internal functions carry out that process. Internal functions can reference the data items in the enclosing scope, in effect creating a program within a program.

In C++, the programmer can use classes to accomplish the same task by creating a class that has private functions for internal use and a public function that provides the entry point. Data shared by the various functions can be part of the class definition. Like Pascal, C++ can be used to create self-contained processes.

To *encapsulate* is to *bind together* the different components that form a single concept or entity, hiding the internal structure of a program component. For example, the *complex* class defines the data structure of a complex number; it also defines the functions that can operate on *complex* values, and makes those functions part of the definition of a *complex*.

You use encapsulation every day. A car consists of several components that are all treated like a single unit for most purposes. In fact, you car contains several encapsulations; your refer to the "engine" or the "brakes," which are actually systems of several parts that work together for a single purpose. Combined with abstraction, encapsulation allows a programmer to combine the components of a larger idea into a single, simplified model.

*Inheritance* allows us to create new classes from existing ones. For example, my *SortableArray* class inherits the characteristics defined by the *Array* class, which defines the core features of arrays. *SortableArray* then adds its own features to support the sorting of arrays. In turn, the *IntArray* class is *derived* (inherits from) the *SortableArray* class, to create a sortable array of *ints*. *Array* is a class defining the common characteristics of all arrays; *SortableArray* adds the ability to sort arrays, and *IntArray* defines a specific type of array. Thus, hierarchies of related classes are built using inheritance.

Inheritance also allows for *polymorphism. Poly* is derived from the Greek word for *many*; *morphus* is from the Greek word *morphous* meaning *to take a form.* Combined with *-ism,* the term polymorphism means *the ability to take on many forms.* In the case of object-oriented programming, a polymorphic data type is one that can have several variants, all of which can be treated in a like manner. For example, the *Array* class is polymorphic; any class derived from it can be treated as a generic *Array*, allowing a program to treat any type of *Array* in a generic fashion.

As I build classes later in this book, I'll be pointing out where and why I used encapsulation, inheritance, and polymorphism.

## 1.3 Cautionary Tales

An old saying goes: The inherent flexibility of C provides the rope with which programmers can hang themselves. Fortunately, good C programmers know how to avoid wrapping the rope around their neck; from experience, they know what should and shouldn't be done in C, and most of them escape unscathed.

The unprecedented freedom of expression allowed by C++ requires a great amount of caution and knowledge on your part. C++ doesn't just supply the rope; it ties the noose, places it over your head, stands you over the trap door with your hand on the release-lever. Am I exaggerating? I suppose so — but only a bit.

It wouldn't be so bad if C++ programmers had as much experience as their C-programming brethren. C programmers learned long ago that certain programming techniques were bad news. Most C++ programmers have been using the language for only a few months, or at most a couple of years; they haven't had enough time to learn right from wrong. In three years of C++ programming, I've hung myself so many times I'm surprised that I can still breathe. I hope that, by passing on what I've learned, I can prevent you from having too many pain-in-the-neck experiences.

### 1.3.1 Trendiness

*It is undesirable to believe a proposition when there is no ground whatever for supposing it true.*
Bertrand Russell (1872-1970), Skeptical Essays (1928)

Every few years, a new programming technique comes along, promising to make software development easier. Like politicians on the campaign trail, the advocates of "a technological breakthrough" eagerly ply us with promises of a better future. The question is, are they (like politicians) promising more than they can deliver?

The champions of object-oriented programming make some pretty big promises. We are told that programs will be easier to build because existing components can be linked together quickly and easily. Using objects will simplify the process of debugging programs because problems can be isolated within given data types. Finally, future changes can be implemented merely by deriving new program components from the existing ones.

In theory, that is. As I've worked with C++ over the past several years, I've come to realize that the additional benefits of object-oriented programming require more design and planning on the part of the software developer. It takes time to analyze an application, identify its components, develop the relationships between those components, and create the network of classes.

Many C programmers tend to "hack" programs together. For whatever reason — be it a lack of design time or a case of machismo — C programmers tend to build on-screen, in real time, with a design consisting of a few scribbled notes. A programmer needs a clear idea of what data types are to be used, how they will be used, and what the relationships are. If you work in an environment where program specifications are rare, and where programs are developed on the fly, C++ is not the language you should be using.

But all those new toys in C++ are inviting, aren't they? There are so many nooks and crannies in C++, you could spend years engaged in exploring C++ without ever completely understanding it. This is both a strength and a weakness. As a strong point, the complexity of C++ makes it powerful; as a weakness, complexity increases the chance of making mistakes.

This doesn't mean that there's anything *wrong* with C++; it merely means that you need to be cautious. Don't jump right in, grabbing every feature you see, just because some pundit (including this one!) tells you that's what you should do. Weigh and consider; experiment and test; observe and contemplate. That's how you learn C++.

### 1.3.2 Inheritance Follies

The most important decision you can make in an object-oriented program is how the classes of objects will be organized. Choosing the wrong organization can be fatal later, when you suddenly discover that you needed a branch here instead of a class there. As with a real tree, you can't take a branch and move it, or change its point of attachment to the tree. Because of this class hierarchies often degenerate into class "thickets" as new classes are patched in. Multiple inheritance can add to this problem by creating multiple paths of ancestry.

When you create a new class by means of multiple inheritance, be aware of the ancestry of the classes that are being combined. For example, Figures 1.1 and 1.2 each show portions of class hierarchies from different vendors' libraries. Vendor A's library provides basic container classes; Vendor B's hierarchy consists of classes that encapsulate numeric data types. Note that the two classes named Object are different.

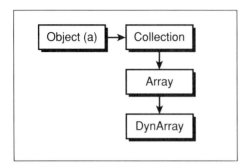

**Figure 1-1. Vendor A's Class Hierarchy.**

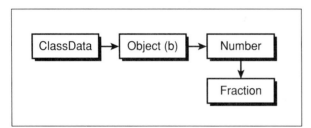

**Figure 1-2. Vendor's B's Class Hierarchy.**

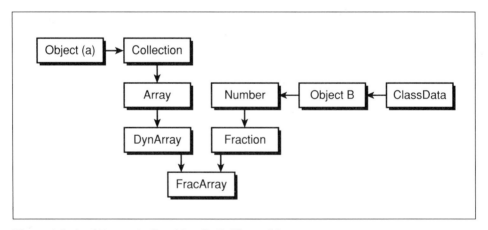

**Figure 1-3. An Attempt to Combine Both Hierarchies.**

What happens when you want to create a new class, named *FracArray,* that is based upon Vendor A's *DynArray* class and Vendor B's *Fraction* class? Figure

1-3 shows the ancestry of the *FracArray* class.

Everything looks okay, until you realize that you have two *different ancestral* classes named *Object*. Were these classes identical, the declaration of *Collection* and *Number* could be modified to declare as a virtual base class. Unfortunately, because the two *Object* classes are different, the virtual mechanism won't work. The compiler will complain about ambiguous base classes; the linker will complain that there are two classes with the same name. And let's not think about the problems with identically named header, source, and object files!

An obvious solution is to rename one or both of the *Object* classes — if you have the source code for the vendors classes. Although it solves the immediate problem, renaming a class requires a substantial amount of work. Because *Object* is likely to be the base for every class in the vendors hierarchies, you'll have to change every reference to *Object*. Even using a sophisticated editor, that's a lot of work! And, when the vendors upgrade their class libraries to new versions, you'll have to choose between renaming the class again, or not upgrading.

I'll assume that changes have been made so that the two conflicting classes are now named *ObjectA* and *ObjectB*, respectively. Everything's okay now, isn't it?

Not by a long shot. The purpose of a single-tree hierarchy is to make the polymorphic manipulation of objects easier. Most *Object*-type classes provide virtual functions for determining an object's class, comparing two objects for equality, obtaining the object's size, and performing I/O on the object. Unfortunately, while the designers of single-tree hierarchies may agree on *what* the *Object* class should define, they probably don't agree on *how* that definition should be implemented.

Something as simple as different naming conventions can cause a major headache. Vendor A defines the virtual member function *PrintOn* in *ObjectA*. Vendor B's *ObjectB* class, however, defines a *PrintTo* virtual member. In all likelihood, *PrintOn* and *PrintTo* have completely different semantics. Your *FracArray* class inherits both of these member functions, and you'll need to provide your own implementations of *PrintOn* and *PrintTo* which are specific to *FracArray*. In addition, the two vendors probably use different names and conventions for class identification, equivalence, and size-calculation member functions. What a mess of redundancies! I don't even want to think about inheriting from *more* than two hierarchies.

### 1.3.3 Single-Tree Hierarchies

A large hierarchy is like a piece of string. Drop a short piece of string to the floor, and it's simple to tell which end of the string lies where. As the string gets longer, it becomes harder and harder to determine which end of the string is which. If the string is long enough, trying to follow it from one end to the other only generates knots. That's how long, complex class hierarchies tie you up later on — particularly when looking at someone else's code, or code that you wrote in the past.

How often do you need to have a data item identify itself? Does every object need to support I/O features? Are generic data structures efficient enough for your application? What are the costs involved in having layers of virtual functions? Don't assume that a purely object-oriented approach is the only route; the best feature of C++ is that it lets you use plain old C when it is needed, and C++ when you want objects. Don't add stuff to your C++ programs just because you can; add it because it's the best option.

### 1.3.4  Do it Twice (At Least!)

How often have you written a piece of software, only to realize that you could have done better? Perhaps you find, after getting into a project, that your original assumptions were wrong. Then you are faced with the choice of making major changes to work already completed, or with producing a kludge. Either way, you aren't going to be happy with the result. Programs (written in C++ or not) always work better the second time they're written.

Inheritance and polymorphism can't hide a bad design. No matter how much the pundits would like you to think you can simply derive new classes to make up for deficiencies in old ones, it simply isn't true. Think about building a house, where the architect, halfway through, finds out that there's a structural flaw in the foundation. He may be able to complete the house by patching the foundation, but the structure will always have an underlying flaw. The same hold true for class hierarchies: If the underlying classes have flaws, derived classes can hide the flaws, but they can't fix them.

Programs are always better the second (or third, or fourth...) time around. It's a simple fact of life that no amount of planning and designing anticipates every possible situation your software will encounter. Although it's often impossible to rewrite existing code — due to time and budget constraints, or because the program simply isn't worth rewriting — you'll end up with a better program if you can take the time to rebuild.

C++ is not for hacker-style programming. If you work in an environment where program specifications are rare or where time is always short, C++ is not the language for you.

## 1.4 Software Components

Computers are built from modular components. Once the hardware has been created, software can manipulate the hardware to direct how it performs a task. Several object-oriented programming enthusiasts have proposed that software be constructed from interchangeable software components, just as computers are constructed from standard chips and circuit cards. The result, they say, will be a new age of perfect software, where programmers simply connect objects together to form new applications.

The assumption being made, of course, is that software is like hardware. A given hardware component is designed to be absolute; a machine has this CPU, these I/O ports, and a specific number of expansion slots. Once a piece of hardware is built it is almost impossible to change it significantly. Let's say, for example, that you want to add a new expansion card to your PC — only to find that all of your expansion slots are full. You can't simply change the design of your motherboard; adding an additional expansion slot would be more work than it's worth. You either have to remove an existing expansion card, or live without your new card.

The problem becomes more complicated when you want to change how your hardware works. With your PC, the ROM BIOS is fixed; you can change it only for another BIOS that works in a very similar way. Once hardware has been built and software has been cast in silicon, making changes is very difficult.

If discrete software functions can be encapsulated into components, we could build programs like we build cars or computers. Programming would consist of developing networks of fixed, unchangeable software ICs. The only difference between software and hardware would be that software would be easier to rearrange than hardware. This would eliminate creativity; programming with software ICs would be as exciting as building structures with tinker toys. And, worse yet, software ICs would eliminate the need for programmers in the first place. Without the human element, programs would become sterile and lifeless, lacking creativity and ingenuity. Assembly-line software may be for some people, but I don't look forward to using it.

A better design method is to create *flexible* and *extensible* objects. A flexible object permits modification. An extensible object can be used as the basis for different objects. The *Array* classes shown later in this book try to use a flexible hierarchy to provide for flexible expansion.

## 1.5 More about Classes

The relationship of two classes can take on one or more of the following forms:

The *is a* relationship. Class B is defined as a variant of Class A. The major characteristics of Class B are inherited from Class A, and Class B objects are often used polymorphically by means of pointers to Class A objects. For example, a class defining an array of *ints* may be derived from a class that specifies the common characteristics of all array types.

The *modifies* relationship. Class B extends or defines the capabilities of Class A. For example, the *SortableArray* class (Chapter 6) adds sorting capabilities to the *Array* class (Chapter 5).

The *made of* relationship. Class A objects are components of Class B. In this case, Class A defines a traditional data type, such as an integer or a complex number, and Class B defines an object type that contains Class A objects.

The *uses* relationship. Class A objects are tools used by Class B objects, such as when a file object is used by another object to store data.

A programmer must know the relationship of classes in a program to be able to determine the types and interactions of classes. This requires that the often-elusive program specification be thoroughly researched. If you make a poor decision about relating your classes, a program can become difficult to understand and maintain.

In subsequent chapters, I'll be presenting several sets of classes. When I discuss how I designed these classes, I'll be referring back to the relationships listed above.

# CHAPTER 2

# A Library of Tools

Every class library contains a set of utilitarian classes and data types. Many common, simple tools can be used over and over again; adding them to a standard library avoids reinventing the wheel.

Before I present the classes later in the book, I want to explain some decisions and issues that affected my designs. No class is an island, entire of itself, to paraphrase the 16th-century poet John Donne.

## 2.1 Switches and Booleans

A program component doesn't have to be complicated to be useful. I've seen too many articles and books that take a simple subject and make it unnecessarily complicated. The simplest data type in my library, switches, can be implemented in a single line of code (if desired); yet, it's turned out to be eminently useful.

I often find that I need a value that tells me whether something is on or off. This isn't quite the same thing as a Boolean expression, where something is true or false. Although, technically speaking, an on/off value is the same as a true/false value, the underlying philosophy of the two differs. People don't say that a light is true or false (or so I should hope!), nor do they say that a logical argument is on or off.

### 2.1.1 A C-like Implementation

How should a on/off switch be implemented? Many C++ programmers would write something like this:

```
#define Switch int

    #define OFF 0
    #define ON  1
```

Or, if they are a bit more sophisticated:

```
typedef int Switch;
```

The designs above lack any sort of protection against the assignment of invalid values to a *Switch*. Also, *#define* constants are obsolete and inefficient in C++, where better tools are available.

### 2.1.2 A C++ Class Implementation

Because *Switch* is a data type, a C++ programmer may decide to create a *Switch* class. Here's one class definition that would do the job:

```
class Switch
      {
      public:
          // constructors
          Switch();
          Switch(int sw);
          Switch(const Switch & sw);

          // assignment operators
          Switch & operator = (int sw);
          Switch & operator = (const Switch & sw);

          // interrogation functions
          int IsOn();
          int IsOff();

          // static data members
          static const Switch On;
          static const Switch Off;

      protected:
          // instance variables
          int Setting;
      };
```

The constants *On* and *Off* need to be defined in a compiled source file, like this:

```
const Switch Switch::On  = 1;
   const Switch Switch::Off = 0;
```

*Switch*'s member functions are very simple, and they should be implemented inline to eliminate the overhead of function calls:

```
inline Switch::Switch()
     {
     Setting = Off.Setting;
     }

  inline Switch::Switch(int sw)
       {
       if (sw == On.Setting)
           Setting = On.Setting;
       else
           Setting = Off.Setting;
       }

  inline Switch::Switch(const Switch & sw)
       {
       Setting = sw.Setting;
       }

  inline Switch & Switch::operator = (int sw)
       {
       if (sw == On.Setting)
           Setting = On.Setting;
       else
           Setting = Off.Setting;

       return *this;
       }

  inline Switch & Switch::operator = (const Switch & sw)
       {
       Setting = sw.Setting;
```

```
        return *this;
        }

inline int Switch::IsOn()
        {
        return (Setting == On.Setting);
        }

inline int Switch::IsOff()
        {
        return (Setting == Off.Setting);
        }
```

This code fragment shows how a *Switch* works:

```
Switch s = Switch::On;

    if (s.IsOn())
        cout << "On\n";
    else
        cout << "Off\n";

    return 0;
```

The *Switch* class avoids invalid assignments, but is it the best possible implementation of a Switch type? All tolled, 64 lines of code are used to define a very simple data type.

### 2.1.3  Using an enum

I always opt for simplicity. A better implementation of *Switch* uses an enumerated type:

```
enum Switch
        {
        OFF = 0,
        ON  = 1
        };
```

Enumerated types are often the most-ignored feature of C++ (and, for that matter, C). Most C++ programmers began as C programmers, and they often overlook the more efficient means in C++ for accomplishing a task.

Using a C++ class to define a *Switch* type is overkill. The *enum* version of *Switch* is concise. Without constructors and member functions, it provides protection against the assignment of invalid values, is easy to use, and doesn't require a source file to define the *On* and *Off* constants used by the class *Switch*. Checking for invalid assignments is performed at compile time, rather than at run time. I use a similar enum to define a Boolean (true/false) data type.

```
enum Boolean
      {
      BOOL_FALSE,
      BOOL_TRUE
      };
```

Why use an enum at all when C++ supports the same Boolean value system (nonzero values are true, zero values are false) as C? It's a matter of taste; the *Boolean* and *Switch* types limit their values to pairs of descriptive identifiers.

Why did I use the BOOL_ prefix on the constants for the Boolean type? I originally used constant names of TRUE and FALSE, only to find that *many* other header files have #define constants named TRUE and FALSE. The processor constants overwrote my constants in the definition of Boolean, leading to syntax errors.

The *Switch* and *Boolean* types are implemented in the files *switch.h* and *boolean.h*, which are listed in Appendix A.

## 2.2 Error Reporting

The latest definition of C++, given in *The Annotated C++ Reference Manual* by Ellis and Stroustrup, includes support for programmer-defined asynchronous error handling by means of exception handlers. Basically, an exception handler is a function that is called when a specific event occurs, such as a division by zero.

Unfortunately, exception handling is too new to be supported by most C++

compilers; at the time of this writing, no compilers for PCs support exception handling. Because errors need to be handled without regard to the compiler being used, I needed to create a different system.

In my view, a class can handle errors in one of two ways. For simple classes, errors can be reported for any object of that class. This is the way intrinsic types work; if a division by zero occurs, a global function is called to display the error. Errors for complicated objects, such as linked lists, should be reported for the object that encountered the error.

My idea was to create an error-reporting object. A static error reporter could be included in classes that use class-wide error handling, while a nonstatic member would be included in each object for object-specific error handling. Here's the class definition that I created:

```
class ErrReporter
    {
    public:
        // constructor
        ErrReporter(const String * lead);

        // destructor
        ~ErrReporter();

        // display warning message
        virtual void Warning(const String & msg);

        // display fatal error message
        virtual void Fatal(const String & msg);

    protected:
        // a function that displays parts of the message
        virtual void MsgOut(const String & msg);

      // pointer to a string used as a message
        String * Leader;
    };
```

*ErrReporter* has six members: a constructor, a destructor, three functions, and a pointer to a string.

When deciding how to present the classes in this book, I encountered a chicken-and-egg problem. The *ErrReporter* class uses *String* objects; my *String* class, however, uses an *ErrReporter* object! Mutual dependancies are common in C++ code, and they make programmers' lives difficult. Which class should be presented first? I decided to show you the *ErrReporter* class first, because it is the simpler of the two.

However, so you can understand the implementation of the *ErrReporter* class, I need to provide you with some basic information on the *String* objects. The *String* class defines a data type that contains a string of characters; it is presented in its entirety in the next chapter. For the purposes of the *ErrReporter* class, I hope it will suffice to say the following things about *Strings*:

> *String* objects can be constructed from *const char \*s*.
> A *String* can be used in place of a *const char \**.
> The *String* class defines a copy constructor.
> The *String* class defines stream I/O functions.

### 2.2.1 Members of ErrReporter

An *ErrReporter* object has a single-instance variable, *Leader*. *Leader* is a pointer to a *String* object. When an *ErrReporter* is told to display an error message, the *String* pointed to by *Leader* is displayed first. The *Leader String* identifies related error messages by giving them a common header text.

The constructor for *ErrReporter* creates a duplicate of the *String* pointed by the *lead* parameter. The duplicated string is allocated with *new*, and its pointer is assigned to *Leader*. If *lead* is *NULL, Leader* is also assigned *NULL*.

```
ErrReporter::ErrReporter(const String * lead)
    {
    if (lead == NULL)
        Leader = NULL;
    else
        Leader = new String(*lead);
    }
```

Why didn't I simply assign *lead* to *Leader*? I consider it to be bad programming practice to store pointers to objects that are outside the scope of a class. If the *String* pointed to by *lead* were deleted, the pointer in the *ErrReporter* object would be invalid.

The destructor deletes the *String* pointed to by *Leader*, if *Leader* is not *NULL*.

```
ErrReporter::~ErrReporter()
    {
    // delete leader if it was allocated
    if (Leader != NULL)
        delete Leader;
    }
```

*ErrReporter* defines the remaining three functions as virtual; all these functions are implemented as empty inline shells.

```
void ErrReporter::Warning(const String & msg)
    {
    // does nothing!
    }

    void ErrReporter::Fatal(const String & msg)
        {
        // does nothing!
        }

    void ErrReporter::MsgOut(const String & msg)
        {
        // does nothing!
        }
```

To display an error message, a program will call either *Fatal* or *Warning*. *Fatal* causes the program to terminate, while the implementation of *Warning* simply displays a message. Because both functions display messages, I created a third function *MsgOut* that performs the actual message display.

In my original implementation, *Warning*, *Fatal*, and *MsgOut* were pure virtual functions. Pure virtual functions made *ErrReporter* an abstract base class. However, it is not possible to create a reference to an abstract class, because it is impossible to create abstract objects. As you'll see below, I use references to *ErrReporter* objects; therefore, I created empty implementations of the three virtual functions and removed the pure virtual function specifiers.

The virtual functions are required so that I can construct *ErrReporter* classes for specific environments. Different environments require different ways of displaying messages. For example, DOS command-line programs often display error messages as line of scrolling text. A program in a windowing environment, however, displays its error messages in a window or display area. Most objects will not know what environment they are working under. It is the job of an *ErrReporter* object to display the error message in a manner compatible with the current environment.

When an object needs to act in different ways under a variety of circumstances, polymorphism is the tool to use. I defined the *ErrReporter* class such that the error display functions are virtual. I derived classes from *ErrReporter* that are specific to various environments. Then, in my programs, I define pointers to *ErrReporter* objects, and assign them the addresses of environment-specific *ErrReporter* derivatives. Calling virtual methods through an *ErrReporter* pointer provides a common interface to all objects of classes derived from *ErrReporter*.

### 2.2.2 An Error Reporter for C++ Streams

An example should make all of this clear. I've defined a class named *DosErrReporter* that displays error messages using C++ streams:

```
class DosErrReporter : public ErrReporter
    {
    public:
        DosErrReporter(const String * lead = NULL,
                            ostream * strm = NULL);

        virtual void Warning(const String & msg);
        virtual void Fatal(const String & msg);

    protected:
        virtual void MsgOut(const String & msg);
```

```
private:
    ostream * Destination;
};
```

*DosErrReporter* is derived from *ErrReporter*. I defined four functions that mirror those defined for *ErrReporter*; I also added a new data element, named *Destination*, that is a pointer to an *ostream*. Destination does not have its own destructor.

The constructor for *DosErrReporter* has two parameters: a *String* pointer and an *ostream* pointer. The *String* pointer is passed to the constructor for *ErrReporter*. If *strm* is *NULL*, *Destination* is set to point to the predefined *cerr* stream. Otherwise, *Destination* is assigned *strm*.

```
DosErrReporter::DosErrReporter(const String * lead,
                                          ostream * strm)
    : ErrReporter(lead)
    {
    if (strm == NULL)
        Destination = &cerr;
    else
        Destination = strm;
    }
```

The three virtual methods send error message *Strings* to *Destination*. The difference between *Warning* and *Fatal* is that *Fatal* calls an exit to stop the program, whereas *Warning* allows the program to continue. *MsgOut* generates the message display.

```
void DosErrReporter::Warning(const String & msg)
    {
    *Destination << "\nWARNING - ";

    MsgOut(msg);
    }
void DosErrReporter::Fatal(const String & msg)
    {
    *Destination << "\nFATAL ERROR - ";
```

```
    MsgOut(msg);

    exit(EXIT_FAILURE);
    }

void DosErrReporter::MsgOut(const String & msg)
    {
    if (Leader == NULL)
        *Destination << msg << endl; // no leader
    else
        *Destination << *Leader << ": " << msg << endl;
    }
```

Note that if *Leader* is *NULL, MsgOut* simply displays the *msg String*. If *Leader* is not *NULL, MsgOut* displays *Leader*, a colon, and then *msg*.

### 2.2.3  Using ErrReporters

Here's an example of using an *ErrReporter* object. The class *Foobar* reports all errors for all *Foobar* objects by means of a static *ErrReporter* member named *ErrOut*.

```
class Foobar
    {
    public:
        ... // various public members

        static void SetErrOut( const ErrReporter & er);

    private:
        static ErrReporter * ErrOut;

        static void ReportError();
    };
```

*ErrOut* needs to be initialized once, somewhere in the program.

```
ErrReporter * Foobar::ErrOut = NULL;
```

When an error occurs in a *Foobar* object, the *ReportError* function is called.

```
void Foobar::ReportError()
    {
    if (ErrOut != NULL)
        ErrOut.Fatal("Error in Foobar object");
    }
```

*ReportError* calls *ErrOut* to display a message only if *ErrOut* points to an *ErrReporter* object. *ErrOut* is assigned a value by means of the *SetErrOut* function.

```
void Foobar::SetErrOut(const ErrReporter & er)
    {
    if (ErrOut != NULL)
        delete ErrOut;

    ErrOut = new ErrReporter(er);
    }
```

If *ErrOut* already points to an *ErrReporter*, that object is deleted. A new *ErrReporter* object is created and assigned to *ErrOut*. Here's how a program could call *SetErrOut*:

```
int main()
    {
    // create a DosErrReporter object
    DosErrReporter * der =
                new DosErrReporter("Foobar error");

    // if the object was create, call SetErrOut
    if (der != NULL)
        {
        // assign object
        Foobar::SetErrOut(*der);

        // delete unneeded object
        delete der;
        }
```

```
    ... // more program!
    }
```

The *ErrReporter* and *DosErrReporter* classes are defined and implemented in the files *err_rptr.h* and *err_rptr.cxx*. I present the complete versions of these files in Appendix A.

## 2.3  Random Number Generation

A random number is just that — a number whose value cannot be predicted in advance of its existence. Although the human mind has been known to be unpredictable, it isn't very good at generating a completely unrelated set of numbers. Try creating a list of twenty random integers selected from the range one through one hundred, inclusive. Are those numbers *really* random? And wouldn't it be tedious if you had to generate a thousand or a million random numbers?

Computers are supposed to be good at reducing tedious numeric operations. Unfortunately, computers perform calculations using algorithms, and truly random numbers cannot be generated by an algorithm. By definition, an algorithm is a specific sequence of operations that produces a predictable output for a given set of parameters. In the case of random numbers, the last thing we want is something predictable!

The best we can do with a computer is create an algorithm that *appears* to generate a random sequence of numbers. The numbers aren't really random; a person with a sharp mind or a calculator could predict the numbers in the sequence by following the algorithm. But the sequence of numbers is very difficult to follow, and a person looking at the values will not be able to see any algorithmic pattern to them. For practical applications, pseudo-random numbers suffice.

### 2.3.1  Choosing an Algorithm

In general, a pseudo-random number generator begins with a *seed* value that begins the sequence. A set of mathematical operations is performed on the seed, generating a value that is reported as a pseudo-random number. That return value is then used as the next seed value.

Researchers have devoted much time to inventing and analyzing pseudo-random number generators. The goal of this research has been to produce the most unpredictable sequence of values possible. Designing a good random number generator involves solving two problems:

1. Increasing the size of the repetition cycle. As the algorithm is applied, the seed eventually returns to its starting value, and the values start repeating themselves. An algorithm that repeats after generating a million numbers is more useful than a generator that repeats itself every hundred numbers.

2. Avoiding predictability. A random number generator that always returns values with the same last digit is worthless. An algorithm that generates only odd numbers is equally useless.

While there are many fancy and complicated algorithms that generate pseudo-random numbers, one of the most commonly used algorithms is also one of the simplest. First introduced by D. Lehmer in 1951, the *linear congruential* method involves only two mathematical operations. Here's a basic implementation of a random number generator for *unsigned shorts*:

```
unsigned short seed = 1u;

    unsigned short randshort()
        {
        const unsigned short k1 = 9821u;
        const unsigned short k2 = 1u;

        seed = seed * k1 + k2;

        return seed;
        }
```

Note that this algorithm truncates after an overflow in a calculation. When seed is multiplied by *k1*, it often overflows, generating a value that is larger than can be held by an *unsigned short*. On most PC-type computers, the extra high-order bits of seed will be dropped, effectively performing a *seed % USHRT_MAX* operation. This algorithm will *not* work on a machine that generates an exception when overflow occurs; in such a case, you'll need to change the algorithm to prevent overflow.

How did I select the constants *k1* and *k2*? Although volumes have been written on the subject, Donald Knuth provided the best analysis in Volume 2 of his series, *The Art of Computer Programming*. Knuth suggests that *k1* should be a "moderately sized" number less than the maximum random value, with no pattern to its digits, and ending in 21. In other words, setting *k1* to 2 or 100 would not make for a good generator. As for *k2*, Knuth states that it must be an odd number, preferably 1. (The underlying numerical analysis that led Knuth to select these values is outside the scope of this book. I suggest you look up his three-volume series; the best programmers consider these to be the bibles of their profession.)

So, looking again at the code above, we see that we have a pseudo-random number generator, right? Wrong! Alas, *randshort* has a nontrivial bug. The first twenty values it generates are:

```
 9822, 58407, 44076,  5117, 53482, 41219, 61464, 51385,
24886, 21663, 22468, 64053, 49986, 47867, 12080, 17521,
41742, 20503, 33372,   877, 27802, 20467,  7496, 21289,
19430, 46735, 35828,  4005, 11506, 16363,  6752, 54497,
48062, 26631, 54412, 65245, 25674, 27363, 34424, 43417
```

At a glance, these numbers don't appear to be related. They do, however, follow a pattern: Odd and even values alternate! And, unfortunately, fiddling with the values of *seed*, *k1*, or *k2* only changes the pattern of alternation. The problem is intrinsic to the algorithm.

Does this mean that the linear congruential method is useless? Certainly not; we merely need to expand our algorithm to avoid the problem:

```
unsigned long seed = 1ul;

unsigned short randshort2()
    {
    const unsigned long k1 = 5709421ul;
    const unsigned long k2 = 1ul;
```

```
seed = seed * k1 + k2;

return (unsigned short)(seed >> 16L);
}
```

The pattern in *randshort2's* values is located in the lowest bits of *seed*. I eliminated this problem by using *unsigned longs* in the calculations, and returning the upper 16 bits of *seed* as *randshort2's* result.

The algorithm above assumes that a *long* is 32 bits and a *short* is 16 bits. This holds true for all PCs and workstations I have used. The shift values and other constants could be defined so that they are adjusted automatically, based on the actual sizes of *shorts* and *longs*.

Starting from a given *seed* value, randshort2 always generates the same sequence of values. Thus, a function to set the seed value can be very useful:

```
void setseed(unsigned long newseed)
    {
    seed = newseed;
    }
```

Setting the *seed* to an unpredictable value, such as the system time, generates an unpredictable set of values:

```
setseed((unsigned long)time(NULL));
```

The ANSI C standard defines the *rand* and *srand* functions, which directly correspond to *randshort2* and *seed* right down to the use of a linear congruential algorithm.

### 2.3.2  A Class for Random Numbers

Hold it! If ANSI C already defines a random number generator, why did I go through this whole discussion? Why not use the ANSI functions?

I've found that C++ classes often provide a better way of accomplishing a task usually performed with standalone functions. From a software-engineering standpoint, *rand* and *srand* have several faults:

**34**

A program must explicitly call *srand* to initialize the *seed*. If *srand* isn't called, the default value of *seed* will be used, and every execution of the program will generate the same sequence of pseudo-random numbers.

Because *srand* and *rand* are two separate functions, *seed* is defined as a global variable. Good programmers avoid global variables, even those that can be hidden using the *static* keyword.

Because there is only one *seed* value, only one sequence of pseudo-random numbers is generated in a program. Often, I like to have separate random number generators for different parts of a program.

The ANSI *rand* function returns values between 0 and UINT_MAX. In most cases, I want to retrieve random values that are within a specific range, say from 1 to 100.

A class can solve all of these problems. Here's the definition of my *RandGen* class:

```
#include "stddef.h"
    #include "time.h"

    class RandGen
        {
        public:
            // constructor
            RandGen(unsigned long initSeed =
                        (unsigned long)time(NULL));

            // set seed value
            void SetSeed(unsigned long newSeed =
                        (unsigned long)time(NULL));

            // get a pseudo-random number from 0 to (lim - 1)
            unsigned short operator () (unsigned short lim);

        private:
            unsigned long Seed;
        };
```

The *RandGen* class encapsulates everything having to do with generating a pseudo-random number sequence. It also demonstrates some unconventional C++ programming techniques.

When a *RandGen* object is created, the constructor assigns a value to *Seed*. I wanted *Seed* to be initialized automatically by the system clock. The ANSI *time* function returns the current time, and I simply included a call to *time* as a default parameter in the prototypes for the constructor and *SetSeed* functions. I implemented the constructor and *SetSeed* inline:

```
inline RandGen::RandGen(unsigned long initSeed)
     {
     Seed = initSeed;
     }

  inline void RandGen::SetSeed(unsigned long newSeed)
     {
     Seed = newSeed;
     }
```

The actual generator function is implemented using the parentheses operators. Within the parentheses, a value can be supplied; a number between 0 and *lim* will be returned. The compiler automatically uses *USHRT_MAX* as the default value of *lim* if an explicit value is not given.

The parentheses function is implemented like this:

```
unsigned short RandGen::operator () (unsigned short lim)
     {
     // get next seed value
     Seed = Seed * 5709421UL + 1UL;

     // return value from 0 to (lim - 1)
     return (unsigned short)((Seed >> 16UL) % lim);
     }
```

I used the modulus operator, %, to limit the returned value to a number between 0 and *lim*. This program sample demonstrates how a *RandGen* object is used:

```
#include "randgen.h"
  #include "iostream.h"

  #define TAB_CHAR '\t'

  int main()
    {
    RandGen rg1; // use the default, time-based seed
    RandGen rg2(1701); // explicitly set the seed

    // print 20 random numbers
    for (int i = 0; i < 20; ++i)
        cout << TAB_CHAR << rg1() << TAB_CHAR << rg2() <<
endl;
  return 0;
    }
```

The program displays two columns of twenty pseudo-random numbers. The first column contains different numbers for each run of the program; however, the second column always displays the same sequence, because it uses a fixed seed value.

As C++ classes go, *RandGen* is nothing fancy. It does, however, provide some capabilities not found in the ANSI function library. In later chapters, you'll see how I use *RandGen* objects in statistical analysis and simulations.

The complete source code for *RandGen* can be found in the file *randgen.h* and *randgen.cxx*, both of which are listed in Appendix A.

# CHAPTER 3

# A String Class

In my previous book for M&T, *Turbo C++ Techniques and Applications* (M&T Books, 1990) , I presented my *String* class. That class has become an integral part of my class library. In the original draft of *C++ Components and Algorithms*, I tried rewriting all of my classes to avoid using the *String* class, because using the *String* class meant that I would need to include it in this new book, duplicating material from my earlier text. Most readers become very annoyed when they buy a new book by an author, only to find that it contains old material from one of that author's previous books.

After working on the book for a while, I realized that I couldn't remove the *String* class without losing the object-oriented feel and integrity of my class-library design. Class libraries are constructed from a set of tools; in my case, the *String* class is a fundamental tool. To satisfy my own sense of correctness, and at the suggestion of several reviewers, I decided to include the discussion of the *String* class in this book, despite its previous publication.

That isn't to say that this is an exact duplication of my original *String* class presentation. The class has grown substantially, has new features, better reliability, and an improved error-handling capability. I've also rewritten this chapter to provide more details about how the *String* class works, and why. However, if you have my earlier work, feel free to simply skim this chapter before moving on to the next.

## 3.1 Design

One of C's primary shortcomings is that it lacks the sophisticated string-handling capacity available in languages such as BASIC. Nearly every program manipulates text data of one type or another, and C's lack of a true string data type has always made it difficult to use for some applications.

Developing a *String* class was one of my first C++ projects, and during the four years since I created it, the class has undergone substantial changes. As my understanding of C++ has grown, so has my ability to build a better class; for example, the *String* class has undergone five major revisions. I'm quite happy with the incarnation presented here, which works well in applications ranging from databases to text editors.

My goal was to create a dynamically allocated *String* class that provides all the functionality of standard, NUL-terminated C character arrays (which I call C-strings). However, I wanted to avoid the pitfalls of C-strings. For instance, errors often occur when working with C-strings because the string library functions fail to do any sort of range or validity checking. In addition, the library functions defined in *string.h* lack important features. In order for strings to be useful in a wide variety of applications, they need to have manipulation routines not normally found in C-function libraries — such as those for inserting and deleting data.

## 3.2 Enumerated Types

The *String* class uses three enumerated types: *StrCompVal*, *StrCompMode*, and *StrError*.

```
enum StrCompVal
      {
      SC_LESS,
      SC_EQUAL,
      SC_GREATER,
      SC_ERROR
      };

   enum StrCompMode
      {
      SM_SENSITIVE,
      SM_IGNORE
      };

   enum StrError
      {
```

```
SE_ALLOC,
SE_TOO_LONG,
SE_INVALID
};
```

*StrCompVal* is the return value of the *Compare* member function (see as follows). *StrCompMode* is used to indicate whether *String* comparisons are case sensitive or not. *StrError* is used by the error-processing function.

I use enumerations for these data types to control the validity of values passed to and returned from member functions. Because some C++ compilers still don't correctly support nested-type definitions, I defined these types outside of the *String* class definition.

## 3.3 Data Members

A String is defined as having three private-instance variables: *Siz, Len,* and *Txt.*

```
class String
    {
    .
    .
    .
    private:
        size_t Siz;
        size_t Len;
        char * Txt;

        static size_t AllocIncr;
    .
    .
    .
    };
```

*Txt* is a pointer to a buffer allocated in dynamic memory; in it are stored the characters that constitute the *String*, as a NUL-terminated array of characters. *Siz* contains the currently allocated length of the buffer pointed to by the *Txt* pointer. *Len* holds the actual number of characters stored in the *String*.

*AllocIncr* is a private static-class member. It defines the "chunk" size used in allocating memory for the *Txt* members of *String* objects. The *Siz* of a *String* is always the smallest multiple of *AllocIncr* that can hold *Len* characters. By default, *AllocIncr* is assigned the value 8 in the implementation file *str.cxx*.

```
size_t String::AllocIncr = 8;
```

## 3.4 Error Handling

Any class that allocates memory should implement an error-reporting mechanism. Between my previous book and this one, I completely changed how the *String* class handles errors. The *String* class uses an *ErrReporter* object (see Chapter 2), the *StrError* enumerated type, and a private function to process errors.

```
class String
    {
    .
    .
    .
    public:
        static void SetErrOut(const ErrReporter & er);

    private:
        static ErrReporter * ErrOut;
        static void ErrorHandler(StrError err);
    .
    .
    .
    };
```

*ErrOut* points to an *ErrReporter* object that is called by the *ErrorHandler* function. Initially, *ErrOut* points to a *DosErrReporter* object that is allocated when the compiler's start-up code begins the program.

```
ErrReporter * String::ErrOut = NULL;
```

The *ErrorHandler* function checks to see if *ErrOut* is *NULL* before calling any member function through it. If *ErrOut* is not *NULL*, *ErrorHandler* calls the *Fatal* method with a message string based on the value of *err*.

```
void String::ErrorHandler(StrError err)
    {
    if (ErrOut != NULL)
        {
        switch (err)
            {
            case SE_ALLOC :
                ErrOut->Fatal("allocation failure");
                break;

            case SE_TOO_LONG :
                ErrOut->Fatal("exceeded character limit");
                break;

            case SE_INVALID :
                ErrOut->Fatal("invalid parameters");
            }
        }
    }
```

Use the *SetErrOut* function to change *ErrOut*. *SetErrOut* deletes the object pointed to by *ErrOut* (if *ErrOut* is not *NULL*), and then allocates a new *ErrReporter* object with *er* as a constructor argument in the call to *new*. Note that if this allocation fails, *ErrOut* will be assigned *NULL* and the *ErrorHandler* function will avoid performing any member-function calls through it.

```
void String::SetErrOut(const ErrReporter & er)
    {
    if (ErrOut != NULL)
        delete ErrOut;

    ErrOut = new ErrReporter(er);
    }
```

## 3.5 Utility Functions

In general, I make class-member functions public to facilitate their use by user-defined objects. In the case of the *String* class, however, some utilitarian functions are used only internally by the class and I defined these as private members.

```
class String
     {
     .
     .
     .
     public:
         static int Version();

         size_t Length() const;
         size_t Size() const;

     private:
         static size_t CalcSiz(size_t needed);
     .
     .
     .
     };
```

*CalcSiz* computes the smallest allocated buffer size for given *String* length. *CalcSize* is not meant to be called from outside of the class scope, so it is declared in the private section of the *String* class definition. Its implementation is inline in the class implementation file (*str.cxx*) to improve efficiency.

```
inline size_t String::CalcSiz(size_t needed)
     {
     size_t x;

     x = ((needed + AllocIncr) / AllocIncr) * AllocIncr;

     return x;
     }
```

The *Length* and *Size* member functions simply return the current length and allocation size of a string, respectively. *Length* corresponds to the ANSI function *strlen*, but it is considerably faster by virtue of its simply returning an already calculated value.

```
inline size_t String::Length() const
     {
     return Len;
     }
```

Originally, *Size* was created to help test the class. Because it is so simple, I just left it in for future use. As I did with *Length*, I defined *Size* as an inline function.

```
inline size_t String::Size() const
     {
     return Siz;
     }
```

## 3.6 Constructors and the Destructor

I defined several constructors for the *String* class.

```
class String
     {
     .
     .
     .
     public:
         // constructors

         // default contructor create empty string
         String();

         // copy constructor
         String(const String & str);

         // create string from char array          String(const
     char * cstr);
```

```
        // create string containg count fillCh
        String(size_t count,   char fillCh = ' ');
    // create string containing formatted output
        String(size_t maxSize, const char * format, ...);

        // destructor
        ~String();
    .
    .
    .
    };
```

The default constructor creates an empty, uninitialized string.

```
String::String()
        {
        Len = 0;
        Siz = 0;
        Txt = NULL;
        }
```

The class also defines a copy constructor to create a new *String* from an existing one:

```
String::String(const String & str)
        {
        Len = str.Len;
        Siz = str.Siz;

        // if source string is empty, so is this string
        if (str.Txt == NULL)
            Txt = NULL;
        else
            {
            // allocate text buffer
            Txt = new char[Siz];

            if (Txt == NULL)
                ErrorHandler(SE_ALLOC);
```

```
        // copy text fom source string
        memcpy(Txt,str.Txt,Len + 1);
        }
    }
```

*String(char * Cstr)* generates a *String* from the value of a character array.

```
String::String(const char * cstr)
    {
    // if given a null char string, create an empty String
    if ((cstr == NULL) || (cstr[0] == '\x00'))
        {
        Len = 0;
        Siz = 0;
        Txt = NULL;
        }
    else
        {
        // calculate length and size
        Len = strlen(cstr);
        Siz = CalcSiz(Len);

        // allocate text buffer
        Txt = new char [Siz];

        if (Txt == NULL)
            ErrorHandler(SE_ALLOC);

        // copy character array into text buffer
        memcpy(Txt,cstr,Len + 1);
        }
    }
```

The constructor *String(char FillCh, unsigned int Count)*, creates a new *String* which contains *Count FillCh* characters:

```
String::String(char fillCh, size_t count)
    {
    // this constructor most store at leat one character
```

```
if (count == 0)
    ErrorHandler(SE_INVALID);

// calculate size and length
Len = count + 1;
Siz = CalcSiz(Len);

// allocate text buffer
Txt = new char[Siz];

if (Txt == NULL)
    ErrorHandler(SE_ALLOC);

// fill text buffer with fillCh
memset(Txt,fillCh,count);

// add terminating NULL
Txt[count] = '\x00';
}
```

The final constructor creates a *String* containing formatted data. It is analogous to the *sprintf* function, which formats a series of data items into a character array. In the *String* class constructor, the first argument specifies the maximum length of the output, and the *format* parameter points to a character array that contains the format specifiers (ala *printf, sprintf,* et al). Following *format* is a variable list of parameters to be formatted into the new *String*.

```
String::String(size_t maxsize, const char * format, ... )
    {
    // allocate temporary buffer
    char * buffer = new char[maxsize];

    if (buffer == NULL)
        ErrorHandler(SE_ALLOC);

    // initialize argument list
    va_list args;
```

```
va_start(args,format);

// format items into buffer based on format
Len = vsprintf(buffer,format,args);

// end argument list processing
va_end(args);

// calculate required Txt length
Siz = CalcSiz(Len);

// allocate Txt
Txt = new char[Siz];

if (Txt == NULL)
    ErrorHandler(SE_ALLOC);

// duplicate data from buffer
strcpy(Txt,buffer);

// delete buffer
delete buffer;
}
```

In the constructor implementation, I allocate a temporary character array (*buffer*) with *maxSize* characters. I used ANSI-standard macros to process the variable-argument list, which, along with with *buffer* and *format*, is passed to the ANSI *vsprintf* function. *Len* is assigned *vsprintf*'s return value, and I calculate *Siz* from *Len*. Finally, *Txt* duplicates *buffer*, and *buffer* is deleted.

Duplicating the buffer may seem like extra work; however, *maxSize* may be (and in fact, should be) larger than the number of characters generated by *vsprintf*. By allocating new space for *Txt* and copying in only the useful contents of *buffer*, I chop off any extraneous characters.

The *String* class requires a destructor to delete the memory allocated to the *Txt* instance variable when a *String* object is destroyed.

```
String::~String()
        {
        if (Txt != NULL)
            delete Txt;
        }
```

## 3.7 Conversion Operator

Often a programmer will want to use a *String* in place of a character array. This conversion can be accomplished with the conversion operator I defined for *String*.

```
class String
        {
        .
        .
        .
        public:
            operator const char * () const;
        .
        .
        .
        };
```

The conversions function allows a *String* to be cast to a *const char \**. This permits *String* objects to be used anywhere that *const char \**s are accepted, such as in ANSI-library functions.

```
inline String::operator const char * () const
        {
        return (const char *)Txt;
        }
```

*Txt* points to a NUL-terminated buffer, and the conversion operator returns the value of *Txt* cast to a *const char \**. I define the conversion operator as a *const* function, so that it can be used with *const Strings*.

The conversion is used like this:

```
String Str = "Hello!";
    puts((const char *)Str);
```

The const specifier is used to prevent modification of the character array pointed to by *Txt*. In other words, the pointer conversion operator can be used to examine the value of *Str*, but it cannot change it.

## 3.8 Assignment Operator

Every class should define an assignment operator.

```
class String
    {
    .
    .
    .
    public:
        String operator = (const String & str);
    .
    .
    .
    };
```

The definition of the assignment operator looks like this:

```
String String::operator = (const String & str)
    {
    Len = str.Len;
    Siz = str.Siz;

    if (Txt != NULL)
        delete Txt;

    if (Siz == 0)
        Txt = NULL;
    else
        {
        Txt = new char[Siz];

        if (Txt == NULL)
            ErrorHandler(SE_ALLOC);

        memcpy(Txt,str.Txt,Len + 1);
```

```
            }

    return *this;
    }
```

## 3.9  Concatenation

I defined the + and += operators to concatenate two *Strings*, performing the same function as the ANSI *strcat* function.

```
class String
        {
        .
        .
        .
        public:
            friend String operator + (const String & str1,
                                       const String & str2);

            friend String operator + (const String & str1, char
    ch);

            void operator += (const String & str);
            void operator += (char ch);
        .
        .
        .
        };
```

The binary + operator concatenates two strings, returning a new *String* object. The function begins by calculating the total length of the combined text, and allocates an appropriately sized *Txt* buffer for *temp* (the return value). The *Txt* buffers in both source strings are then copied into *temp.Txt*, and the length of *temp* is calculated. The function returns *temp* as its result.

```
String operator + (const String & str1,
                   const String & str2)
        {
        // create an empty string
        String temp;
```

```
// calculate length of new string
unsigned long totalLen = str1.Len + str2.Len;

// if both source strings are empty, so is the result
if (totalLen == 0)
    return temp;

// if length is greater than maximum string length
if (totalLen > UINT_MAX)
    String::ErrorHandler(SE_TOO_LONG);


temp.Len = 0;
temp.Siz = String::CalcSiz((size_t)totalLen);

// allocate text buffer for result
temp.Txt = new char[temp.Siz];

if (temp.Txt == NULL)
    String::ErrorHandler(SE_ALLOC);


// copy str1 to result    if (str1.Txt != NULL)
    {
    memcpy(temp.Txt,str1.Txt,str1.Len);
    temp.Len = str1.Len;
    }

// copy str2 to result
if (str2.Txt != NULL)
    {
    memcpy(&temp.Txt[temp.Len],str2.Txt,str2.Len + 1);
    temp.Len += str2.Len;
    }

// return new string
return temp;
}
```

I defined the shorthand operator as a call to the binary operator.

```
inline void String::operator += (const String & str)
    {
    *this = *this + str;
    }
```

If a character array is passed to either of these member functions, the conversion constructor converts it to a temporary *String* object before calling the function.

Two other member functions employ the + operator to concatenate a single character to a *String*.

```
inline void String::operator += (char ch)
    {
    *this = *this + ch;
    }

String operator + (const String & str, char ch)
    {
    String temp;

    if (str.Txt == NULL)
        {
        // if str is empty, the result is a string containing
ch
        temp.Len = 1;
        temp.Siz = String::AllocIncr;

        // allocate text buffer
        temp.Txt = new char [temp.Siz];

        if (temp.Txt == NULL)
            String::ErrorHandler(SE_ALLOC);

        // insert ch and terminating NUL
        temp.Txt[0] = ch;
        temp.Txt[1] = '\000';
        }
    else
```

```
      {
      // if string is max length, can't add any more
      // characters
      if (str.Len == UINT_MAX)
          String::ErrorHandler(SE_TOO_LONG);

      // increment string length
      temp.Len = str.Len + 1;

      // if Len is larger than Siz, increase Siz
      if (temp.Len == str.Siz)
          temp.Siz = str.Siz + String::AllocIncr;
      else
          temp.Siz = str.Siz;

      // allocate text buffer
      temp.Txt = new char[temp.Siz];

      if (temp.Txt == NULL)
          String::ErrorHandler(SE_ALLOC);

      // copy str.Txt to text buffer
      memcpy(temp.Txt,str.Txt,str.Len);

      // append ch
      temp.Txt[str.Len]  = ch;
      temp.Txt[temp.Len] = '\000';
      }

   return temp;
   }
```

## 3.10 Comparison Operators

Several comparison operators are defined for *Strings*.

```
class String
      {
      .
      .
```

```
          .
     public:
          int String::operator <  (const String & str) const
          int String::operator <= (const String & str) const
          int String::operator == (const String & str) const
          int String::operator != (const String & str) const
          int String::operator >= (const String & str) const
          int String::operator >  (const String & str) const
          .
          .
          .
     };
```

The symbolic comparison operators are most efficiently implemented inline, and they all call the *Compare* member function:

```
inline int String::operator <  (const String & str) const
     {
     return (Compare(str) == SC_LESS);
     }

   inline int String::operator >  (const String & str) const
        {
        return (Compare(str) == SC_GREATER);
        }

   inline int String::operator <= (const String & str) const
        {
        return (Compare(str) != SC_GREATER);
        }

   inline int String::operator >= (const String & str) const
        {
        return (Compare(str) != SC_LESS);
        }

   inline int String::operator == (const String & str) const
        {
        return (Compare(str) == SC_EQUAL);
        }
```

```
inline int String::operator != (const String & str) const
    {
    return (Compare(str) != SC_EQUAL);
    }
```

These member functions use symbolic comparison operators as a shell over the
*Compare* member function. I originally implemented individual comparison functions for each operator, only to see that all of the functions were virtually identical.
*Compare* combines all the comparisons into a single function, and the inline operator
functions return appropriate results. No efficiency is lost, code size is reduced, and
a program using these operators looks more natural when read.

*Compare* compares two *Strings* character for character, returning an enumeration value of type *StrCompVal*, which indicates the relationship between the two
values. This works very much like the ANSI function *strcmp*, with the exception that
the *caseChk* parameter determines whether the comparison is case sensitive. The
implementation of *Compare* is:

```
StrCompVal String::Compare(const String & str,
                           StrCompMode caseChk) const
    {
    // handle special cases where one string is empty
    if (Txt == NULL)
        if (str.Txt == NULL)
            return SC_EQUAL;
        else
            return SC_LESS;

    if (str.Txt == NULL)
        return SC_GREATER;

    // compare the # of characters in the shorter string
    size_t count;

    if (str.Len < Len)
        count = str.Len;
    else
```

```
        count = Len;

    // working variables
    char    c1, c2;
    size_t i;
    if (caseChk == SM_IGNORE)
        {
        // case insensitive comparison
        for (i = 0; i < count; ++i)
            {
            // convert both characters to lowercase
            c1 = (char)tolower(Txt[i]);
            c2 = (char)tolower(str.Txt[i]);

            // if characters differ
            if (c1 != c2)
                {
                // select appropriate result
                if (c1 < c2)
                    return SC_LESS;
                else
                    return SC_GREATER;
                }
            }
        }
    else
        {
        for (i = 0; i < count; ++i)
            {
            c1 = Txt[i];
            c2 = str.Txt[i];

            // if characters differ
            if (c1 != c2)
                {
                // select appropriate result
                if (c1 < c2)
                    return SC_LESS;
                else
                    return SC_GREATER;
```

```
            }
         }
      }

   // at this point, no differences were found
   if (Len == str.Len)
      return SC_EQUAL;
   else
      {
      // is lengths differ, shorter string < longer one
      if (Len < str.Len)
         return SC_LESS;
      else
         return SC_GREATER;
      }
   }
```

## 3.11 SubString Searches

Many programs look for one string inside another. The more frequently programs need to perform a task, the more time is spent by computer scientists in trying to find a better algorithm for accomplishing that task. Several algorithms provide techniques for searching one string for another string. In this book, I'll discuss two algorithms: a brute-force algorithm for one-shot searches and a powerful, fast algorithm for performing multiple searches.

### 3.11.1 A Brute-force Algorithm

Brute-force algorithms accomplish their task by the most direct (and usually inefficient) way possible. This implementation of the member function *Find* duplicates the purpose of the ANSI library function *strstr*, by locating a given *String* within another *String*.

```
class String
      {
      .
      .
      .
      public:          size_t Find(const String & str,
```

```
                    size_t & pos,
                    StrCompMode caseChk = SM_IGNORE) const;
    .
    .
    .
};
```

*Find* returns an index that indicates where the substring begins. Like *Compare*, the *caseChk* parameter defaults to *SM_IGNORE* to indicate a case-insensitive comparison. The search can be made case-sensitive by specifying the *Case* parameter as *SM_SENSITIVE*.

This is the implementation of *Find*:

```
Boolean String::Find(const String & str,
                     size_t & pos,
                     StrCompMode caseChk) const
    {
    // uses the brute force method
    if (Len < str.Len)
        return BOOL_FALSE;

    // duplicate buffers
    char * target = new char[Len + 1];

    if (target == NULL)
        ErrorHandler(SE_ALLOC);

    strcpy(target,Txt);

    char * pattern = new char[str.Len + 1];

    if (pattern == NULL)
        ErrorHandler(SE_ALLOC);

    strcpy(pattern,str.Txt);

    // create return value variable
    Boolean result;
```

```
// convert to all lowercase if case-insensitive search
if (caseChk == SM_IGNORE)
    {
    strlwr(target);
    strlwr(pattern);
    }

// calculate last position in *this where str could be
size_t end = Len - str.Len;
size_t p, t;

// start at the beginning of ttarget
pos = 0;

for (;;)
    {
    p = 0;   // beginning of pattern
    t = pos; // beginning of search position in target

    // while characters match
    // and we're not at the end of the strings

    while ((pattern[p] == target[t])
        && (pattern[p] != 0)
        && (target[t]  != 0))
        {
        // move to next character
        ++t;
        ++p;
        }

    // if we've reached the end of pattern
    //     we've found pattern in target

    if (pattern[p] == 0)
        {
        result = BOOL_TRUE;
        break;
        }
```

```
            // if we've reached the end of target
            // or we've searched far enough
            //     pattern has not been found

            if ((target[t] == 0) || (pos >= end))
                {
                result = BOOL_FALSE;
                break;
                }

            // keep looking, starting at the mismatch

            ++pos;
            }

    // delete temporary buffers
    delete target;
    delete pattern;

    // outa here
    return result;
    }
```

Brute-force algorithms, like the one used in *Find* above, work in a direct and simplistic manner. The brute-force string-searching algorithm examines every possible position in the target string for the pattern string.

For example, let's assume that I've written an application which searches an electronic copy of Dante's *The Divine Comedy*. When the brute-force algorithm is asked to find the pattern string "unto" in the target string "Pure and disposed to mount unto the stars" (from canto XXXIII, line 145), the search begins like this:

```
target:   Pure, disposed to mount unto the stars
pattern:    unto
```

The algorithm can best be understood by placing the pattern parallel to the target. The algorithm compares the characters in the pattern to those direcly above it in the target. For example, the *u* in "unto" does not match the corresponding *p* in the target. This is not a match, and the algorithm moves the pattern right one character.

```
target:  Pure, disposed to mount unto the stars
pattern:    unto
```

The *us* in both strings match — but the second character of the pattern, *n*, does not match the corresponding character in the target, *r*. So the algorithm moves the pattern right one more character.

```
target:  Pure, disposed to mount unto the stars
pattern:     unto
```

The brute-force algorithm keeps looking for the pattern string by sliding it to the right one character every time the pattern is not found. After several more comparisons, the pattern is situated below the u in mount:

```
target:  Pure, disposed to mount unto the stars
pattern:                 unto
```

Four comparisons (one for each character in the pattern) are made before the algorithm realizes it hasn't got a a match. The pattern is moved right four more times before it finally lands under the matching word.

```
target:  Pure, disposed to mount unto the stars
pattern:                      unto
```

In the example, the brute-force algorithm performs 32 comparisons to locate the pattern string. In a worst-case situation, where the pattern isn't found in a target, the brute-force algorithm will need to perform *strlen(target) - strlen(pattern)* comparisons — and more comparisons if there are any partial matches. When performing a search many times, or when the target string is very large, the brute-force algorithm is brutally slow.

### 3.11.2 Boyer-Moore String Searching

One goal of computer science is to develop algorithms that operate using rudimentary intelligence. Robert S. Boyer and J. Strother Moore developed a very intelligent (and efficient) string-searching algorithm in 1977.

The basic implementation of the Boyer-Moore algorithm builds a table used to make decisions while searching for a substring. The table contains a number of values equal to the size of the character set being used. In most environments, characters are represented by 8-bit values; this requires a table of 256 entries to hold values for all possible characters. In an ASCII environment, the value associated with *A* would be in entry 65; the value for space would be located in entry 32.

Initially, the array should contain zeros in all entries. Then, a "delta" value is computed for each character in the pattern, as shown by this pseudo-code:

```
for index = 1 to (pattern_length)
      delta [pattern [ index - 1 ] ] = pattern_length -
   index
```

The delta value for a character is the leftmost position occurrence of that character, relative to the end of pattern. For the word "unto", *u* would be assigned 3, *n* would be assigned 2, *t* would be assigned 1, and *o* would be assigned zero.

In the brute-force algorithm, comparisons are performed from left to right; the first character of the pattern is compared against the first search position in the target, and then the second character in the pattern is compared against the second target character, and so on. The Boyer-Moore algorithm is a right-to-left algorithm; it begins by comparing the *last* character in the pattern to the corresponding character in the target.

```
target:   Pure, disposed to mount unto the stars
pattern:      unto
```

*o* is not equal to *e*; the pattern must be moved to the right. The pattern is moved to the right the number of characters from the entry in the delta table that corresponds to the target character from the mismatch. Because *e* does not appear in the pattern string its delta value is 4 (the length of the pattern), and the pattern is moved four characters left, relative to the target string.

```
target:   Pure, disposed to mount unto the stars
pattern:        unto
```

Again, the o in the pattern fails to match the corresponding character in the target. Because *i* is not in the pattern, the pattern is again moved four positions right.

```
target:   Pure, disposed to mount unto the stars
pattern:            unto
```

Another mismatch. Again, the pattern is shifted right by its length, where it reaches this position.

```
target:   Pure, disposed to mount unto the stars
pattern:                unto
```

Although the pattern's *o* does not match the corresponding *u* in the target string, the *t* does match a character in the pattern. Again, the pattern is shifted right by the delta value for *t,* which is 1.

```
target:   Pure, disposed to mount unto the stars
pattern:                 unto
```

The last two characters of the pattern match the target, but *n* does not match a space. The pattern is once again shifted by its length.

```
target:   Pure, disposed to mount unto the stars
pattern:                     unto
```

The *o* does not match the *u* in the target. *u* is a member of the string "unto," and its table entry has a delta value of 3. So the pattern is shifted right by three characters, placing the *u*s in the target and pattern strings together.

```
target:   Pure, disposed to mount unto the stars
pattern:                           unto
```

The *o* in "unto" does not match the corresponding space in the target. Again, the pattern is shifted right by its length.

```
target:   Pure, disposed to mount unto the stars
pattern:                               unto
```

And the pattern is found! Where the brute-force algorithm required more than 30 comparisons for finding the pattern, the Boyer-Moore algorithm needs only 13.

The Boyer-Moore algorithm is faster because it has information about the pattern string stored in the delta table. The character that caused the mismatch in the target string tells Boyer-Moore how to move the pattern in relation to the target. If the mismatching character in the target does not exist in the pattern, Boyer-Moore can safely move the pattern its length to the right, because it is a waste of time to compare the pattern against a character that it doesn't contain. When the mismatched character in the target is also resident in the pattern, the delta value for that character aligns the rightmost occurrence of that character in the pattern with the character in target.

### 3.11.3 The Boyer-Moore Class

Once the delta table has been created, it can be used to search for the pattern string in any target string. The overhead of creating the table is such that I wanted to create the table only once, and use it again and again. In the case where searches are being performed for several patterns, I wanted to be able to define unique delta tables for each pattern.

A class that defines a Boyer-Moore delta table is exactly what I needed. The *BoyerMoore* class is defined like this:

```
class BoyerMoore
    {
    public:
```

```
// constructors
BoyerMoore(const String & pattern);
BoyerMoore(const BoyerMoore & bm);

// destructor
~BoyerMoore();

// assignment operator
void operator = (const BoyerMoore & bm);

// get character from pattern string
char operator [] (size_t index) const;

// get delta value from table
size_t GetDelta(char ch) const;

// get length of pattern used to create table
size_t GetPatternLen() const;

// Assign an exception handler
static void SetErrOut(const ErrReporter & er);

private:

// error display object
static ErrReporter * ErrOut;

// pointer to error handler
static void ReportError();

// size of delta table
static const size_t DeltaSize;

// pointer to delta table
size_t * Delta;
String Pattern;
};
```

Inside a *BoyerMoore* object is a pointer, *Delta*, that references a dynamically allocated table of delta values. A *BoyerMoore* object also includes a duplicate of the pattern *String*, named *Pattern*. The static constant *DeltaTableSize* contains the number of characters in the character set; in this case, I assume that characters are 8-bit values, and initialize *DeltaTableSize* to 256.

```
const size_t BoyerMoore::DeltaSize = 256;
```

Because *BoyerMoore* objects allocate memory, they need to use an *ErrReporter* object to report any problems. The error-handling scheme is the same as that used by the *String* class.

```
ErrReporter * BoyerMoore::ErrOut = NULL;

    // report an error
    void BoyerMoore::ReportError()
        {
        if (ErrOut != NULL)
            ErrOut->Fatal("Boyer-Moore allocation failure");
        }

    // Assign an exception handler
    void BoyerMoore::SetErrOut(const ErrReporter & er)
        {
        if (ErrOut != NULL)
            delete ErrOut;

        ErrOut = new ErrReporter(er);
        }
```

A *BoyerMoore* object can be created only from a pattern *String* or another existing *BoyerMoore* object. The primary constructor duplicates the pattern *String*, and then builds a delta table from it.

```
BoyerMoore::BoyerMoore(const String & pat)
        : Pattern(pat)
        {
        // allocate delta table
        Delta = new size_t [DeltaSize];
```

```
    if (Delta == NULL)
        ReportError();

    // clear table
    size_t i;

    // get length of pattern
    size_t patlen = Pattern.Length();

    for (i = 0; i < DeltaSize; ++i)
        Delta[i] = patlen;

    // set table values
    for (i = 1; i < patlen; ++i)
        Delta[(size_t)Pattern[i - 1]] = patlen - i;

    // set value for last pattern character
    Delta[(size_t)Pattern[patlen - 1]] = 1;
    }
```

The copy constructor simply duplicates the *Delta* table of the source object.

```
BoyerMoore::BoyerMoore(const BoyerMoore & bm)
        : Pattern(bm.Pattern)
        {
        // allocate delta table
        Delta = new size_t [DeltaSize];

        if (Delta == NULL)
            ReportError();

        // copy contents of source
        memcpy(Delta,bm.Delta,DeltaSize);
        }
```

The destructor deletes the Delta table when the object is destroyed.

```
inline BoyerMoore::~BoyerMoore()
        {
        delete Delta;
        }
```

I defined an assignment operator for *BoyerMoore* objects.

```
void BoyerMoore::operator = (const BoyerMoore & bm)
     {
     Delta = bm.Delta;
     }
```

Three interrogation functions provide information about the pattern and its delta table. The *[ ]* operator is an inline function that returns a character from the *Pattern String*. *PatternLen* is also an inline function that returns the value from calling the *String::Length* function for *Pattern*.

```
// get length of pattern used to create table
    inline size_t BoyerMoore::GetPatternLen() const
        {
        return Pattern.Length();
        }

    inline char BoyerMoore::operator [] (size_t index) const
        {
        return Pattern[index];
        };
```

Why not derive *BoyerMoore* from *String*? I wanted to limit the types of operations that could be performed on the pattern *String*. Any modifications to the *Pattern* after it has been used to create the delta table will invalidate that table. The pattern *String* can only be examined; it cannot be changed or manipulated in any other fashion.

The remaining interrogation function returns the value from *Delta* for the character *ch*.

```
inline size_t BoyerMoore::GetDelta(char ch) const
     {
     return Delta[size_t(ch)];
     }
```

### 3.11.4  Boyer-Moore Searching for String

I created a second *Find* function that takes a *BoyerMoore* object as a parameter.

```
class String
    {
    .
    .
    .
    public:
        // Boyer-Moore string search
        Boolean Find(const BoyerMoore & bm, size_t & pos);
    .
    .
    .
    };
```

The Boyer-Moore *Find* function is implemented like this:

```
Boolean String::Find(const BoyerMoore & bm, size_t & pos)
    {
    size_t i, j, patlen;

    // store pattern length locally (it gets used a lot)
    patlen = bm.GetPatternLen();

    // i is the index into the target
    i = patlen;

    while (i <= Len)
        {
        // j is an index into pattern
        j = patlen;

        // while corresponding characters match
        while (bm[j - 1] == Txt[i - 1])
            {
            if (j > 1)
                {
                // move left one character for next comparison
```

```
                         -j;
                         -i;
                         }
             else
                 {
                 // we've reached the beginning of the pattern
                 // pattern found!
                 pos = i - 1;
                 return BOOL_TRUE;
                 }
             }

         // move target index by delta value of
         // mismatched character
         i += bm.GetDelta(Txt[i - 1]);
         }

    return BOOL_FALSE;
    }
```

The delta table in the *BoyerMoore* object is used to change the position in the target string where the pattern is being compared. The function returns BOOL_FALSE if the pattern was not found. If the pattern was found, BOOL_TRUE is returned, and the variable parameter *pos* is set to hold the index within the target at which the first occurrence of the pattern was found.

## 3.12 Substring Deletion

The *Delete* member function removes a specified number of characters from a string.

```
class String
    {
    .
    .
    .
    public:
```

```
void String::Delete(size_t pos, size_t count = 1);
    .
    .
    .
};
```

The parameter *pos* provides the index of the first character to be deleted, and the *count* parameter indicates how many characters are to be deleted. If count isn't specified, it defaults to one, so the *Delete* operator removes a single character from the string. Here is the implementation of *Delete*:

```
void String::Delete(size_t pos, size_t count)
    {
    if (Txt == NULL)
        return;

    size_t newLen, i;

    // error if deleting outside of string
    if ((pos + count - 1) > Len)
        ErrorHandler(SE_INVALID);

    // length of new string
    newLen = Len - count;

    if ((Siz - newLen) > AllocIncr)
        {
        // allocation size has changed
        // calculate new size

        Siz = CalcSiz(newLen);

        // create new buffer

        char * temp = new char[Siz];

        if (temp == NULL)
            ErrorHandler(SE_ALLOC);
```

```
            // copy characters into new buffer
            char * tptr = temp;

            for (i = 0; i <= Len; ++i)
                {
                // when count is reached, skip deleted characters
                if (i == pos)
                    i += count;

                *tptr = Txt[i];
                ++tptr;
                }

            // delete old buffer
            delete Txt;

            // assign new buffer
            Txt = temp;
            }
        else
            {
            // just "slide" characters down
            for (i = pos + count; i <= Len; ++i)
                Txt[i] = Txt[i + count];
            }

        Len = newLen;
        }
```

## 3.13 String Insertion

Characters and strings can be inserted into a *String* at any position using the *Insert* member functions.

```
    class String
        {
        .
        .
        .
        public:
            void Insert(size_t pos, char ch);
```

**74**

```
        void Insert(size_t pos, const String & str);
    .
    .
    .
    };
```

The first *Insert* member function listed inserts a single character:

```
void String::Insert(size_t pos, char ch)
    {
    if (pos > Len)
        ErrorHandler(SE_INVALID);

    if (Txt == NULL)
        {
        // an empty string == ch
        Len = 1;
        Siz = AllocIncr;

        Txt = new char [Siz];

        if (Txt == NULL)
            String::ErrorHandler(SE_ALLOC);

        Txt[0] = ch;
        Txt[1] = '\000';
        }
    else
        {
        size_t newLen = Len + 1;
        size_t i;

        if (newLen == Siz)
            {
            // need a larger buffer
            Siz += AllocIncr;

            // create temporary buffer
            char * temp = new char[Siz];
```

```
            char * tptr = temp;

            if (temp == NULL)
                ErrorHandler(SE_ALLOC);

            // copy in old buffer, inserting ch when needed
            for (i = 0; i <= Len; ++i)
                {
                if (i == pos)
                    {
                    *tptr = ch;
                    ++tptr;
                    }

                *tptr = Txt[i];
                ++tptr;
                }

            // delete old buffer
            delete Txt;

            // assign new buffer and length
            Txt = temp;
            Len = newLen;
            }
        else
            {
            // slide characters right
            for (i = newLen; i > pos; --i)
                Txt[i] = Txt[i-1];

            // insert character
            Txt[pos] = ch;

            // adjust length
            Len = newLen;
            }
        }
    }
```

The second inserts an entire *String*:

```
void String::Insert(size_t pos, const String & str)
    {
    if (str.Txt == NULL)
        return;

    if (pos > Len)
        ErrorHandler(SE_INVALID);

    if (Txt == NULL)
        {
        // empty string = str
        *this = str;
        }
    else
        {
        // calculate new length
        unsigned long totalLen = str.Len + Len;

        if (totalLen > UINT_MAX)
            ErrorHandler(SE_TOO_LONG);

        size_t i, j;

        // if new  length > current size
        if (totalLen > Siz)
            {
            // allocate new buffer
            Siz = CalcSiz((size_t)totalLen);

            char * temp = new char [Siz];
            char * tptr = temp;

            // copy buffers from source strings
            for (i = 0; i <= Len; ++i)
                {
                if (i == pos)
                    {
                    for (j = 0; j < str.Len; ++j)
```

```
                    {
                    *tptr = str.Txt[j];
                    ++tptr;
                    }
                }

            *tptr = Txt[i];
            ++tptr;
            }

        // delete old buffer
        delete Txt;

        // assign new buffer
        Txt = temp;
        }
    else
        {
        // slide section old buffer to right
        for (i = Len + str.Len; i > pos + str.Len; —i)
            Txt[i] = Txt[i - str.Len];

        // insert new string
        for (i = 0; i < str.Len; ++i)
            Txt[pos + i] = str.Txt[i];
        }

    Len = (size_t)totalLen;
    }
}
```

Once again, the conversion constructor permits the use of a character array in place of the *String* parameter in both *Insert* member functions.

## 3.14 Substring Extraction

The various "cut" member functions extract portions of a string.

```
class String
    {
    .
    .
    .
    public:
        String Cut(size_t start, size_t count);
        String CutHead(size_t count);
        String CutTail(size_t count);
    .
    .
    .
    };
```

The *Cut* function extracts *count* characters beginning at start.

```
String String::Cut(size_t start, size_t count)
    {
    if ((start + count) > Len)
        ErrorHandler(SE_INVALID);

    String temp;

    if ((start < Len) && (count > 0))
        {
        temp.Len = count;
        temp.Siz = CalcSiz(count);
        temp.Txt = new char[temp.Siz];

        if (temp.Txt == NULL)
            ErrorHandler(SE_ALLOC);

        memcpy(temp.Txt,&Txt[start],count);

        temp.Txt[count] = '\000';
        }

    return temp;
    }
```

*CutHead* cuts *count* characters from the front of the *String*, and *CutTail* extracts *count* characters from the end of a *String*.

```
String String::CutHead(size_t count)
      {
    if (count > Len)
        ErrorHandler(SE_INVALID);

    String temp;

    if (count > 0)
        {
        temp.Len = count;
        temp.Siz = CalcSiz(count);
        temp.Txt = new char[temp.Siz];

        if (temp.Txt == NULL)
            ErrorHandler(SE_ALLOC);

        memcpy(temp.Txt,Txt,count);

        temp.Txt[count] = '\000';
        }

    return temp;
    }

    String String::CutTail(size_t count)
      {
    if (count > Len)
        ErrorHandler(SE_INVALID);

    String temp;

    if (count > 0)
        {
        temp.Len = count;
        temp.Siz = CalcSiz(count);
        temp.Txt = new char[temp.Siz];
```

```
        if (temp.Txt == NULL)
            ErrorHandler(SE_ALLOC);

        memcpy(temp.Txt,&Txt[Len - count - 1],count);

        temp.Txt[count] = '\000';
        }

    return temp;
    }
```

All of these member functions create a new string that contains the characters extracted from the implicit object.

## 3.15 Indexing

Single characters at indexed positions within a *String* can be examined with the operator [] function.

```
class String
        {
        .
        .
        .
        public:
            char operator [] (size_t pos) const;
        .
        .
        .
        };
```

The String operator function [] is used exactly as the [] operators are used on a C-like array of characters. However, while you can index outside a C-like string, the [] operator implementation prevents indexing into areas outside a *String*'s boundaries. If the position given is beyond the last character of the *String*, a NUL character is returned. I implement the [] operator inline.

```
inline char String::operator [] (size_t pos) const
        {
        if (pos >= Len)
            return '\x00';
        else
            return Txt[pos];
        }
```

## 3.16 Case Conversion

The last four member functions for *String* are *ToUpper*, *ToLower*, *AsUpper*, and *AsLower*.

```
class String
        {
        .
        .
        .
        public:
            void ToUpper();
            void ToLower();

            String AsUpper();
            String AsLower();
        .
        .
        .
        .
        };
```

These member functions convert all of the characters in a *String* to uppercase or lowercase. The *To...* functions change the *String* object directly.

```
void String::ToUpper()
        {
        if (Txt != NULL)
            strupr(Txt);
        }

    void String::ToLower()
```

```
        {
        if (Txt != NULL)
            strlwr(Txt);
        }
```

The *As...* functions return a new *String* with the same text as the original but with the case changed.

```
String String::AsUpper()
        {
        String temp = *this;

        if (temp.Txt != NULL)
            strupr(temp.Txt);

        return temp;
        }

    String String::AsLower()
        {
        String temp = *this;

        if (temp.Txt != NULL)
            strlwr(temp.Txt);

        return temp;
        }
```

## 3.17 Stream I/O

C++ permits the creation of operators that read and write objects to I/O streams. For the *String* class, I defined input and output operator functions.

```
class String
        {
        .
        .
        .
        public:
            friend ostream & operator << (ostream & strm,
```

```
                                        const String & str);

        friend istream & operator >> (istream & strm,
                                      String & str);
        .
        .
        .
        };
```

The output function is very simple; it uses the character array insertion function to write *str.Txt* to *strm*.

```
inline ostream & operator << (ostream & strm, const String & str)
        {
        strm << str.Txt;

        return strm;
        }
```

The input function was more difficult to implement. I wanted to avoid overflowing *str.Txt*, but I also wanted to allow for the creation of a string of whatever length was input. I reached a compromise in my implementation of the stream extraction operator:

```
istream & operator >> (istream & strm, String & str)
        {
        static char buf[128];

        if ((str.Txt == NULL) || (str.Len == 0))
            {
            strm >> setw(128) >> buf;

            #ifdef __ZTC__
                str = (const char *)buf;
            #else
                str = buf;
            #endif
            }
        else
```

```
strm >> setw(str.Siz) >> str.Txt;


  return strm;
  }
```

If *str* is empty, I create a temporary buffer of 128 characters in length, insert characters into that buffer from *strm*, and then duplicate the contents of *buffer* in *Txt* and assign values to *Len* and *Siz* based on the input data. If *str* has already allocated *Txt*, I use the *Siz* of that buffer as the maximum length of the input. In both cases, I use the *setw* manipulator to prevent overflow of the input array.

I'm certain this isn't a perfect solution, but it has worked well enough for me to live with it.

## 3.18 Moving On

The *String* class has been immensely useful to me. I now use *Strings* everywhere I can to replace C's NUL-terminated character arrays. In particular, the searching, substring, insertion, and deletion features of *String* objects make them useful for interactive programs such as word processors and data-entry programs. *Strings* are also more reliable than character arrays; common program bugs with *char* arrays include a failure to allocate a large enough space, forgetting to add the terminating NUL, or simply writing into an area of a *char* array which is outside of the array bounds. The *String* class is an example of how a C++ class can improve programs by providing reliable and powerful new data types.

# PART II

# Arrays

# CHAPTER 4

# Ranges and Indexes

## 4.1 Ranged Values

In some cases, it's valuable to have an integral numeric data type that is bounded by a high and low value. Pascal and Modula-2 support subrange data types that allow the programmer to define the specific range for an integral value. In the case of C++, classes can provide the means for creating a subrange feature.

### 4.1.1 Data Members

I prefer to begin simply, by creating a data type that defines the upper and lower bounds of an *int* value. The class needs data elements which contain the upper and lower values of the *int*. For algorithmic purposes, the number of values in the range should be stored.

Error reporting requires the inclusion of a static *ErrReporter* object. Error checking produces overhead, however. To eliminate that overhead, I included two mechanisms for removing error checking.

A static *Switch* value is included so that error checking can be turned on and off at run time. For example, you may want error checking in place for some sections of a program, but not for others. Setting the *Switch* to *OFF* prevents the error-checking code from being executed.

To remove the error-checking code completely at compile time, you can define the symbol RANGE_CHK_OFF. The error-checking code is not included when RANGE_CHK_OFF is defined.

The data definition of a *Range* looks like this:

```
class Range
    {
    protected:
```

```
        // minimum and maximum value
        int Minimum;
        int Maximum;
    // difference of min and max
        unsigned int Magnitude;

        // members used in error reporting
        #ifndef RANGE_CHK_OFF
            static ErrReporter * ErrOut;
            static Switch RangeCheck;
        #endif
    .
    .
    .
    };
```

If RANGE_CHK_OFF is not defined, the static members *RangeCheck* and *ErrOut* need to be initialized.

```
#ifndef RANGE_CHK_OFF
ErrReporter * Range::ErrOut = NULL;Switch Range::RangeCheck =
OFF;
```

### 4.1.2 Constructors

I provided *Range* with three constructors.

```
class Range
    {
    .
    .
    .
    public:
        Range(int rmin, int rmax);
        Range(int rmax);
        Range(const Range & r);
    .
    .
    .
    };
```

The first constructor is given both the minimum and maximum bounds for the *Range*. An error is reported if *rmax* is less than the *rmin*; otherwise, *Minimum* is assigned *rmin*, *Maximum* is assigned *rmax*, and *Magnitude* is calculated.

```
Range::Range(int rmin, int rmax)
    {
    #ifndef RANGE_CHK_OFF
        if (RangeCheck == ON)
            {
            if (rmax < rmin)
                ErrExit.Handler("construction with max <
min");
            }
    #endif

    Minimum = rmin;
    Maximum = rmax;

    if (Minimum < 0)
        {
        if (Maximum < 0)
            Magnitude = (unsigned int)(Minimum - Maximum);
        else
            Magnitude = (unsigned int)(-Minimum)
                        + (unsigned int)Maximum;
        }
    else
        Magnitude = Maximum - Minimum;

    ++Magnitude;
    }
```

The second constructor assumes that the *Minimum* value is 1. The *rmax* value defines the upper bound of the *Range*.

```
Range::Range(int rmax)
    {
    #ifndef RANGE_CHK_OFF
```

```
        if (RangeCheck == ON)
            {
            if (rmax <= 1)
                ErrExit.Handler("invalid construction");
            }
    #endif

    Minimum   = 1;
    Maximum   = rmax;
    Magnitude = rmax + 1;
    }
```

The last constructor is the obligatory copy constructor. I almost always define a copy constructor, even though the compiler can generate one for me. In this case, the copy constructor simply copies the instance variables of the source object. Simple constructors like this can be implemented inline.

```
inline Range::Range(const Range & r)
    {
    Minimum   = r.Minimum;
    Maximum   = r.Maximum;
    Magnitude = r.Magnitude;
    }
```

### 4.1.3 Operators

Four operator functions are defined for *Range*.

```
class Range
    {
    .
    .
    .
    public:
        Range & operator = (const Range & r);

        friend Range operator + (const Range & r1,
                                  const Range & r2);

        int operator == (const Range & r) const;
```

```
int operator != (const Range & r) const;

    .
    .
    .

};
```

The assignment operator looks very similar to the copy constructor. It returns a pointer to *this* so that assignments can be chained (e.g., a = b = c).

```
inline Range & Range::operator = (const Range & r)
    {
    Minimum   = r.Minimum;
    Maximum   = r.Maximum;
    Magnitude = r.Magnitude;

    return *this;
    }
```

Note: Although the assignment operator and the copy constructor look the same, they serve very different purposes. The assignment operator assigns the value of an object to an existing object, and the copy constructor creates a new object from an existing object.

Two *Ranges* can be combined using the + operator. The lower bound of *r1* is used as the *Minimum* value for the new *Range*; the *Magnitude* of *r2* is added to the *Maximum* value of *r1* to obtain the new *Range's Maximum*.

```
Range operator + (const Range & r1, const Range & r2)
    {
#ifndef RANGE_CHK_OFF
    if (Range::RangeCheck == ON)
        {
        if ((INT_MAX - r1.Maximum) < r2.Magnitude)
            Range::ErrExit.Handler(
                "range addition out of range");
        }
#endif

    Range result(r1.Minimum,r1.Maximum + r2.Magnitude);
```

```
return result;
}
```

*Ranges* can be compared using the == and != operators. Two *Ranges* are equal if they have the same *Minimum* and *Maximum*. The comparison functions are declared *const* so that they can be used to compare constant *Ranges*. These simple functions are implemented inline.

```
inline int Range::operator == (const Range & r) const
    {
    return ((Minimum == r.Minimum) &&
                 (r.Maximum == r.Maximum));
    }

   inline int Range::operator != (const Range & r) const
      {
      return ((Minimum != r.Minimum)
                  || (r.Maximum != r.Maximum));
      }
```

### 4.1.4 Interrogation Functions

It's bad C++ programming practice to make the data members of a class public. Although a public data member can be read easily when needed, it can also be modified directly from outside of the class scope. Using interrogation functions allows data members to be read without leaving them open to modification.

```
class Range
    {
    .
    .
    .
    public:
        int GetMin() const;
        int GetMax() const;

        unsigned int GetMagnitude() const;
    .
    .
    .
    };
```

These functions return, respectively, the *Minimum*, *Maximum*, and *Magnitude* members of a *Range*. Implementing these functions inline actually produces smaller (and vastly faster) code than does the use of callable functions.

```
inline int Range::GetMin() const
    {
    return Minimum;
    }

    inline int Range::GetMax() const
        {
        return Maximum;
        }

    inline unsigned int Range::GetMagnitude() const
        {
        return Magnitude;
        }
```

### 4.1.5 Checking Values

Five functions can compare an *int* value against a *Range*.

```
class Range
    {
    .
    .
    .
    public:
        void Check(int n) const;

        int Includes(int n) const;
        int Includes(const Range & r) const;

        int Excludes(int n) const;
        int Excludes(const Range & r) const;
    .
    .
    .
    };
```

If the given *int* is out of range, the *Check* function uses *ErrExit* to display an error message.

```
void Range::Check(int n) const
    {
    #ifndef RANGE_CHK_OFF
        if ((RangeCheck == ON)

    && ((n < Minimum) || (n > Maximum)))
            ErrExit.Handler("value out of range");
    #endif
    }
```

The *Includes* functions return a nonzero value if the given *int* or *Range* is within bounds; otherwise, they return 0. The *Excludes* functions return 0 if the parameter is in bounds; otherwise, they return 1. These four functions are implemented inline.

```
inline int Range::Includes(int n) const
    {
    return ((n >= Minimum) && (n <= Maximum));
    }

inline int Range::Includes(const Range & r) const
    {
    return ((Minimum <= r.Minimum) && (Maximum >= r.Maximum));
    }

inline int Range::Excludes(int n) const
    {
    return ((n < Minimum) || (n > Maximum));
    }

inline int Range::Excludes(const Range & r) const
    {
    return ((Minimum > r.Minimum) || (Maximum < r.Maximum));
    }
```

### 4.1.6 Range-Checking Control

Range checking can be turned on and off — and its current state can be determined — with these functions.

```
class Range
    {
    .
    .
    .
    public:
        static void CheckOn();
        static void CheckOff();

        static Switch GetCheck();
    .
    .
    .
    };
```

These are simple functions that set or return the value of *RangeCheck*; as such, they've been implemented inline.

```
inline void Range::CheckOn()
    {
    #ifndef RANGE_CHK_OFF
        RangeCheck = ON;
    #endif
    }

  inline void Range::CheckOff()
    {
    #ifndef RANGE_CHK_OFF
        RangeCheck = OFF;
    #endif
    }

  inline Switch Range::GetCheck()
    {
```

```
#ifndef RANGE_CHK_OFF
    return RangeCheck;
#else
    return OFF
#endif
}
```

The class definition and inline functions for *Range* are in the file *range.h*. The non-inline functions and static initializations are located in the file *range.cxx*. These two files are listed in their entirety in Appendix A.

### 4.1.7 Error Handling

I used the error handling technique discussed in Chapter 1, where an *ErrReporter* object (pointed to by a static class member) is used by an error-reporting function to display messages.

```
class Range
    {
    .
    .
    .
public:
    #ifndef RANGE_CHK_OFF
        static Boolean SetErrOut(const ErrReporter & er);
    #endif

protected:
    #ifndef RANGE_CHK_OFF
        static ErrReporter * ErrOut;

        static void ReportError(const String & str);
    #endif
    .
    .
    .
    };
```

*ErrOut* is initialized with *NULL*, as shown in section 4.1.1. The *ReportError* function checks the value of *ErrOut*; if *ErrOut* is not equal to *NULL*, then *ReportError* uses the *ErrReporter* object to display the *msg* string.

```
#ifndef RANGE_CHK_OFF
    void Range::ReportError(const String & msg)
        {
        if (ErrOut != NULL)
            ErrOut->Fatal(msg);
        }
    #endif
```

Error messages are displayed only if *ErrOut* points to an *ErrReporter* object. The *SetErrOut* function performs this task.

```
#ifndef RANGE_CHK_OFF
    Boolean Range::SetErrOut(const ErrReporter & er)
        {
        // delete any object pointed to by ErrOut
        if (ErrOut != NULL)
            delete ErrOut;

        ErrOut = new ErrReporter(er);

        if (ErrOut == NULL)
            return BOOL_FALSE;
        else
            return BOOL_TRUE;
        }
    #endif
```

*SetErrOut* allocates a new *ErrReporter* object from *er*. To make sure that *er* points to a valid *ErrReporter* object, I defined it as a reference. A program that will display *Range* errors must create an *ErrReporter* object and assign it to *ErrOut* by means of *SetErrOut*.

```
ErrReporter * RangeErr = new DosErrReporter("Range error");
    Range::SetErrOut(RangeErr);
    delete RangeErr;
```

It is inefficient to create an object, pass it to a function, have that function duplicate the object, and then delete the original. However, because this is done only once in a program, and the creation of an *ErrReporter* object is trivial, the effect on program performance is minimal.

In exchange for a small performance penalty, my technique allows a program to select the type of *ErrReporter* used by *Range* objects. In the example above, a *DosErrReporter* object is created and assigned to *ErrOut*, presumably in a text-based program. For a program that operates under a windowed environment, a program could define a class that is a window-based derivative of *ErrReporter*, assigning a "window *ErrReporter*" object to *ErrOut* such that all *Range* error messages will be displayed in a window.

## 4.2 Indexes

Arrays have a lower and upper bound; the index used to reference array elements should be within these bounds. Keeping a value within bounds is the job of a *Range* object.

### 4.2.1 Data Members

An *Index* data type is essentially a *Range* that has a specific value. Thus, I derived the *Index* class from *Range*, adding a new data member named *Value*.

```
class Index : public Range
     {
     .
     .
     .
     protected:
         int Value;
     .
     .
     .
     };
```

98

### 4.2.2 Constructors

Four constructors build *Index* objects.

```
class Index : public Range
        {
        .
        .
        .
        public:
            Index(int imin, int imax);
            Index(const Range & r);
            Index(const Range & r, int i);
            Index(const Index & i);
        .
        .
        .
        };
```

The first constructor calls the *Range* constructor with *rmin == imin* and *rmax == imax*. It then sets *Value* equal to *imin*.

```
inline Index::Index(int imin, int imax)
        : Range(imin,imax)
        {
        Value = Minimum;
        }
```

The second constructor creates an *Index* from a *Range*. As you'll see in subsequent chapters, a constant *Range* can be used to define consistent bounds for *Arrays* and their related *Indexes*. The initial *Value* is *Minimum*.

```
inline Index::Index(const Range & r)
        : Range(r)
        {
        Value = Minimum;
        }
```

A variation of the second constructor allows an *Index* to be created from a *Range* with a *Value* other than *Minimum*.

```
Index::Index(const Range & r, int i)
      : Range(r)
      {
      #ifndef RANGE_CHK_OFF
          if (RangeCheck == ON)
              {
              if ((i < Minimum) || (i > Maximum))
                  ErrExit.Handler("assignment out of range");
              }
      #endif

      Value = i;
      }
```

The last constructor is the copy constructor.

```
inline Index::Index(const Index & i)
      : Range(i)
      {
      Value = i.Value;
      }
```

### 4.2.3 Conversions

The *Index* class defines two conversion operators.

```
class Index : public Range
      {
      .
      .
      .

      public:
          operator int() const;          // returns exact value
          operator unsigned int() const; // returns relative
    value
      .
      .
      .
      };
```

The *int()* operator returns *Value*; it is an inline function.

```
inline Index::operator int () const
        {
        return Value;
        }
```

The *unsigned int()* operator returns the value of the *Index* relative to zero. As you'll see in the next chapter, the *unsigned int()* conversion is very useful when indexing from a pointer.

```
Index::operator unsigned int () const
        {
        unsigned long result;

        if (Minimum < 0)
            {
            result = (unsigned int)(-Minimum);

            if (Value < 0)
                result -= (unsigned int)(-Value);
            else
                result += (unsigned int)Value;
            }
        else
            result = (unsigned int)(Value - Minimum);

        return result;
        }
```

### 4.2.4 Setting and Checking Values

These four functions are used to handle special *Values* of an *Index*.

```
class Index : public Range
        {
        .
        .
        .
```

```
public:
    int IsMin() const;
    int IsMax() const;

    void SetMin();
    void SetMax();
    .
    .
    .
};
```

Two Boolean interrogation functions check to see if *Value* is equal to *Minimum* or *Maximum*.

```
inline int Index::IsMin() const
    {
    return (Value == Minimum);
    }

    inline int Index::IsMax() const
        {
        return (Value == Maximum);
        }
```

The last two functions set *Value* to *Minimum* or *Maximum*. This makes it easier to handle "unknown" *Index* objects that are passed as parameters to functions.

```
inline void Index::SetMin()
    {
    Value = Minimum;
    }
```

### 4.2.5 Operators

These functions define assignment, addition, and subtraction operations.

```
class Index : public Range
    {
    .
    .
```

```
public:
    Index & operator = (int n);
    Index & operator = (const Index & i);

    Index operator + (const Index & i);
    Index operator - (const Index & i);

    Index operator + (int i);
    Index operator - (int i);

    Index & operator += (const Index & i);
    Index & operator -= (const Index & i);

    Index & operator += (int n);
    Index & operator -= (int n);

    Index & operator ++ ();
    Index & operator - ();
    .
    .
    .
    };
```

When an *int* is assigned to an *Index*, the class reports an error if it is not within bounds.

```
Index & Index::operator = (int i)
    {
    #ifndef RANGE_CHK_OFF
        if (RangeCheck == ON)
            {
            if ((i < Minimum) || (i > Maximum))
                ErrExit.Handler("assignment out of range");
            }
    #endif

    Value = i;

    return *this;
    }
```

The assignment of one *Index* to another may not be executed exactly as you would expect. Only the *Value* of the source *Index* is copied; the destination retains its *Minimum*, *Maximum*, and *Magnitude*. This allows *Indexes* with overlapping ranges to be mutually assignable. An error will be reported if the source *Value* is out of range.

```
Index & Index::operator = (const Index & i)
      {
      this->Range::operator = (i);

      Value = i.Value;

      return *this;
      }
```

*Index* defines both the binary and shorthand forms of addition and subtraction; *ints* and *Indexes* can be used as operands.

The operators that add and subtract *ints* and *Indexes* are implemented like this:

```
Index Index::operator + (int i)
      {
#ifndef RANGE_CHK_OFF
      if (RangeCheck == ON)
          {
          if (i < 0)
             {
             if ((Value - Minimum) < -i)
                 ErrExit.Handler("underflow in addition");
             }
          else
             {
             if ((Maximum - Value) < i)
                 ErrExit.Handler("overflow in addition");
             }
          }
#endif
```

```
        Index result(*this);

        result.Value += i;

        return result;
        }

    Index Index::operator - (int i)
        {
    #ifndef RANGE_CHK_OFF
        if (RangeCheck == ON)
            {
            if (i > 0)
                {
                if ((Value - Minimum) < i)
                    ErrExit.Handler
                            ("underflow in subtraction");
                }
            else
                {
                if ((Maximum - Value) < -i)
                    ErrExit.Handler
                            ("overflow in subtraction");
                }
            }
    #endif

        Index result(*this);

        result.Value -= i;

        return result;
        }
```

The operators that work with *Indexes* — and the shorthand operators — are built on the functions above and implemented inline.

```
inline Index Index::operator + (const Index & i)
    {
    return *this + i.Value;
    }

    inline Index Index::operator - (const Index & i)
        {
        return *this - i.Value;
        }

    inline Index & Index::operator += (const Index & i)
        {
        return *this += i.Value;
        }

    inline Index & Index::operator -= (const Index & i)
        {
        return *this -= i.Value;
        }

    inline Index & Index::operator += (int i)
        {
        return *this = *this + i;
        }

    inline Index & Index::operator -= (int i)
        {
        return *this = *this - i;
        }
```

Incrementing and decrementing are the operations most often performed on an *Index*. As do the addition and subtraction operators, increment and decrement report an error if the calculation results in an out-of-range *Value*.

```
Index & Index::operator ++ ()
    {
    #ifndef RANGE_CHK_OFF
        if (RangeCheck == ON)
            {
```

```
                if (Value == Maximum)
                    ErrExit.Handler("overflow on increment");
                }
    #endif

    ++Value;

    return *this;
    }

Index & Index::operator - ()
    {
    #ifndef RANGE_CHK_OFF
        if (RangeCheck == ON)
            {
            if (Value == Minimum)
                ErrExit.Handler("underflow on decrement");
            }
    #endif

    -Value;

    return *this;
    }
```

### 4.2.6 Comparisons

*Indexes* can be compared against other *Indexes* and *ints* using these operator functions.

```
class Index : public Range
    {
    .
    .
    .
    public:
        int operator >  (const Index & i) const;
        int operator >= (const Index & i) const;
        int operator == (const Index & i) const;
        int operator != (const Index & i) const;
```

```
        int operator <= (const Index & i) const;
        int operator <  (const Index & i) const;

        int operator >  (int i) const;
        int operator >= (int i) const;
        int operator == (int i) const;
        int operator != (int i) const;
        int operator <= (int i) const;
        int operator <  (int i) const;
        .
        .
        .
};
```

All of these operator functions are simple enough to be implemented inline.

```
inline int Index::operator > (const Index & i) const
    {
    return (Value > i.Value);
    }

    inline int Index::operator >= (const Index & i) const
        {
        return (Value >= i.Value);
        }

    inline int Index::operator == (const Index & i) const
        {
        return (Value == i.Value);
        }

    inline int Index::operator != (const Index & i) const
        {
        return (Value != i.Value);
        }

    inline int Index::operator <= (const Index & i) const
        {
        return (Value <= i.Value);
        }
```

```
inline int Index::operator < (const Index & i) const
    {
    return (Value < i.Value);
    }

inline int Index::operator > (int i) const
    {
    return (Value > i);
    }

inline int Index::operator >= (int i) const
    {
    return (Value >= i);
    }

inline int Index::operator == (int i) const
    {
    return (Value == i);
    }

inline int Index::operator != (int i) const
    {
    return (Value != i);
    }

inline int Index::operator <= (int i) const
    {
    return (Value <= i);
    }

inline int Index::operator < (int i) const
    {
    return (Value < i);
    }
```

### 4.2.7  Using Indexes

In C++ parlance, an *Index* is a type of iterator. Iterators are objects used to reference the elements of aggregate types, such as arrays. Different types of iterators are useful in different situations; Chapter 5 discusses another type of iterator, the array element pointer.

Once I implemented the *Index* class, I discovered a problem in its use. The traditional loop for an *int* index looks something like this:

```
int minimum = 1;
    int maximum = 10;

    for (int i = minimum; i <= maximum; ++i)
        cout << i << endl;
```

The *int* loop prints the numbers from 1 to 10. If you write an *Index* loop like this:

```
Range r(1,10);

    for (Index i(r); i <= r.GetMax(); ++i)
        cout << (int)i << endl;
```

it will print the numbers 1 through 10, and then generate a range-checking error!

In the *int* loop, the value of *i* is incremented past the *maximum* value. The increment operator for the *Index* loop, however, will generate an error when it tries to increment a *Maximum Index*. In a *for* loop, the "operation" part of the statement (in this case, *i++*) takes place before the loop-ending condition *(i <= r.GetMax())* is executed. How do we get around this problem?

Several solutions present themselves. For me, the best solution was the clearest one.

```
Range r(1,10);

    Index i(r);

    for (;;) // infinite loop
        {
```

```
cout << (int)i << endl;

if (i.IsMax())
    break;

++i;
}
```

The loop above generates code that is just as efficient as a *for* loop, but it avoids the range-checking problem. (Loops of this type appear often in subsequent chapters.)

I know that some programmers will miss the simplicity of a C-style *for* loop. Using *Indexes*, however, protects a program from referencing values outside of a specified range. Many a C program has entered an infinite loop with code like this:

```
unsigned char c;
    for (c = 0; c < 256; ++c)
        // do something
```

*C* will never reach 256 to end the loop; when *c* is 255 and it is incremented, an overflow occurs. The code fragment becomes an infinite loop on hardware where overflow wraps values back to zero, or an error where overflow generates an exception.

In my software design, I strive for program reliability over simplicity in coding. Like all people, I make mistakes, and any device (like *Indexes*) that prevents mistakes is invaluable.

The class definition and inline functions for *Index* are in the file *index.h*. The non-inline functions and static initializations are located in the file *index.cxx*. These two files are listed in their entirety in Appendix A.

CHAPTER 5

# Building Blocks for Arrays

The goal in creating a C++ class is to build upon other classes and the data types intrinsic to the language. In other words, we either want to add a new data type (such as complex) or we want to create a "better" version of an existing data type. In the first case, we are expanding our tools; in the second case, we are enhancing them. In some situations — such as that of the Array classes being presented here — a new class enhances an existing part of the language while adding new features.

## 5.1 Examining C-style Arrays

A review of C-style arrays will help us to see how a C++ array class should be designed, and where C++ can improve upon C. If you're an experienced C programmer with a solid feel for the intricacies of arrays, feel free to skip over this section to the discussion in section 5.2 on implementing an array class in C++.

Programs often need to work with homogeneous sets of data. In a financial application, you may need to keep track of the profits for each month in a year. This type of data is often represented in a program by an array. In C++, arrays are the same as C arrays; as such, C++ arrays inherit the limitations and problems of C arrays. Fortunately, a C++ class can be used to improve upon the traditional C-style array.

### 5.1.1 Array Basics

Let's work with my example of a financial application that stores a monthly numeric value. In C, we could declare an array of twelve doubles, like this:

```
double profit[12];
```

The variable *profit* designates an area of memory in which twelve *doubles* are stored. Each *double* is an element of the array, and an integer value can be used as

**113**

an *Index* to specify an array element. The elements of an array are numbered from 0; thus, the elements of the *profit* array have integer *Indexes* ranging from 0 to 11. For example:

```
profit[1]  = 1200.00; // the second element (February)
profit[11] = 1750.00; // the last   element (December)
profit[4]  = 2398.00; // the fifth  element (May)
profit[0]  =  900.00; // the first  element (January)
```

### 5.1.2 Pointers and Arrays

Pointers and arrays are intimately related; in many cases, they are interchangeable. The name of an array can be used as the address of the array's first element. For example:

```
double * profPtr = profit;
```

*profPtr* is initialized with the address of the first element of *Profit*, so both of these statements assign the value 500 to the first element of *Profit*:

```
*profPtr = 500.00;
Profit[0] = 500.00;
```

An *Index* can be used to treat a pointer as if it were an array identifier. This statement

```
profPtr[9] = 3215.00;
```

is equivalent to the statements

```
*(profPtr + 9 * sizeof(double)) = 3215.00;
```

or

```
*(profPtr + 72) = 3215.00;
```

which refer to the 10th element of *Profit* (assuming, of course, that *profPtr* is equal to the address of the first element of *Profit*).

Pointer arithmetic can be useful when working with arrays. This statement

```
++profPtr;
```

increments *profPtr* by the size of the type it points to; in this case, we'll assume that we're working with an IEEE double-precision implementation of *double* (used by PCs and other computers), which is 8 bytes in size. Incrementing *profPtr* adds 8 to it; *profPtr* now points to the second element of *Profit*.

Note: Although the name of an array can be used to determine the array's base address, it is not a pointer. The identifier *Profit* cannot be manipulated arithmetically.

Access to an array by means of an *Index* is defined by access through a pointer. This statement:

```
Profit[i] = 0.0;
```

is guaranteed to be equivalent to this statement:

```
*(Profit + i * sizeof(double)) = 0.0;
```

### 5.1.3 Array Parameters

An array can be processed either by *Indexing* or by means of a pointer. However, the array does not include any information on its size; the programmer is responsible for knowing the size of the array. Usually, a constant is used to define the number of elements in an array, as in this example:

```
const int MON_PER_YR = 12;

    double Profit[MON_PER_YR];

    // fill Profit with zeros
    for (int i = 0; i < MON_PER_YR; ++i)
        Profit[i] = 0.0;
```

When passing an array as a function argument, things get a bit stickier. You can't specify the exact size of an array in the function declaration. Instead, you must specify a blank set of brackets, as in this function:

```
void ClearProfits(double prof[])
    {
    for (int i = 0; i < MON_PER_YR; ++i)
        prof[i] = 0.0;
    }
```

Or, because array arguments are passed as pointers, you could use this declaration:

```
void ClearProfits(double * prof)
    {
    for (int i = 0; i < MON_PER_YR; ++i)
        prof[i] = 0.0;
    }
```

This function definition is illegal:

```
void ClearProfits(double prof[MON_PER_YR])
    {
    // does something
    }
```

Remember: A C-style array does not keep track of the number of elements it contains. Unlike Pascal and Modula-2, a C++ compiler cannot perform a check to see if the number of elements specified for the parameter matches the number of elements in the argument. So, a function that handles an array of fixed size would have to make an assumption that the array argument has the expected number of elements:

```
void ShowMonthlies(double prof[])
    {
    for (int i = 0; i < MON_PER_YR; ++i)
        prof[i] = 0.0;
    }
```

If you want a function that can work with any size array, the number of elements in the array will have to be passed as an addition argument. For example, a function that prints an array of doubles might look like this:

```
void PrintDoubleArray(double darray[], int size)
    {
    for (int i = 0; i < size; ++i)
        cout << "element " << i << " = " << darray[i];
    }
```

### 5.1.4 Arrays of Objects

An array of objects is created in the same fashion as an array of an intrinsic type:

```
class Integer
    {
    private:
        int Value;
    public:
        // constructor
        Integer(int i = 0) { Value = i; };

        // other function members
    };

    Integer IntGroup[10];
```

In this case, the compiler generates calls to the default constructor *Integer(int i)* with *i* equal to the default value of *0* for each element of *IntArray*. If you want to assign specific values to each member of *IntArray*, you can provide explicit constructor values:

```
Integer IntGroup[10] = { Integer(1), Integer(2),
                          Integer(3), Integer(4),
                           Integer(5), Integer(6),
                          Integer(7), Integer(8),
                           Integer(9), Integer(10));
```

If a class does not have a default constructor, an array of that class's objects must be created using explicit constructor values.

### 5.1.5 Pros and Cons

Arrays and pointers are very efficient; your program works directly with the underlying memory map of the data. Unfortunately, this efficiency comes with a cost: arrays are error prone.

### 5.1.5.1 Caught Out of Bounds

If you try to *Index* outside the bounds of an array, C++ will not complain. This statement will compile without so much as a peep from your C++ compiler:

```
Profit[20] = 0.0; // set value of 21st element
```

However, if you run a program containing the above statement, what will happen is anybody's guess. *Profit* has only 12 elements; the memory in the "21st element" may be a piece of executable code, or it might be a part of another data item. When a function like *PrintDoubleArray* is passed to an array address and size, problems are likely. If the size is too small, some array elements will be ignored. If the size is too large, memory outside the array will be manipulated. And manipulating pointers has always involved the risk of wandering outside the memory owned by an array.

Whenever a program dies mysteriously, or your data is corrupted, you can bet that an out-of-bounds array reference or pointer is to blame.

### 5.1.5.2 Convenience

Arrays are not only dangerous; they are inconvenient. You can't simply assign one array to another, as in these statements:

```
double Profit1[MON_PER_YR];
   double Profit2[MON_PER_YR];

   // assign values to Profit1
   for (int i = 0; i < MON_PER_YR; ++i
```

```
    Profit1 = 0.0;

  // copy Profit1 into Profit2
  Profit2 = Profit1; // ERROR!
```

Instead, you have to either copy one array to another, element by element:

```
for (int i = 0; i < MON_PER_YR; ++i)
     Profit2[i] = Profit1[i];
```

Or, you can use a library function like memcpy:

```
memcpy(Profit2,Profit1,MON_PER_YR * sizeof(double));
```

In either case, it is the programmer's responsibility to ensure that the correct number of elements is copied, and that the two arrays are compatible.

### 5.1.5.3 Arrays as Groups

One reason to use an array is so that several items of the same data type can be handled as a group. When collecting data into an array, it's often necessary to apply the same operation or function to each element. Using C-type arrays, a loop must be used:

```
// function prototype
   double Adjust(double n);

   for (int i = 0; i < MON_PER_YR; ++i)
        Profit[i] = Adjusted(Profit[i]);
```

Again, it's necessary to know the number of array elements, and you need to put a loop in the program every time you want to perform the same operation on all of an array's elements.

### 5.1.5.4 Based from Zero

Arrays are always indexed beginning with zero. This is inconvenient, to say the least, when working with values that are not normally numbered from zero. The months of the year would be better *index*ed from 1 through 12, rather than from 0 to 11 as is required by a C-style array. And, in some cases, you may want to number the elements of an array from a different base, say from 1981 through 2001. Unfortunately, the only base value allowed for arrays is zero.

### 5.1.5.5 Comparisons

You can't compare two arrays with a simple statement:

```
if (Profit2 == Profit1) // won't work!
      // do something
```

In some cases, we want to know if all the elements in one array equal those in another array of the same size and type. Also, it can be very useful to know how the corresponding elements of two arrays compare. Again, the comparison of two C-type arrays requires the use of loops and the knowledge of an array's size.

## 5.2 A Basic Array Class

Can you use a C++ class to create a "better" array type? Of course you can! Otherwise, I wouldn't be writing this book....

### 5.2.1 Design

Before building the *Array* class, I developed a list of goals that I wanted to accomplish:

- I need to create type-specific *Arrays*.

- An *Array* will be similar in use to C-type arrays. It will be possible to convert a C-type array to an Array, and vice versa.

- An *Array* will know its upper and lower bounds and prevent access to "elements" outside those bounds.

120

- When an *Array* is created, it will be possible to assign values to its elements, similar to the way in which constructors are used to assign initial values to the elements of a C-type object array.

- The *Indexes* used to reference an *Array* will have a programmer-defined base value, rather than always being based from zero.

- It will be possible to compare *Arrays* as a whole and on an element-by-element basis.

- Arithmetic operators will be defined to apply the same operation to all *Array* elements.

A base class, named *Array*, provides a common foundation from which type-specific *Array* classes are built. To keep things simple, I decided to define an *Array* as a C-style array with enhancements. Thus, an *Array* object contains a member that is a pointer to a traditional array; another data member stores the size of the C-style array, which is dynamically allocated. I added a *Range* member (see Chapter 2) to specify the upper and lower bounds of the array. To keep the base class generic, an *Array* also needs a member that stores the size of an element. *Arrays* report errors through an *ErrReporter* object member (see Chapter 2).

The *Array* class defines member functions that create, destroy, and copy *Arrays*; type-specific *Array* classes inherit these functions. The *Array* class also provides several interrogation functions. *Array* does not define mathematical or comparison operators; the implementation of these members is dependent upon the type of data being stored in the *Array*. Virtual functions can be used to create a generic interface to mathematical and comparison operations, but at a significant loss in efficiency. Also, different types have unique operational characteristics. So, each type-specific *Array* class will define its own mathematical and comparison operators.

### 5.2.2 Data Elements and Error Reporting

The data elements of an *Array* are:

```
class Array
     {
     .
     .
     .
     protected:
         Range  IndexRange;
         char * Buffer;
         size_t ElementSize;
         size_t BufferSize;
         unsigned int Count;

         static ErrReporter * ErrOut;

         ElemDestroy DestroyFunc;
     .
     .
     .
     };
```

*IndexRange* defines the upper and lower bounds of the *Array*. *Buffer* is a pointer to the dynamically allocated memory that holds the *Array* elements. *ElementSize* contains the number of bytes in each element, and *BufferSize* is the number of bytes allocated to *Buffer*. *Count* is an information value that holds the number of elements in the *Array*. The *ElemDestroy* member is used by the *Array* destructor, and it will be discussed in detail in the next section.

The static member *ErrOut* must be initialized with a statement such as this:

```
ErrReporter * Array::ErrOut = NULL;
```

Two functions use ErrOut in conjunction with error reporting.

```
class Array
     {
     .
     .
     .
     public:
```

```
     static Boolean SetErrOut(const ErrReporter & er);

 protected:
     static void ReportError(const String & msg);
 .
 .
 .
 };
```

These two function are implemented as follows:

```
void Range::ReportError(const String & msg)
    {
    if (ErrOut != NULL)
        ErrOut->Fatal(msg);
    }

  Boolean Range::SetErrOut(const ErrReporter & er)
    {
    // delete any object pointed to by ErrOut
    if (ErrOut != NULL)
        delete ErrOut;

    ErrOut = new ErrReporter(er);

    if (ErrOut == NULL)
        return BOOL_FALSE;
    else
        return BOOL_TRUE;
    }
```

If, by means of *SetErrOut*, *ErrOut* is assigned to point to an *ErrReporter* object, the *ReportError* function uses *ErrOut* to display error message. See Chapter 2 for an explanation of implementing error reporting.

For the *Range* and *Index* classes, I used a preprocessor constant to control the inclusion of error-checking code. I decided not to provide for the elimination of error-checking code in the *Array* classes. The overhead of error checking is insignificant when compared to the body of code in most *Array* functions, and its existence prevents common mistakes (such as comparing two arrays with different numbers of elements).

### 5.2.3 Utility Functions

Classes often contain functions that are used only internally for utilitarian tasks. In the case of *Array*, two private utility functions are *Kill* and *Copy*.

```
class Array
    {
    .
    .
    .
    private:
        void Kill();
        void Copy(const Array & a);
    .
    .
    .
    };
```

*Kill* destroys the contents of an *Array*. In most classes, deletion of the object's contents is performed by the destructor. The *Array* class, however, needs to delete the contents of an *Array* when it is destroyed or when an *Array* is assigned the value of another *Array*.

```
void Array::Kill()
    {
    if (DestroyFunc != NULL)
        {
        // for each element in the Array, call DestroyFunc
        for (size_t n = 0; n < IndexRange.GetMagnitude(); ++n)
            DestroyFunc((void *)(Buffer + n * ElementSize));
        }

    delete [BufferSize] Buffer;
    }
```

*Copy* duplicates the contents of one *Array* into another *Array; Copy* assumes that the destination *Array* is either new or that its contents have been erased by a call to *Kill*. The copy constructor and the assignment operator call *Copy*.

```
void Array::Copy(const Array & a)
    {
    BufferSize = a.BufferSize;

    // allocate a buffer
    Buffer = (char *)new char[BufferSize];

    if (Buffer == NULL)
        ReportError("unable to allocate buffer");

    // copy the contents of a's buffer
    memcpy(Buffer, a.Buffer, BufferSize);

    // copy other instance variables
    IndexRange  = a.IndexRange;
    ElementSize = a.ElementSize;
    DestroyFunc = a.DestroyFunc;
    Count       = a.Count;
    }
```

Isolating these utility functions eliminates the need for duplicating code.

### 5.2.4 Constructors and the Destructor

*Array* defines four constructors and a destructor. All of these are protected members; they are used only by derived classes. Also, without a public constructor, *Array* objects can be created only as parts of derived class objects.

```
class Array
    {
    .
    .
    .
    protected:
        Array::Array(const Range & r, size_t elemSize,
```

```
                        ElemCreate create, ElemDestroy destroy)
        .
        .
        .
        };
```

The primary constructor creates a new *Array* based on a *Range*, the size of each element, and the addresses of a pair of functions.

```
Array::Array(const Range & r, size_t elemSize,
             ElemCreate create, ElemDestroy destroy)
    : IndexRange(r)
    {
    // ensure that we're inline
    if (r.GetMagnitude() > UINT_MAX / elemSize)
        ReportError("capacity exceeded in construction");

    // allocate buffer space
    BufferSize = elemSize * r.GetMagnitude();

    Buffer = (char *)new char[BufferSize];

    if (Buffer == NULL)
        ReportError("unable to allocate buffer");

    // assign remaining elements
    ElementSize = elemSize;
    Count       = IndexRange.GetMagnitude();
    DestroyFunc = destroy;

    // call create function for each element, if create !=
NULL
    if (create != NULL)
        {
        for (size_t n = 0; n < r.GetMagnitude(); ++n)
            create((void *)(Buffer + n * elemSize));
        }
    }
```

The constructor begins by making sure that the size of the *Array* does not exceed the maximum amount of memory that can be allocated. It then calculates *BufferSize*, and allocates the *Buffer. ElementSize, Count,* and *DestroyFunc* are assigned values, and *create* is called for each element in the *Array*.

*ElemCreate* and *ElemDestroy* are types that define pointers to functions used, respectively, in creating and destroying *Array* elements.

```
typedef void * (* ElemCreate)(void *);
   typedef void * (* ElemDestroy)(void *);
```

If *create* is not equal to *NULL*, it is called for each element in the *Array*. The destroy parameter is stored in *DestroyFunc* for use by the *Kill* function. If *DestroyFunc* is not *NULL, Kill* calls it for each member of the *Array* before *Buffer* is deleted.

Why use *ElemCreate* and *ElemDestroy* instead of the constructor and destructor for the data type of the *Array* elements? First, intrinsic types like *int* and *double* do not have constructors and destructors. Second, a constructor does not have an address.

The copy constructor simply calls the *Copy* function, and it is implemented inline.

```
inline Array::Array(const Array & a)
      : IndexRange(a.IndexRange)
      {
      Copy(a);
      }
```

Two *Arrays* can be concatenated as a new *Array* with this constructor:

```
Array::Array(const Array & a1, const Array & a2)
      : IndexRange(a1.IndexRange + a2.IndexRange)
      {
      if (a1.ElementSize != a2.ElementSize)
          ReportError("construction using incompatible Array
   types");
```

```
            // determine the size needed to hold both source arrays
    BufferSize = a1.ElementSize * IndexRange.GetMagnitude();

            // allocate a buffer
            Buffer = (char *)new char[BufferSize];

            if (Buffer == NULL)
                ReportError("unable to allocate buffer");

            // assign remaining elements
            ElementSize = a1.ElementSize;
            DestroyFunc = a1.DestroyFunc;

            // copy a1's buffer
            memcpy(Buffer,
                    a1.Buffer,
                    a1.BufferSize);

            // copy a2's buffer after a1's
            memcpy(Buffer + a1.BufferSize,
                    a2.Buffer,
                    a2.BufferSize);
            }
```

Note that the *IndexRange* of the new *Array* will be from the minimum *IndexRange* value for *a1* to the maximum, or *a1*'s *IndexRange* plus the number of elements in *a2*.

An *Array* can be created from a subrange of an existing *Array* with this constructor:

```
Array::Array(const Array & a,
                const Index & first,
                const Index & last)
        : IndexRange((int)first,(int)last)
        {
        // check to see if indexes are within the array
        if ((Range(first) == a.IndexRange)
        &&  (Range(last)  == a.IndexRange))
            {
```

```
        // calculate required buffer size
        BufferSize = a.ElementSize *
IndexRange.GetMagnitude();

        // allocate buffer
        Buffer = (char *)new char[BufferSize];

        if (Buffer == NULL)
            ReportError("unable to allocate buffer");

        // assign elements
        ElementSize = a.ElementSize;
        DestroyFunc = a.DestroyFunc;

        // copy elements from source array to new array
        memcpy(Buffer,
                a.Buffer + (unsigned int)first * ElementSize,
                ((unsigned int)last - (unsigned int)first)
                            * ElementSize);
        }
    else
        ReportError("construction with incompatible Indexes");
    }
```

The bounds are defined by *first* and *last*, which are used to create the *IndexRange* for the new *Array*. *memcpy* copies the elements of the two source *Arrays* into the newly created *Array*.

The *Array* destructor is implemented inline as a call to *Kill*.

```
inline Array::~Array()
        {
        Kill();
        }
```

### 5.2.5  Interrogation Functions

Several functions provide information about an *Array*.

```
class Array
      {
      .
      .
      .
      public:
          Index MakeIndex() const;
          Range GetRange() const;
          unsigned int GetCount() const;
          size_t GetElemSize() const;
          ElemDestroy GetDestroyFunc() const;
      .
      .
      .
      };
```

*MakeIndex* is a convenience function; it returns an *Index* built from the *IndexRange* of the *Array*. Thus *Indexes* can be created without having to know anything about the *Array*. *MakeIndex* is implemented inline.

```
inline Index Array::MakeIndex() const
      {
      return Index(IndexRange);
      }
```

*GetRange*, *GetCount*, *GetElemSize*, and *GetDestroyFunc* simply return the values of the data members *IndexRange*, *Count*, *ElementSize*, and *DestroyFunc*. All four functions are implemented inline.

```
inline Range Array::GetRange() const
      {
      return IndexRange;
      }

   inline size_t Array::GetElemSize() const
      {
      return ElementSize;
      }
```

```
inline ElemDestroy Array::GetDestroyFunc() const
    {
    return DestroyFunc;
    }

inline unsigned int Array::GetCount() const
    {
    return Count;
    }
```

*GetElemSize* and *GetDestroyFunc* are used only in the *Matrix* class constructor that converts an *Array* into a vector matrix (see Chapter 8).

### 5.2.6 Assignment Operator

The assignment operator allows one *Array* to be assigned to another.

```
class Array
    {
    .
    .
    .
    protected:
        Array & operator = (const Array & r);
    .
    .
    .
    };
```

It is implemented like this:

```
Array & Array::operator = (const Array & a)
    {
    Kill();
    IndexRange = a.IndexRange;

    Copy(a);
    return *this;
    }
```

### 5.2.7 Element Access Functions

Four functions provide access to the members of an *Array*.

```
class Array
    {
    .
    .
    .
    protected:
        void * GetElement(const Index & i);
        void * GetElement(int i);

        const void * ReadElement(const Index & i) const;
        const void * ReadElement(int i) const;
    .
    .
    .
    };
```

The *Get...* functions return a pointer to an element specified by either an *Index* or an *int*.

```
void * Array::GetElement(const Index & i)
    {
    void * result;

    if (IndexRange == Range(i))
        result = (void *)(Buffer + ElementSize *
                        (unsigned int)i);
    else
        ReportError("invalid Index");

    return result;
    }

inline void * Array::GetElement(int i)
    {
    return GetElement(Index(IndexRange,i));
    }
```

I didn't want to allow the modification of a const *Array*'s elements. So, I created the *Read...* functions, which are declared *const*, to return *const* pointers to *Array* elements.

```
const void * Array::ReadElement(const Index & i) const
    {
    const void * result;

    if (IndexRange == Range(i))
        result = (const void *)(Buffer + ElementSize *
                        (unsigned int)i);
    else
        ReportError("invalid Index");

    return result;
    }

inline const void * Array::ReadElement(int i) const
    {
    return ReadElement(Index(IndexRange,i));
    }
```

Of course, while the *Get...* functions can be used only with non-*const Arrays*, the *Read...* functions can be used with both *const* and non-*const Arrays*.

Why didn't I overload the [] operator to allow *Indexing* of an *Array* with standard notation? It was an aesthetic matter for me. Type-specific *Array* class will be calling the base-class functions from overloaded [] operator functions. Calling a base class operator function is ugly, and because the *Array* class is going to be used only as the basis for other classes, I decided to use non-operator functions for accessing *Array* elements.

The class definition and inline functions for *Array* are in the file *Array.h*. The non-inline functions and static initializations are located in the file *Array.cpp*. These two files are listed in their entirety in Appendix A.

## 5.3 Array Pointers

Using an *Index* to reference an element in an *Array* prevents out-of-bounds problems. However, it isn't very efficient; every time an *Array* element is referenced, a multiplication must be performed in order to find the element. Multiplication is the slowest mathematical operation.

### 5.3.1 Design

What I needed was a data type that simulated the use of pointers to access *Array* elements. In designing the *ArrayPtr* class, I made the following design choices:

An *ArrayPtr* should know (and stay within) the upper and lower bounds of the *Array* it is referencing.

An *ArrayPtr* is tied to a specific *Array*; therefore, an *ArrayPtr* can be created only by an *Array*, or from another *ArrayPtr*.

The programmer should be able to increment, decrement, assign, and otherwise manipulate *ArrayPtrs*.

De-referencing an *ArrayPtr* should work in the same fashion as de-referencing a pointer.

*ArrayPtrs* are created by an *Array* because the *ArrayPtr* must know the bounding range of the *Array* it is referencing. However, the *Array* class doesn't create *ArrayPtrs*, because there is never a standalone *Array* object in a program. For each type-specific *Array* class there is a corresponding type-specific *ArrayPtr* class; the *IntArray* class in Chapter 5 will generates *IntArrayPtr* objects.

Because *Arrays* are typeless, the basic *ArrayPtr* class doesn't define a de-referencing operator function. Each of the type-specific *ArrayPtr* classes defines a de-referencing operator that returns a reference to the appropriate data type. If it sounds confusing now, don't worry. In Chapter 5, where I implement the *IntArray* class, you'll see how all of this comes together.

### 5.3.2 Data Elements

These data elements are included in *ArrayPtr:*

```
class ArrayPtr
     {
     .
     .
     .
     protected:
         size_t ElemSize;
         Range  ElemRange;

         char * ElemFirst;
         char * ElemLast;

         char * ElemPtr;
     .
     .
     .
     };
```

*ElemPtr* points to the selected element of the *Array. ElemSize* is the size of an element in the *Array* referenced by this *ArrayPtr;* it is used primarily as the number of bytes added or subtracted from *ElemPtr* when incrementing or decrementing the *ArrayPtr.*

*ElemRange* is the *Range* of the *Array,* and it is used to check *Index* and *int* assignments against the bounds of the *Array. ElemFirst* and *ElemLast* are also used for range checking; *ElemFirst* points to the first element in the *Array,* and *ElemLast* points to the last element.

### 5.3.3 Constructors and Destructors

*ArrayPtr* defines two constructors.

```
class ArrayPtr
     {
     .
     .
```

```
    .
public:
    ArrayPtr(const ArrayPtr & aptr);
protected:
    ArrayPtr(char * base, size_t esize, const Range & r);
    .
    .
    .
    .
};
```

The copy constructor creates an exact copy of an existing *ArrayPtr*.

```
ArrayPtr::ArrayPtr(const ArrayPtr & aptr)
    : ElemRange(aptr.ElemRange)
    {
    ElemSize  = aptr.ElemSize;
    ElemFirst = aptr.ElemFirst;
    ElemLast  = aptr.ElemLast;
    ElemPtr   = aptr.ElemPtr;
    }
```

The constructor used to create original *ArrayPtr* objects is declared protected.

```
ArrayPtr::ArrayPtr(char * base, size_t esize, const Range & r)



    : ElemRange(r)
    {
    ElemSize  = esize;
    ElemFirst = base;
    ElemLast  = ElemFirst + ElemSize *
                  (ElemRange.GetMagnitude() - 1);
    ElemPtr   = ElemFirst;
    }
```

This constructor is called only by functions defined by type-specific *Array* to generate *ArrayPtrs*. As such, type-specific *ArrayPtr* classes need to declare the corresponding type-specific *Array* class as a friend. Chapter 6 shows how this works.

**136**

### 5.3.4 Assignment Operators

*ArrayPtr* defines three assignment operators.

```
class ArrayPtr
        {
        .
        .
        .
        public:
            ArrayPtr & operator = (const ArrayPtr & aptr);
            ArrayPtr & operator = (const Index & i);
            ArrayPtr & operator = (int i);
        .
        .
        .
        };
```

The copy assignment copies the data elements of one *ArrayPtr* into another.

```
ArrayPtr & ArrayPtr::operator = (const ArrayPtr & aptr)
        {
        ElemSize  = aptr.ElemSize;
        ElemRange = aptr.ElemRange;
        ElemFirst = aptr.ElemFirst;
        ElemLast  = aptr.ElemLast;
        ElemPtr   = aptr.ElemPtr;

        return *this;
        }
```

Both *Indexes* and *ints* can be used to set an *ArrayPtr* to a specific element of an *Array*. Bounds checking is performed against *ElemRange*.

```
ArrayPtr & ArrayPtr::operator = (const Index & i)
        {
        if (ElemRange == Range(i))
            ElemPtr = ElemFirst + ElemSize * (unsigned int)i;

        return *this;
```

```
      }

  ArrayPtr & ArrayPtr::operator = (int i)
      {
      ElemRange.Check(i);

      ElemPtr = ElemFirst + ElemSize * i;

      return *this;
      }
```

### 5.3.5 Increment and Decrement

*ArrayPtrs* can be incremented and decremented.

```
  class ArrayPtr
      {
      .
      .
      .
      public:
          ArrayPtr & operator ++ ();
          ArrayPtr & operator - ();
      .
      .
      .
      };
```

When incrementing an *ArrayPtr, ElemPtr* is checked against *ElemLast* to ensure that *ElemPtr* is not incremented beyond the end of the *Array*. When decrementing, *ElemPtr* is compared with *ElemFirst* to avoid decrementing below the *Array*. These functions are implemented inline.

```
  inline ArrayPtr & ArrayPtr::operator ++ ()
      {
      if (ElemPtr != ElemLast)
          ElemPtr += ElemSize;

      return *this;
```

```
        }

    inline ArrayPtr & ArrayPtr::operator - ()
        {
        if (ElemPtr != ElemFirst)
            ElemPtr -= ElemSize;

        return *this;
        }
```

### 5.3.6 Special Value Functions

Four functions handle values of an *ArrayPtr* that represent the first and last elements of an *Array*.

```
class ArrayPtr
        {
        .
        .
        .
    public:
        void SetFirst();
        void SetLast();

        int IsFirst();
        int IsLast();
        .
        .
        .
        };
```

The Boolean functions *IsFirst* and *IsLast* check to see if *ElemPtr* is equal to *ElemFirst* and *ElemLast*, respectively. These functions are implemented inline.

```
inline void ArrayPtr::SetFirst()
        {
        ElemPtr = ElemFirst;
        }

    inline void ArrayPtr::SetLast()
```

```
        {
        ElemPtr = ElemLast;
        }
```

*SetFirst* sets *ElemPtr* to *ElemFirst*, and *SetLast* sets *ElemPtr* to *ElemLast*. These are inline functions.

```
inline int ArrayPtr::IsFirst()
        {
        return (ElemPtr == ElemFirst);
        }

    inline int ArrayPtr::IsLast()
        {
        return (ElemPtr == ElemLast);
        }
```

### 5.3.7 Comparison Operators

*ArrayPtrs* can be compared with the == and != operators.

```
class ArrayPtr
        {
        .
        .
        .
        public:
            int operator == (const ArrayPtr & aptr);
            int operator != (const ArrayPtr & aptr);
        .
        .
        .
        };
```

Two *ArrayPtrs* are equal if their *ElemPtrs* reference the same location in memory. I implemented these functions inline.

```
inline int ArrayPtr::operator == (const ArrayPtr & aptr)
        {
```

```
    return (ElemPtr == aptr.ElemPtr);
    }

inline int ArrayPtr::operator != (const ArrayPtr & aptr)
    {
    return (ElemPtr != aptr.ElemPtr);
    }
```

### 5.3.8 Using ArrayPtrs

An *ArrayPtr* is a type of iterator, like an *Index* (see Chapter 4). *ArrayPtrs* can be used to sequence through the elements of an *Array*, just as a pointer can be used to process the element of a C-type *Array*. In Chapter 6, the *IntArray* and *IntArrayPtr* classes are respectively derived from the *Array* and *ArrayPtr* classes. *IntArray* defines a function named *MakePtr* that creates an *IntArrayPtr*; a de-referencing operator defined by *IntArray* allows direct access to the *int* element of the *IntArray* begin referenced.

To process all the elements of an *IntArray* by means of an *IntArrayPtr*, the following syntax can be used:

```
Range r(1,10);
    IntArray iArray(r);

    IntArrayPtr iptr = iArray.MakePtr();

    // set all elements of iArray to 1
    for (;;)
        {
        *iptr = 1;

        if (iptr.IsLast())
            break;

        ++iptr;
        }
```

A loop that uses an *Index* looks very similar:

```
Index i = iArray.MakeIndex();

    for (;;)
        {
        iArray[i] = 1;

        if (i.IsMax())
            break;

        ++i;
        }
```

Although the syntaxes are very similar, the underlying code is not. Incrementing an *ArrayPtr* is done inline, as is de-referencing an *ArrayPtr* as a reference to an int. Referencing an *IntArray* element with an *Index* requires a function call that includes a multiplication. My tests have shown that *ArrayPtrs* are five times faster than *Indexes* at sequentially processing *Arrays*; in fact, the overhead of range checking makes *ArrayPtrs* only slightly slower than traditional pointers. *Indexes* have the advantage of convenience; they can be used to directly access any element of an *Array*.

*ArrayPtrs* are trickier to use but faster in action than *Indexes*. However, *Indexes* are safer than *ArrayPtrs*. An *Index* can never be used to reference elements in an *Array* that has been destroyed. However, an *ArrayPtr* is indirectly associated with an *Array*; if the *Array* is destroyed, the *ArrayPtr* will not know. It's possible to create an *ArrayPtr*, destroy its associated *Array*, and then still use the *ArrayPtr* to reference what is now freed memory.

The class definition and inline functions for *ArrayPtr* are in the file *array.h;* the non-inline functions are in the file *array.cxx*. These two files are listed in their entirety in Appendix A.

# CHAPTER 6

# Sortable Arrays

It can be useful to sort the elements of some types of Arrays, particularly those that contain numeric data. Sorting is one of the most analyzed subjects in computing; entire books have been written about sorting algorithms.

Creating a sort for a few items isn't difficult — in fact, it can be downright trivial. For example, a function that sorts two *ints* can be written like this:

```
void sort2(int & a, int & b)
    {
    int temp;

    if (a > b)
        {
        temp = a;
        a = b;
        b = temp;
        }
    }
```

A similar technique can be used to sort three items:

```
void sort3(int & a, int & b, int & c)
    {
    int temp;
    if (a > b)
        {
        temp = a;
        a = b;
        b = temp;
        }
```

```
if (a > c)
    {
    temp = a;
    a = c;
    c = temp;
    }

if (b > c)
    {
    temp = b;
    b = c;
    c = temp;
    }
}
```

Once we get beyond three items, sorting becomes complicated. The books I own describe insertion sorts, selection sorts, heap sorts, and all sorts of sorts. Because this isn't a book on computer science, I'll leave the discussion of less generally useful sorting algorithms to college-level texts. Instead, here I will discuss the fastest and most widely used sorting algorithm, which is appropriately named QuickSort.

Note: I use the general term "array" to refer to a ANSI-standard, C-type array that is indexed by *ints*. The identifier *Array* is used when referring to the *Array* classes presented in this book.

## 6.1 Understanding QuickSort

Sorting involves two actions: comparing values and exchanging values. An efficient sorting routine will minimize the number of comparisons and exchanges. QuickSort is just such an algorithm, invented by C. A. R. Hoare in 1960. Although several minor improvements have been made to QuickSort since then, no one has developed a sorting algorithm that is faster or more elegant.

The premise of the basic QuickSort algorithm can be stated simply. Let's assume that we have an array. An array element is selected as the pivot value. All elements less than the pivot value are moved to its left; all of the elements that come after the pivot value are placed on the right. The pivot value is then placed in the appropriate position within the array. Then, the elements to the left of the pivot are processed using the same technique, as are the elements to the right of the pivot. This goes on, with smaller and smaller sections being processed, until the entire array is sorted.

Let's see how this works, using a simple 11-element array of characters.

| index: | 0 | 1 | 2 | 3 | 4 | 5 | 6 | 7 | 8 | 9 | 10 |
|--------|---|---|---|---|---|---|---|---|---|---|----|
| value: | S | T | A | N | J | F | U | B | X | R | G |

Any element can be chosen for the pivot value; in this case, I'll use the right-most element in the array, G. Two indexes will scan the array; one will begin with the left-most element, and the other will start with the element just to the left of the pivot value. So, the left index begins at 0 and the right index begins at 9.

The left index is incremented when the element it references is less than the pivot value. In other words, all the elements that are already less than the pivot value are ignored; what we're interested in is an element that is out of place by virtue of being greater than the pivot value G. In the example above, the very first element is S, so the left index simply stays at 0. The right index is decremented until it references an element that is less that the pivot value; in this case, it stops on B with a value of 7.

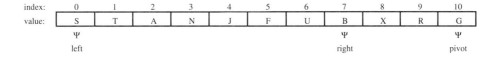

B and S are out of order; therefore, they need to be swapped. Subsequently, the left and right indexes must be moved to start scanning anew. The array now looks like this:

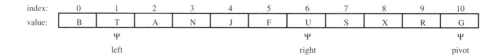

The left and right indexes begin scanning again from their new positions. The left index stays on element 1 (T) and the right index moves to element 5 (F).

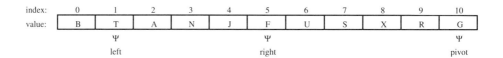

Again, the elements are swapped, and the indexes are moved to continue the scanning.

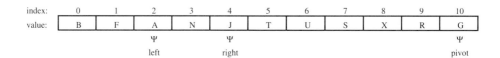

The scan continues. The left index stops at element 3 (N), and the right index stops at 2 (A).

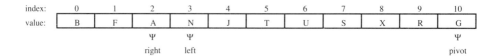

At this point, the indexes have passed each other, and the scanning is complete. All that remains to be done is to swap the pivot element with the element in the position where the left index stopped.

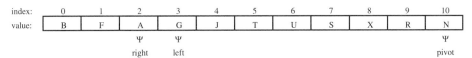

All of the elements to the left of G are smaller than it; all of the elements larger than G are now on its right. What we have just done is known as partitioning the array.

The partially sorted array can now be viewed as two pieces that need to be sorted further by partitioning off the elements to the right of G, and the elements to its left. It doesn't matter which section is partitioned first; for example's sake, I use the right partition. When partitioning begins, the section looks like this:

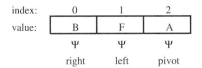

This section doesn't take much time to partition! The right index stays just where it is, pointing to B (which is larger than the pivot value, A). The left index moves to point to B also, ending the partitioning process.

A is then swapped with B as the final act of the partitioning process.

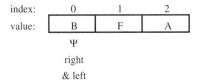

**147**

This leaves two sections: A by itself, and B with F. A single-element section can be ignored, because it can't be sorted. So the two-element section needs to be partitioned, beginning like this:

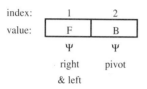

The right and left indexes have nowhere to go; all that needs to be done is to swap the pivot value (B) with the value pointed to by the left index (F). This ends the processing of everything to the left of G, and the array now looks like this:

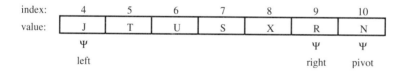

Now the elements to the left of G need to be processed by the partitioning routine. Here's how the pivot and indexes start out:

The left index will scan to element 5 (T), and the right index will scan to element 4(J)— ending the scanning process. The only thing that will happen is that the pivot element (N) is exchanged with T.

| index: | 4 | 5 | 6 | 7 | 8 | 9 | 10 |
|--------|---|---|---|---|---|---|----|
| value: | J | N | U | S | X | R | T |
|        | Ψ | Ψ |   |   |   |   |    |
|        | right | left |   |   |   |   |    |

Because J is in a section by itself, it doesn't need any further processing. Partitioning the section containing elements 6 through 10 begins like this:

| index: | 6 | 7 | 8 | 9 | 10 |
|--------|---|---|---|---|----|
| value: | U | S | X | R | T |
|        | Ψ |   |   | Ψ | Ψ |
|        | left |   |   | right | pivot |

The indexes start out referencing elements that need to be exchanged. After the exchange, the next scan begins like this:

| index: | 6 | 7 | 8 | 9 | 10 |
|--------|---|---|---|---|----|
| value: | R | S | X | U | T |
|        |   | Ψ | Ψ |   | Ψ |
|        |   | left | right |   | pivot |

After scanning, the indexes will be positioned like this:

| index: | 6 | 7 | 8 | 9 | 10 |
|--------|---|---|---|---|----|
| value: | R | S | X | U | T |
|        |   | Ψ | Ψ |   | Ψ |
|        |   | right | left |   | pivot |

The left and right indexes have crossed, and the scanning ends. To complete the partitioning, element 8 (X) will be exchanged with the pivot value T.

| index: | 6 | 7 | 8 | 9 | 10 |
|---|---|---|---|---|---|
| value: | R | S | T | U | X |

$\Psi$ (right, under 7), $\Psi$ (left, under 8), $\Psi$ (pivot, under 10)

Although the entire array is sorted, the two-element sections will still be partitioned, because the program doesn't know that they are already in order. The end result of all this is that the array now looks like this:

| index: | 0 | 1 | 2 | 3 | 4 | 5 | 6 | 7 | 8 | 9 | 10 |
|---|---|---|---|---|---|---|---|---|---|---|---|
| value: | A | B | F | G | J | N | R | S | T | U | X |

From this, it may not appear obvious that QuickSort is efficient. Sometimes, sections that are already sorted are partitioned, which is useless. Indexes scan back and forth through the data, often scanning over the same item several times.

QuickSort is fast because it performs very few comparisons and exchanges. Incrementing and decrementing indexes does not use CPU time; comparing values and moving data does, however. In the example, only seven swaps were required to sort eleven elements.

Overall, empirical testing has shown that QuickSort is by far the fastest sorting routine so far invented — unless the wrong circumstances get it into trouble, for QuickSort has an Achilles heel that can turn it into SlowSort.

Sorted arrays and QuickSort are not compatible. For example, let's say that we tried to QuickSort this array:

| index: | 0 | 1 | 2 | 3 | 4 | 5 | 6 | 7 | 8 | 9 | 10 |
|---|---|---|---|---|---|---|---|---|---|---|---|
| value: | A | B | C | D | E | F | G | H | I | J | K |

Although it may seem silly to sort sorted data, it often happens that incoming data is either sorted or nearly sorted.

QuickSort begins as it did before picking a pivot value and the starting points for right- and left-scanning indexes.

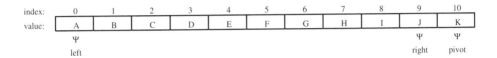

The left index scans forward until it reaches the first element that is greater than or equal to the pivot element (K); the right index stays right where it is, because J is less than K.

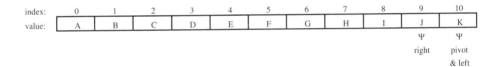

The left and right indexes pass each other, ending the partitioning process. Because the left index now points to the pivot element, no exchanges take place.

Because there are no elements to the right of the pivot element, QuickSort proceeds to partition the elements on the left, 0 through 9

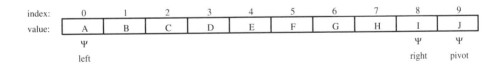

Again, the left index slides all the way over to the left, and the right index remains stationary. No exchanges take place.

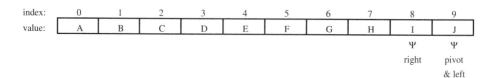

If you see a pattern developing, you're right! QuickSort continues to partition sections of the array that are one element smaller than the last section. Lots of comparisons are performed, but no exchanges take place. The end result? QuickSort takes a very long time to sort sorted information. It doesn't matter which element is selected as the pivot value; changing the pivot selection changes the order of partitioning, but it doesn't reduce the amount of work that is done.

All is not lost, however. A simple improvement to QuickSort can make it perform very quickly on sorted arrays. That, however, is a subject we'll discuss later in this chapter. First, let's implement the basic QuickSort algorithm before we proceed to improve upon it.

## 6.2 A Simple Implementation

To simplify the exploration of QuickSort, I'll demonstrate how it can be implemented for sorting a C-type array of *ints*. This eliminates some additional complexities introduced when incorporating QuickSort into the *Array* class.

The basic algorithm can be expressed like this:

```
void quicksort1(int array[], int l, int r)
    {
    int temp, pivot, scanl, scanr;

    if (r > l)
        {
        // select pivot element
        pivot = array[r];

        // set scanning indexes
        scanl = l;
```

```
    scanr = r - 1;

    for (;;)
        {
        // scan from left
        while (array[scanl] < pivot)
            ++scanl;

        // scan from right
        while (array[scanr] > pivot)
            —scanr;

        // if scans have met, exit inner loop
        if (scanl >= scanr)
            break;

        // exchange elements
        temp        = array[scanl];
        array[scanl] = array[scanr];
        array[scanr] = temp;

        // move scans to next elements
        ++scanl;
        —scanr;
        }

    if (scanl != r)
        {
        // exchange final element
        temp        = array[r];
        array[r]     = array[scanl];
        array[scanl] = temp;
        }

    // process the sections
    quicksort1(array,l,scanl - 1);
    quicksort1(array,scanl + 1,r);
    }
}
```

The *pivot* value is selected as the rightmost element in the section. The *for* loop partitions the segment. *scanl* begins by pointing to the first element in the section, and it scans to the right, looking for elements that are greater than *pivot*. *scanr* begins with the element just to the right of the pivot element; it scans to the left looking for elements that are less than the pivot element. If *scanl* and *scanr* cross each other, the partitioning process ends. Otherwise, two out-of-order elements have been found, and they are swapped.

Once the partitioning process is complete, *quicksort1* calls itself to partition the sections *l* through *scanl - 1* and *scanl + 1* through *r*. This makes the *quicksort1* function recursive. The statement *if (r > l)* ends the recursive cycle; once *quicksort1* is called with a section containing less than two elements, it returns without calling itself.

## 6.3 Removing Recursion

Recursion is expensive. Every time *quicksort1* is called, a pointer and two integers must be pushed onto the stack, and a function call is executed. When each call to *quicksort1* ends, it must remove arguments from the stack and return to the function call that invoked it. In any environment, this is expensive in terms of time and resources. Pushing, calling, popping, and returning all take time. Arguments on the stack use (what may be) limited stack space.

Removing recursion isn't difficult. Analysis by computer scientists has shown that any algorithm that can be expressed recursively can be also be expressed iteratively. So, we need to replace the recursion in *quicksort1* with a loop that tracks the sizes of partitions.

Most recursive routines call themselves only once, making it easier to remove recursion. Let's look at a simple example before removing recursion from QuickSort.

A *factorial* is the value obtained when multiplying a whole number by all of the whole numbers that proceed it in a sequence. For example, the factorial of 4 (4! in mathematical notation) is 4 * 3 * 2 * 1, or 26. And, 5! is 5 * 4 * 3 * 2 * 1, or 120. An observant person will notice a pattern here:

```
for x > 1, x! = x * (x - 1)!
for x = 1, x! = 1;
```

The last statement declares that the factorial of 1 is defined explicitly as 1. All other factorials can be defined in terms of other factorials leading to this recursive implementation of a factorial function:

```
int factorial(int n)
    {
    if (n == 1)
        return 1;
    else
        return n * factorial(n - 1);
    }
```

The function calls itself with successively smaller values of $n$, until $n$ equals 1. When $n == 1$, the recursion "unfolds," providing the correct answer.

While the recursive implementation is very simple, it isn't fast. Assuming a large range for an *int*, it's possible that the factorial of a very large number could cause a stack overflow. And, as I mentioned before, function calls are not generally efficient.

The solution is to remove the recursion by implementing *factorial* as an iterative function:

```
int factorial(int n)
    {
    int result = 1;

    while (n > 1)
        {
        result *= n;
        —n;
        }

    return result;
    }
```

The iterative version of *factorial* is longer, and it looks more complex than does its recursive cousin. However, we have removed the need for functions calls and stack overhead.

Note: Actually, the factorial function could be implemented as a table look-up, removing the need for repeated multiplications at the expense of allocating static memory for the table. But that's a story for another book.

The same principles can be applied to create an iterative version of *quicksort1*. The task is complicated by the fact that *quicksort1* calls itself twice, rather than just once as in *factorial*. So, what we need is a mechanism that allows us to store information on sections that have not yet been partitioned. Information on one section can be imparted through variables; information on the other section needs to be stored so that it can be retrieved.

The solution is to use a simple internal stack. Create two arrays of *ints* that represent the left and right bounds of sections that need to be processed. An index can be used as a stack pointer to indicate how many sections are stored in the arrays. Then, once partitioning is done, the bounds of one partition can be stored in the internal stack, and the other bounds can be used to reset the parameters of the loop that replaces recursion.

This is how the QuickSort function looks after I removed the recursion by adding a loop and a stack:

```
// set the size of the stack based on the size of an int
const int STKSZ = sizeof(int) * CHAR_BIT;

void quicksort2(int array[], int l, int r)
    {
    int temp, pivot, scanl, scanr;

    // stack data
    int stackl[STKSZ], stackr[STKSZ], sptr = 0;

    for (;;)
        {
        while (r > l)
            {
            // select pivot element
            pivot = array[r];
```

```
// set scanning indexes
scanl = l;
scanr = r - 1;

for (;;)
    {
    // scan from left
    while (array[scanl] < pivot)
        ++scanl;

    // scan from right
    while (array[scanr] > pivot)
        —scanr;

    // if scans have met, exit inner loop
    if (scanl >= scanr)
        break;

    // exchange elements
    temp        = array[scanl];
    array[scanl] = array[scanr];
    array[scanr] = temp;

    // move scans to next elements
    ++scanl;
    —scanr;
    }

if (scanl != r)
    {
    // exchange final element
    temp        = array[r];
    array[r]     = array[scanl];
    array[scanl] = temp;
    }

// place left-side section on stack
++sptr;

if (sptr == STKSZ)
```

```
            {
            cerr << "\aError: stack overflow";
            exit(EXIT_FAILURE);
            }

        stackl[sptr] = l;
        stackr[sptr] = scanl - 1;

        l = scanl + 1;
        }

    // iterate with values from the stack (if any)
    if (sptr)
        {
        l = stackl[sptr];
        r = stackr[sptr];

        —sptr;
        }
    else
        break;
    }
}
```

The core of *quicksort2* is the same as the core of *quicksort1*: A *for* loop performs partitioning on a section of the array. When the loop is done, the left and right bounds of the section to the left of the pivot are stored in the arrays *stackl* and *stackr*. The stack pointer, *sptr*, keeps track of the number of sections stored in the stack arrays. The right-side section has bounds of *scanl + 1* and *r*; to iterate, I simply assign *scanl + 1* to *l,* and loop back. The looping continues, storing data on the left-side section in the stack and iterating with the bounds of the right-side section, until the right-side section contains less than two elements. At that point, the values stored in *stackl* and *stackr* are retrieved to start the loop process for the unpartitioned sections. When the stack arrays are empty, the iteration ends, and the array is sorted.

The number of bits in the index data type determines the maximum size of the array, and thus the size of the stack; in this case, for a C-type array, *ints* are used as indexes. The size of an *int*, in bytes, is multiplied by the number of bits-per-byte to obtain the size of the stack. Because QuickSort is essentially a binary algorithm dividing sections into two smaller sections the average number of sections stored in the stack arrays should be no larger than *log2(sizeof(int))*, or, the number of bits in an *int*.

*CHAR_BIT* was created by the ANSI standard as a constant representing the number of bits in a *char*. It is defined in the header file *limits.h*.

Of course, when sorting an already sorted array, the number of sections to be stored equals the number of elements in the array. Clearly, we don't want to create an internal stack large enough to handle the largest possible sorted array. In 16-bit MS-DOS programs, an array of ints may have as many as 30,000+ elements, requiring two stack arrays of 30,000+ elements. Fortunately, we can make a simple modification to QuickSort that eliminates the need to store all that section information.

## 6.4 Minor Improvements

In my tests, *quicksort2* performs slightly faster than *quicksort1*. However, *quicksort2* has a hard-coded limitation: its internal stack may not be adequate when QuickSort degenerates into SlowSort on ordered arrays.

In every case, *quicksort2* stores information on the left-side section and iterates using the right-side section. When the data in an array causes *quicksort2* to generate small left-side partitions and large right-side partitions, a stack overflow is bound to occur. An ordered (or nearly ordered) array can cause just this behavior in *quicksort2*.

The largest partition needs to be placed on the stack every time. Where *quicksort2* has these statements:

```
// place left-side section on stack
++sptr;

if (sptr == STKSZ)
    {
    cerr << "\aError: stack overflow";
    exit(EXIT_FAILURE);
    }
```

```
stackl[sptr] = l;
stackr[sptr] = scanl - 1;

l = scanl + 1;
```

*quicksort3* has these statements:

```
// place largest section on stack
if ((scanl - l) > (r - scanl))
    {
    // ignore 1-element sections
    if ((scanl - l) > 1)
        {
        ++sptr;

        if (sptr == STKSZ)
            {
            cerr << "\aError: stack overflow";
            exit(EXIT_FAILURE);
            }

        stackl[sptr] = l;
        stackr[sptr] = scanl - 1;
        }

    // ignore 1-element sections
    if (rsize != 0)
        l = scanl + 1;
    else
        break;
    }
else
    {
    // ignore 1-element sections
    if ((r - scanl) > 1)
        {
        ++sptr;

        if (sptr == STKSZ)
            {
```

```
        cerr << "\aError: stack overflow";
        exit(EXIT_FAILURE);
        }

    stackl[sptr] = scanl + 1;
    stackr[sptr] = r;
    }

// ignore 1-element sections
if (lsize != 0)
    r = scanl - 1;
else
    break;
}
```

The sizes of the left and right sections are compared, and the larger of the two is placed on the stack. The smaller section is then used to iterate the partitioning loop. This guarantees that no more than *log2(sizeof(int))* elements will be needed in the stack arrays. As an additional benefit, the program now avoids iterating or storing partitions with less than two elements. The overall gain in speed is about 5%.

With a sorted array, *quicksort3* will place the largest section on the stack; the smallest section, consisting of a single element, will end the loop. *quicksort3* will then retrieve the largest section from the stack and process it. In other words, for a sorted array, *quicksort3* uses only one element of stack space for iteration. It isn't very efficient, but we avoid the problem of overrunning the stack.

## 6.5 Median-of-three Partitioning

Now it's time to solve QuickSort's problem with ordered arrays. The solution to the problem involves finding a better way of selecting the pivot element. Two techniques have been presented in various texts:

Use a random number generator to pick an element for the pivot value. Picking a random element avoids the possibility that a consistent selection (e.g. always using the right-most element in a section) will generate lots of partitions.

Pick three elements, sort them, and pick the middle-most element for the pivot value. This is known as median of three partitioning.

Good random number functions use multiplication or division to generate values. Multiplication and division are the most costly operations that can be performed on two numbers; I like to avoid costly math whenever possible. Also, I don't like hit-and-miss techniques for solving problems; I prefer to use an empirical method that leaves as little as possible to chance.

For these reasons, I decided to implement median-of-three partitioning. For a theoretical section, let L represent the index of the left-most argument, R represent the index of the right-most argument, and M represent the index of the middle element.

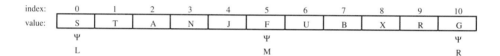

I begin by sorting L, M, and R into order relative to each other.

Then, the middle-most element is exchanged with the element just to the left of the right-most element.

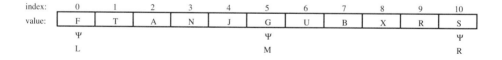

Partitioning now proceeds, with the left scan starting at L + 1 and the right scan at R - 2.

| index: | 0 | 1 | 2 | 3 | 4 | 5 | 6 | 7 | 8 | 9 | 10 |
|--------|---|---|---|---|---|---|---|---|---|---|----|
| value: | F | T | A | N | J | R | U | B | X | G | S |

Ψ (index 0) → L  
Ψ (index 5) → M  
Ψ (index 10) → R

It may not seem obvious, at first, how median-of-three partitioning could improve QuickSort's performance. Why does shuffling a few elements make QuickSort run faster?

QuickSort performs best when the pivot value is the median of the values in a section. The original QuickSort algorithm always picked the right-most element in a section as the pivot element. For an unordered section, any element has an equal chance of being close to the median value; thus, always picking the right-most element (or any other element, for that matter) works well. When a section is sorted or almost sorted, the right-most element will be the largest value, causing a SlowSort to occur.

Median-of-three selects the median of three values in a section, increasing the chance of picking a good pivot value. It's easier to see how this helps when we look at how median-of-three partitioning affects a sorted array like this one:

| index: | 0 | 1 | 2 | 3 | 4 | 5 | 6 | 7 | 8 | 9 | 10 |
|--------|---|---|---|---|---|---|---|---|---|---|----|
| value: | A | B | C | D | E | F | G | H | I | J | K |

After performing the median-of-three operation, the array and its scanning indexes look like this before partitioning begins:

| index: | 0 | 1 | 2 | 3 | 4 | 5 | 6 | 7 | 8 | 9 | 10 |
|--------|---|---|---|---|---|---|---|---|---|---|----|
| value: | A | B | C | D | E | F | G | H | I | J | K |

Without a median-of-three setup, partitioning begins like this:

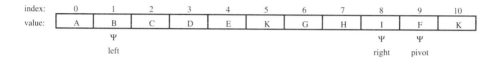

Median-of-three partitioning selects a pivot value of F, which is closer to being a median value than is the element K selected without using the median-of-three setup. Strange as it may seem, median-of-three partitioning improves sorting performance by "unsorting" sorted data!

For small sections, the added overhead for median-of-three partitioning overshadows the benefits. In testing, I saw the best performance when I used median-of-three partitioning for sections with eight or more elements. I defined a variable named *Threshold* which defines the size of the largest section that is not partitioned using the median-of-three arrangement.

Note: *Threshold* should not be set to a value less than 3, because you need at least three elements (right, left, and middle) for median-of-three partitioning.

In the earlier QuickSort functions, the following three lines were used to set the pivot and index values for partitioning:

```
pvidx = r;
scanl = l;
scanr = r - 1;
```

To implement median-of-three partitioning, *quicksort4* replaces the above lines with these lines:

```
if ((r - l) > Threshold)
   {
   // "median-of-three" partitioning
   mid = (l + r) / 2;

   // three-sort left, middle, and right elements
```

```
    if (array[l] > array[mid])
        {
        temp      = array[l];
        array[l]  = array[mid];
        array[mid] = temp;
        }

    if (array[l] > array[r])
        {
        temp     = array[l];
        array[l] = array[r];
        array[r] = temp;
        }

    if (array[mid] > array[r])
        {
        temp       = array[mid];
        array[mid] = array[r];
        array[r]   = temp;
        }

    // select pivot element index
    pvidx = r - 1;

    // exchange pivot with the middle element
    temp         = array[mid];
    array[mid]   = array[pvidx];
    array[pvidx] = temp;

    // set-up for partitioning
    scanl = l + 1;
    scanr = r - 2;
    }
else
    {
    // select pivot element index
    pvidx = r;

    // set scanning indexes
```

```
scanl = 1;
scanr = r - 1;
}
```

The *if* statement chooses between median-of-three partitioning and normal partitioning after comparing the difference in *r* and *l* to *Threshold*.

When writing *quicksort4*, I realized that the sizes of the left and right sections could be precalculated. In the earlier QuickSort functions, three subtractions are performed when storing a section in the internal stack. Precalculating the sizes of the sections eliminates duplicate subtractions. The speed gain is minimal, but every little bit helps.

The complete *quicksort4* function looks like this:

```
// set the size of the stack based on the size of an int
const int STKSZ = sizeof(int) * CHAR_BIT;

// minimum size of a section for median-of-3 processing
const int Threshold = 7;

void quicksort4(int array[], int l, int r)
    {
    int temp, pivot, scanl, scanr, mid, pvidx, lsize, rsize;

    // stack data
    int stackl[STKSZ], stackr[STKSZ], sptr = 0;

    for (;;)
        {
        while (r > l)
            {
            if ((r - l) > Threshold)
                {
                // "median-of-three" partitioning
                mid = (l + r) / 2;

                // three-sort left, middle, and right elements
                if (array[l] > array[mid])
                    {
```

```
        temp      = array[l];
        array[l]  = array[mid];
        array[mid] = temp;
        }

    if (array[l] > array[r])
        {
        temp      = array[l];
        array[l] = array[r];
        array[r] = temp;
        }

    if (array[mid] > array[r])
        {
        temp      = array[mid];
        array[mid] = array[r];
        array[r]  = temp;
        }

    // select pivot element index
    pvidx = r - 1;

    // exchange pivot with the middle element
    temp       = array[mid];
    array[mid]  = array[pvidx];
    array[pvidx] = temp;

    // setup for partitioning
    scanl = l + 1;
    scanr = r - 2;
    }
else
    {
    // select pivot element index
    pvidx = r;

    // set scanning indexes
    scanl = l;
    scanr = r - 1;
    }
```

```
// select pivot element
pivot = array[pvidx];

for (;;)
    {
    // scan from left
    while (array[scanl] < pivot)
        ++scanl;

    // scan from right
    while (array[scanr] > pivot)
        —scanr;

    // if scans have met, exit inner loop
    if (scanl >= scanr)
        break;

    // exchange elements
    temp        = array[scanr];
    array[scanr] = array[scanl];
    array[scanl] = temp;

    // move scans to next elements
    ++scanl;
    —scanr;
    }

if (scanl != pvidx)
    {
    // exchange final element
    temp        = array[pvidx];
    array[pvidx] = array[scanl];
    array[scanl] = temp;
    }

// calculate section sizes
lsize = scanl - 1;
rsize = r - scanl;

// place largest section on stack
```

```
if (lsize > rsize)
    {
    // ignore 1-element sections
    if (lsize > 1)
        {
        ++sptr;

        if (sptr == STKSZ)
            {
            cerr << "\aError: stack overflow";
            exit(EXIT_FAILURE);
            }

        stackl[sptr] = l;
        stackr[sptr] = scanl - 1;
        }

    // ignore 1-element sections
    if (rsize != 0)
        l = scanl + 1;
    else
        break;
    }
else
    {
    // ignore 1-element sections
    if (rsize > 1)
        {
        ++sptr;

        if (sptr == STKSZ)
            {
            cerr << "\aError: stack overflow";
            exit(EXIT_FAILURE);
            }

        stackl[sptr] = scanl + 1;
        stackr[sptr] = r;
        }
```

```
                        // ignore 1-element sections
                        if (lsize != 0)
                            r = scanl - 1;
                        else
                            break;
                        }
                    }

            // iterate with values from the stack (if any)
            if (sptr)
                {
                l = stackl[sptr];
                r = stackr[sptr];

                —sptr;
                }
            else
                break;
            }
        }
```

## 6.6 What I Didn't Do

Some texts talk about using alternate sorting routines for small partitions. It makes logical sense to handle small sections using simpler sorts. For example, a two-element section can be sorted with a simple *if* statement; three-element partitions can be sorted used the three-sort method I showed at the beginning of this chapter. Some texts suggest that, for partitions of less than 20 elements, a simple insertion or selection sort will be faster than the partitioning process.

I wrote versions of QuickSort that used alternate sorts for array elements ranging in size from 2 to 10 elements. In every case, the alternate sorts produced a slower QuickSort. Profiling the results, I found that the overhead of additional conditional statements was sufficient to cancel out the advantage of having little sorts for small sections.

I'm a firm believer in analysis. When I create what appears to be an optimization, I test it with a profiler to be certain that I really did improve my program's performance. You should never make assumptions when it comes to computers; what may run fast on a Macintosh may run slower than molasses on a PC. What may look good in a theoretical paper may not perform well on an architecture that has specific performance pluses and minuses. Always test your assumptions.

## 6.7 The SortableArray Class

Speaking of assumptions, my design for a simple QuickSort function quickly caused me problems when I implemented it for *Arrays*. While I was developing the sorting routines for C-type arrays, I assumed that it would be easy to modify the best routine for use with an *Array*. How wrong I was! Decisions that I made about the workings of an *Array* did not mesh with the way *quicksort4* goes about its task.

For example, it is possible that the *scanl* and *scanr* indexes will be incremented or decremented outside the bounds of the array during the partitioning process. This doesn't cause a problem when working with C-type arrays, because they don't perform bounds checking. An *Index* object, however, knows what its bounds are and will report an error when those bounds are crossed. That meant that I had to add several checks to be sure that increments and decrements did not exceed the ranges of *Indexes* for a given *Array*.

I wanted to write one sorting function that could be used by any *Array* type; my goal was to create a sort function that could transparently handle everything from ints to *doubles* to *strings*. QuickSort performs two actions that are dependent on the type of data being sorted: comparisons and exchanges. So, in an object-oriented fashion, I defined virtual functions for comparing and exchanging elements.

Then there was the burning question: Should the sort, compare, and exchange member functions be incorporated into *Array*, or should they be added in a class derived from *Array*? In the former case, all *Arrays* would be sortable; in the later, sortable Arrays would need to be derived from a class derived from *Array*. I chose to derive a new class, named *SortableArray*, that implements the additional members needed to sort an *Array*.

### 6.7.1 Creating a Stack of Indexes

The most intractable problem arose when I tried to create arrays of *Indexes* that would be used to store the bounds of unprocessed sections. For sorting C-type arrays, which use int values for indexes, simple arrays would do the trick. *Indexes* are more complicated than *ints*. For example, an array of *Indexes* can't be created easily, because there isn't a default constructor for the *Index* class. An *Index* can be created only from a *Range* or another *Index*.

The *Indexes* used in sorting the *Array* must be defined using the *IndexRange* of the *Array* to ensure that the *Indexes* have the appropriate *Range*. The number of elements in an array of Indexes, however, depends upon the maximum number of elements in an *Array* which is dependent upon the number of bits in an *int* (see section 6.4).

I decided to dynamically create the stack of *Index*es at run time, thereby eliminating the need to statically allocate an area of memory for the stack (which limits it to a specific size).

Each element in the stack is a structure, containing two Indexes that represent the left and right bounds of a section in the *Array*.

```
struct stackItem
    {
    Index left;
    Index right;
    };
```

When sorting begins, an array of *stackItems* is created dynamically, based on the number of bits in an *int*. Of course, using the *struct* above doesn't get us around the need to specify values for the left and right *Index* members for each element of the array. I solved that problem by adding two more members to *stackItem*:

```
struct stackItem
    {
    Index left;
    Index right;

    static Range lrRange;

    stackItem(); // a default constructor
    };
```

172

The constructor creates the left and right *Indexes* using *lrRange*:

```
inline stackItem::stackItem()
    : left(lrRange), right(lrRange)
    {
    // does nothing else
    }
```

*lrRange* is provided with a default value when it is defined:

```
Range stackItem::lrRange(0,1);
```

Before the array of *stackItems* is created, *lrRange* needs to be set to the *Range* of the *Array* that is being sorted. The default constructor automatically creates left and right *Indexes* with the correct *Range*. Ta-da! We have an array of appropriate *Indexes* for storing section data.

Why didn't I use a *class* instead of a *struct*? The *stackItem* structure is a kludge to get around restrictions in C++. A class simply wouldn't make *stackItem* work any better.

Why isn't *stackItem* a part of the *SortableArray* class? It was a practical matter; I wanted *stackItem* to be private to the internal workings of *SortableArray*. The current MS-DOS C++ compilers do not enforce access specifiers for *structs* and other types declared inside of a *class*. So, for security, I created the *stackItem* structure in the source file that implements the non-inline functions for *SortableArray*.

### 6.7.2 Inline Functions

The *SortableArray* class is derived from the *Array* class. *SortableArray* does not add any data elements to those it inherits; however, it needs to implement constructors and the assignment operator, which are not inherited from *Array*.

```
class SortableArray : public Array
    {
    .
    .
    .
    protected:
```

**173**

```
SortableArray(const Range & r,
              size_t elemsize,
              ElemCreate  create  = NULL,
              ElemDestroy destroy = NULL);

SortableArray(const SortableArray & a);

// concatenate
SortableArray(const SortableArray & a1,
              const SortableArray & a2);

// subrange
SortableArray(const SortableArray & a,
              const Index & first,
              const Index & last);

SortableArray & operator = (const SortableArray & a);
    .
    .
    .
};
```

Because *SortableArray* doesn't have any initialization requirements of its own, these functions can be implemented as inline shells that call the base-class constructors and the assignment operator.

```
inline SortableArray::SortableArray(const Range & r,
                                    size_t elemsize,
                                    ElemCreate  create,
                                    ElemDestroy destroy)
    : Array(r,elemsize,create,destroy)
    {
    // does nothing else
    }

inline SortableArray::SortableArray(const SortableArray & a)
    : Array(a)
    {
    // does nothing else
    }
```

```
inline SortableArray::SortableArray(const SortableArray & a1,
                                    const SortableArray & a2)
    : Array(a1,a2)
    {
    // does nothing else
    }

inline SortableArray::SortableArray(const SortableArray & a,
                                    const Index & first,
                                    const Index & last)
    : Array(a,first,last)
    {
    // does nothing else
    }

inline SortableArray & SortableArray::operator =
                       (const SortableArray & a)
    {
    this->Array::operator = (a);

    return *this;
    }
```

This situation occurs often in C++: The derived class adds functionality — but not data — to the elements inherited from the base class. In spite of this, the derived class must implement constructors and assignment operators, because those types of member functions are not inherited from the base class.

### 6.7.3 Virtual Functions

As mentioned earlier in the chapter, QuickSort performs two actions that are dependent upon the type of data being sorted — comparison and exchange. When a general function like QuickSort is dependent upon the type of data being manipulated, a virtual function is called for.

```
class SortableArray : public Array
    {
    .
    .
    .
    private:
        virtual int  IsBefore(const Index & i1,
                                  const Index & i2) = 0;

        virtual void Exchange(const Index & i1,
                                  const Index & i2) = 0;
    .
    .
    .
    };
```

A type-specific *Array* will need to implement *IsBefore* and *Exchange* for the type of data the *Array* holds.

*IsBefore* is the comparison function; if it returns a true (nonzero) result, then the item at *Index i1* should be sorted before the item in element at *Index i2*; otherwise, it returns *false* (zero). I named this function *IsBefore* because, in some cases, the sorting order may not be based on a less-than/greater-than relationship; this is particularly true of *Arrays* of structures.

*Exchange* should simply swap the items at *Indexes i1* and i2. In Chapter 6, you'll see how *IsBefore* and *Exchange* are implemented for the *IntArray* class, which should clarify their use.

### 6.7.4 The Sort Function

The meat of the *SortableArray* class is the *Sort* function, which implements the QuickSort algorithm using *IsBefore*, *Exchange*, and the *stackItem* struct.

```
class SortableArray : public Array
    {
    .
    .
    .
    public:
```

```
      void Sort();
    .
    .
    .
    };
```

*Sort* is the only public function in *SortableArray*. Its implementation looks like this:

```
void SortableArray::Sort()
    {
    //———
    // create stack
    //———

    stackItem::lrRange = IndexRange;

    const size_t stackSize = CHAR_BIT * sizeof(int);

    stackItem * stack = new stackItem [stackSize];

    if (stack == NULL)
        ErrExit.Handler("cannot allocate stack for sorting");

    size_t stackPtr = 0;

    //————————————————
    // size of minimum partition to median-of-three
    //————————————————

    const int Threshold = 7;

    //————————————
    // sizes of left and right partitions
    //————————————

    int lsize, rsize;

    //———————
    // create working indexes
    //———————
```

```cpp
Index l(IndexRange),       // left    partition index
      r(IndexRange),       // right   partition index
      mid(IndexRange),     // middle partition index
      scanl(IndexRange),   // index scanning from left
      scanr(IndexRange),   // index scanning from right
      pivot(IndexRange);   // pivot element index

//————————
// set initial values
//————————

l.SetMin();
r.SetMax();

//————
// main loop
//————

for (;;)
    {
    while (r > l)
        {
        if (((int)r - (int)l) > Threshold)
            {
            //————————————
            // "median-of-three" partitioning
            //————————————

            mid = ((int)l + (int)r) / 2;

            //————————————————
            // three-sort left, middle, and right elements
            //————————————————

            if (IsBefore(mid,l))
                Exchange(mid,l);

            if (IsBefore(r,l))
                Exchange(r,l);
```

```
    if (IsBefore(r,mid))
        Exchange(r,mid);

    //—————————
    // setup for partitioning
    //—————————

    pivot = r - 1;
    Exchange(mid,pivot);

    scanl = l + 1;
    scanr = r - 2;
    }
else
    {
    //—————————
    // setup for partitioning
    //—————————

    pivot = r;
    scanl = l;
    scanr = r - 1;
    }

for (;;)
    {
    //————————————
    // scan from left for element >= to pivot
    //————————————

    while (IsBefore(scanl,pivot) && (scanl < r))
        ++scanl;

    //————————————
    // scan from right for element <= to pivot
    //————————————

    while (IsBefore(pivot,scanr) && (scanr > l))
        —scanr;
```

```
        //————————————
        // if scans have met, exit inner loop
        //————————————

        if (scanl >= scanr)
            break;

        //————————
        // exchange elements
        //————————
        Exchange(scanl,scanr);

        if (scanl < r)
            ++scanl;

        if (scanr > l)
            —scanr;
        }

//————————
// exchange final element
//————————

Exchange(pivot,scanl);

//————————————
// place largest partition on stack
//————————————

lsize = (int)scanl - (int)l;
rsize = (int)r - (int)scanl;

if (lsize > rsize)
    {
    if (lsize != 1)
        {
        ++stackPtr;

        if (stackPtr == stackSize)
            ErrExit.Handler("stack overflow (left)");
```

```
                        stack[stackPtr].left  = l;
                        stack[stackPtr].right = scanl - 1;
                        }

                if (rsize != 0)
                    l = scanl + 1;
                else
                    break;
                }
        else
            {
            if (rsize != 1)
                {
                ++stackPtr;

                if (stackPtr == stackSize)
                    ErrExit.Handler(
                        "stack overflow (right)");

                stack[stackPtr].left  = scanl + 1;
                stack[stackPtr].right = r;
                }

            if (lsize != 0)
                r = scanl - 1;
            else
                break;
            }
        }

//————————————
// iterate with values from stack
//————————————

if (stackPtr)
    {
    l = stack[stackPtr].left;
    r = stack[stackPtr].right;

    —stackPtr;
```

```
        }
    else
        break;
    }

delete [stackSize] stack;
}
```

*Sort* begins by assigning a value to *stackItem::lrRange* and creating an array of *stackItems* that is *sizeof(int) * CHAR_BIT* elements in length. At one point, I tried implementing an *IndexArray* class, which would have been a more object-oriented approach than creating an array of structs. I found that the added complexity added nothing to the program's performance; in fact, the *IndexArray* class actually made the program more complicated and confusing.

Once *stack* has been created and a *stack pointer* has been set, *Sort* looks pretty much like *quicksort4*. The primary differences are that the manual exchanges in *quicksort4* are replaced by calls to *Exchange*, and the comparisons are replaced by calls to *IsBefore*. I also added checks to avoid out-of-range *Indexes*.

The virtual function calls and checks for out-of-range *Indexes* make *Sort* slower than *quicksort4* but not by much. Still, it's a whole lot faster than I am....

CHAPTER 7

# Integer Arrays

I present two useful array types in this book: *IntArray* and *DblArray*, which, respectively, hold *ints* and *doubles*. The *IntArray* is the simpler of the two, and *IntArray* objects are used by *DblArray* objects. So, I begin by describing *IntArray*.

## 7.1 The Int Array Class

An *IntArray* contains *ints*. The goal of this decision was to minimize the number of classes in the library. An *int* is (in theory) the optimum integer size for the given compiler and hardware. When working with standard MS-DOS, an *int* will contain 16 bits and have a range of -32,768 through 32,767. 32-bit operating systems, such as DOS extenders, will support a 32-bit *int* with a range of -2,147,483,648 to 2,147,483,647. Note that, if you're using Borland C++, templates could be used to define a "integral" Array template, which could define an array of any integral type (*int*, *long*, *short*, etc.) according to the programmer's desire. Unfortunately, most C++ compilers have yet to support templates, so I will leave them out of this book.

The class should support all the standard mathematical operations associated with ints: addition, subtraction, multiplication, division, bit-wise, and logical in binary and shorthand forms. The class should also provide for various comparisons of two *IntArrays*. *IntArrays* will be sortable, so the class will be derived from *SortableArray*.

Upon creation, a new *IntArray* will contain zeros unless the programmer specifies a different initial value. I also decided that all numeric array classes should support "fill" functions that generate values for array elements. It should be possible to fill all elements with a single value or with a sequence of numbers generated by arithmetic, geometric, or recursive progression.

### 7.1.1 Constructors

Five constructors build *IntArrays*; four of these are mere shells for constructors inherited from *SortableArray*. Because *SortArray*'s constructors are inline function shells that call the constructors for the *Array* class, most *IntArray* constructors are directly implemented as calls to *Array* constructors.

```
class IntArray : public SortableArray
    {
    .
    .
    .
    private:
        static int InitValue;

    public:
        IntArray(const Range & r);
        IntArray(const IntArray & ia);

        IntArray(const int * a);

        // concatenate
        IntArray(const IntArray & a1,
                const IntArray & a2);

        // subrange
        IntArray(const IntArray & a,
                const Index & first,
                const Index & last);
    .
    .
    .
    .
    };
```

The first constructor builds a new *IntArray*, filling it with the value *InitValue*.

```
inline IntArray::IntArray(const Range & r)
        : SortableArray(r,sizeof(int),(ElemCreate)IntArray::Set)
        {
```

```
      // does nothing
      }
```

The second constructor is the copy constructor.

```
inline IntArray::IntArray(const IntArray & ia)
      : SortableArray(ia)
      {
      // does nothing
      }
```

The third constructor creates a new *IntArray* that contains the same values as a traditional array of *ints*. It is passed a pointer to an array in *a* along with the number of elements in *len*. Note that it is impossible to verify the length of *a*, and that care must be taken by the programmer to ensure that *len* is correct.

```
IntArray::IntArray(const int * a)
      : SortableArray(Range(0,sizeof(a) - 1),sizeof(int))
      {
      memcpy(Buffer,a,BufferSize);
      }
```

The fourth constructor concatenates two *IntArrays*. (Refer to Chapter 4 for details on how this is accomplished.)

```
inline IntArray::IntArray(const IntArray & a1,
                          const IntArray & a2)
      : SortableArray(a1,a2)
      {
      // does nothing else
      }
```

The final constructor creates an *IntArray* that contains a "slice" of an existing *IntArray*. (Again, see Chapter 4 for how this is accomplished in the base *Array* class.)

```
inline IntArray::IntArray(const IntArray & a,
                          const Index & first,
                          const Index & last)
```

```
    : SortableArray(a,first,last)
    {
    // does nothing else
    }
```

### 7.1.2 Conversions

A standard C-type array can be generated from an *IntArray*.

```
class IntArray : public SortableArray
    {
    .
    .
    .
    public:
        operator int * ();
    .
    .
    .
    };
```

The conversion function allocates a block of memory, and then copies into that the contents of the *IntArray*.

```
IntArray::operator int * ()
    {
    int * result;

    result = new int[BufferSize];

    if (result == NULL)
        ReportError("cannot allocate memory for int []");

    memcpy(result,Buffer,BufferSize);

    return result;
    }
```

A conversion operator function can return only one piece of information, that is, the new type generated from the object being converted. Thus, the size of the array returned by the above conversion is not immediately known. However, a call to the *GetCount* function (defined in *Array*) provides the number of elements in the *IntArray*, and thus the number of elements in the newly-created C-type array.

```
Range r(0,10);
   IntArray ia(r);

   // generate a c-type array from ia
   int * ca = (int *)ia;

   // get the number of elements in ia
   sizeof calen = ia.GetCount();
```

Also note that, because the array is dynamically allocated, it is the responsibility of the programmer to ensure that the array is deleted from memory when it is no longer required.

### 7.1.3 Assignment

The assignment operator assigns the contents of one array to another.

```
class IntArray : public SortableArray
      {
      .
      .

      .
      public:
          IntArray & operator = (const IntArray & ia);
      .
      .

      .
      };
```

As with the constructors, the assignment operator is implemented as an inline call to the base-class assignment operator.

```
inline IntArray & IntArray::operator = (const IntArray & ia)
        {
        this->SortableArray::operator = (ia);

        return *this;
        }
```

### 7.1.4 Generating Pointers

As discussed in Chapter 4, the type-specific *Array* classes need to define derivatives of the *ArrayPtr* class for type-specific *Array* pointers. In the case of *IntArray*, two pointer classes are created, *IntArrayPtr* and *IntArrayConstPtr*, which access the elements of non-*const* and *const IntArrays*, respectively. (I describe the implementation of these two classes in sections 7.2 and 7.3, below.)

The *IntArray* class needs to generate *IntArrayPtrs* and *IntArrayConstPtrs*, and it does so using these two functions:

```
class IntArray : public SortableArray

        {
        .
        .
        .
public:
        IntArrayPtr MakePtr();
        IntArrayConstPtr MakeConstPtr() const;
        .
        .
        .
        };
```

These functions return *IntArrayPtr* and *IntArrayConstPtrs* that know the bounds of the *IntArray* to which they are applied. I implemented these functions like this:

```
inline IntArrayPtr IntArray::MakePtr()
        {
        return IntArrayPtr(Buffer,ElementSize,IndexRange);
        }
```

```
inline IntArrayConstPtr IntArray::MakeConstPtr() const
    {
    return IntArrayConstPtr(Buffer,ElementSize,IndexRange);
    }
```

Further discussion of these functions comes later in this chapter.

### 7.1.5 Indexing

In designing the IntAr*ray* class, I found myself in a quandary.

I wanted to implement the [] operators for indexing *IntArrays*. The indexing operators return an *int* reference, so that the specified element of the array can be modified.

Then I wrote a function with a *const IntArray* and as a parameter. The [] operators I had defined were not declared *const*, so I couldn't index the elements of the *const IntArray*. Declaring the indexing operator functions as *const* permitted me to read the elements of a *const IntArray* using an *Index*. It also allowed for the possible modification of *IntArray* elements as well as an unacceptable loss of data security.

My first thought was to create two sets of [] operators, the difference being that one set is declared with the *const* qualifier and returns a *const int* reference. A function declared as *const* has a *const this* pointer, whereas a non-*const* function has a non-*const this* pointer. Because *this* is an implied parameter, and a *const this* is different from a non-*const this*, it should have worked.

It didn't. My C++ compilers distinguish between different overloaded functions by their parameters but they look at only the explicitly declared parameters and not at *this*. Growl!

My ultimate solution was to create a pair of *const* functions, named *Read*, that returned *const int* references. The [] operators can be used to index non-*const IntArrays*, and the *Read* functions provide read-only access to elements of *const* (and non-*const*, for that matter) *IntArrays*. This explains why the base *Array* class defines *GetElement* and *ReadElement* member functions (see Chapter 4).

```
class IntArray : public SortableArray
    {
    .
    .
    .
    public:
        int & operator [] (const Index & i);
        int & operator [] (int i);

        const int & Read(const Index & i) const;
        const int & Read(int i) const;
    .
    .
    .
    };
```

I implemented these four functions as inline calls to the *GetElement* and *ReadElement* functions inherited from the *Array* class.

```
inline int & IntArray::operator [] (const Index & i)
    {
    return *((int *)(GetElement(i)));
    }

inline int & IntArray::operator [] (int i)
    {
    return *((int *)(GetElement(i)));
    }

inline const int & IntArray::Read(const Index & i) const
    {
    return *((const int *)(ReadElement(i)));
    }

inline const int & IntArray::Read(int i) const
    {
    return *((const int *)(ReadElement(i)));
    }
```

### 7.1.6 Unary Operators

Four unary operations are defined by the *IntArray* class.

```
class IntArray : public SortableArray
    {
    .
    .
    .
    public:
        IntArray operator + ();
        IntArray operator - ();

        IntArray operator ~ ();
        IntArray operator ! ();
    .
    .
    .
    };
```

The unary plus operator is defined for completeness; as when applied to any other numeric value, a unary plus does nothing. In essence, the unary plus merely returns a copy of the *IntArray* object to which it is applied. Being a very simple function, the unary plus is implemented inline.

```
inline IntArray IntArray::operator + ()
    {
    return *this;
    }
```

The other three unary operators create a copy of the subject *IntArray*, and then apply their operation to each element of the copy. The copy is then returned as the function's result.

```
IntArray IntArray::operator - ()
    {
    IntArray result(*this);
```

```
        IntArrayPtr ptr = result.MakePtr();

        for (;;)
            {
            *ptr = -(*ptr);

            if (ptr.IsLast())
                break;

            ++ptr;
            }

        return result;
        }

IntArray IntArray::operator ~ ()
        {
        IntArray result(*this);

        IntArrayPtr ptr = result.MakePtr();

        for (;;)
            {
            *ptr = ~(*ptr);

            if (ptr.IsLast())
                break;

            ++ptr;
            }

        return result;
        }

IntArray IntArray::operator ! ()
        {
        IntArray result(*this);

        IntArrayPtr ptr = result.MakePtr();
```

```
for (;;)
    {
    *ptr = !(*ptr);

    if (ptr.IsLast())
        break;

    ++ptr;
    }

return result;
}
```

### 7.1.7 Binary Mathematical Operators

The C++ language defines a surprisingly large number of mathematical, bitwise, and logical operators for application to *int* values. I have defined functions that implement all of these operations for *IntArrays*.

```
class IntArray : public SortableArray
    {
    .
    .
    .
public:
    IntArray operator + (const IntArray & ia);
    IntArray operator + (int n);

    IntArray operator - (const IntArray & ia);
    IntArray operator - (int n);

    IntArray operator * (const IntArray & ia);
    IntArray operator * (int n);

    IntArray operator / (const IntArray & ia);
    IntArray operator / (int n);

    IntArray operator % (const IntArray & ia);
    IntArray operator % (int n);
```

```
IntArray operator << (const IntArray & ia);
IntArray operator << (int n);

IntArray operator >> (const IntArray & ia);
IntArray operator >> (int n);

IntArray operator & (const IntArray & ia);
IntArray operator & (int n);

IntArray operator | (const IntArray & ia);
IntArray operator | (int n);

IntArray operator ^ (const IntArray & ia);
IntArray operator ^ (int n);
       .
       .
       .
    };
```

For each operator function, I have created two implementations. The first argument is always an *IntArray*, which appears to the left of the operation symbol. To the right of the operation symbol there can be either an *IntArray* or a single *int* value. For example:

```
Range r(1,20);
   IntArray ia1(r), ia2(r), ia3(r);

   ia3 = ia1 + ia2; // add two IntArrays
   ia3 = ia1 + 10;  // add an IntArray and an int
```

The two binary + functions are implemented thus:

```
IntArray IntArray::operator + (const IntArray & ia)
       {
       if (IndexRange != ia.IndexRange)
          ReportError("incompatible arrays: +");

       IntArray result(*this);
```

```
    IntArrayPtr dest = result.MakePtr();

    IntArrayConstPtr src = ia.MakeConstPtr();

    for (;;)
        {
        *dest += *src;

        if (dest.IsLast())
            break;

        ++dest;
        ++src;
        }

    return result;
    }

IntArray IntArray::operator + (int n)
    {
    IntArray result(*this);

    IntArrayPtr ptr = result.MakePtr();

    for (;;)
        {
        *ptr += n;

        if (ptr.IsLast())
            break;

        ++ptr;
        }

    return result;
    }
```

When two *IntArrays* are added, initially a copy is made of the first one, to which the corresponding elements of the second array are added. The resulting array is the return value. Note that the "add two *IntArrays*" function displays an error if the two *IntArrays* have different *Ranges*.

When the parameter is an *int*, a copy of the subject *IntArray* is made and the *int* value is added to each of its elements.

I implemented the other binary operators using the same logic as I used for the + operator. You can find the complete listings for these functions in Appendix A.

### 7.1.8 Shorthand Mathematical Operators

There is a shorthand form of every binary operator.

```
class IntArray : public SortableArray
    {
    .
    .
    .
    public:
        IntArray & operator += (const IntArray & ia);
        IntArray & operator += (int n);

        IntArray & operator -= (const IntArray & ia);
        IntArray & operator -= (int n);

        IntArray & operator *= (const IntArray & ia);
        IntArray & operator *= (int n);

        IntArray & operator /= (const IntArray & ia);
        IntArray & operator /= (int n);

        IntArray & operator %= (const IntArray & ia);
        IntArray & operator %= (int n);

        IntArray & operator <<= (const IntArray & ia);
        IntArray & operator <<= (int n);

        IntArray & operator >>= (const IntArray & ia);
        IntArray & operator >>= (int n);

        IntArray & operator &= (const IntArray & ia);
        IntArray & operator &= (int n);
```

```
IntArray & operator |= (const IntArray & ia);
IntArray & operator |= (int n);

IntArray & operator ^= (const IntArray & ia);
IntArray & operator ^= (int n);
.
.
.
};
```

In keeping with the style used for the binary operator, the shorthand operators each have two variants with *IntArray* and *int* parameters. The implementations are nearly identical, so I shall present only the implementation of the += operator here:

```
IntArray & IntArray::operator += (const IntArray & ia)
    {
    // verify that the arrays have the same ranges
    if (IndexRange != ia.IndexRange)
        ReportError("incompatible arrays: +=");
    // create pointers to elements of the arrays
    IntArrayPtr      dest = MakePtr();
    IntArrayConstPtr src  = ia.MakeConstPtr();

    for (;;)
        {
        // add elements of source array to
        // corresponding elements of destination
        *dest += *src;

        if (dest.IsLast())
            break;

        // go to next element
        ++dest;
        ++src;
        }

    return *this;
    }
```

```
IntArray & IntArray::operator += (int n)
    {
    // create pointer to subject array
    IntArrayPtr dest = MakePtr();

    for (;;)
        {
        // add n to the element in the array
        *dest += n;

        if (dest.IsLast())
            break;

        // move to next element
        ++dest;
        }

    return *this;
    }
```

### 7.1.9 Absolute Value Functions

I've often found it useful to retrieve the absolute value of the elements in an *IntArray*.

```
class IntArray : public SortableArray
    {
    .
    .
    .
    public:
        IntArray & abs();

        friend IntArray abs(const IntArray & ia);
    .
    .
    .
    };
```

The first implementation performs the *abs* function on each element in the *IntArray* to which it is applied.

```
//——————
   // absolute value functions
   //——————

   IntArray & IntArray::abs()
       {
       IntArrayPtr ptr = MakePtr();

       for (;;)
           {
           // apply function to element of array
           // assign the result of the element to the array
           *ptr = ::abs(*ptr);

           if (ptr.IsLast())
               break;

           ++ptr;
           }

       return *this;
       }
```

The second *abs* implementation creates a new array that contains the same values as the subject *IntArray*, with the *abs* operation applied to each element.

```
   IntArray abs(const IntArray & ia)
       {
       // create new array
       IntArray result(ia);

       // create pointer to new array
       IntArrayPtr ptr = result.MakePtr();

       for (;;)
           {
           // perform calculation on element of result
           *ptr = ::abs(*ptr);
```

```
            if (ptr.IsLast())
                break;

            // move to next element
            ++ptr;
            }

        return result;
        }
```

The syntax for using the *abs* functions depends upon where you want the result to be stored. To perform an absolute-value operation on each element of an *IntArray*, storing the value in the same array, use the first *abs* member function in this fashion:

```
ia.abs();
```

To obtain a new *IntArray* that contains the absolute values of the elements in another *IntArray*, the second *abs* member function is used with this syntax:

```
ia2 = abs(ia1);
```

This follows the form of the standard C-library function *abs*, which returns a new *int* value that is the absolute value of its parameter. The *DblArray* class, presented in the next chapter, uses this technique for dozens of member functions.

When I initially developed these classes, I had the bright idea of cutting down on code and simplifying matters by including a member function such as this:

```
typedef int (* IntFunc)(int);

    class IntArray : public SortableArray
        {
        public:
            IntArray Apply(IntFunc func);
        };

    IntArray IntArray::Apply(IntFunc func)
        {
```

```
// create new array
IntArray result(ia);

// create pointer to new array
IntArrayPtr ptr = result.MakePtr();

for (;;)
    {
    // apply functions to element in array
    *ptr = func(*ptr);

    if (ptr.IsLast())
        break;

    // move to next element
    ++ptr;
    }

return result;
}
```

In essence, the *Apply* function calls *func* for every element in an *IntArray*, returning a new *IntArray* containing the results. To obtain an array containing the absolute values of the elements of another *IntArray*, I could simply have done this:

```
IntArray absvalues = ia.Apply(abs);
```

This passes the address of the ANSI *abs* functions to *Apply*, which then generates a new *Array* containing the absolute values of the elements of *ia*.

It didn't work! Why? Because *abs* is not necessarily a function. Sometimes, a call to *abs* is generated as inline code by the compiler. In other cases, *abs* may be defined as a macro. Because you can't obtain the address of a macro or a compiler-generated inline function, some compilers couldn't pass an address for *abs* to *Apply*.

When you look at the implementation of the *DblArray* class in the next chapter, you'll note that it has dozens of similar-looking functions for logarithms, trigonometry, and such. Again, an *Apply* function would have allowed me to define one function that could be called with the address of an appropriate numeric function if many of the floating-point math functions were not compiled inline by many compilers!

So much for the *Apply* function....

### 7.1.10 Fill Functions

I designed a variety of functions that fill an *IntArray* with values.

```
class IntArray : public SortableArray
     {
     .
     .
     .
     public:
         typedef int (* IA_FillRecFunc)(int);
         typedef int (* IA_FillByFunc)(const Index & i);

         static void SetInit(int i);

         void Fill(int i = InitValue);

         void FillArithmetic(int first, int incr);
         void FillGeometric(int first,  int mult);
         void FillRecursive(int first,  IA_FillRecFunc func);

         void FillRandom(RandGen & rg);
         void FillRandomBounded(int low, int high, RandGen &
                                                       rg);

         void FillBy(IA_FillByFunc func);
     .
     .
     .
     };
```

The *SetInit* function assigns its parameter to *InitValue*. *InitValue* (see section 7.1.1) are the default values assigned to the elements of a newly created array. *SetInit* is an inline function.

```
inline void IntArray::SetInit(int d)
      {
      InitValue = d;
      }
```

The *Fill* function assigns the same value to each element in an *IntArray*. The default value for *i* is *InitValue*, and *Fill* can thus be used to reinitialize an *IntArray* to its creation values.

```
void IntArray::Fill(int n)
      {
      IntArrayPtr ptr = MakePtr();

      for (;;)
          {
          *ptr = n;

          if (ptr.IsLast())
              break;

          ++ptr;
          }
      }
```

It's often useful to assign a progression of values to an *IntArray*. The *FillArithmetic* function assigns *init* to the first element of the array; each succeeding element is assigned the value of the previous element plus *incr*. *FillGeometric* uses a similar technique, except that each succeeding element is the value of the previous element multiplied by *mult*.

```
void IntArray::FillArithmetic(int first, int incr)
      {
      int value;

      IntArrayPtr ptr = MakePtr();

      value = first;
```

```
    *ptr = value;

    if (!ptr.IsLast())
        {
        ++ptr;

        for (;;)
            {
            value += incr;

            *ptr = value;

            if (ptr.IsLast())
                break;

            ++ptr;
            }
        }
    }

void IntArray::FillGeometric(int first,  int mult)
    {
    int value;

    IntArrayPtr ptr = MakePtr();

    value = first;

    *ptr = value;

    if (!ptr.IsLast())
        {
        ++ptr;

        for (;;)
            {
            value *= mult;

            *ptr = value;
```

```
        if (ptr.IsLast())
            break;

        ++ptr;
        }
    }
}
```

In *FillRecursive*, the function specified by the *func* parameter is called for each element after the first, with the value of the previous element. *func* should return the next value in a sequence.

```
void IntArray::FillRecursive(int first, IA_FillRecFunc func)
    {
    int value;

    IntArrayPtr ptr = MakePtr();

    value = first;

    *ptr = value;

    if (!ptr.IsLast())
        {
        ++ptr;

        for (;;)
            {
            value = func(value);

            *ptr = value;

            if (ptr.IsLast())
                break;

            ++ptr;
            }
        }
    }
```

For example, this program fills an *IntArray* with a *Fibonacci* sequence:

```
int main()

      {
      Range r (1,10);
      IntArray ia(r);

      // fill ia with Fibonacci sequence
      ia.FillRecursive(1,FibFill);

      // do other things...

      return 0;
      }

   int FibFill(int n)
      {
      // note: this is a one-shot function!
      // in a real program, x would need to be
      // reinitialized to 0 after each Fill
      // using this function.

      static int x = 0;
      int res;

      if (x == 0)
         {
         res = 1;
         x = 1;
         }
      else
         {
         res = x + n;
         x = n;
         }

      return res;
      }
```

The *FillRandom* function has a *RandGen* object (see Chapter 2) for a parameter. The *RandGen* object is called to supply random values for each element in the *IntArray*. *FillRandomBounded* is similar, but it fills the *IntArray* with values between *low* and *high*, inclusive.

```
void IntArray::FillRandom(RandGen & rg)
    {
    IntArrayPtr ptr = MakePtr();

    for (;;)
        {
        *ptr = (int)rg(INT_MAX);

        if (ptr.IsLast())
            break;

        ++ptr;
        }
    }

    void IntArray::FillRandomBounded(int low, int high,
                                         RandGen & rg)
    {
    if (high <= low)
        ReportError("high bound <= low bound");

    int x = high - low + 1;

    IntArrayPtr ptr = MakePtr();

    for (;;)
        {
        *ptr = (int)(rg(x)) + low;

        if (ptr.IsLast())
            break;

        ++ptr;
        }
    }
```

*FillBy* calls *func* with the Index value for each element in the *IntArray*, and assigns the return value to the corresponding element.

```
void IntArray::FillBy(IA_FillByFunc func)
    {
    Index i(IndexRange);

    for (;;)
        {
        (*this)[i] = func(i);

        if (i.IsMax())
            break;

        ++i;
        }
    }
```

### 7.1.11 Private Functions

*IntArray* defines a pair of utility functions.

```
class IntArray : public SortableArray
    {
    .
    .
    .
    private:
        static void Set(int * i);

        static void FriendErrExit(const char * msg);
    .
    .
    .
    };
```

The primary constructor for *IntArray* passes the address of the *Set* function to the constructor inherited from *Array*. For each element in the new *IntArray*, *Set* is called to assign to it an *InitValue*. Because its address is required, I defined *Set* as a callable function.

```
void IntArray::Set(int * i)
      {
      *i = InitValue;
      }
```

*FriendErrExit* was created to solve problems with an MS-DOS C++ compiler, which would not allow friends of the *IntArray* class to access the *ErrOut* member object. It provides an inline shell that calls *ErrOut*.

```
inline void IntArray::FriendErrExit(const char * msg)
      {
      ReportError(msg);
      }
```

### 7.1.12 Sorting Functions

Because *IntArray* is derived from *SortableArray*, it must define implementations for the pure virtual methods it inherits.

```
class IntArray : public SortableArray
      {
      .
      .
      .
      public:
          virtual int  IsBefore(const Index & i1,
                                const Index & i2);

          virtual void Exchange(const Index & i1,
                                const Index & i2);
      .
      .
      .
      };
```

These functions provide the ability to sort an *IntArray* in ascending order.

```
int IntArray::IsBefore(const Index & i1, const Index & i2)
    {
    return ((*this)[i1] < (*this)[i2]);
    }

  void IntArray::Exchange(const Index & i1, const Index & i2)
    {
    int temp = (*this)[i1];

    (*this)[i1] = (*this)[i2];
    (*this)[i2] = temp;
    }
```

I considered implementing a "selectable" *IsBefore* function that would allow for ascending and descending sorts. So far, though, I've needed to sort *IntArrays* only into ascending order.

### 7.1.13 Comparisons

The *IntArray* class defines member functions to implement the six standard comparison operators.

```
class IntArray : public SortableArray
    {
    .
    .
    .
    public:
        int Equals(const IntArray & ia) const;

        friend IntArray operator <  (const IntArray &ia1,
                                     const IntArray &ia2);

        friend IntArray operator <= (const IntArray &ia1,
                                     const IntArray &ia2);
```

```
friend IntArray operator == (const IntArray &ia1,
                             const IntArray &ia2);

friend IntArray operator != (const IntArray &ia1,
                             const IntArray &ia2);

friend IntArray operator >= (const IntArray &ia1,
                             const IntArray &ia2);

friend IntArray operator >  (const IntArray &ia1,
                             const IntArray &ia2);
    .
    .
    .
};
```

*Equals* compares two *IntArrays* for complete equality — the same *Ranges* and identical values in the elements. If the two arrays are equal, 1 is returned; otherwise, *Equals* returns 0.

```
int IntArray::Equals(const IntArray & ia) const
    {
    int result = 1;

    if (IndexRange == ia.IndexRange)
        {
        IntArrayConstPtr left  = MakeConstPtr();
        IntArrayConstPtr right = ia.MakeConstPtr();

        for (;;)
            {
            if (*left != *right)
                {
                result = 0;
                break;
                }
```

```
            if (left.IsLast())
                break;

            ++left;
            ++right;
            }
        }
    else
        result = 0;

    return result;
    }
```

*Equals* isn't the same thing as the == operator. For the standard comparison operators, the comparison of two *IntArrays* results in the creation of a new *IntArray*. Each element in the result contains the result of comparing the corresponding elements of *ia1* and *ia2*. In other words, the resulting *IntArray* contains zero and nonzero values based on the comparison of parallel elements in the two elements being compared.

This is how the == operator is implemented:

```
IntArray operator == (const IntArray & ia1,
                      const IntArray & ia2)
    {
    if (ia1.IndexRange != ia2.IndexRange)
        IntArray::FriendErrExit("incompatible arrays: ==");

    IntArray result(ia1.IndexRange);

    IntArrayPtr      dest  = result.MakePtr();
    IntArrayConstPtr left  = ia1.MakeConstPtr();
    IntArrayConstPtr right = ia2.MakeConstPtr();

    for (;;)
        {
        *dest = *left == *right;

        if (dest.IsLast())
            break;
```

```
        ++dest;
        ++left;
        ++right;
        }

    return result;
    }
```

The other comparison operators functions are nearly identical to ==, and they are shown in Appendix A.

## 7.2 Pointers for IntArrays

As I mentioned in section 7.1, two different derivatives of the *ArrayPtr* class are needed to complement the *IntArray* class. Just as two different sets of indexing functions are required (see section 7.1) to handle non-*const* and *const IntArrays*, so too are a pair of classes for *const* and non-*const* pointers required.

### 7.2.1 The IntArrayPtr class

*IntArrayPtr* objects can be used only to reference elements in non-*const IntArrays*. I created this limitation by defining the constructor for an *IntArrayPtr* as private, with *IntArray* as a friend class. The non-*const MakePtr* member function of *IntArray* creates *IntArrayPtrs*, preventing *IntArrayPtrs* from being created for *const IntArrays*.

The class definition looks like this:

```
class IntArrayPtr : public ArrayPtr
        {
        friend class IntArray;

        public:

            //————
            // copy constructor
            //————
```

```
        IntArrayPtr(const IntArrayPtr & aptr);
        IntArrayPtr(const ArrayPtr & aptr);

        //————————
        // assignment operators
        //————————

        IntArrayPtr & operator = (const IntArrayPtr & aptr);
        IntArrayPtr & operator = (const Index & i);
        IntArrayPtr & operator = (int i);

        //————————————
        // increment and decrement
        //————————————

        IntArrayPtr & operator ++ ();
        IntArrayPtr & operator - ();

        //————————
        // get pointer value
        //————————

        operator int * () const;

        //————————
        // dereference
        //————————

        int & operator * ();

protected:

        //————————
        // constructor
        //————————

        IntArrayPtr(char * base, size_t esize, const Range & r);
};
```

All of the real work is accomplished by the base *ArrayPtr* class. *IntArray*'s primary contibution is that of de-referencing operator functions that return *int* references to elements in the *IntArray*. Because *IntArrayPtr*'s functions are merely shells for those inherited from *ArrayPtr*, all of them are implemented inline:

```
inline IntArrayPtr::IntArrayPtr(char * base,
                                size_t esize,
                                const Range & r)
     : ArrayPtr(base,esize,r)
     {
     // empty
     }

//————
// copy constructor
//————

inline IntArrayPtr::IntArrayPtr(const IntArrayPtr & aptr)
     : ArrayPtr(aptr)
     {
     // empty
     }

inline IntArrayPtr::IntArrayPtr(const ArrayPtr & aptr)
     : ArrayPtr(aptr)
     {
     // empty
     }

//————
// assignment operators
//————

inline IntArrayPtr & IntArrayPtr::operator =
                                (const IntArrayPtr & aptr)
     {
     this->ArrayPtr::operator = (aptr);

     return *this;
```

```
        }

    inline IntArrayPtr & IntArrayPtr::operator = (const Index & i)
        {
        this->ArrayPtr::operator = (i);

        return *this;
        }

    inline IntArrayPtr & IntArrayPtr::operator = (int i)
        {
        this->ArrayPtr::operator = (i);

        return *this;
        }

//——————————
// increment and decrement
//——————————

    inline IntArrayPtr & IntArrayPtr::operator ++ ()
        {
        this->ArrayPtr::operator ++ ();

        return *this;
        }

    inline IntArrayPtr & IntArrayPtr::operator — ()
        {
        this->ArrayPtr::operator — ();

        return *this;
        }

//——————
// get pointer value
//——————

    inline IntArrayPtr::operator int * () const
        {
```

```
    return (int *)ElemPtr;
    }

//———
// dereference
//———

inline int & IntArrayPtr::operator * ()
    {
    return *((int *)ElemPtr);
    }
```

### 7.2.2 The IntArrayConstPtr class

*IntArrayConstPtr* is nearly identical to *IntArrayPtr*, save for two points: *IntArrayConstPtr* objects can be created only for *const IntArrays* (with the *MakeConstPtr* member function), and the return value from de-referencing an *IntArrayConstPtr* is a *const int &*.

Here is the class definition:

```
class IntArrayConstPtr : public ArrayPtr
    {
    friend class IntArray;

    public:

        //———
        // copy constructor
        //———

        IntArrayConstPtr(const IntArrayConstPtr & aptr);
        IntArrayConstPtr(const ArrayPtr & aptr);

        //———
        // assignment operators
        //———

        IntArrayConstPtr & operator =
                        (const IntArrayConstPtr & aptr);
```

```
            IntArrayConstPtr & operator = (const Index & i);
            IntArrayConstPtr & operator = (int i);

            //———————————
            // increment and decrement
            //———————————

            IntArrayConstPtr & operator ++ ();
            IntArrayConstPtr & operator - ();

            //——————
            // get pointer value
            //——————

            operator const int * () const;

            //——————
            // dereference
            //——————

            const int & operator * ();

        protected:
            IntArrayConstPtr(char * base, size_t esize,
                            const Range & r);
        };
```

And these are the inline function definitions:

```
inline IntArrayConstPtr::IntArrayConstPtr(char * base,
                                          size_t esize,
                                          const Range & r)
        : ArrayPtr(base,esize,r)
        {
        // empty
        }

    //——————
    // copy constructor
    //——————
```

```
inline IntArrayConstPtr::IntArrayConstPtr(const
IntArrayConstPtr & aptr)
    : ArrayPtr(aptr)
    {
    // empty
    }

inline IntArrayConstPtr::IntArrayConstPtr(const ArrayPtr &
aptr)
    : ArrayPtr(aptr)
    {
    // empty
    }

//——————
// assignment operators
//——————

inline IntArrayConstPtr & IntArrayConstPtr::operator = (const
IntArrayConstPtr & aptr)
    {
    this->ArrayPtr::operator = (aptr);

    return *this;
    }

inline IntArrayConstPtr & IntArrayConstPtr::operator = (const
Index & i)
    {
    this->ArrayPtr::operator = (i);

    return *this;
    }

inline IntArrayConstPtr & IntArrayConstPtr::operator = (int i)
    {
    this->ArrayPtr::operator = (i);

    return *this;
    }
```

```
//——————————
// increment and decrement
//——————————

inline IntArrayConstPtr & IntArrayConstPtr::operator ++ ()
    {
    this->ArrayPtr::operator ++ ();

    return *this;
    }

inline IntArrayConstPtr & IntArrayConstPtr::operator — ()
    {
    this->ArrayPtr::operator — ();

    return *this;
    }

//——————
// get pointer value
//——————

inline IntArrayConstPtr::operator const int * () const
    {
    return (const int *)ElemPtr;
    }

//——————
// dereference
//——————

inline const int & IntArrayConstPtr::operator * ()
    {
    return *((const int *)ElemPtr);
    }
```

# CHAPTER 8

# Floating-point Arrays

The *IntArray* class (presented in Chapter 7) demonstrates the issues and solutions that are required when creating a type-specific, numeric *Array* derivative. Although *IntArrays* are useful in some applications, many real-world problems involve real numbers, not integers. So, the next logical step is to create an *Array* type that contains floating-point values.

## 8.1 The DblArray Class

Herein I present my *DblArray* class, which defines an *Array* of *doubles*. I chose *doubles* over *floats* for a practical reason: at present, most C++ compilers supply only complete functional support for *doubles*. In many ways, an *Array* of *doubles* is no different than an *Array* of *ints*; in fact, some sections of this chapter will read like similar sections of Chapter 7. Like its integer sibling, the *DblArray* class needs to support construction, destruction, and the application of basic mathematical operations. Although *doubles* are not subject to bitwise and logical operators, they are manipulated by a wide variety of mathematical (e.g., trigonometric and logarithmic) functions.

The *DblArray* class is derived from the *SortableArray* class, because *doubles* can be sorted into order. Like *IntArray*, *DblArray* also needs to support fill functions, array pointers, and indexing.

### 8.1.1 Constructors

I defined five constructors for *DblArrays*.

```
class DblArray : public SortableArray
     {
     .
```

```
        .
        .
public:
      // constructors
      DblArray(const Range & r);
      DblArray(const DblArray & da);
      DblArray(const IntArray & ia);
      DblArray(const double * a);

      // concatenate
      DblArray(const DblArray & a1,
               const DblArray & a2);

      // subrange
      DblArray(const DblArray & a,
               const Index & first,
               const Index & last);
        .
        .
        .
};
```

The first constructor builds a new *DblArray*, filling it with the value *InitValue* by means of the private *Set* function (see below).

```
inline DblArray::DblArray(const Range & r)
      :
   SortableArray(r,sizeof(double),(ElemCreate)DblArray::Set)
      {
      // does nothing
      }
```

The second constructor is the copy constructor.

```
inline DblArray::DblArray(const DblArray & da)
      : SortableArray(da)
      {
      // does nothing
      }
```

A *DblArray* can be created from an *IntArray* using this conversion constructor:

```
DblArray::DblArray(const IntArray & ia)
        : SortableArray(ia.GetRange(),sizeof(double),
                        (ElemCreate)NULL)
        {
        Index i(IndexRange);

        for (;;)
            {
            (*this)[i] = (double)ia.Read(i);

            if (i.IsMax())
                break;

            ++i;
            }
        }
```

As you'll see later in this chapter, the conversion constructor allows *IntArrays* to be used as parameters wherever *DblArrays* are valid.

The next constructor creates a new *DblArray* that contains the same values as a traditional array of *doubles*. It is passed a pointer to an array in *a* along with the number of elements in *len*. Note that it is impossible to verify the length of *a*, and that care must be taken by the programmer to ensure that *len* is correct.

```
DblArray::DblArray(const double * a)
        : SortableArray(Range(0,sizeof(a) - 1),sizeof(double))
        {
        memcpy(Buffer,a,BufferSize);
        }
```

The fourth constructor concatenates two *DblArrays*. See Chapter 4 for details on how this is accomplished.

```
inline DblArray::DblArray(const DblArray & da1,
                                const DblArray & da2)
        : SortableArray(da1,da2)
```

```
      {
      // does nothing else
      }
```

The final constructor creates a *DblArray* that contains a subset of an existing *DblArray*. Again, see Chapter 4 for how this is accomplished in the base *Array* class.

```
inline DblArray::DblArray(const DblArray & a,
                          const Index & first,
                          const Index & last)
        : SortableArray(a,first,last)
        {
        // does nothing else
        }
```

### 8.1.2 Conversions

A standard C-type array can be generated from a *DblArray*.

```
class DblArray : public SortableArray
        {
        .
        .
        .
        public:
            operator double * ();
        .
        .
        .
        };
```

The conversion function allocates a block of memory, and then copies the contents of the *DblArray* into that block of memory.

```
DblArray::operator double * ()
        {
        double * result;

        result = new double[BufferSize];
```

```
if (result == NULL)
    ReportError("cannot allocate memory for double []");

memcpy(result,Buffer,BufferSize);

return result;
}
```

A conversion operator function can return only one piece of information, that is, the new type generated from the object being converted. Thus, the size of the array returned by the above conversion is not immediately known. A call to the *GetCount* function (defined in *Array*), however, provides the number of elements in the *DblArray*, and thus the number of elements in the newly created C-type array.

```
Range r(0,10);
   DblArray da(r);

   // generate a c-type array from ia
   double * ca = (double *)ia;

   // get the number of elements in ia
   sizeof calen = ia.GetCount();
```

Also note that, because the array is dynamically allocated, it is the responsibility of the programmer to ensure that the array is deleted from memory when it is no longer required.

### 8.1.3 Assignment Operator

The assignment operator assigns the contents of one *DblArray* to another *DblArray* already in existence.

```
class DblArray : public SortableArray
     {
     .
     .
     .
```

```
public:
    DblArray & operator = (const DblArray & da);
    .
    .
    .
};
```

I implemented the assignment operator as an inline call to the assignment operator inherited from *SortableArray*.

```
inline DblArray & DblArray::operator = (const DblArray & da)
    {
    this->SortableArray::operator = (da);

    return *this;
    }
```

### 8.1.4 Generating Pointers

Two *ArrayPtr* classes are created for *DblArrays*: *DblArrayPtr* (for non-*const DblArrays*) and *DblArrayConstPtr* (for *const DblArrays*). Sections 8.2 and 8.3 describe these two classes in detail.

As with the *IntArray* class, *DblArray* needs to define functions that generate array pointers for a given *DblArray*.

```
class DblArray : public SortableArray
    {
    .
    .
    .
    public:
        DblArrayPtr MakePtr();
        DblArrayConstPtr MakeConstPtr() const;
    .
    .
    .
    };
```

I implemented these functions as inline calls to the constructors for the two array pointer classes:

```
inline DblArrayPtr DblArray::MakePtr()
    {
    return DblArrayPtr(Buffer,ElementSize,IndexRange);
    }

  inline DblArrayConstPtr DblArray::MakeConstPtr() const
    {
    return DblArrayConstPtr(Buffer,ElementSize,IndexRange);
    }
```

### 8.1.5 Indexing

Indexing a *DblArray* is accomplished using the [] operator and the *Read* functions.

```
class DblArray : public SortableArray
    {
    .
    .
    .
    public:
        double & operator [] (const Index & i);
        double & operator [] (int i);

        const double & Read(const Index & i) const;
        const double & Read(int i) const;
    .
    .
    .
    };
```

The [] operators are used to return references to the elements of non-*const DblArrays*. The *Read* functions return *const* references to the elements of const *DblArrays*. I implemented these four functions as inline calls to the *GetElement* and *ReadElement* functions inherited from the *Array* class through *SortableArray*.

```
inline double & DblArray::operator [] (const Index & i)
        {
        return *((double *)(GetElement(i)));
        }

   inline double & DblArray::operator [] (int i)
        {
        return *((double *)(GetElement(i)));
        }

   inline const double & DblArray::Read(const Index & i) const
        {
        return *((const double *)(ReadElement(i)));
        }

   inline const double & DblArray::Read(int i) const
        {
        return *((const double *)(ReadElement(i)));
        }
```

### 8.1.6 Unary Operators

The *DblArray* class defines functions to implement the + and - unary operators.

```
class DblArray : public SortableArray
        {
        .
        .
        .
        public:
            DblArray operator + ();
            DblArray operator - ();
        .
        .
        .
        };
```

228

The unary plus does nothing more than return a copy of the *DblArray* it is applied to.

```
inline DblArray DblArray::operator + ()
        {
        return *this;
        }
```

The unary - operator creates a copy of the subject *DblArray*, and applies the unary - to each element in the copy. The copy is then returned as the function's result.

```
DblArray DblArray::operator - ()
        {
        DblArray result(*this);

        DblArrayPtr ptr = result.MakePtr();

        for (;;)
            {
            *ptr = -(*ptr);

            if (ptr.IsLast())
                break;

            ++ptr;
            }

        return result;
        }
```

### 8.1.7 Binary Mathematical Operators

The *DblArray* class defines functions that support addition, subtraction, multiplication, and division operators.

```
class DblArray : public SortableArray
        {
        .
        .
```

```
public:
    DblArray operator + (const DblArray & da);
    DblArray operator + (double n);

    DblArray operator - (const DblArray & da);
    DblArray operator - (double n);

    DblArray operator * (const DblArray & da);
    DblArray operator * (double n);

    DblArray operator / (const DblArray & da);
    DblArray operator / (double n);
    .
    .
    .
};
```

Using member functions, I created two implementations for each mathematical operation. The first argument is always a *DblArray*, which appears to the left of the operation symbol. To the right of the operation symbol can be either a *DblArray* or a single *double* value. For example:

```
Range r(1,20);
   DblArray da1(r), da2(r), da3(r);

   da3 = da1 + da2; // add two DblArrays
   da3 = da1 + 10;  // add a DblArray and an int
```

The two binary + functions are implemented like this:

```
DblArray DblArray::operator + (const DblArray & da)
      {
      if (IndexRange != da.IndexRange)
         ReportError("incompatible arrays: +");

      DblArray result(*this);

      DblArrayPtr      dest = result.MakePtr();
      DblArrayConstPtr src  = da.MakeConstPtr();
```

```
    for (;;)
        {
        *dest += *src;

        if (dest.IsLast())
            break;

        ++dest;
        ++src;
        }

    return result;
    }

DblArray DblArray::operator + (double n)
    {
    DblArray result(*this);

    DblArrayPtr ptr = result.MakePtr();

    for (;;)
        {
        *ptr += n;

        if (ptr.IsLast())
            break;

        ++ptr;
        }

    return result;
    }
```

The first function, which adds two *DblArrays*, begins by making a copy of the first array; it then adds the corresponding elements of the second array to the elements of the copy. The copy is the return value. If the two *DblArrays* have different Ranges, an error message is called for.

When the parameter is a *double*, a copy of the subject *DblArray* is made and the *double* value is added to each of its elements.

**231**

The -, *, and / operators are implemented in a nearly identical fashion; complete listings of those functions can be found in Appendix A.

### 8.1.8  Shorthand Mathematical Operators

There is a shorthand form of every binary operator.

```
class DblArray : public SortableArray
    {
    .
    .
    .
    public:
        DblArray & operator += (const DblArray & da);
        DblArray & operator += (double n);

        DblArray & operator -= (const DblArray & da);
        DblArray & operator -= (double n);

        DblArray & operator *= (const DblArray & da);
        DblArray & operator *= (double n);

        DblArray & operator /= (const DblArray & da);
        DblArray & operator /= (double n);
    .
    .
    .
    };
```

In keeping with the style used for the binary operator, the shorthand operators each have two variants with *DblArray* and *double* parameters. The implementations are nearly identical, so I shall present only the implementation of the += operator here:

```
DblArray & DblArray::operator += (const DblArray & da)
    {
    if (IndexRange != da.IndexRange)
        ReportError("incompatible arrays: +=");
```

```
    DblArrayPtr      dest = MakePtr();
    DblArrayConstPtr src  = da.MakeConstPtr();

    for (;;)
        {
        *dest += *src;

        if (dest.IsLast())
            break;

        ++dest;
        ++src;
        }

    return *this;
    }

DblArray & DblArray::operator += (double n)
    {
    DblArrayPtr ptr = MakePtr();

    for (;;)
        {
        *ptr += n;

        if (ptr.IsLast())
            break;

        ++ptr;
        }

    return *this;
    }
```

### 8.1.9 Comparison Functions

The *DblArray* class defines member functions to implement comparison operators.

```
class DblArray : public SortableArray
     {
     .
     .
     .
     public:
          int Equals(const DblArray & da) const;

          friend IntArray operator <  (const DblArray &da1,
                                       const DblArray &da2);

          friend IntArray operator <= (const DblArray &da1,
                                       const DblArray &da2);

          friend IntArray operator == (const DblArray &da1,
                                       const DblArray &da2);

          friend IntArray operator != (const DblArray &da1,
                                       const DblArray &da2);

          friend IntArray operator >= (const DblArray &da1,
                                       const DblArray &da2);

          friend IntArray operator >  (const DblArray &da1,
                                       const DblArray &da2);

     .
     .
     .
     };
```

*Equals* compares two *DblArrays* for complete equality — the same *Ranges* and identical values in the elements. If the two arrays are equal, 1 is returned; otherwise, *Equals* returns 0.

```
int DblArray::Equals(const DblArray & da) const
    {
    int result = 1;

    if (IndexRange == da.IndexRange)
        {
        DblArrayConstPtr ptr1 = MakeConstPtr();
        DblArrayConstPtr ptr2 = da.MakeConstPtr();

        for (;;)
            {
            if (*ptr1 != *ptr2)
                {
                result = 0;
                break;
                }

            if (ptr1.IsLast())
                break;

            ++ptr1;
            ++ptr2;
            }
        }
    else
        result = 0;

    return result;
    }
```

The comparison operators generate an *IntArray* result that represents the comparison of corresponding elements in the two *DblArray* parameters. The *IntArray* contains zero and nonzero values based on the comparison of the elements of *ia1* and *ia2*. The two arrays must have the same range, or an error message will be requested from *ReportError*.

This is how the == operator is implemented:

```
IntArray operator == (const DblArray & da1,
                      const DblArray & da2)
    {
    if (da1.IndexRange != da2.IndexRange)
        DblArray::FriendErrExit("incompatible arrays: ==");

    IntArray result(da1.IndexRange);

    IntArrayPtr      dest  = result.MakePtr();
    DblArrayConstPtr left  = da1.MakeConstPtr();
    DblArrayConstPtr right = da2.MakeConstPtr();

    for (;;)
        {
        *dest = *left == *right;

        if (dest.IsLast())
            break;

        ++dest;
        ++left;
        ++right;
        }

    return result;
    }
```

NCEG defines several new comparison operators. The Table 8-1 shows the results obtained from the ANSI and NCEG operators.

|  | | *relationship* | | | | |
|:---:|:---|:---:|:---:|:---:|:---:|:---:|
| *operator* | *description* | > | < | = | ? | *error?* |
| < | less | F | T | F | F | yes |
| > | greater | T | F | F | F | yes |
| <= | less or equal | F | T | T | F | yes |
| >= | greater or equal | T | F | T | F | yes |
| == | equal | F | F | T | F | no |
| != | unordered, less, or greater | T | T | F | T | no |

**Table 8-1. Results from the ANSI and NCEG operators.**

The table consists of seven columns. The first column contains the operator symbol, and the descriptive name of that symbol is given in column two. The four *relations* columns show the results of a comparison, for each, of four possible relationships between two operands: greater than (>), less than (<), equal(=), and unordered (?).

All of the comparison operators functions are defined using the same syntax as is ==, and they are shown in Appendix A.

### 8.1.10 Mathematical Functions

C++ defines a library of several dozen floating-point functions, which calculate triginometric, logarithmic, and other values.

```
class DblArray : public SortableArray
      {
      .
      .
      .
      public:
            //——————————
            // trigonometric functions
            //——————————

            DblArray & cos();
            friend DblArray cos(const DblArray & da);

            DblArray & cosh();
            friend DblArray cosh(const DblArray & da);

            DblArray & acos();
            friend DblArray acos(const DblArray & da);

            DblArray & sin();
            friend DblArray sin(const DblArray & da);

            DblArray & sinh();
            friend DblArray sinh(const DblArray & da);

            DblArray & asin();
            friend DblArray asin(const DblArray & da);

            DblArray & tan();
            friend DblArray tan(const DblArray & da);
```

```
DblArray & tanh();
friend DblArray tanh(const DblArray & da);

DblArray & atan();
friend DblArray atan(const DblArray & da);

DblArray & atan2(const DblArray & den);

friend DblArray atan2(const DblArray & num,
                      const DblArray & den);

//——————
// logarithmic functions
//——————

// natural logarithm

DblArray & log();
friend DblArray log(const DblArray & da);

// natural exponentiation

DblArray & exp();
friend DblArray exp(const DblArray & da);

// base-10 logarithm

DblArray & log10();
friend DblArray log10(const DblArray & da);

// exponentiation
```

```
friend DblArray pow(const DblArray & da,
                         double p);

DblArray & pow(double p);

DblArray & pow(const DblArray & p);

friend DblArray pow(const DblArray & da,
                         const DblArray & p);

// square root

DblArray & sqroot();
friend DblArray sqroot(const DblArray & da);

//————
// sign functions
//————

// absolute value

DblArray & abs();
friend DblArray abs(const DblArray & da);

// copy sign

//—————
// power of 2 functions
//—————

// multiply by power of 2

friend DblArray ldexp(const DblArray & da,
                          int p);

DblArray & ldexp(int p);

DblArray & ldexp(const IntArray & p);

friend DblArray ldexp(const DblArray & da,
                          const IntArray & p);
```

```
// get fraction and power of 2

DblArray & frexp(IntArray & pow2);

friend DblArray frexp(const DblArray & da,
                             IntArray & pow2);


//————————
// rounding functions
//————————

// round toward negative infinity

DblArray & floor();
friend DblArray floor(const DblArray & da);

// round toward positive infinity

DblArray & ceil();
friend DblArray ceil(const DblArray & da);


//————————
// miscellaneous functions
//————————

// compute remainder

friend DblArray fmod(const DblArray & da,
                            double div);

DblArray & fmod(double div);

DblArray & fmod(const DblArray & div);

friend DblArray fmod(const DblArray & da,
                            const DblArray & div);

// get fractional and integer parts

DblArray & modf(DblArray & ipart);
```

```
friend DblArray modf(const DblArray & da,
                      DblArray & ipart);



      .
      .
      .
};
```

I defined two or more versions of each function, which provide different data sources and result destinations. The syntax for using these functions depends upon where you want the result to be stored. To obtain the sine of each element in a *DblArray*, storing the value in the same array, use the first *sin* member function in this fashion:

```
da.sin();
```

To obtain a new *DblArray* that contains the sines of the elements in another *DblArray*, the second *sin* member function is used by means of this syntax:

```
da2 = sin(da1);
```

This follows the form of the standard C++ library function *sin*, which returns a new *double* value that is the absolute value of its parameter. The *DblArray* class, presented in the next chapter, uses this technique for dozens of member functions.

Here are the implementations of the two *sin* functions:

```
DblArray & DblArray::sin()
      {
      DblArrayPtr ptr = MakePtr();

      for (;;)
          {
          *ptr = ::sin(*ptr);

          if (ptr.IsLast())
              break;
```

```
        ++ptr;
        }

    return *this;
    }

DblArray sin(const DblArray & da)
    {
    DblArray result(da);

    DblArrayPtr      dest = result.MakePtr();
    DblArrayConstPtr src = da.MakeConstPtr();

    for (;;)
        {
        *dest = ::sin(*src);

        if (dest.IsLast())
            break;

        ++dest;
        ++src;
        }

    return result;
    }
```

Those functions that return a single *double* answer for a single *double* input (that is, *sin, tan, log10,* and others) are implemented using the same technique as the two *sin* functions. Some functions, however, are a bit more complicated.

For example, the standard library function *pow* requires two *double* values: the base and the power. I implement four different versions of *pow* for *DblArray*:

A function that raises the elements of *DblArray* to the same power.

A function that returns a new array that contains the elements of the subject *DblArray* raised to the same power.

A function that raises the elements of one *DblArray* to powers stored in another *DblArray*.

A function that returns a new *DblArray* that contains the values of raising the elements of one *DblArray* to powers stored in another *DblArray*.

These four functions are implemented like this:

```
DblArray & DblArray::pow(double p)
    {
    DblArrayPtr ptr = MakePtr();

    for (;;)
        {
        *ptr = ::pow(*ptr,p);

        if (ptr.IsLast())
            break;

        ++ptr;
        }

    return *this;
    }

DblArray pow(const DblArray & da, double p)
    {
    DblArray result(da.IndexRange);

    DblArrayPtr      dest = result.MakePtr();
    DblArrayConstPtr src = da.MakeConstPtr();

    for (;;)
        {
        *dest = ::pow(*src,p);

        if (dest.IsLast())
            break;
```

```
        ++dest;
        ++src;
        }

    return result;
    }

DblArray & DblArray::pow(const DblArray & p)
    {
    if (IndexRange != p.IndexRange)
        ReportError("incompatible arrays: pow(1)");

    DblArrayPtr      base = MakePtr();
    DblArrayConstPtr pwr  = p.MakeConstPtr();

    for (;;)
        {
        *base = ::pow(*base,*pwr);

      · if (base.IsLast())
            break;

        ++base;
        ++pwr;
        }

    return *this;
    }

DblArray pow(const DblArray & da, const DblArray & p)
    {
    if (da.IndexRange != p.IndexRange)
        DblArray::FriendErrExit("incompatible arrays:
pow(2)");

    DblArray result(da.IndexRange);

    DblArrayPtr      dest = result.MakePtr();
    DblArrayConstPtr base = da.MakeConstPtr();
    DblArrayConstPtr  pwr = p.MakeConstPtr();
```

```
        for (;;)
            {
            *dest = ::pow(*base,*pwr);

            if (dest.IsLast())
                break;

            ++dest;
            ++base;
            ++pwr;
            }

        return result;
        }
```

I used a similar set of variant implementations when defining other multiparameter functions, such as *fmod* and *remquo*. The complete source code for the mathematical functions is presented in Appendix A, in the file *darraym.cxx*.

### 8.1.11 Fill Functions

I designed a variety of functions that fill a *DblArray* with values.

```
class DblArray : public SortableArray
        {
        .
        .
        .
    public:
        typedef double (* DA_FillRecFunc)(double);
        typedef double (* DA_FillByFunc)(const Index & i);

        static void SetInit(double d);

        void Fill(double d = InitValue);

        void FillArithmetic(double first, double incr);
        void FillGeometric(double first,  double mult);
        void FillRecursive(double first,  DA_FillRecFunc
    func);
```

```
void FillRandom(RandGen & rg);
void FillRandomBounded(double low, double high,
                       RandGen & rg);

void FillBy(DA_FillByFunc func);
    .
    .
    .
};
```

The *SetInit* function assigns its parameter to *InitValue*. *InitValue* (see section 8.1.1) is the default value assigned to the elements of a newly created array. *SetInit* is an inline function.

```
inline void DblArray::SetInit(double d)
    {
    InitValue = d;
    }
```

The *Fill* function assigns the same value to each element in a *DblArray*. The default value for *i* is *InitValue*, and *Fill* can thus be used to reinitialize a *DblArray* to its creation values.

```
void DblArray::Fill(double d)
    {
    DblArrayPtr dest = MakePtr();

    for (;;)
        {
        *dest = d;

        if (dest.IsLast())
            break;

        ++dest;
        }
    }
```

It's often useful to assign a progression of values to a *DblArray*. The *FillArithmetic* function assigns *init* to the first element of the array; each succeeding element is assigned the value of the previous element plus *incr*. *FillGeometric* uses a similar technique, except that each succeeding element is the value of the previous element multiplied by *mult*.

```
void DblArray::FillArithmetic(double first, double incr)
    {
    double value;

    DblArrayPtr dest = MakePtr();

    value = first;

    *dest = value;

    if (!dest.IsLast())
        {
        ++dest;

        for (;;)
            {
            value += incr;

            *dest = value;

            if (dest.IsLast())
                break;

            ++dest;
            }
        }
    }
void DblArray::FillGeometric(double first,  double mult)
    {
    double value;

    DblArrayPtr dest = MakePtr();
```

```
value = first;

*dest = value;

if (!dest.IsLast())
    {
    ++dest;

    for (;;)
        {
        value *= mult;

        *dest = value;

        if (dest.IsLast())
            break;

        ++dest;
        }
    }
}
```

In *FillRecursive*, the function specified by the *func* parameter is called for each element after the first, with the value of the previous element. *func* should return the next value in a sequence.

```
void DblArray::FillRecursive(double first, DA_FillRecFunc func)
    {
    double value;

    DblArrayPtr dest = MakePtr();

    value = first;

    *dest = value;

    if (!dest.IsLast())
        {
        ++dest;
```

```
        for (;;)
            {
            value = func(value);

            *dest = value;

            if (dest.IsLast())
                break;

            ++dest;
            }
        }
    }
```

My discussion of the *IntArray* class demonstrates how the *FillRecursive* function is employed.

The *FillRandom* function has a *RandGen* object (see Chapter 2) for a parameter. The *RandGen* object is called to supply random values for each element in the *DblArray*. *FillRandomBounded* is similar, but it fills the *DblArray* with values between *low* and *high*, inclusive.

```
void DblArray::FillRandom(RandGen & rg)
    {
    DblArrayPtr dest = MakePtr();

    for (;;)
        {
        *dest = double(rg(UINT_MAX)) / double(UINT_MAX);

        if (dest.IsLast())
            break;

        ++dest;
        }
    }

void DblArray::FillRandomBounded(double low, double high,
RandGen & rg)
    {
```

```
    if (high <= low)
        ReportError("high bound <= low bound");

    double range = high - low;

    DblArrayPtr dest = MakePtr();

    for (;;)
        {
        *dest = double(rg(UINT_MAX)) / double(UINT_MAX) *
range + low;

        if (dest.IsLast())
            break;

        ++dest;
        }
    }
```

*FillBy* calls *func* with the *Index* value for each element in the *DblArray*, and assigns the return value to the corresponding element.

```
void DblArray::FillRandom(RandGen & rg)
    {
    DblArrayPtr dest = MakePtr();

    for (;;)
        {
        *dest = double(rg(UINT_MAX)) / double(UINT_MAX);

        if (dest.IsLast())
            break;

        ++dest;
        }
    }

void DblArray::FillRandomBounded(double low, double high,
RandGen & rg)
    {
```

```
    if (high <= low)
        ReportError("high bound <= low bound");

    double range = high - low;

    DblArrayPtr dest = MakePtr();

    for (;;)
        {
        *dest = double(rg(UINT_MAX)) / double(UINT_MAX) *
range + low;

        if (dest.IsLast())
            break;

        ++dest;
        }
    }
```

### 8.1.12 Sorting Functions

Because *DblArray* is derived from *SortableArray*, it must define implementations for the pure virtual methods it inherits.

```
class DblArray : public SortableArray
    {
    .
    .
    .

    public:
        virtual int  IsBefore(const Index & i1,
                                const Index & i2);

        virtual void Exchange(const Index & i1,
                                const Index & i2);
    .
    .
    .
    };
```

These functions make it possible to sort a *DblArray* in ascending order.

```
int DblArray::IsBefore(const Index & i1, const Index & i2)
    {
    return ((*this)[i1] < (*this)[i2]);
    }

   void DblArray::Exchange(const Index & i1, const Index & i2)
    {
    int temp = (*this)[i1];

    (*this)[i1] = (*this)[i2];
    (*this)[i2] = temp;
    }
```

I considered implementing a "selectable" *IsBefore* function that allows for ascending and descending sorts. So far, however, I have needed to sort *DblArrays* only into ascending order.

### 8.1.13 Private Functions

*DblArray* defines a pair of utility functions.

```
class DblArray : public SortableArray
    {
    .
    .
    .
    protected:
        static void Set(double * d);

        static void FriendErrExit(const char * msg);
    .
    .
    .
    };
```

The primary constructor for *DblArray* passes the address of the *Set* function to the constructor inherited from *Array*. For each element in the new *DblArray*, *Set* is called to assign it *InitValue*. Because its address is required, I defined *Set* as a callable function.

```
void DblArray::Set(double * i)
      {
      *d = InitValue;
      }
```

*FriendErrExit* was created to solve problems with some MS-DOS C++ compilers that would not allow friends of the *DblArray* class to access the *ReportError* member object. It provides an inline shell that calls *ReportError*.

```
inline void DblArray::FriendErrExit(const char * msg)
      {
      ReportError(msg);
      }
```

## 8.2 Pointers for DblArrays

As I mentioned in section 8.1, two different derivatives of the *ArrayPtr* class are needed to complement the *DblArray* class. Just as two different sets of indexing functions are required (see section 8.1) to handle non-*const* and *const DblArrays*, so to are a pair of classes for *const* and non-*const* pointers required.

### 8.2.1 The DblArrayPtr class

*DblArrayPtr* objects can only be used to reference elements in non-const *DblArrays*. I created this limitation by defining the constructor for a *DblArrayPtr* as private, with *DblArray* as a friend class. The non-const *MakePtr* member function of *DblArray* creates *DblArrayPtrs*, preventing *DblArrayPtrs* from being created for const *DblArrays*.

The class definition looks like this:

```
class DblArrayPtr : public ArrayPtr
      {
      friend class DblArray;
```

```
public:
    DblArrayPtr(const DblArrayPtr & aptr);
    DblArrayPtr(const ArrayPtr & aptr);

    DblArrayPtr & operator = (const DblArrayPtr & aptr);
    DblArrayPtr & operator = (const Index & i);
    DblArrayPtr & operator = (int i);

    DblArrayPtr & operator ++ ();
    DblArrayPtr & operator - ();

    operator double * () const;

    double & operator * ();

protected:
    DblArrayPtr(char * base, size_t esize, const Range &
                                                     r);
};
```

All of the real work is accomplished by the base *ArrayPtr* class. *DblArray*'s primary contribution is that of de-referencing operator functions that return *int* references to elements in the *DblArray*. Because *DblArrayPtr*'s functions are merely shells for those inherited from *ArrayPtr*, all of them are implemented inline:

```
inline DblArrayPtr::DblArrayPtr(char * base,
                                size_t esize,
                                const Range & r)
    : ArrayPtr(base,esize,r)
    {
    // empty
    }

inline DblArrayPtr::DblArrayPtr(const DblArrayPtr & aptr)
    : ArrayPtr(aptr)
    {
    // empty
    }
```

```
inline DblArrayPtr::DblArrayPtr(const ArrayPtr & aptr)
    : ArrayPtr(aptr)
    {
    // empty
    }

inline DblArrayPtr & DblArrayPtr::operator = (const
DblArrayPtr & aptr)
    {
    this->ArrayPtr::operator = (aptr);

    return *this;
    }

inline DblArrayPtr & DblArrayPtr::operator = (const Index & i)
    {
    this->ArrayPtr::operator = (i);

    return *this;
    }

inline DblArrayPtr & DblArrayPtr::operator = (int i)
    {
    this->ArrayPtr::operator = (i);

    return *this;
    }

inline DblArrayPtr & DblArrayPtr::operator ++ ()
    {
    this->ArrayPtr::operator ++ ();

    return *this;
    }

inline DblArrayPtr & DblArrayPtr::operator − ()
    {
    this->ArrayPtr::operator − ();

    return *this;
```

```
        }

    inline DblArrayPtr::operator double * () const
        {
        return (double *)ElemPtr;
        }

    inline double & DblArrayPtr::operator * ()
        {
        return *((double *)ElemPtr);
        }
```

### 8.2.2 The DblArrayConstPtr class

*DblArrayConstPtr* is nearly identical to *DblArrayPtr*, save for two points: *DblArrayConstPtr* objects can be created only for *const DblArrays* (with the *MakeConstPtr* member function), and the return value from de-referencing a *DblArrayConstPtr* is a *const int &*.

Here is the class definition:

```
class DblArrayConstPtr : public ArrayPtr
        {
        friend class DblArray;

        public:
            DblArrayConstPtr(const DblArrayConstPtr & aptr);
            DblArrayConstPtr(const ArrayPtr & aptr);

            DblArrayConstPtr & operator =
                            (const DblArrayConstPtr & aptr);
            DblArrayConstPtr & operator = (const Index & i);
            DblArrayConstPtr & operator = (int i);

            DblArrayConstPtr & operator ++ ();
            DblArrayConstPtr & operator - ();

            operator const double * () const;
```

```
        const double & operator * ();

    protected:
        DblArrayConstPtr(char * base, size_t esize,
                         const Range & r);
    };
```

And these are the inline function definitions:

```
inline DblArrayConstPtr::DblArrayConstPtr(char * base,
                                          size_t esize,
                                          const Range & r)
    : ArrayPtr(base,esize,r)
    {
    // empty
    }

    inline DblArrayConstPtr::DblArrayConstPtr(const
    DblArrayConstPtr & aptr)
        : ArrayPtr(aptr)
        {
        // empty
        }

    inline DblArrayConstPtr::DblArrayConstPtr(const ArrayPtr &
    aptr)
        : ArrayPtr(aptr)
        {
        // empty
        }

    inline DblArrayConstPtr & DblArrayConstPtr::operator =
                    (const DblArrayConstPtr & aptr)
        {
        this->ArrayPtr::operator = (aptr);

        return *this;
        }
```

```
inline DblArrayConstPtr & DblArrayConstPtr::operator =
                         (const Index & i)
    {
    this->ArrayPtr::operator = (i);

    return *this;
    }

inline DblArrayConstPtr & DblArrayConstPtr::operator = (int i)
    {
    this->ArrayPtr::operator = (i);

    return *this;
    }

inline DblArrayConstPtr & DblArrayConstPtr::operator ++ ()
    {
    this->ArrayPtr::operator ++ ();

    return *this;
    }

inline DblArrayConstPtr & DblArrayConstPtr::operator - ()
    {
    this->ArrayPtr::operator - ();

    return *this;
    }

inline DblArrayConstPtr::operator const double * () const
    {
    return (const double *)ElemPtr;
    }

inline const double & DblArrayConstPtr::operator * ()
    {
    return *((const double *)ElemPtr);
    }
```

## 8.3 Wrapping Up

All the class definitions and inline functions discussed in this chapter are contained in the file *darray.h*; most of the functions are defined in the file *darray.cxx*, and the functions listed in section 8.1.11 are defined in the file *darraym.cxx*. Look in Appendix A for complete listings of these files.

The next, most obvious question is: What can be done with these arrays? Well, for one thing, I have used these arrays for statistical analysis. And that is the subject of the next chapter.

# CHAPTER 9

# Basic Statistics

The preceeding chapters introduced a set of classes for manipulating arrays of numeric values. One goal of using classes is to allow for the easy introduction of expanded capabilities. For example, I recently have been required to use the *DblArray* class in statistical calculations.

The field of statistics is far too broad for me to cover in great detail. The copious shelving in my office contains dozens of books that discuss the ins and outs of determining exactly what a set of numbers might mean. That, after all, is the purpose of statistics: to find out what numbers signify and how if at all different numbers are related.

Statistics is by far the grayest area of mathematics, in that it deals with intangibles. What a statistician tries to do is apply certain mathematical principles to a set of data, generating a characteristic value that can be examined by a thoughtful human. Statistics in and of themselves prove nothing; a human brain is required to determine if the statistics mean anything.

## 9.1 Design Decisions

How should a set of statistical functions be implemented? In a C program, there are no design choices: individual functions are written to calculate statistical values from C-style arrays of *doubles*. C++, however, offered me two choices. I could develop a C-like library of functions that manipulates *DblArrays*, or I could derive a new class from *DblArray* that provides member functions.

I chose to derive a new class, named *DblStatArray*, because the solution "felt" better than creating a set of functions. I like the idea of binding a function to data; to my way of thinking, it made more sense to create a new *Array* type that defines new operations for a *DblArray*.

Implementing statistical calculations in a set of functions would work just as well as using my *DblStatArray* class. I made my design choice based on personal preference, not technical dogma. Use your common sense and gut feeling when designing classes and you'll be more comfortable with the results.

For the purposes of this book, I have reduced the complexity of the *DblStatArray* class presented herein. The class I use has more than 40 statistical functions, and many of those require a large library of functions for working with differential equations and integration. What I have done is condense the *DblStatArray* class, so that it provides simple statistical tools that can be described fully in this text.

The *DblStatArray* class is derived from *DblArray*. *DblStatArray* does not define any data members; it defines only new functions. Each of the following sections describes a set of related functions.

## 9.2 Constructors and Assignments

A *DblStatArray* is nothing more than a *DblArray* with extra member functions. It is constructed, copied, destroyed, and assigned in the same manner as a *DblArray*. However, constructors and the assignment operator are not inherited from a base class; thus, *DblStatArray* must define constructors in order to call the constructors for its base class, *DblArray*.

```
class DblStatArray : public DblArray
    {
    .
    .
    .
public:
    DblStatArray(const Range & r);
    DblStatArray(const DblArray & da);
    DblStatArray(const DblStatArray & dsa);
    DblStatArray(const IntArray & ia);

    DblStatArray(const DblStatArray & a1,
                 const DblStatArray & a2);
```

```
       DblStatArray(const DblStatArray & a,
                    const Index & first,
                    const Index & last);

       DblStatArray & operator = (const DblStatArray & da);
       .
       .
       .
       };
```

I implemented the constructors and the assignment operator as inline shells which call only the corresponding functions inherited from *DblArray*.

```
inline DblStatArray::DblStatArray(const Range & r)
    : DblArray(r)
    {
    // empty
    }

inline DblStatArray::DblStatArray(const DblArray & da)
    : DblArray(da)
    {
    // empty
    }

inline DblStatArray::DblStatArray(const DblStatArray & dsa)
    : DblArray(dsa)
    {
    // empty
    }

inline DblStatArray::DblStatArray(const IntArray & ia)
    : DblArray(ia)
    {
    // empty
    }

inline DblStatArray::DblStatArray(const DblStatArray & a1,
                                  const DblStatArray & a2)
```

```
        : DblArray(a1,a2)
        {
        // does nothing else
        }

inline DblStatArray::DblStatArray(const DblStatArray & a,
                                  const Index & first,
                                  const Index & last)
        : DblArray(a,first,last)
        {
        // does nothing else
        }

//————————
// assignment operator
//————————

inline DblStatArray & DblStatArray::operator = (const
DblStatArray & da)
        {
        this->DblArray::operator = (da);

        return *this;
        }
```

As you may have noticed, *DblStatArray* defines a conversion constructor to create a *DblStatArray* from a *DblArray*. This might seem a bit odd; after all, isn't *DblStatArray* nearly the same thing as a *DblArray*?

No!

An object of a derived class can be used as if it were an object of its base class, because the derived class is a superset of the base class. It follows that a base-class object cannot be used as a derived-class object, because the derived class may have members and needs that do not exist for the base class. Even though *DblStatArray* adds only functions to *DblArray*, it still requires a conversion constructor to convert a *DblArray* to a *DblStatArray*. The conversion takes place as an inline call to the copy constructor inherited from *DblArray*.

## 9.3 Finding the Range of Values

It can be very useful to know the highest and lowest values in a data set. These four functions provide that capability for *DblStatArrays*.

```
class DblStatArray : public DblArray
    {
    .
    .
    .
    public:
        // minimum, maximum, and range determination
        double Min() const;
        double Max() const;

        void MinMax(double & minimum, double & maximum) const;

        double RangeOf() const;
    .
    .
    .
    };
```

*Min* and *Max* return the minimum (smallest) and maximum (largest) values, respectively, in the array.

```
double DblStatArray::Min() const
    {
    DblArrayConstPtr ptr = MakeConstPtr();

    double result = *ptr;

    for (;;)
        {
        if (ptr.IsLast())
            break;

        ++ptr;
```

```
            if (*ptr < result)
                result = *ptr;
            }

        return result;
        }


double DblStatArray::Max() const
    {
    DblArrayConstPtr ptr = MakeConstPtr();

    double result = *ptr;

    for (;;)
        {
        if (ptr.IsLast())
            break;

        ++ptr;

        if (*ptr > result)
            result = *ptr;
        }

    return result;
    }
```

I created *MinMax* to return both the minimum and maximum values with one function call.

```
void DblStatArray::MinMax(double & minimum, double & maximum)
const
    {
    DblArrayConstPtr ptr = MakeConstPtr();

    maximum = *ptr;
    minimum = *ptr;

    for (;;)
```

```
    {
    if (ptr.IsLast())
        break;

    ++ptr;

    if (*ptr < minimum)
        minimum = *ptr;

    if (*ptr > maximum)
        maximum = *ptr;
    }
  }
```

*RangeOf* returns the difference between the minimum and maximum values, showing how far the values range within the array. If you already have the minimum and maximum values you can calculate this value without calling this function.

```
double DblStatArray::RangeOf() const
    {
    double minimum, maximum;

    MinMax(minimum,maximum);

    return ::fabs(maximum - minimum);
    }
```

## 9.4 Series Calculations

Often I've found it useful to be able to generate a product or sum of an array's elements. Although these aren't statistical functions, they are used by other members of *DblStatArray*.

```
class DblStatArray : public DblArray
    {
    .
    .
    .
```

```
public:
    double Sum() const;
    double Product() const;
.
.
.
};
```

The *Sum* represents the addition of all the elements in an array. The function calculates the result by cycling through the array from the first to the last element, adding each value to a result.

```
double DblStatArray::Sum() const
    {
    double result = 0.0;

    DblArrayConstPtr ptr = MakeConstPtr();

    for (;;)
        {
        result += *ptr;

        if (ptr.IsLast())
            break;

        ++ptr;
        }

    return result;
    }
```

The *Product* is calculated by multiplying together all the elements in a *DblStatArray*. It uses the same programming techniques as *Sum*, using multiplication instead of addition for calculating the result.

```
double DblStatArray::Product() const
    {
    double result = 1.0;
```

```
DblArrayConstPtr ptr = MakeConstPtr();

for (;;)
    {
    result *= *ptr;

    if (ptr.IsLast())
        break;

    ++ptr;
    }

return result;
}
```

## 9.5 Moments of Distribution

A *moment of distribution* is a single value that describes a data set. These are the most fundamental values used in statistics. The *DblStatArray* defines member functions to calculate the most commonly used moments of distribution.

```
class DblStatArray : public DblArray
    {
    .
    .
    .
public:
    // calculate moments of distribution
    double Mean() const;
    double Median() const;
    double MedianSort();

    double Variance() const;

    double StdDeviation() const;
    double AvgDeviation() const;

    void Moment(double & mean,
                double & avgdev,
```

```
                    double & stddev,
                    double & var) const;
        .
        .
        .
    };
```

I'll explain the meaning and calculation of each value in its own section.

### 9.5.1 Mean

The *mean* is commonly known as the average; it is the sum of all elements in the set, divided by the number of elements.

$$\bar{x} = \frac{1}{N} \sum_{j=1}^{N} x_j$$  (Equation 9-1)

The mean is a simple yardstick for determining the most common value in a data set. It is calculated by dividing the result of the *Sum* function by the number of elements in the array.

```
double DblStatArray::Mean() const
    {
    return Sum() / (double)Count;
    }
```

### 9.5.2 Median

The *median* also tries to tell you what the most common element in the set is, by returning the middle-most value. This involves sorting the *DblStatArray*, and then returning the value of the element that falls in the middle of the array. For example, in this array of data:

```
1, 1, 2, 4, 5, 5, 6, 7, 9, 10, 10
```

The median will be 5, because that value is located in the middle of the data set.

The median can be calculated easily only if the elements of the array are sorted. This can be a problem when you don't want the data in your array to be rearranged by sorting. To limit the problem, I developed two implementations of the *median* function. The first creates a temporary copy of a *DblStatArray*, sorts it, and returns the median.

```
double DblStatArray::Median() const
    {
    DblStatArray temp(*this);

    int middle = (IndexRange.GetMin() + IndexRange.GetMax()) / 2;

    temp.Sort();

    return temp[middle];
    }
```

The advantage of *Median* is that it does not affect the ordering of elements in the *DblStatArray* to which it is applied. However, creating a second duplicate array can be problematic, particularly when the array is very large. Also, the work that goes into sorting the array is thrown away once the median is calculated. But, because *Median* does not alter its object, it can be used for constant *DblStatArrays*.

The second implementation, *MedianSort*, directly sorts the *DblStatArray* and returns the median.

```
double DblStatArray::MedianSort()
    {
    int middle = (IndexRange.GetMin() + IndexRange.GetMax()) / 2;

    Sort();

    return Read(middle);
    }
```

*MedianSort* does not create a temporary array, but it does sort the *DblStatArray* being examined. Your choice of a median function depends upon your requirements for maintaining the order of the elements in an array.

### 9.5.3 Variance and Standard Deviation

It's often useful to know how widely the data in a set varies from the mean. The most common characterization of differences in a data set is known as *variance*, which is calculated using the following formula:

$$Var = \frac{1}{N-1} \sum_{j=1}^{N} \left( x_j - \bar{x} \right)^2$$

(Equation 9-2)

The variance represents the average square of the differences between the elements of an array and the array's mean. I implemented it like this:

```
double DblStatArray::Variance() const
    {
    double temp, result = 0.0;

    double m = Mean();

    DblArrayConstPtr ptr = MakeConstPtr();

    for (;;)
        {
        temp = *ptr - m;

        result += temp * temp;

        if (ptr.IsLast())
            break;

        ++ptr;
        }
```

```
result /= ((double)(Count - 1));

return result;
}
```

The square root of the variance is called the standard deviation; it is represented by the greek letter σ.

$$\sigma = \sqrt{Var}$$

(Equation 9-3)

Note that the standard deviation represents the common range in which most data points will be found: between *mean* - s and *mean* + s. In other words, the standard deviation is an indicator of how far the data ranges from the mean.

I implemented the *StdDeviation* function as an inline function:

```
inline double DblStatArray::StdDeviation() const
    {
    return sqrt(Variance());
    }
```

### 9.5.4 Average Deviation

Another estimator of the variablity in data is the average deviation, which is calcuated by taking the average of the difference between each data point and the mean of the array.

$$\text{average deviation} = \frac{1}{N} \sum_{j=1}^{N} \left| x_j - \bar{x} \right|$$

(Equation 9-4)

The *AvgDeviation* function implements the above equation in this fashion:

```
double DblStatArray::AvgDeviation() const
    {
    double result = 0.0;
    double m = Mean();
```

**273**

```
DblArrayConstPtr ptr = MakeConstPtr();

for (;;)
    {
    result += fabs(*ptr - m);

    if (ptr.IsLast())
        break;

    ++ptr;
    }

result /= (double)Count;

return result;
}
```

### 9.5.5 Moment

I developed much of the code above based on an amazing text called *Numerical Recipes in C*, by Press, Flannery, Teukolsky, and Vetterling (Cambridge Press, 1988). This volume contains a treasure trove of mathematical formulas, concepts, and tools that are of indescribable value to a mathematical programmer.

The above-mentioned authors suggest that a single function be used to calculate several moments of distribution simultaneously. Statisticians generally require more than one of these values, and using the individual functions discussed above can be *very* inefficient. For example, calculating the *Variance* and then calling *StdDeviation* will result in two calls to *Variance* and *Mean*. Generally, a statistician needs to know several of the above values. So, I created the *Moment* function, which returns the mean, average deviation, standard deviation, and variance in one fell swoop.

```
void DblStatArray::Moment(double & mean,
                          double & avgdev,
                          double & stddev,
                          double & var) const
    {
    double temp, cnt;
```

```
cnt    = (double)Count;
mean   = Mean();
var    = 0.0;
avgdev = 0.0;

DblArrayConstPtr ptr = MakeConstPtr();

for (;;)
    {
    temp = *ptr - mean;

    var    += temp * temp;
    avgdev += fabs(temp);

    if (ptr.IsLast())
        break;

    ++ptr;
    }

var    /= cnt - 1.0;
avgdev /= cnt;
stddev = sqrt(var);
}
```

## 9.6 Understanding Individual Values with Z-scores

Let's say that we have the set values shown in Table 9.1, representing the rainfall in Sagecliff, Colorado, for the month of July, for the last twenty years.

Looking at the data that follows, can we tell if the 1991 data is highly unusual? It appears to be so, but is that data any more unlikely than the data for 1988, when it rained 3.5 inches? Is the two-tenths of an inch reported in 1983 unusual, or is that a normal figure? Is the rainfall of 2.5 inches in 1979 above or below normal?

A value called a *z-score* can help answer questions like these. A z-score is calculated for any individual member of the data set using the formula in Equation 9-5.

$$z_j = \frac{x_j - \overline{x}}{\sigma}$$

(Equation 9-5)

275

The z-score represents the number of "standard deviations" a given value is from the average (mean) value. A negative z-score tells us that the value is below the norm, and a positive z-score says that the value is above normal. In most cases, a "normal" value should have a z-score between -1 and +1, indicating that it is within the range of the standard deviation from the mean. A z-score with an absolute value greater than 1 is calculated for values that fall outside of the normal data distribution. The higher the absolute z-score, the more unusual the value is.

| Year | Rainfall |
|------|----------|
| 1970 | 1.5" |
| 1971 | 2.3" |
| 1972 | 2.1" |
| 1973 | 7.5" |
| 1974 | 3.0" |
| 1975 | 2.4" |
| 1976 | 1.9" |
| 1977 | 1.8" |
| 1978 | 2.0" |
| 1979 | 2.5" |
| 1980 | 2.3" |
| 1981 | 2.4" |
| 1982 | 3.0" |
| 1983 | 0.2" |
| 1984 | 1.9" |
| 1985 | 2.5" |
| 1986 | 2.1" |
| 1987 | 2.6" |
| 1988 | 3.5" |
| 1989 | 1.8" |
| 1990 | 2.1" |
| 1991 | 6.0" |

Table 9-1. Set values representing the rainfall in Sagecliff, Colorado.

I created two functions that calculate Z-scores:

```
class DblStatArray : public DblArray
    {
    .
    .
    .
    public:
        double ZScore(const Index & i) const;
        double ZScore(int i) const;

        DblStatArray ZScore() const;      .
    .
    .
    };
```

The first two of these functions calculate the z-score for any element of the array that is selected either by *Index* or *int* index. These two functions are implemented as follows:

```
double DblStatArray::ZScore(const Index & i) const
    {
    double result = 0.0;

    double sd = StdDeviation();

    if (sd == 0.0)
        result = 0.0;
    else
        result = (Read(i) - Mean()) / sd;

    return result;
    }

double DblStatArray::ZScore(int i) const
    {
    double result = 0.0;
```

```
double sd = StdDeviation();

if (sd == 0.0)
    result = 0.0;
else
    result = (Read(i) - Mean()) / sd;

return result;
}
```

Note that the result of these functions is zero when the standard deviation is zero. This avoids a divide overflow that would otherwise terminate the program.

The third *ZScore* function creates a new *DblStatArray* that contains z-scores for every element in the target array. This is a quick way of getting all the z-scores in one function call. Its implementation follows:

```
DblStatArray DblStatArray::ZScore() const
    {
    DblStatArray result(IndexRange);

    double sd = StdDeviation();

    if (sd == 0.0)
        result.Fill(0.0);
    else
        {
        DblArrayConstPtr  src = MakeConstPtr();
        DblArrayPtr      dest = result.MakePtr();

        double m  = Mean();

        for (;;)
            {
            *dest = (*src - m) / sd;
```

```
          if (src.IsLast())
              break;

          ++src;
          ++dest;
          }
      }

  return result;
  }
```

The z-score is 2.3 for the 6 inches of rain recorded in 1991. That's more than 1, telling me that 1991's July rainfall was unusually high. For the 3.5 inches of rain recorded in 1988, however, the z-score is only 0.6, meaning that that amount is well within the expected range. For 1983, when only 0.2 inches of rain fell, a z-score of -1.6 indicates an unusually dry July.

## 9.7 Correlation

Statisticians are always trying to determine whether two sets of data are related. For example: Is there a connection between the average temperature and average rainfall in Sagecliff? Table 9-2 shows the average monthly temperatures for Sagecliff during the same period as that for which the rainfall data was collected.

When two data sets follow a similar pattern of peaks and valleys in their structure, they are said to be "positively correlated." If the high values in one data set correspond to the low values in the other data set (and vice versa), the two are said to be "negatively correlated." If there is no relationship, then it is said that there is "no correlation" between the two data sets.

| Year | Rainfall |
|------|----------|
| 1970 | 1.5" |
| 1971 | 2.3" |
| 1972 | 2.1" |
| 1973 | 7.5" |
| 1974 | 3.0" |
| 1975 | 2.4" |
| 1976 | 1.9" |
| 1977 | 1.8" |
| 1978 | 2.0" |
| 1979 | 2.5" |
| 1980 | 2.3" |
| 1981 | 2.4" |
| 1982 | 3.0" |
| 1983 | 0.2" |
| 1984 | 1.9" |
| 1985 | 2.5" |
| 1986 | 2.1" |
| 1987 | 2.6" |
| 1988 | 3.5" |
| 1989 | 1.8" |
| 1990 | 2.1" |
| 1991 | 6.0" |

Table 9-2. Set values representing the temperature in Sagecliff, Colorado.

To correlate two data sets, we compare the z-scores of corresponding elements. Using z-scores instead of actual values eliminates scaling problems; it allows us to look at the two data sets based on how much they vary from their means. I have implemented a function name *Correlation* to perform this calculation for a *DblStatArray*.

```
class DblStatArray : public DblArray
    {
    .
    .
    .
    public:
        double Correlation(const DblStatArray & dsa);
    .
    .
    .
    };
```

A correlation value is obtained using the following formula:

$$cor = \frac{1}{N} \sum_{j=1}^{N} \frac{\left(x_j - \bar{x}\right)\left(y_j - \bar{y}\right)}{\sigma_x \sigma_y}$$

(Equation 9-6)

In other words, the correlation of two data sets can be calculated by summing the products of corresponding z-scores, and dividing the sum by the number of elements in the data sets. I implemented the *Correlation* function like this:

```
double DblStatArray::Correlation(const DblStatArray & dsa)
    {
    if (IndexRange != dsa.IndexRange)
        ReportError("Incompatible arrays in Correlation");

    DblArrayConstPtr ptr1 = MakeConstPtr();
    DblArrayConstPtr ptr2 = dsa.MakeConstPtr();

    double result = 0.0;

    double  m1 = Mean();
    double  m2 = dsa.Mean();
    double div = StdDeviation() * dsa.StdDeviation();

    if ((sd1 == 0.0) || (sd2 == 0.0))
        {
        if (sd1 == sd2)
            result = 1.0;
        else
            result = 0.0;
        }
    else
        {
        for (;;)
            {
            result += ((*ptr1 - m1) * (*ptr2 - m2)) / div;
```

```
        if (ptr1.IsLast())
            break;

        ++ptr1;
        ++ptr2;
        }

    result /= Count;
    }

return result;
}
```

## 9.8 An Example

Using the climate data for Sagecliff, I built a small program to demonstrate the use of *DblStatArrays*.

```
                        rain.cxx
        Performs statistical analysis on rainfall amounts for
                     Sagecliff, Colorado.
```

```
#include "iostream.h"
#include "dsarray.h"

const Range DataRange(1970,1991);

double RainValues[] =
    {
    1.5, 2.3, 2.1, 7.5, 3.0, 2.4, 1.9, 1.8, 2.0, 2.5, 2.3,
    2.4, 3.0, 0.2, 1.9, 2.5, 2.1, 2.6, 3.5, 1.8, 2.1, 6.0
    };
```

```
double TempValues[] =
    {
    91, 81, 84, 75, 79, 81, 81, 88, 87, 80, 83,
    81, 79, 94, 77, 79, 78, 82, 90, 73, 77, 76
    };

DblStatArray RainData(DataRange);
DblStatArray TempData(DataRange);

int main()
    {
    // fill arrays with data
    DblArrayPtr rainPtr = RainData.MakePtr();
    DblArrayPtr tempPtr = TempData.MakePtr();

    int n = 0;

    for (;;)
        {
        *rainPtr = RainValues[n];
        *tempPtr = TempValues[n];

        if (rainPtr.IsLast())
            break;

        ++rainPtr;
        ++tempPtr;
        ++n;
        }

    double mean, var, sd, ad, skew, kurt, z;
```

```
RainData.Moment(mean,ad,sd,var,skew,kurt);

cout << "\nRainData has a mean of " << mean
     << " and a standard deviation of " << sd << "\n\n";

z = RainData.ZScore(1973);

cout << "In 1973: "
     << RainData[1973]
     << " inches of rain represents a z-score of "
     << z << '\n';

z = RainData.ZScore(1977);

cout << "In 1977: "
     << RainData[1977]
     << " inches of rain represents a z-score of "
     << z << '\n';

z = RainData.ZScore(1983);

cout << "In 1983: "
     << RainData[1983]
     << " inches of rain represents a z-score of "
     << z << '\n';

z = RainData.ZScore(1988);

cout << "In 1988: "
     << RainData[1988]
     << " inches of rain represents a z-score of "
     << z << '\n';
```

```
z = RainData.ZScore(1991);

cout << "In 1991: "
    << RainData[1991]
    << " inches of rain represents a z-score of "
    << z << "\n\n";

TempData.Moment(mean,ad,sd,var,skew,kurt);

cout << "TempData has a mean of " << mean
    << " and a standard deviation of " << sd << "\n\n";

double cor = RainData.Correlation(TempData);

cout << "The correlation between rain and temp data is: "
    << cor << "\n";

return 0;
}
```

The program creates two *DblStatArrays RainData* and *TempData* and fills them with data. The program displays the mean and standard deviation for both arrays. For *RainData*, the program calculates z-scores for several values in *RainData*. Finally, the program correlates *RainData* and *TempData*. The output looks like this:

```
RainData has a mean of 2.60909 and a standard deviation of 1.5010

In 1973: 7.5 inches of rain represents a z-score of  3.25826
In 1977: 1.8 inches of rain represents a z-score of -0.539005
In 1983: 0.2 inches of rain represents a z-score of -1.6049
In 1988: 3.5 inches of rain represents a z-score of  0.593511
In 1991: 6.0 inches of rain represents a z-score of  2.25898

TempData has a mean of 81.6364 and a standard deviation of 5.4296

The correlation between rain and temp data is: -0.449105
```

A value of -0.45 tells us that there is *not* a strong correlation between rainfall and temperature in Sagecliff.

Be careful in making assumptions based on statistical data. If the correlation between rainfall and temperature had been closer to -1 (say -0.95), that would have told us only that the two quantities follow an inverse pattern of high and low values. It wouldn't *prove* that higher temperatures result in lower rainfall; it would merely suggest that such a supposition *might* be right.

## 9.9 Where To From Here?

That's it, then, for our discussion of various types of arrays. I hope these classes have been useful, and even interesting. Now it's time to turn our attention to a completely new subject: file handling. More than anything else, programs process sets of information stored in files.

# PART III

# Indexing, Hashing, and Filing

CHAPTER 10

# Persistent Objects

File handling is arguably the most important component of a software application. Most useful programs are capable of storing and retrieving file-based information in a speedy and reliable manner. Yet file handling is often overlooked — particularly by C++ library vendors. They give us classes for matrices, user interfaces, and containers, but fail to provide for the handling of data.

One of my goals in building my library of C++ classes was to create a powerful library of file-handling classes. I wanted a class library that was flexible, general, extensible, and understandable. So what else is new?

## 10.1 Persistent Objects

If you read the literature about object-oriented programming, you'll find discussions of *persistent* objects. A persistent object is one that can be stored outside of the program, to be retrieved at a later time. Such objects are called persistent objects because their state persists between instances of an application. In essence, persistent objects are objects that can be stored in files. However, storing objects isn't as easy as storing structures.

It's easy — and incomplete — to view objects as data structures with associated functionality. An object is a program component that has an identity and a state. The identity and state involves relationships to other objects, static class members, virtual functions, and base classes. In storing a persistent object, the identity and state of the object must be preserved.

Only an object itself can know how to preserve its state; thus, only an object can be responsibile for controlling the storage of its components. When the object is retrieved, it should be able to construct itself based on the data that was stored.

A consequence of this is that objects read from files must be new objects, constructed from the retrieved data. This ensures that state information — such as base classes, component objects, and virtual function tables — are built correctly for the object being retrieved. In other words, my design has persistent objects being read from a file using a special constructor.

## 10.2 Approaches to Persistence

It isn't easy to implement persistent objects; notice the scarcity of books and articles that cover the subject in detail. When I began looking at the problem, I saw three routes to a solution: extending the iostreams library, using templates, and using inheritance.

### 10.2.1 Extending iostreams

The primary advantage of streams is that they can be extended to handle new data types by overloading the << and >> operators. For example, the *String* class in Chapter 3 defines stream I/O operators. The C-based *printf* family of functions cannot be easily modified to handle new data types.

In the case of iostreams, expanded capability means decreased performance and increased complexity. I see iostreams as a complex, general-purpose library designed for the display and storage of text. The stream library is specifically designed to handle a linear sequence of data moving to or from a stream. Binary-file operations, which involve the search for specific file locations, are not in the "spirit" of the iostreams library.

Although C++ streams provide excellent tools for formatting textual output, I find them clumsy when used for binary-data handling. When I designed my *Persistent* class library, I wanted a library tailored to the storage of objects in a variety of environments.

### 10.2.2 Parameterized Types

Parameterized types, or templates, allow classes and functions to be defined by parameters. For example, this template defines a generic-number class template:

```
template <class T>
class Object
```

```
    {
public:
    // constructor
    Object(const T & v) { Value = v; }

    // conversion operator
    operator T () { return Value; }

protected:
    T Value;
};
```

A class type must be included in the definition of an *Object* instance:

```
Object<int> n(1); // creates an Object that uses int for Value
```

Wherever you used a macro in a C program, a template can probably do the same job in C++. Macros can be used to easily define symbolic constants and simple function-like statements, but they are clumsy when used to create a new data type. Templates define types or functions, are more flexible than macros, and provide type checking. For example, by using a template, the compiler automatically knows that two *Object<int>s* are compatible.

Templates could be used to define persistent objects. For example:

```
template<class File>
class Object
    {
    .
    .
    .
    public:
        Object(File & f);

        void Write(File & f);
    .
    .
    .
    };
```

The *Object* class is defined in terms of the *File* type used for the storage and retrieval of *Objects*. New *Objects* are created from information retrieved using the constructor; *Objects* are stored through the *Write* function.

The problem with the use of templates is that the *Object* class must make the assumption that *File* provides the appropriate tools for converting objects to and from their storage format. A common *File* base class could solve that problem by defining pure virtual functions that would implement required operations. However, a common base class may — depending on its design — limit the nature of the "files" that can store persistent objects. As you'll see in future chapters, I use the common concept of persistence when storing objects in linked lists, hash tables, trees, and (of course) files.

I avoid the use of templates in my code, for two reasons. One, although the ANSI C++ committee has approved templates for inclusion in the forthcoming C++ standard, several recent discussions have concerned problems with the current definition and semantics of templates. It is a very real possibility that changes will occur in templates before a final C++ standard emerges. Second, templates are not universally available. My programs often run on a variety of hardware and software platforms — where the local C++ compiler may or may not have templates. My code needs to be reasonably portable, so I avoid new language features that are implemented by only a few vendors.

### 10.2.3 Inheriting Persistence

How a file goes about its business should be transparent to the objects that use it. An object should not be concerned with how or where its data is stored or retrieved. All the object needs to know is that it formats itself and stores that data to a file from which the data can later be retrieved to reconstruct the object.

Conversely, a file should never need to know anything about the objects it stores. A file should receive a chunk of data from an object and store it without regard for what that data represents. In this fashion, files become independent of the data which is stored in them.

Furthermore, files should not be limited to disk-based storage. I've worked with systems that use tapes and solid-state memories for data storage. In one application,

I built a file system that resided entirely inside battery-backed RAM. Where and how a file is stored should never concern an object being stored, and a persistent object should be able to treat different file types as equivalent. By making files and objects independent, file handling becomes more generalized.

I see two broad categories of components that are needed to support persistence: persistent objects and storage objects. To provide a bridge between persistent and storage objects, I defined an intermediate type. Persistent objects can convert themselves to and from the intermediate type; storage objects store the intermediate type directly. Persistent objects have full control over how they are represented in the intermediate type; storage objects are free to handle the intermediate type, so long as they preserve its contents.

It may seem like a considerable amount of work to use an intermediate type, but I've found that it provides sufficient flexibility and performance for my needs.

## 10.3 Generic Data

The *DataBlock* class can be thought of as a translator. Persistent objects create *DataBlocks*, which are collected by a storage object. Storage objects, in turn, return *DataBlocks*, which are then used to construct objects.

### 10.3.1 Object Signatures

I needed a simple mechanism for type verification of the data in *DataBlocks*. Somehow, an object needed to know that it was being built from the right kind of *DataBlock*. The problem is that type information cannot be stored in a file; so far as a file is concerned, a block of data is a set of bytes, and it is the program's responsibility to assign some meaning to those bytes.

My solution was to store a signature with each *DataBlock*. The signature is an *unsigned long* that should be unique for each persistent object class. When a persistent object builds an *DataBlock* of itself, it should store the appropriate signature value. When an object is constructed from an *DataBlock*, the signature can be checked to ensure that this data block goes with this kind of object.

*Signatures* are not foolproof. It's possible for two different object types to have the same signature. But it's a better system than having no type checking at all. If a file is going to contain objects of several different types, it is the programmer's responsibility to guarantee that those objects have different identifiers. When we get into real programs later in the book, I'll demonstrate techniques for selecting reliable object signatures.

The *DataBlock* class is completely defined in the files *persist.h* and *persist.cxx*. (both of which are presented in their entirety in Appendix A). In *file.h* I define the *Signature* data type as:

```
typedef unsigned long Signature;
```

I also defined some contant values for Signatures:

```
const Signature SIG_USER_BASE = 0x00000000;
const Signature SIG_USER_MAX  = SYS_SIG_BASE - 1;
const Signature SIG_SYS_BASE  = 0xF0000000;
const Signature SIG_DELETED   = 0xFFFFFFFF;
```

"User" Signatures are those that can be used by user-defined classed; "System" signatures are those used internally by various classes in my persistence library. In other words, objects that define persistent objects can use any value between 0 and *SIG_USER_MAX* for their signature. *SIG_DELETED* is a system signature that defines a deleted block in a storage object; it will be explained later, in more detail.

### 10.3.2 The DataBlock Class Definition

I defined the *DataBlock* class like this:

```
class DataBlock
    {
    public:
        // constructors
        DataBlock();

        DataBlock(Signature sig,
                  size_t sz,
                  const void * data);
```

```
        DataBlock(const DataBlock & db);

        // destructor
        ~DataBlock();

        // assignment
        void operator = (const DataBlock & db);

        // interrogation
        Signature    GetSignature() const;
        size_t       GetSizeOf() const;
        const void * GetBufferPtr() const;

        // check for NULL block
        Boolean IsNull() const;

        // change error reporter
        static void SetErrOut(const ErrReporter & er);

    protected:
        Signature BlockSig;
        size_t    BufferSize;
        void *    BufferPtr;

        static ErrReporter * ErrOut;

        static void ReportError();
    };
```

A *DataBlock* consists of a *Signature*, a *size_t* value named *BufferSize*, and a block of data named *BufferPtr*. The block of data is *BufferSize* bytes in length. I also included a static *ErrorReporter* object (see Chapter 2) that is used to display memory-allocation error messages. The *ReportError* and *SetErrOut* functions follow the functionality set forth by similar functions in earlier chapters.

```
    void DataBlock::ReportError()
        {
        if (ErrOut != NULL)
```

```
                    ErrOut->Fatal("memory allocation failure");
            }

    void DataBlock::SetErrOut(const ErrReporter & er)
            {
            if (ErrOut != NULL)
                delete ErrOut;

            ErrOut = new ErrReporter(er);
            }
```

A new *DataBlock* is constructed from a *Signature*, a *size_t* value, and a pointer to a block of memory.

```
    DataBlock::DataBlock(Signature sig, size_t sz, const void *
    data)
            {
            BufferSize = sz;
            BlockSig   = sig;

            BufferPtr = (void *)new char[sz];

            if (BufferPtr == NULL)
                ReportError();

            if (data == NULL)
                memset(BufferPtr,0,sz);
            else
                memcpy(BufferPtr,data,sz);
            }
```

An error is reported if the constructor cannot allocate enough memory to duplicate the data block. If the *data* argument is *NULL*, the memory block pointed to by *BufferPtr* is filled with zeros.

The default constructor creates a *DataBlock* for which all values are zero. A *DataBlock* with no data and a zero signature is known as a null block.

```
inline DataBlock::DataBlock()
    {
    BufferSize = 0;
    BufferPtr  = NULL;
    BlockSig   = 0;
    }
```

*DataBlocks* can also be constructed from other *DataBlocks* using a copy constructor.

```
DataBlock::DataBlock(const DataBlock & db)
    {
    BufferSize = db.BufferSize;
    BlockSig   = db.BlockSig;

    BufferPtr  = (void *)new char[BufferSize];

    if (BufferPtr == NULL)
        ReportError();

    memcpy(BufferPtr,db.BufferPtr,BufferSize);
    }
```

The destructor deletes *Buffer*.

```
inline DataBlock::~DataBlock()
    {
    if (BufferPtr != NULL)
        delete BufferPtr;
    }
```

*DataBlocks* can be assigned to each other.

```
void DataBlock::operator = (const DataBlock & db)
    {
    BufferSize = db.BufferSize;
    BlockSig   = db.BlockSig;
```

```
    if (BufferPtr != NULL)
        delete BufferPtr;

    BufferPtr = (void *)new char[BufferSize];

    if (BufferPtr == NULL)
        ReportError();

    memcpy(BufferPtr,db.BufferPtr,BufferSize);
    }
```

Several interrogation functions return the values of a *DataBlock*'s data members. The *IsNull* function returns a *Boolean* indicating if the block in question is a null block.

```
inline Signature DataBlock::GetSignature() const
    {
    return BlockSig;
    }

inline size_t DataBlock::GetSizeOf() const
    {
    return BufferSize;
    }

inline const void * DataBlock::GetBufferPtr() const
    {
    return BufferPtr;
    }

inline Boolean DataBlock::IsNull() const
    {
    if (BufferSize == 0)
        return BOOL_TRUE;
    else
        return BOOL_FALSE;
    }
```

*GetDataPtr* returns a constant pointer to *BufferPtr*, thus preventing the data from being changed by a user of a *DataBlock*. Once a *DataBlock* has been created, it cannot be changed (other than by assignment).

Later, I'll show you functions that return *DataBlocks* from storage objects. When those functions encounter an error, they return a null block. To simplify returning a null block, I defined a global constant named *NULL_BLOCK* that is (surprise, surprise!) a null *DataBlock*.

```
// default constructor automatically
// makes this a null block
const DataBlock NULL_BLOCK;
```

## 10.4 Defining Persistence

A persistent class must be able to create *DataBlocks* from existing objects and construct new objects from *DataBlocks*. I defined this capability in the *Persistent* class.

```
class Persistent
    {
    public:
        //****************************************
        // all persistent classes should define a
        // a constructor that converts a DataBlock
        // to an object:
        //
        // Persistent(const DataBlock & db);
        //****************************************

        virtual operator DataBlock () const = 0;
    };
```

*Persistent* is what I call a characteristic class: it defines a set of characteristics imparted to those classes derived from it. Classes whose objects are persistent will have *Persistent* as a base class. The functions defined for *Persistent* define what a persistent object needs to be able to do. The pure virtual function in *Persistent* requires the derived class to define a *DataBlock* conversion operator.

A persistent object can create *DataBlocks*, using the conversion operator defined by *Persistent*. These blocks are then passed to file objects for storage. When a file object retrieves a *DataBlock*, it can be passed to the constructor from which a new object will be made.

The comment is a reminder that a conversion constructor must be defined by the derived class. Unlike a pure virtual method, there is no C++ technique for compelling a class to define a constructor with a given set of arguments, so a reminder will have to do.

## 10.5 Strings as Keys

Some data can be identified by a *key* value. The type of key depends upon the data being stored and the requirements for retrieval. For example, a financial program would identify data by an account number. Most often, data is identified by a piece of text, such as a name. I created the *KeyString* class to define a *String*-based key.

```
class KeyString : public Persistent
    {
  public:
      KeyString(const String & str);
      KeyString(const DataBlock & db);
      KeyString(const KeyString & key);

      const String & GetString() const;

      virtual operator DataBlock() const;

      int operator <  (const KeyString & key);
      int operator <= (const KeyString & key);
      int operator == (const KeyString & key);
      int operator != (const KeyString & key);
      int operator >= (const KeyString & key);
      int operator >  (const KeyString & key);

    protected:
      static const Signature Sig;
```

```
private:
    String KStr;
};
```

*KeyStrings* are persistent objects, because they need to be collected in storage objects that store and retrieve persistent objects using a key value.

A *KeyString* contains a *String* object. The choice to have *KeyString* contain a *String* rather than being derived from the *String* class is philosophical; I view a *KeyString* as a key that contains a character string for identifying another object. It would be just as legitimate to have *KeyString* based on *String* and to think of it as a *String* that can be used as a key. Decisions like this are a matter of personal taste.

Note that a template class could be used to make *Key* classes for various types:

```
template <class T>
class Key : Persistent
    {
    .
    .
    .
    public:
        Key (const T & k);

        T GetValue() const;

    private:
        T Value
    .
    .
    .
    };
```

A static constant named *Sig* is the *Signature* used when creating *DataBlocks* from *KeyStrings*. *Sig* is defined relative to *SIG_SYS_BASE:*

```
const Signature KeyString::Sig = SYS_SIG_BASE + 1;
```

*KeyStrings* are constructed from *Strings*, *DataBlocks*, or other *KeyStrings*:

```
inline KeyString::KeyString(const String & str)
    : KStr(str)
    {
    // void
    }

inline KeyString::KeyString(const KeyString & keystr)
    : KStr(keystr.KStr)
    {
    // void
    }
```

Constructing a *KeyString* from a *String* or *KeyString* is very simple; conversion from a *DataBlock* involves constructing a *String* from the NULL-terminated character array stored in the *DataBlock*. If the *DataBlock* does not have the expected *Signature*, a *KeyString* with a blank *KStr* is created.

```
KeyString::KeyString(const DataBlock & db)
    {
    if (db.GetSignature() == Sig)
        KStr = (const char *)db.GetBufferPtr();
    };
```

Persistence requires that the *Keystrings* be convertible to *DataBlocks* for storage. The *DataBlocks* created vary in size; their length is the length of the NULL-terminated character array generated by conversion from *KStr*.

```
KeyString::operator DataBlock() const
    {
    return DataBlock(Sig,(size_t)(KStr.Length() + 1),
                ((const void *)((const char *)KStr)));
    }
```

*Keys* are often compared to determine the order of objects. The *KeyString* class defines the six standard comparison operators in terms of inline calls to the operators defined for *String*.

```
inline int KeyString::operator <  (const KeyString & key)
    {
    return (KStr < key.KStr);
    }

inline int KeyString::operator <= (const KeyString & key)
    {
    return (KStr <= key.KStr);
    }

inline int KeyString::operator == (const KeyString & key)
    {
    return (KStr == key.KStr);
    }

inline int KeyString::operator != (const KeyString & key)
    {
    return (KStr != key.KStr);
    }

inline int KeyString::operator >= (const KeyString & key)
    {
    return (KStr >= key.KStr);
    }

inline int KeyString::operator >  (const KeyString & key)
    {
    return (KStr > key.KStr);
    }
```

I defined a characteristic class named *KeyByString* that defines a class of objects for which keys can be generated.

```
class KeyByString
    {
    public:
        virtual KeyString MakeKey() const = 0;
    };
```

## 10.6 Data File Classes

Different types of storage objects have very different requirements. For example, a hash table is used differently from a binary tree, and these are different from files stored on disks or in memory.

I defined a basic set of classes for disk-based data files. Basing these classes on the ANSI-standard file I/O functions provided portability. The following discussion assumes that you understand the workings of *fopen*, *fclose*, *fseek*, *fread*, and *fwrite* as defined by ANSI C.

The hierarchy consists of four classes: a base class that defines the characteristics of all files, a class for sequential-output files, a class for sequential-input files, and a powerful data-file class designed for randomly accessing records.

### 10.6.1 The Data File Base

*DataFileBase* is the base for the data-file classes:

```
class DataFileBase
    {
    public:
        // constructor
        DataFileBase(const char * name = NULL,
                     FileMode m       = FM_TEMPORARY,
                     size_t bufsiz    = 0);

        // destructor
        ~DataFileBase();

        // set error-reporting object
        static Boolean SetErrOut(const ErrReporter & er);
```

```
protected:
    // data members
    FileMode Mode;      // file mode
    char *   FileName;  // file name
    FILE *   Data;      // structure used by I/O functions
    char *   Buffer;    // I/O buffer
    size_t   BufferSize; // size of I/O buffer
    char     DosMode[4]; // mode string used in fopen call

    // error-reporting mechanisms
    static ErrReporter * ErrOut;

    static void ReportError(const String & msg);
};
```

*DataFileBase* defines a common data structure used by all data file classes. The *FileMode* enumeration defines the possible modes in which a file can be opened:

```
enum FileMode
    {
    FM_NEW,       // new file
    FM_EXISTING,  // file must already exist
    FM_TEMPORARY  // new file, deleted when closed
    };
```

The constructor begins by duplicating the file name pointed to by the parameter *name*. It then constructs the contents of *DosMode* from the *FileMode* value *m*. The *fopen* function uses *DosMode* to determine how a file is opened (new, existing, etc.). Once the file name and mode have been stored, the file is opened, and its pointer is assigned to *Data*. If *bufsize* is zero, the file is unbuffered; otherwise, memory is allocated so that the *Buffer* points to a block of *bufsize* bytes, and the ANSI *setvbuf* function assigns that buffer to the file.

```
DataFileBase::DataFileBase(const char * name,
                           FileMode m,
                           size_t bufsize)
    {
    // store file name
```

**305**

```
if (name == NULL)
    ReportError("file name not specified");

FileName = new char[strlen(name) + 1];

if (FileName == NULL)
    ReportError("cannot allocate memory for file name");

strcpy(FileName,name);

// generate DosMode string
Mode = m;

DosMode[1] = 'b';
DosMode[2] = 0;

switch (Mode)
    {
    case FM_NEW:
    case FM_TEMPORARY:
        DosMode[0] = 'w';
        DosMode[2] = '+';
        DosMode[3] = 0;
        break;

    case FM_EXISTING:
        DosMode[0] = 'r';
        DosMode[2] = '+';
        DosMode[3] = 0;
        break;

    default:
        ReportError("invalid file mode");
    }

BufferSize = bufsize;

int failed;

// open file
Data = fopen(FileName,DosMode);
```

```
    if (Data == NULL)
        ReportError("cannot open file");

    // create buffer (if needed)
    if (BufferSize == 0)
        {
        // unbuffered file
        Buffer = NULL;

        failed = setvbuf(Data,NULL,_IONBF,0);
        }
    else
        {
        // buffered file
        Buffer = new char[BufferSize];

        if (Buffer == NULL)
            failed = 1;
        else
            failed = setvbuf(Data,Buffer,_IOFBF,BufferSize);
        }

    if (failed)
        ReportError("cannot set file buffer");
    }
```

The destructor closes the file, frees the memory allocated to *Buffer* and *FileName*, and deletes the file from disk if it was temporary.

```
DataFileBase::~DataFileBase()
    {
    // close up!
    fclose(Data);

    // delete buffer if allocated
    if (Buffer != NULL)
        delete Buffer;

    // if temp file, delete it!
```

```
if (Mode == FM_TEMPORARY)
    remove(FileName);

// delete file name buffer (if any)
if (FileName != NULL)
    delete FileName;
}
```

As in past classes, the *DataFileBase* class implements error reporting by means of a static *ErrReporter* object named *ErrOut*.

```
ErrReporter * DataFileBase::ErrOut = NULL;

Boolean DataFileBase::SetErrOut(const ErrReporter & er)
    {
    if (ErrOut != NULL)
        delete ErrOut;

    ErrOut = new ErrReporter(er);

    if (ErrOut == NULL)
        return BOOL_FALSE;
    else
        return BOOL_TRUE;
    }

void DataFileBase::ReportError(const String & msg)
    {
    if (ErrOut != NULL)
        ErrOut->Fatal(msg);
    }
```

### 10.6.2 Sequential Output Files

The *DataFileOutput* class adds a single output function to the functions it inherits from *DataFileBase*.

```
class DataFileOutput : virtual public DataFileBase
    {
```

```
public:
    DataFileOutput(const char * name = NULL,
                   size_t bufsiz    = 0,
                   FileMode m        = FM_NEW);

    Boolean Write(const DataBlock & db);
};
```

Because *DataBlocks* come in various sizes, *DataFileOutput* stores variable-length records. Every record has a header, defined by the *RecordHeader* structure, that contains the size of the record and a *Signature* value extracted from the *DataBlock*.

```
struct RecordHeader
    {
    size_t RecSize;
    Signature RecSig;
    };
```

The constructor simply passes its arguments to the constructor for *DataFileBase*.

```
inline DataFileOutput::DataFileOutput(const char * name,
                                      size_t bufsiz,
                                      FileMode m)
    : DataFileBase(name,m,bufsiz)
    {
    // void
    }
```

The *Write* function stores the information in a *DataBlock* at the current location in a file. It creates a record header from the *DataBlock*'s values, and stores that header. Then it writes the data portion of the *DataBlock*. Note that every I/O operation is followed by a check for success and that *Write* returns *BOOL_FALSE* if something goes wrong.

```
Boolean DataFileOutput::Write(const DataBlock & db)
    {
```

```
        RecordHeader hdr;

        hdr.RecSig  = db.GetSignature();
        hdr.RecSize = db.GetSizeOf();

        // store record header
        size_t n = fwrite(&hdr,sizeof(RecordHeader),1,Data);

        if (n == 0)
            return BOOL_FALSE;

        // store data
        n = fwrite(db.GetBufferPtr(),hdr.RecSize,1,Data);

        if (n == 0)
            return BOOL_FALSE;

        return BOOL_TRUE;
        }
```

*DataFileOutput* sequentially writes *DataBlocks* into a file. There are no provisions for deleting records or selecting the file position where records are written. For many applications, the simple sequential output of data is more than adequate; however, for applications (such as database programs) that require random access to data, the *DataFile* class in Chapter 12 provides the necessary capabilities.

### 10.6.3 Sequential Input Files

The *DataFileInput* adds three functions to *DataFileBase*.

```
    class DataFileInput : virtual public DataFileBase
        {
        public:
            DataFileInput(const char * name = NULL,
                          size_t bufsiz     = 0);

            DataBlock Read() const;
```

```
        Boolean Rewind();
        Boolean Skip();
    };
```

Like *DataFileOutput*, the constructor merely passes arguments to the base-class constructor.

```
    inline DataFileInput::DataFileInput(const char * name,
                                            size_t bufsiz)
        : DataFileBase(name,FM_EXISTING,bufsiz)
        {
        // a shell for calling the base-class constructor
        }
```

The *Read* function complements *DataFileOutput*'s *Write* function. *Records* are read sequentially, and the *Read* function assumes that the file pointer is positioned at the beginning of a record. The *DataFileInput* class is designed to complement and work with the *DataFileOutput* class. Files written with the *DataOutput* class are structured such that they can be read by the *DataFileInput* class.

*Read* begins by reading a record header from the file. Then, based on *hdr.RecSize*, it allocates a buffer into which data is read. The buffer and header information is used to construct a *DataBlock* that is returned as the function's value. If an error occurs, the constant value *NULL_BLOCK* (defined in the *DataBlock* class) is returned.

```
    DataBlock DataFileInput::Read() const
        {
        if (feof(Data))
            return NULL_BLOCK;

        RecordHeader hdr;
        size_t res;

        // read record header
        res = fread(&hdr,sizeof(RecordHeader),1,Data);

        if (res == 0)
```

```
        return NULL_BLOCK;

    // allocate buffer to hold data
    void * buf = (void *)new char[hdr.RecSize];

    if (buf == NULL)
        return NULL_BLOCK;

    // read data
    res = fread(buf,hdr.RecSize,1,Data);

    if (res == 0)
        return NULL_BLOCK;

    // create a DataBlock
    DataBlock result(hdr.RecSig,hdr.RecSize,buf);

    // delete the data buffer
    delete buf;

    // outta here
    return result;
    }
```

The *Skip* function reads a record header, and then moves the file pointer past the record's data — in effect, skipping a record.

```
Boolean DataFileInput::Skip()
    {
    RecordHeader hdr;
    size_t res;

    // read record header
    res = fread(&hdr,sizeof(RecordHeader),1,Data);

    if (res == 0)
        return BOOL_FALSE;

    // skip data
```

```
    if (0 != fseek(Data,hdr.RecSize,SEEK_CUR))
        return BOOL_FALSE;

return BOOL_TRUE;
    }
```

The *Rewind* function places the file pointer at the beginning of the file.

```
    Boolean DataFileInput::Rewind()
        {
        if (rewind(Data))
            return BOOL_FALSE;
        else
            return BOOL_TRUE;
        }
```

The *DataFileBase*, *DataFileOutput*, and *DataFileInput* classes are defined and implemented in the files *datafile.h* and *datafile.cxx*. Those files are listed in their entirety in Appendix A.

## 10.7 An Example of Persistence

This short program demonstrates how persistent objects and data files work together. I began by defining a class named *Object*, which is derived from *Persistent*.

```
    class Object : public Persistent
        {
        public:
            Object(const String & name, const String & adr);
            Object(const DataBlock & db);
            Object(const Object & obj);

            void operator = (const Object & obj);

            virtual operator DataBlock() const;

            friend ostream & operator << (ostream & strm,
                                          const Object & obj);
```

313

```
private:
    String Name;
    String Address;

    static const Signature Sig;
};
```

The static constant member *Sig* is assigned a value based on SIG_USER_BASE. *Sig* is the *Signature* value used to identify a *DataBlock* that contains an *Object*.

```
const Signature Object::Sig = USER_SIG_BASE + 1701;
```

An *Object* contains two *Strings*: a name and an address. An *Object* can be constructed from a pair of *Strings*, a *DataBlock*, or another *Object*.

```
Object::Object(const String & name, const String & adr)
    : Name(name), Address(adr)
    {
    // empty
    }

Object::Object(const DataBlock & db)
    {
    if (Sig != db.GetSignature())
        cout << "\aIllegal object signature!";

    char * ptr = (char *)db.GetBufferPtr();

    Name = ptr;

    ptr += Name.Length() + 1;

    Address = ptr;
    }
```

```
Object::Object(const Object & obj)
    : Name(obj.Name), Address(obj.Address)
    {
    // empty
    }
```

The second constructor builds a new *Object* from a *DataBlock*. If the *Signature* of the block is okay, the *DataBlock* is assumed to contain two consecutive, NULL-terminated strings — which is the format of a *DataBlock* created by this conversion function:

```
Object::operator DataBlock() const
    {
    size_t blen = Name.Length() + Address.Length() + 2;

    char * blk = new char[blen];

    if (blk == NULL)
        cout << "\acannot allocate space for new object!";

    // store name
    strcpy(blk,Name);

    // store address
    strcpy(blk + Name.Length() + 1,Address);

    return DataBlock(Sig,blen,(void *)blk);
    }
```

The assignment operator assigns the value of one *Object* to another.

```
void Object::operator = (const Object & obj)
    {
    Name    = obj.Name;
    Address = obj.Address;
    }
```

I defined a stream-output operation for *Objects*.

```
ostream & operator << (ostream & strm, const Object & obj)
    {
    strm << obj.Name << " of " << obj.Address;

    return strm;
    }
```

The program begins by generating an array of *Objects* that will be stored in a file.

```
const size_t objCount = 20;

Object obj[objCount] =
    {
    Object("Larry",       "Los Angeles"),
    Object("John",        "San Mateo"),
    Object("Karl",        "Boston"),
    Object("Fred",        "Philadelphia"),
    Object("Lucy",        "Seattle"),
    Object("Jerry",       "Newark"),
    Object("Adam",        "Houston"),
    Object("Carmichael",  "Lincoln"),
    Object("Scott",       "Colorado Springs"),
    Object("Maria",       "Colorado Springs"),
    Object("Rebecca",     "Colorado Springs"),
    Object("Elora",       "Colorado Springs"),
    Object("Rudolph",     "North Pole"),
    Object("Robert",      "Somerset"),
    Object("Mark",        "Phoenix"),
    Object("Abercrombie", "Tucson"),
    Object("Ed",          "Salt Lake City"),
    Object("Theodore",    "Boise"),
    Object("Everett",     "Portland"),
    Object("Edwin",       "Cheyenne")
    };
```

A *DataFileOutput* object is created, and the *Objects* in the array are written to it. Each *Object* is displayed as it is written.

```
const char * fn = "tsio.dat";
size_t n;

//————————————————————————
cout << "\nCreating output file object\n";

DataFileOutput * ofile = new DataFileOutput(fn);

for (n = 0; n < objCount; ++n)
    {
    cout << "Writing record #" << n << " : " << obj[n] << endl;
    ofile->Write(obj[n]);
    }

delete ofile;
```

The output file object is deleted, and a *DataFileInput* object is created. The program constructs *Objects* from the *DataBlocks* read from the input file, and the objects are displayed.

```
//————————————————————————
cout << "Creating input file object\n";

Object * dataIn;

if (dataIn == NULL)
    {
    cout << "\acan't allocated input object array!\n";
    exit(EXIT_FAILURE);
    }

DataFileInput * ifile = new DataFileInput(fn);

for (n = 0; n < objCount; ++n)
    {
```

```
    if (n == 7)
        ifile->Skip();
    else
        {
        cout << "Reading record #" << n << " : ";

        dataIn = new Object(ifile->Read());

        cout << *dataIn[n] << '\n';

        delete dataIn;
        }
    }

delete ifile;
```

Later chapters also include further examples of using my persistent object classes. Note that there are many ways to handle persistent objects; the *DataBlock* and *Persistent* classes work very well in my environment where I am storing large amounts of homogeneous data.

*DataBlocks* and *Persistent* objects are not the only solution to persistence. For example, a text file could be defined to contain *String* objects, not *DataBlocks*. No one solution to persistence will handle all types of data and containers; you need to design tools appropriate to the task at hand.

## 10.7 Effectively using DataBlocks

The use of *DataBlocks* in the example program is inefficient, for the sake of simplicity. To keep a copy of an object in memory *and* in a *DataBlock and* in a *DataFile* is a waste of memory. In general, *DataBlocks* are best created when needed and destroyed when they are no longer required. In most applications, this won't be difficult to accomplish. For example, a data-entry program could follow this pattern of actions:

1. Create a dynamic data object from user input
2. Create a dynamic *DataBlock* from the data object

3. Delete the data object
4. Store the *DataBlock*
5. Delete the *DataBlock*

To retrieve data by key, a similar algorithm could be followed:
1. Create a dynamic blank *DataBlock*
2. Read information for a container into the *DataBlock*
3. Create a data object from the *DataBlock*
4. Delete the *DataBlock*

Remember: A *DataBlock* is only an intermediate object form. Once a *DataBlock* has been stored or used to create a data object, the *DataBlock* should be discarded. If dynamic allocation is a problem, encapsulate the reading and writing of objects in functions where automatic *DataBlocks* will be created on function entry and destroyed on function exit.

# CHAPTER 11

# Hash Tables

Chapter 10 described my implementation of persistent objects through the abstract *Persistent* class. The *DataFileInput* and *DataFileOutput* classes defined file objects in which *Persistent* objects could be stored for later retrieval. Objects are written in a sequential manner to *DataFileOutput* objects, and read sequentially from *DataFileInput* objects.

Although sequential data storage is useful for many applications, many programs need the ability to store and retrieve data based on a key value. A key identifies a specific piece of data. For example, in an application that handles personnel data it would be very useful to be able to access a specific record by the person's name. The name is a key by which personnel records are found.

Computer scientists have invented techniques for associating keys and data. In this book, I'll cover two techniques for handling keyed data: hash tables and trees. I'll begin with hash tables.

## 11.1 What is Hashing?

A *hash table* contains a fixed number of *buckets*. A bucket either contains data associated with a key or it is empty. To find the data for a key, a bucket number is calculated from the key value by a *hash function*. The hash function always generates the same bucket number for a given key, so that a key always retrieves the same data from the same bucket.

To see how this works, let's examine simple hash tables. A 26-bucket hash table could contain data associated with each letter of the alphabet, using the ordinal value of the letter as a bucket index. The hash function would look like this:

```
int Hash(char ch)
    {
```

```
// return ordinal value of character relative to 'A'
return (int)ch - 'A';
}
```

Single letters make simple keys, but they aren't very useful in identifying most real-world information. In many financial applications, information is identified by a number such as an account number, social security number, or a ZIP code.

It isn't practical to define a hash table for 5-digit ZIP codes where there is a bucket for each code; such a table would have hundreds of thousands of entries! A table with 256 buckets would be manageable; in that case, a ZIP could be converted to a bucket number with a hash function like this one:

```
int Hash(unsigned long ZIP)
    {
    return (int)(ZIP & 0xFF); // return lowest 8 bits of ZIP
    }
```

Using the function above, a ZIP of 80901 (Colorado Springs) would "hash" to bucket number 5. The ZIP code 80901 in hexadecimal is 13C05, and the *Hash* function returns the lowest 8 bits, which are 05. A ZIP of 10019 (Manhattan) would Hash to bucket 194.

## 11.2 Collisions and Duplicates

When the number of buckets is smaller than the number of possible keys, two or more keys may hash to the same bucket value. This is known as a *collision*. For example, the ZIP codes 21509 and 80901 hash to the number 5 bucket. When this happens, you have two choices: to expand buckets to hold more than one entry, or to disallow multiple-bucket entries.

Disallowing multiple-bucket entries is *not* a good solution, because it forces us to make very large hash tables to avoid collisions. In most cases, collisions are best handled by allowing each bucket to hold a list of entries that are hashed to that location.

Each bucket can contain a simple linked list of entries; empty buckets have an empty list, and new entries for a bucket are appended to the end of their bucket list.

## 11.3 Hash Algorithms

A good hash algorithm distributes data evenly among the buckets, which avoids collisions and limits the number of entries per bucket. The effectiveness of a hash algorithm is affected by the nature of data used as key values. For example, if all your numbers end in the same set of digits, or the data is restricted to a specific range, your hash algorithm must take that information into account when distributing keys among buckets.

Where keys are evenly distributed numeric values, the best hashing algorithm is one of the simplest:

```
int Hash(unsigned long ZIP, int buckets)
    {
    return (int)(ZIP % buckets);
    }
```

The modulus operator returns the remainder of one number divided by another. In the function above, the remainder of dividing the ZIP by the number of buckets generates an index of between 0 and *buckets - 1*. Choosing the number of buckets is important; a prime number will distribute remainders more uniformly than nonprimes (according to mathematical nature).

Much of the data manipulated by programs is identified by a string. Fortunately, C++, like C, treats characters as numeric values. Thus, the algorithm above could be modified to handle strings in a variety of ways:

```
int Hash(const char * key, int buckets)
    {
    unsigned long n = 0;

    for (char * ptr = key; *ptr; ++ptr)
      {
      n <<= 1;
        n += *ptr;
      }

    return (int)(n % buckets);
    }
```

The function sums the characters in the string, shifting itself left one bit before each character is added. The left shift helps distribute keys evenly by lessening the impact of common character sequences.

## 11.4 Classes for Hash Tables

These are the characteristics of a hash table:

A hash table contains a list of buckets.

A hash function calculates the bucket for data based on a key.

The hash function should be unique for each type of data.

Each bucket contains zero or more key/data entries, stored in a linked list.

At this point, I decided to implement my hash-table class hierarchy with these core classes:

| | |
|---|---|
| *HashErrorBase* | A common static base class used to process errors from all hash-table classes. |
| *HashEntryBase* | A base class defining the common characteristics of entries in a bucket's linked list. Each type of entry will contain a key, which can be compared to keys from other similar entries. A hash function will convert the key into a bucket number. |
| *HashBucket* | A class defining the basic bucket type. Each bucket contains a linked list of *HashEntryBase* pointers. New entries can be added by key, existing entries can be deleted by key, and searches can be performed for specific key values. |
| *HashTableBase* | A base class defining the common characteristics of all hash tables. The hash table contains an array of *HashBuckets*, into which entries are stored. New entries can be added by key, existing entries can be deleted by key, and searches can be performed for specific key values. |

### 11.4.1 HashErrorBase

I wanted to tie together the error reporting for all hash table-related classes. To do that, I created a common base class named *HashErrorBase*.

```
class HashErrorBase
    {
    public:
        static void SetErrOut(const ErrReporter & er);

    protected:
        static ErrReporter * ErrOut;

        static void ReportError(HashError herr);
    };
```

*HashErrorBase* implements the same error-reporting scheme used by classes earlier in this book. Because all of its members are static, all classes derived from *HashErrorBase* will share a single instance of its members.

The *ErrOut* pointers is initialized to *NULL*, and the *SetErrOut* function dynamically creates a new *ErrReporter* object from the supplied parameter.

```
ErrReporter * HashErrorBase::ErrOut = NULL;

void HashErrorBase::SetErrOut(const ErrReporter & er)
    {
    if (ErrOut != NULL)
        delete ErrOut;

    ErrOut = new ErrReporter(er);
    }
```

The *HashError* enumerated type defines the values for hash table errors.

```
enum HashError
    {
    HE_ALLOC,     // fatal:   memory allocation failure
    HE_ZEROSIZE,  // fatal:   created bucket w/ zero buckets
    HE_CORRUPTED, // fatal:   table / list has been corrupted
    HE_BADTYPES,  // fatal:   mismatched data types
    HW_TOOSMALL,  // warning: about very small table sizes
    HW_DUPEKEY,   // warning: about duplicate keys
    };
```

The *ReportError* function reports a different error for each *HashError* constant.

```
void HashErrorBase::ReportError(HashError herr)
    {
    if (ErrOut != NULL)
        {
        switch (herr)
            {
            case HE_ALLOC:
                ErrOut->Fatal("memory allocation failure");
                break;

            case HE_ZEROSIZE:
                ErrOut->Fatal("cannot create zero-size table");
                break;

            case HE_CORRUPTED:
                ErrOut->Fatal("corrupted");
                break;

            case HE_BADTYPES:
                ErrOut->Fatal("mismatched types");
                break;

            case HW_TOOSMALL:
                ErrOut->Warning("# of buckets is very small");
                break;

            case HW_DUPEKEY:
                ErrOut->Warning("duplicate key ignored");
                break;

            default:
                ErrOut->Fatal("unknown");
                break;
            }
        }
    }
```

### 11.4.2 HashEntryBase

Buckets contain entries stored as a linked list. The abstract struct *HashEntryBase* defines a list entry.

```
struct HashEntryBase : public HashErrorBase
    {
    HashEntryBase * Prev;
    HashEntryBase * Next;

    HashEntryBase();

    virtual HashKeyType GetKeyType() const = 0;

    virtual size_t Hash(size_t buckets) const = 0;

    virtual int KeyEquals(const HashEntryBase * entry) const = 0;
    };
```

Why is *HashEntryBase* a *struct* instead of a *class*? *HashEntryBase* objects are linked into lists that are parts of a *HashBucket* object. Because of this, a *HashBucket* object needs easy access to the *Next* and *Prev* members of a *HashEntryBase*. Providing member-access functions in *HashEntryBase* complicates the class; making those members public simplifies the program.

A *HashEntryBase* object contains two pointers, referencing the previous and next entries in the list. A singly-linked list could have been used, with each entry pointing only to the next entry in the list. Deleting an entry from the middle of a singly-linked list, however, is more complicated that deleting an entry from a doubly-linked list. So, I opted to trade some data space for algorithmic simplicity.

The constructor is defined inline; it merely assigns NULL values to the *Next* and *Prev* pointers. Nearly all the *structs* in my program include default constructors that automatically initialize the members to a "null" state. It makes programming simpler, and prevents some common errors.

```
inline HashEntryBase::HashEntryBase()
    {
    Prev = NULL;
    Next = NULL;
    }
```

Any class derived from *HashEntryBase* needs to define versions of the three virtual functions corresponding to the type of key value being used.

### 11.4.3 HashEntryStr and HashEntryStrDB

The most common type of key is a string of characters; therefore, my standard implementation of hash tables automatically includes a *String*-based hash entry class named *HashEntryStr*.

```
struct HashEntryStr : public HashEntryBase
    {
    KeyString Key;

    HashEntryStr(const KeyString & k);
    HashEntryStr(const HashEntryStr & e);

    virtual HashKeyType GetKeyType() const;

    virtual size_t Hash(size_t buckets) const;

    virtual int KeyEquals(const HashEntryBase * entry) const;

    protected:
        HashEntryStr();
    };
```

The default constructor doesn't contain any explicit code. It automatically calls the *KeyString* constructor to create an empty *KeyString*. I defined it as protected because I wanted only classes derived from *HashEntryStr* to be able to create "null" objects.

The other constructors create the *Key* value from either a given *KeyString* or another *HashEntryStr*.

```
inline HashEntryStr::HashEntryStr()
    {
    // void
    }

inline HashEntryStr::HashEntryStr(const KeyString & k)
    : Key(k)
    {
    // void
    }

inline HashEntryStr::HashEntryStr(const HashEntryStr & e)
    : Key(e.Key)
    {
    // void
    }
```

A derived class must define a virtual function using the return type and parameter list inherited from the base class. In the *KeyEquals* function, which compares the key of one entry to another, I needed to be sure that the two *HashEntryBase* objects in question were using the same type of key. If the key types are the same, the result of comparing the two keys can be returned.

```
int HashEntryStr::KeyEquals(const HashEntryBase * e) const
    {
    // make sure key types match
    if (KEY_STRING != e->GetKeyType())
        ReportError(HE_BADTYPES);

    // compare keys
    return (Key == ((const HashEntryStr *)e)->Key);
    }
```

The virtual *GetKeyType* function returns a *HashKeyType* value:

```
HashKeyType HashEntryStr::GetKeyType() const
    {
    return KEY_STRING;
    }
```

The enumerated values for key types include specific values for *Strings*, *ints*, and *longs*, as well as generic "user" values for identifying other key types.

```
enum HashKeyType
    {
    KEY_STRING,
    KEY_INT,
    KEY_LONG,
    KEY_USER1,
    KEY_USER2,
    KEY_USER3,
    KEY_USER4
    };
```

The hash function for a *HashEntryStr* uses the *String*-to-bucket number algorithm discussed above.

```
size_t HashEntryStr::Hash(size_t buckets) const
    {
    unsigned long n = 0;
    const String & str = Key.GetString();
    size_t len = str.Length();

    for (size_t i = 0; i < len; ++i)
        {
        n <<= 1;
        n += str[i];
        }

    return size_t(n % (unsigned long)buckets);
    }
```

To store persistent data using a *String* key, I derived an additional class that includes a *DataBlock* with a *HashEntryStr*.

```
struct HashEntryStrDB : public HashEntryStr
    {
    DataBlock Data;

    HashEntryStrDB(const KeyString & k, const DataBlock & db);
    };
```

The only function *HashEntryStrDB* defines is a constructor; all other functions are inherited through *HashEntryStr*.

```
struct HashEntryStrDB : public HashEntryStr
    {
    DataBlock Data;

    HashEntryStrDB(const KeyString & k, const DataBlock & db);
    };
```

### 11.4.4 HashBucket

A HashBucket contains a list of entries.

```
class HashBucket : virtual public HashErrorBase
    {
    public:
        HashBucket();
        ~HashBucket();

        Boolean AddEntry(HashEntryBase * newe);
        Boolean DelEntry(const HashEntryBase * dele);
        Boolean IsDupe(const HashEntryBase * dupe);

        const HashEntryBase * FindEntry
                                (const HashEntryBase * finde);

        Boolean Traverse(const HashTableBase & table,
                        HashTravFunc func);

    protected:
        HashEntryBase * First;
    };
```

The *First* pointer addresses the first entry in the linked list. If *First* is NULL, the list is empty. The constructor simply assigns NULL to *First*; thus, every new *HashBucket* is automatically empty.

```
inline HashBucket::HashBucket()
    {
    First = NULL;
    }
```

The destructor deletes all the entries in the list if there are any. *HashTableEntries* are created by a hash table and added to a *HashBucket*; this allows the hash table to define derivatives of *HashEntryBase* that reflect the data to be stored in that table. Those entries, through their virtual functions, are treated polymorphically by a *HashBucket*. Once an entry's address has been added to a *HashBucket*, the *HashBucket* is responsible for deleting that entry from memory when that entry is no longer required.

```
HashBucket::~HashBucket()
    {
    if (First != NULL)
        {
        HashEntryBase * e, * enext;

        e = First;

        while (e != NULL)
            {
            enext = e->Next;

            delete e;

            e = enext;
            }
        }
    }
```

The *AddEntry* function adds a *HashTableEntry* to the list. If the list is empty *(First == NULL)*, the entry becomes the head of the list. Otherwise, *AddEntry* appends the entry to the end of the list.

```
Boolean HashBucket::AddEntry(HashEntryBase * newe)
    {
    if (newe == NULL)
        return BOOL_FALSE;

    if (First == NULL)
        First = newe;
    else
        {
        HashEntryBase * e = First;

        // search for last entry in list
        while (e != NULL)
            {
            // watch for duplicate keys
            if (e->KeyEquals(newe))
                {
                ReportError(HW_DUPEKEY);
                return BOOL_FALSE;
                }

            if (e->Next == NULL)
                {
                // link entry to end of list
                e->Next = newe;
                newe->Prev = e;

                break;
                }

            e = e->Next;
            }
        }

    return BOOL_TRUE;
    }
```

**333**

The *DelEntry* function deletes an entry from the list. It searches the list for an entry whose key equals the key in the entry given by the parameter *dele*. If the entry is not found or *dele* is *NULL*, *DelEntry* returns *BOOL_FALSE*. Otherwise, it removes the entry from the linked list and returns *BOOL_TRUE*.

```
Boolean HashBucket::DelEntry(const HashEntryBase * dele)
    {
    if (dele == NULL)
        return BOOL_FALSE;

    HashEntryBase * e = First;

    // search for key in list
    while (e != NULL)
        {
        // if key found, delete it
        if (e->KeyEquals(dele))
            {
            if ((e->Prev == NULL) && (e->Next == NULL))
                First = NULL;
            else
                {
                // remove entry from list
                if (e->Prev == NULL)
                    First = e->Next;
                else
                    e->Prev->Next = e->Next;

                if (e->Next != NULL)
                    e->Next->Prev = e->Prev;
                }

            // delete entry
            delete e;

            // a success!
            return BOOL_TRUE;
            }
```

```
        e = e->Next;
        }

    return BOOL_FALSE;
    }
```

The *IsDupe* function checks to see if the key in *dupe* is found in the entries for a *HashBucket*.

```
Boolean HashBucket::IsDupe(const HashEntryBase * dupe)
    {
    if ((dupe == NULL) || (First == NULL))
        return BOOL_FALSE;

    HashEntryBase * e = First;

    // search for key in list
    while (e != NULL)
        {
        // if key found, return it
        if (e->KeyEquals(dupe))
            return BOOL_TRUE;

        e = e->Next;
        }

    return BOOL_FALSE;
    }
```

*FindEntry* is almost identical to *IsDupe*. Whereas *IsDupe* returns a true/false value indicating whether a certain key was found among a bucket's entries, *FindEntry* returns a pointer to the entry in which the key was found. If the key was not found, *FindEntry* returns *NULL*.

```
const HashEntryBase * HashBucket::FindEntry
                            (const HashEntryBase * finde)
    {
    if ((finde == NULL) || (First == NULL))
```

```
        return NULL;

    HashEntryBase * e = First;

    // search for key in list
    while (e != NULL)
        {
        // if key found, return it
        if (e->KeyEquals(finde))
            return e;

        e = e->Next;
        }

    return NULL;
    }
```

The *Traverse* function passes the address of every entry in a bucket to the function pointed to by *func*. Only the table that created an entry will know how to handle it; therefore, *HashTravFunc* is defined as a pointer to a *HashTable* member function that accepts a *HashEntryBase* pointer as a parameter.

```
    typedef Boolean (HashTableBase::*HashTravFunc)
                            (const HashEntryBase * e) const;


    Boolean HashBucket::Traverse(const HashTableBase & table,
                            HashTravFunc func)
        {
        Boolean result;

        HashEntryBase * e = First;

        while (e != NULL)
            {
            result = (table.*func)(e);

            if (result == BOOL_FALSE)
```

```
        break;

    e = e->Next;
    }

  return result;
  }
```

*HashTableBase* defines a virtual function that matches *HashTravFunc*; as you'll see below, type-specific hash tables derived from *HashTableBase* will define a type-specific version of this function.

### 11.4.5 HashTableBase

The *HashTableBase* class defines the characteristics and functionality of hash tables. Nearly everything a hash table needs is defined by *HashTableBase*; derived classes simply enhance the *inherited* functionality. Hereafter, when I refer to a non-class-specific hash table, I'm referring to any class derived from *HashTableBase*.

```
class HashTableBase : public HashErrorBase
    {
    public:
        HashTableBase(size_t buckets);
        ~HashTableBase();

    protected:
        Boolean AddEntry(HashEntryBase * newe);
        Boolean DelEntry(const HashEntryBase * dele);
        Boolean IsDupe(const HashEntryBase * dupe);

        const HashEntryBase * FindEntry
                        (const HashEntryBase * finde);

        Boolean Traverse();

        virtual Boolean TravCallback
                        (const HashEntryBase * e) const = 0;
```

```
        // data members
        size_t NoOfBuckets;

        HashBucket * * Table;
    };
```

A hash table has two data members: A number of buckets, and a dynamically allocated array of pointers to buckets. The constructor allocates *Table* to have *NoOfBuckets* elements. If the number of buckets is zero or very small, an error or warning is reported. An error is also reported if the *Table* cannot be allocated. If the *Table* is allocated, each element is assigned the address of a dynamically allocated *HashBucket*. The constructor for *HashBucket* ensures that all buckets are empty when the *Table* is created.

```
    HashTableBase::HashTableBase(size_t buckets)
        {
        // verify number of buckets
        if (buckets == 0)
            ReportError(HE_ZEROSIZE);

        if (buckets < 9)
            ReportError(HW_TOOSMALL);

        // store number of buckets
        NoOfBuckets = buckets;

        // allocate Table
        Table = new HashBucket * [NoOfBuckets];

        if (Table == NULL)
            ReportError(HE_ALLOC);

        // assign empty buckets to table
        for (size_t b = 0; b < NoOfBuckets; ++b)
            {
            Table[b] = new HashBucket;

            if (Table[b] == NULL)
```

```
                ReportError(HE_ALLOC);
            }
        }
```

The destructor's job is to delete the entries in *Table* before deleting *Table* iself.

```
HashTableBase::~HashTableBase()
    {
    // delete buckets
    for (size_t b = 0; b < NoOfBuckets; ++b)
        delete Table[b];

    // delete table
    delete[] Table;
    }
```

The functions that add, delete, and find entries follow a similar implementation pattern. Each accepts a pointer to a *HashEntryBase* object; if that pointer is not a *NULL*, a bucket number is obtained from the *Hash* function for the entry. The bucket number indexes a pointer to a *HashBucket* in *Table*; through that pointer, a call is made to the corresponding function for the operation being performed. For example, *HashTableBase::AddEntry* calls *HashBucket::Entry*.

```
Boolean HashTableBase::AddEntry(HashEntryBase * newe)
    {
    if (newe == NULL)
        return BOOL_FALSE;

    size_t bucket = newe->Hash(NoOfBuckets);

    return Table[bucket]->AddEntry(newe);
    }


Boolean HashTableBase::DelEntry(const HashEntryBase * dele)
    {
    if (dele == NULL)
```

```
            return BOOL_FALSE;

        size_t bucket = dele->Hash(NoOfBuckets);

        return Table[bucket]->DelEntry(dele);
        }



    Boolean HashTableBase::IsDupe(const HashEntryBase * dupe)
        {
        if (dupe == NULL)
            return BOOL_FALSE;

        size_t bucket = dupe->Hash(NoOfBuckets);

        return Table[bucket]->IsDupe(dupe);
        }



    const HashEntryBase * HashTableBase::FindEntry
                                    (const HashEntryBase * finde)
        {
        if (finde == NULL)
            return NULL;

        size_t bucket = finde->Hash(NoOfBuckets);

        return Table[bucket]->FindEntry(finde);
        }
```

The *Traverse* function calls the *HashBucket::Traverse* function for each *HashBucket* in *Table*. The address of the virtual function *TravCallBack* is passed to the *HashBucket*; *TravCallBack* is called by the *HashBucket* for each entry in its list. Classes derived from *HashTableBase* need to provide their own implementations of *TravCallBack*, because it is a pure virtual function.

```
Boolean HashTableBase::Traverse()
    {
    Boolean result;

    for (size_t n = 0; n < NoOfBuckets; ++n)
        {
        result = Table[n]->Traverse
                        (*this,&HashTableBase::TravCallback);

        if (result == BOOL_FALSE)
            break;
        }

    return result;
    }
```

### 11.4.6 HashTableStrDB

Now it's time to look at a practical, useful implementation of a hash table. Most of the work is already defined by the classes above; the *HashTableStrDB* class merely needs to fill in the blanks.

```
class HashTableStrDB : private HashTableBase
    {
    public:
        HashTableStrDB(size_t buckets);

        Boolean Insert(const KeyString & key,
                       const DataBlock & db);

        Boolean Delete(const KeyString & key);

        DataBlock LookUp(const KeyString & key);

        Boolean Enumerate(HashEnumFuncStrDB func);

    protected:
        virtual Boolean TravCallback
                            (const HashEntryBase * e)
```

```
const;

        HashEnumFuncStrDB EnumCallback;
    };
```

The constructor is an inline function that simply calls the base-class constructor. The *HashTableBase* destructor handles deletion of the table, and *HashTableStrDB* does not need (or define) its own destructor.

```
inline HashTableStrDB::HashTableStrDB(size_t buckets)
    : HashTableBase(buckets)
    {
    // void
    }
```

In previous classes, I used names like *AddEntry* and *FindEntry*. Those were low-level functions that work directly with *TableEntryBase* objects.

The interface to *HashTableStrDB* is defined in terms of high-level, user-oriented objects. *HashTableStrDB* is defined in terms of *KeyStrings* and *DataBlocks*; therefore, I used different names for the add, delete, find, and traverse function in an attempt to differentiate between a high-level interface and the internal interface of base classes.

For example, the function which adds data to a *HashTableStrDB* is named *Insert*. *Insert* accepts a *KeyString* and an associated *DataBlock*. These parameters are used to create a *HashEntryStrDB*, the address of which is passed to *HashTableBase::AddEntry*.

```
Boolean HashTableStrDB::Insert(const KeyString & key,
                               const DataBlock & data)
    {
    // create new HashEntryStrDB
    HashEntryStrDB * entry = new HashEntryStrDB(key,data);

    if (entry == NULL)
        ReportError(HE_ALLOC);
```

```
// insert into table
return AddEntry(entry);
}
```

The *Delete* function uses a *KeyString* to create a *HashEntryStr* object. *HashTableBase::DelEntry* is called to delete any bucket entry whose key matches that of the parameter.

```
Boolean HashTableStrDB::Delete(const KeyString & key)
    {
    // create new HashEntryStr
    HashEntryStr * entry = new HashEntryStr(key);

    if (entry == NULL)
        ReportError(HE_ALLOC);

    // insert into table
    Boolean result = DelEntry(entry);

    delete entry;

    return result;
    }
```

The *LookUp* function uses the same techniques as *Insert* and *Delete* for using base-class functions. The result of *HashTableBase::FindEntry* is a pointer to a *HashEntryBase* object; because *AddEntry* only adds *HashEntryStrDB* objects to the table, *LookUp* can safely cast the returned pointer to a *HashStrDB* pointer. The *DataBlock* stored in that entry is returned.

```
DataBlock HashTableStrDB::LookUp(const KeyString & key)
    {
    // create new HashEntryStr
    HashEntryStr * entry = new HashEntryStr(key);

    if (entry == NULL)
        ReportError(HE_ALLOC);
```

```
const HashEntryStrDB * e =
        (const HashEntryStrDB *)FindEntry(entry);

delete entry;

if (e == NULL)
    return NULL_BLOCK;
else
    return e->Data;
}
```

A *HashTableStrDB* doesn't know what type of data is stored in the *DataBlocks* it handles. This requires that *DataBlocks* be handled by a user-defined function that knows the contents of the block. The virtual *HashTravCallBack* function is defined such that it calls a *HashEnumFuncStrDB* function.

```
typedef Boolean (* HashEnumFuncStrDB)(const KeyString & k,
                                      const DataBlock & db);
```

The *Enumerate* function stores the pointer to a *HashEnumFuncStrDB* in the data member *EnumCallback*. It then calls *HashTableBase::Traverse*, which calls *TravCallBack* for each entry in the table. *TravCallBack* calls the function address stored in *EnumCallback* with the *KeyString* and *DataBlock* stored in an entry.

```
Boolean HashTableStrDB::Enumerate(HashEnumFuncStrDB func)
    {
    if (func == NULL)
        return BOOL_FALSE;

    EnumCallback = func;

    return Traverse();
    }

Boolean HashTableStrDB::TravCallback
                            (const HashEntryBase * e)
const
```

```
    {
    if (e == NULL)
        return BOOL_FALSE;
    else
        {
        HashEntryStrDB * e2 = (HashEntryStrDB *)e;

        return EnumCallback(e2->Key, e2->Data);
        }
    }
```

## 11.5 Hash Tables in Action

All of this may seem complicated — and it is! I've developed a half-dozen hash-table libraries in my career, and the class hierarchy above works wonderfully. Remember: The purpose of the four base classes is to define the functionality of a *HashTable*. The higher level classes (such as *HashTableStrDB*) are defined in such a manner that all the internal workings are hidden. Using a *HashTableStrDB* object is easy — here's a sample program to show how a *HashTableStrDB* works. It uses the *Object* class and *obj* array from Chapter 10.

```
#include "hash.h"
#include "iostream.h"
#include "str.h"
#include "string.h"
#include "stdlib.h"

static const String ErrLdr("Hash Test");

static DosErrReporter ErrHandler(&ErrLdr);

//─────────────────────────────
// Object class
//─────────────────────────────

class Object : public Persistent, public KeyByString
    {
```

```
public:
    Object(const String & name, const String & adr);
    Object(const DataBlock & db);
    Object(const Object & obj);

    void operator = (const Object & obj);

    virtual operator DataBlock() const;

    virtual KeyString MakeKey() const;

    String GetName();
    String GetAddress();

    friend ostream & operator << (ostream & strm,
                                  const Object & obj);

private:
    String Name;
    String Address;

    static const Signature Sig;
};

const Signature Object::Sig = USER_SIG_BASE + 1701;

Object::Object(const String & name, const String & adr)
    : Name(name), Address(adr)
    {
    // empty
    }

Object::Object(const DataBlock & db)
    {
    if (Sig != db.GetSignature())
        cout << "\aIllegal object signature!";

    char * ptr = (char *)db.GetBufferPtr();

    Name = ptr;
```

```
    ptr += Name.Length() + 1;

    Address = ptr;
    }

Object::Object(const Object & obj)
    : Name(obj.Name), Address(obj.Address)
    {
    // empty
    }

void Object::operator = (const Object & obj)
    {
    Name    = obj.Name;
    Address = obj.Address;
    }

Object::operator DataBlock() const
    {
    size_t blen = Name.Length() + Address.Length() + 2;

    char * blk = new char[blen];

    if (blk == NULL)
        cout << "\acannot allocate space for new object!";

    // store name
    strcpy(blk,Name);

    // store address
    strcpy(blk + Name.Length() + 1,Address);

    return DataBlock(Sig,blen,(void *)blk);
    }

inline KeyString Object::MakeKey() const
    {
    return KeyString(Name);
    }
```

```cpp
inline String Object::GetName()
    {
    return Name;
    }

inline String Object::GetAddress()
    {
    return Address;
    }

ostream & operator << (ostream & strm, const Object & obj)
    {
    strm << obj.Name << " of " << obj.Address;

    return strm;
    }

//——————————————————————
//  main program
//——————————————————————


Boolean ShowThem(const KeyString & key, const DataBlock & db);

int main()
    {
    const size_t objCount = 20;

    Object obj[objCount] =
        {
        Object("Larry",      "Los Angeles"),
        Object("John",       "San Mateo"),
        Object("Karl",       "Boston"),
        Object("Fred",       "Philadelphia"),
        Object("Lucy",       "Seattle"),
        Object("Jerry",      "Newark"),
        Object("Adam",       "Houston"),
        Object("Carmichael", "Lincoln"),
        Object("Scott",      "Colorado Springs"),
        Object("Maria",      "Colorado Springs"),
```

```
        Object("Rebecca",     "Colorado Springs"),
        Object("Elora",       "Colorado Springs"),
        Object("Rudolph",     "North Pole"),
        Object("Robert",      "Somerset"),
        Object("Mark",        "Phoenix"),
        Object("Abercrombie","Tucson"),
        Object("Ed",          "Salt Lake City"),
        Object("Theodore",    "Boise"),
        Object("Everett",     "Portland"),
        Object("Edwin",       "Cheyenne")
        };

// set error handlers
HashErrorBase::SetErrOut(ErrHandler);
String::SetErrOut(ErrHandler);

// create hash table
HashTableStrDB ht(23);

//————————————————————
size_t n;

// insert elements of obj into ht
for (n = 0; n < objCount; ++n)
    ht.Insert(obj[n].MakeKey(),obj[n]);

// display all entries in the table
ht.Enumerate(ShowThem);

// Look for an entry with the key "Rebecca"
String name1("Rebecca");

KeyString key1(name1);

DataBlock db1(ht.LookUp(key1));

// if db1 is a null block, Rebecca wasn't found
if (db1.IsNull())
    {
    cout << "\aCOULD NOT FIND " << name1 << endl;
```

```
            exit(EXIT_FAILURE);
            }

    // if Rebecca was found, create an OBject from the DataBlock
    Object obj1(db1);

    // display Rebecca object
    cout << "\nFOUND: " << obj1 << endl << endl;

    // delete object with key "Rebecca" from tree
    if (BOOL_FALSE == ht.Delete(key1))
        {
        cout << "\aCOULD NOT DELETE " << name1 << endl;
        exit(EXIT_FAILURE);
        }

    cout << endl << "DELETED: " << name1 << endl << endl;

    // show all data in hash table
    ht.Enumerate(ShowThem);

    return 0;
    }

// HashEnumFuncStrDB / callback function
Boolean ShowThem(const KeyString & key, const DataBlock & db)
    {
    Object obj(db);

    cout << "key = "    << key.GetString()
        << "\tdata = " << obj << endl;

    return BOOL_TRUE;
    }
```

# CHAPTER 12

# Indexing Files with Hash Tables

The previous chapters have described persistent objects, files, and hash tables. The *HashTableStrDB* class provides tools for storing and retrieving objects, in the form of *DataBlocks* identified by a *KeyString*. The drawback to *HashTableStrDB* is that it keeps copies of objects (as *DataBlocks*) in internal memory. Even with today's multimegabyte computers, internal memory is a limited resource that should be used with caution.

When large numbers of sizeable objects need to be stored, it is best to use external storage, such as a disk file. Instead of storing a *HashTable's DataBlocks* in the table entries, a file-based implementation stores a reference to the *DataBlock's* location in a file. To accomplish this, we need to extend the file classes from Chapter 10 and create a new type of hash table.

## 12.1 Random Access Files

Chapter 10 introduced two file classes: *DataFileInput* and *DataFileOutput*. Information is written sequentially to *DataFileOutput* objects, and read sequentially from *DataFileInput* objects. For many applications, the sequential file I/O is sufficient.

Sequential files have limitations. Once data is stored, it cannot be retrieved, changed, or deleted. The data can be retrieved only in the same order in which it was written. New data is simply appended to the end of a file.

In an application where data is referred to by a key, the program needs to locate data by its position within a file. Most applications need the ability to delete and change records, too. Because the two existing file classes don't support these features, a new file class is required.

For the purposes of this discussion, I'll use the term *record* to refer to a distinct piece of data stored at a specific location in a file.

### 12.1.1 Variable-Length Records

Files can contain fixed-length or variable-length records. Fixed-length records are simple; every record is of the same length, so moving through the file is merely a matter of incrementing the current file pointer by the size of the record currently being pointed to. The *DataFile* classes automatically handle variable-length records, because the *DataBlocks* are stored with length information.

### 12.1.2 File Pointers and Indexing

A *file pointer* is a value that references a location in a file. Every file has a *current file pointer* that points to the locations where I/O operations are performed. Each record is located at a specific file pointer. Files that allow records to be read and written to in any position are known as *random-access files*.

An *index* is a data structure that associates a key value with a file pointer. The file pointer for a record is found by looking up the record's key in the index.

A hash table used for indexing is sometimes referred to as a *scatter table* or an *indirect hash table*. When a record is written to a file, we need to obtain its file pointer within the file. That value, along with a key, is stored in an index so that the key can be used to find the record again.

### 12.1.3 Record Deletion and Insertion

How should records be deleted from a file? One scheme would be to remove the deleted record from the file, shifting other records to eliminate the now-empty space. This method can be very inefficient; for example, deleting the second record in a thousand-record file would mean moving 998 other records! Furthermore, moving the records would require the regeneration of any index that references the file pointers for those records.

It makes more sense to reuse deleted record space rather than remove it. Deleted records simply can be marked as such. When new records are written to the file, a

352

program can check to see if any of the deleted record spaces is large enough to hold the new record. If so, the new record is written into the same place as a deleted record. Otherwise, the new record is appended to the end of the file. No records move, so indexes for "live" records don't need to change.

A file can use a linked list to keep track of deleted records. In the file's header, the linked list keeps a file pointer to the first deleted record in the list. Each deleted record contains a file pointer to the next deleted record in the list; the last record in the list has a value to indicate that no more deleted records exist. When a record is deleted, it stores the deleted file pointer for the header, and the header contains the file pointer for the newly deleted record. In other words, newly deleted records are inserted at the head of the list. This type of list is called a *deleted list*.

When a new record is inserted into the file, it searches the list of deleted records, looking for a deleted record space into which it fits. The first deleted record space that is the same size or larger than the new record becomes the new record's home. The deleted record is removed from the linked list. If no records are in the linked list, or the new record is too large to fit into the spaces of any deleted records, the new record is appended to the file.

Reusing deleted record space has only one drawback: it leaves dead space in the file. Deleted records occupy space in the file until a new record is written into their location. Because we are using variable-length records, new records usually are shorter than the deleted records they overwrite, leaving various sized "holes" in the file.

Periodically, it makes sense to *compact* the file, removing the wasted space and eliminating deleted records. This can be accomplished by simply rewriting the file, record by record, using exact record lengths and ignoring deleted records.

However, when a file is compacted, every record could change positions within the file. In the case of an indexed file, where a table stores keys and file pointers, a new index needs to be built to reflect the new record positions.

## 12.2 The DataFile Class

I created a new class, named *DataFile*, that implements a random-access file as described above. It is based on the *DataFileBase* class, and it provides the capabilities to read, write, and delete records in a file. The class definition is:

```
class DataFile : public DataFileBase
    {
    public:
        // constructor
        DataFile(const char * name,
                FileMode m    = FM_EXISTING,
                size_t bufsiz = 0);

        // write a record
        DataFilePtr Write(const DataBlock & db);

        // read a record
        DataBlock Read() const;

        // commit data to disk
        Boolean Commit();

        // delete a record
        Boolean Delete();

        // move to next record
        Boolean Skip();

        // return to beginning of file
        Boolean Rewind();

        // remove blanks and wasted space
        Boolean Compact(DFCompFunc func = NULL);

        // go to  position in file
        DataFilePtr Seek(DataFilePtr pos) const;

        // get current file position
        DataFilePtr CurrentPtr() const;

    protected:
        DataFileHdr Hdr;
    };
```

### 12.2.1 Support Structures

The *DataFile* file pointer type is defined by *DataFilePtr*. *DataFilePtr* is a *long* because that is the value defined by ANSI for file pointers. A *long* allows files of up to 2 billion bytes to be created; this should be large enough for most applications.

```
typedef long DataFilePtr;
```

The deleted list uses *DataFilePtrs* to link deleted records. The end of the list is marked by the constant value *DFP_MARKER*.

```
const DataFilePtr DFP_MARKER = -1;
```

Functions that return *DataFilePtrs* must be able to return an error indication. I use the constant *DFP_ERROR* for that purpose.

```
#define DFP_ERROR DFP_MARKER
```

A *DataFile* needs a header record that contains the number of the first record in the deleted list. If there are no deleted records, *FirstEmpty* is set to *DFP_MARKER*.

```
struct DataFileHdr
    {
    DataFilePtr FirstEmpty;
    };
```

The records in *DataFileInput/DataFileOutput* files have a header that contains a signature and the size of the record. *DataFile* records need two more pieces of header information: the size of the space occupied by the original record, and a pointer to the next deleted record.

```
struct IORecordHeader : public RecordHeader
    {
    size_t Size;
    DataFilePtr NextDeleted;
    };
```

The *Size* value contains the number of bytes in the original record. When a record is written into a new location in the file, *Size* and *RecSize* are the same. When a new record is written into a deleted record, *RecSize* contains the size of the new record, and *Size* contains the number of bytes in the overwritten record.

In addition to making the record a part of the deleted list, a deleted record is indicated by a special *Signature* value, named *SIG_DELETED*.

```
const Signature   SIG_DELETED = 0xFFFFFFFF;
```

## 12.2.2 Constructors and Destructors

The constructor for a *DataFile* needs to create a header record if the file is new or temporary; otherwise, it needs to read the existing header from disk. A copy of the header record is always kept in the *Hdr* data member.

```
DataFile::DataFile(const char * name,
                   FileMode m,
                   size_t bufsiz)
    : DataFileBase(name,m,bufsiz)
    {
    size_t n;

    if ((m == FM_NEW) || (m == FM_TEMPORARY))
        {
        Hdr.FirstEmpty = DFP_MARKER;

        n = fwrite(&Hdr,sizeof(DataFileHdr),1,Data);

        if (n == 0)
            ReportError("cannot create file header");
        }
    else
        {
        n = fread(&Hdr,sizeof(DataFileHdr),1,Data);

        if (n == 0)
            ReportError("cannot read file header");
        }
    }
```

*DataFile* doesn't need a destructor; the base-class constructor automatically closes the file.

### 12.2.3 Writing Records

The *Write* function adds new records to the file. It searches the deleted list for the first deleted record that is large enough to hold the new record.

```
DataFilePtr DataFile::Write(const DataBlock & db)
    {
    // search for first open record that can hold this one
    IORecordHeader rechdr;
    DataFilePtr ptr;
    int res;
    size_t n;

    if (Hdr.FirstEmpty == DFP_MARKER)
        {
        // append new data to end of file
        res = fseek(Data,0,SEEK_END);

        if (res)
            return DFP_ERROR;

        ptr = ftell(Data);

        rechdr.Size = db.GetSizeOf();
        }
    else
        {
        // start with first empty record
        DataFilePtr prev = DFP_MARKER;

        ptr = Hdr.FirstEmpty;

        for (;;)
            {
            // set file pointer
            res = fseek(Data,ptr,SEEK_SET);
```

```
if (res)
    return DFP_ERROR;

// read record header
n = fread(&rechdr,sizeof(IORecordHeader),1,Data);

if ((n == 0) || (rechdr.RecSig != SIG_DELETED))
    return DFP_ERROR;

// is it big enough?
if (rechdr.Size >= db.GetSizeOf())
    {
    // go to previous record
    if (prev == DFP_MARKER)
        {
        // change entry in header
        Hdr.FirstEmpty = rechdr.NextDeleted;

        // go to beginning of file
        fseek(Data,0,SEEK_SET);

        // write new header
        n = fwrite(&Hdr,sizeof(DataFileHdr),1,Data);

        if (n == 0)
            return DFP_ERROR;
        }
    else
        {
        // adjust chain by putting next in prev
        res = fseek(Data,prev,SEEK_SET);

        if (res)
            return DFP_ERROR;

        // read previous record's header
        IORecordHeader prevhdr;

        n = fread(&prevhdr,sizeof(IORecordHeader),
                1,Data);
```

```
        if (n == 0)
            return DFP_ERROR;

        // change next deleted reference
        prevhdr.NextDeleted = rechdr.NextDeleted;

        // rewrite prev. header
        res = fseek(Data,prev,SEEK_SET);

        if (res)
            return DFP_ERROR;

        // read previous record's header
        n = fwrite(&prevhdr,sizeof(IORecordHeader),
                    1,Data);

        if (n == 0)
            return DFP_ERROR;
        }

    // set pointer to beginning of ptr record
    fseek(Data,ptr,SEEK_SET);
    break;
    }

// save pointer
prev = ptr;

if (rechdr.NextDeleted == DFP_MARKER)
    {
    // append new data to end of file
    res = fseek(Data,0,SEEK_END);

    if (res)
        return DFP_ERROR;

    ptr = ftell(Data);

    rechdr.Size = db.GetSizeOf();
```

```
                break;
                }
            else
                ptr = rechdr.NextDeleted;
            }
        }

    rechdr.RecSig      = db.GetSignature();
    rechdr.RecSize     = db.GetSizeOf();
    rechdr.NextDeleted = DFP_MARKER;

    // store signature
    n = fwrite(&rechdr,sizeof(IORecordHeader),1,Data);

    if (n == 0)
        return DFP_ERROR;

    // store data
    n = fwrite(db.GetBufferPtr(),rechdr.RecSize,1,Data);

    if (n == 0)
        return DFP_ERROR;

    // return location data was written to
    return ptr;
    }
```

If *Write* finds a deleted record in which the new record can be written, it removes that record from the deleted list and writes the new record.

If *Write* can't fit the new record into a deleted slot, it appends the new record to the end of the file.

### 12.2.4 Reading Records

Reading records is much simpler than writing them. *Read* assumes that the current file pointer is positioned at the beginning of a record.

```
DataBlock DataFile::Read() const
    {
    if (feof(Data))
        return NULL_BLOCK;

    size_t n;

    IORecordHeader rechdr;

    for (;;)
        {
        // read record header
        n = fread(&rechdr,sizeof(IORecordHeader),1,Data);

        // this may indicate end-of-file
        if (n == 0)
            return NULL_BLOCK;

        // return null for deleted record
        if (rechdr.RecSig == SIG_DELETED)
            fseek(Data,rechdr.Size,SEEK_CUR);
        else
            break;
        }

    // allocate buffer to hold data
    void * buf = (void *)new char[rechdr.RecSize];

    if (buf == NULL)
        return NULL_BLOCK;

    // read data
    n = fread(buf,rechdr.RecSize,1,Data);

    if (n == 0)
        return NULL_BLOCK;

    // create a DataBlock
    DataBlock result(rechdr.RecSig,rechdr.RecSize,buf);
```

```
    // skip over any "waste" characters
    if (rechdr.RecSize < rechdr.Size)
        fseek(Data,rechdr.Size - rechdr.RecSize, SEEK_CUR);

    // delete the data buffer
    delete buf;

    // outta here
    return result;
    }
```

If the record is marked as deleted (by having a *Signature* of *SIG_DELETED*), *Read* skips to the next record. If *Read* encounters the end of the file or an error occurs, it returns *DFP_ERROR*.

### 12.2.5 Deleting Records

Like *Read*, the *Delete* function assumes that the current file pointer is located at the beginning of a record. *Delete* marks a record as deleted, and adds the record's file pointer to the deleted list. *Delete* returns *BOOL_TRUE* if a record is deleted, and *BOOL_FALSE* if an error occurs.

```
Boolean DataFile::Delete()
    {
    size_t n;
    int res;
    IORecordHeader rechdr;

    // save this position
    DataFilePtr curptr = ftell(Data);

    // make sure we're not in the header
    if (curptr < sizeof(DataFileHdr))
        return BOOL_FALSE;

    // read header
    n = fread(&rechdr,sizeof(IORecordHeader),1,Data);
```

```
if (n == 0)
    return BOOL_FALSE;

// mark as deleted
if (rechdr.RecSig != SIG_DELETED)
    {
    // update record header
    rechdr.RecSig     = SIG_DELETED;
    rechdr.NextDeleted = Hdr.FirstEmpty;

    // write record header
    res = fseek(Data,curptr,SEEK_SET);

    if (res)
        return BOOL_FALSE;

    n = fwrite(&rechdr,sizeof(IORecordHeader),1,Data);

    if (n == 0)
        return BOOL_FALSE;

    // modify header
    Hdr.FirstEmpty = curptr;

    res = fseek(Data,0,SEEK_SET);

    if (res)
        return BOOL_FALSE;

    n = fwrite(&Hdr,sizeof(DataFileHdr),1,Data);

    if (n == 0)
        return BOOL_FALSE;
    }

// move back to start of deleted record
res = fseek(Data,curptr,SEEK_SET);

if (res)
    return BOOL_FALSE;
```

```
    else
        return BOOL_TRUE;
    }
```

The *FirstEmpty* member of the *DataFile* header contains the file pointer of the
first record in the deleted list. When *Delete* "deletes" a record, it sets the record's
*Signature* to *SIG_DELETED*, stores the current value of *Hdr.FirstEmpty* in
*NextDeleted*, and sets *Hdr.FirstEmpty* to the file pointer of the record. Thus, as
records are deleted they are added to the beginning of the deleted list.

### 12.2.6 Moving Around the File

The current file pointer is used by the *Read* and *Delete* functions. The *Seek*
function sets the current file pointer.

```
DataFilePtr DataFile::Seek(DataFilePtr pos) const
    {
    // make sure position is outside of header
    if (pos < sizeof(DataFileHdr))
        return DFP_ERROR;

    // get current position
    DataFilePtr ptr = ftell(Data);

    // move to new position
    int res = fseek(Data,pos,SEEK_SET);

    // check for error
    if (res)
        {
        // try to restore previous position
        fseek(Data,ptr,SEEK_SET);

        ptr = DFP_ERROR;
        }

    // done
    return ptr;
    }
```

A program can obtain the current file pointer with the inline *CurrentPtr* function.

```
inline DataFilePtr DataFile::CurrentPtr() const
    {
    return ftell(Data);
    }
```

The *Rewind* function sets the current file pointer to the beginning of the first record in the file, basically, at the byte directly after the header record.

```
Boolean DataFile::Skip()
    {
    IORecordHeader rechdr;
    int res;
    size_t n;

    // read record header
    n = fread(&rechdr,sizeof(IORecordHeader),1,Data);

    if (n == 0)
        return BOOL_FALSE;

    // skip data
    res = fseek(Data,rechdr.Size,SEEK_CUR);

    if (res)
        return BOOL_FALSE;
    else
        return BOOL_TRUE;
    }
```

The current file pointer is moved to the beginning of the next record by the *Skip* function.

```
Boolean DataFile::Skip()
    {
    IORecordHeader rechdr;
    int res;
```

```
size_t n;

// read record header
n = fread(&rechdr,sizeof(IORecordHeader),1,Data);

if (n == 0)
    return BOOL_FALSE;

// skip data
res = fseek(Data,rechdr.Size,SEEK_CUR);

if (res)
    return BOOL_FALSE;
else
    return BOOL_TRUE;
}
```

### 12.2.7 Committing Data Functions

If a file is buffered, some information may be resident in buffer memory, not having been written to the external file. Should the program suddenly crash or the computer lose power, data in the buffer is lost. Some applications can't afford to take risks, and they can use the *Commit* function to force data to be written from the buffer to disk.

```
Boolean DataFile::Commit()
    {
    if (Buffer != NULL)
        {
        int res = fflush(Data);

        if (res)
            return BOOL_FALSE;
        }

    return BOOL_TRUE;
    }
```

*Commit* does not do anything if the file is not buffered.

### 12.2.8 Compacting a DataFile

In 12.1.3, I discussed wasted space caused by the deletion and insertion of variable-length records. An active file, where deletions and insertions are common, develops significant amounts of wasted space. The *Compact* function can be used to eliminate dead space in a *DataFile*.

```
Boolean DataFile::Compact(DFCompFunc func)
    {
    if (BOOL_FALSE == Commit())
        return BOOL_FALSE;

    // generate temporary file name
    char tname[32];

    sprintf(tname,"%lx.TMP",time(NULL));

    // open temporary file
    FILE * newfile = fopen(tname,"wb");

    if (newfile == NULL)
        return BOOL_FALSE;

    // read and copy header
    int res = fseek(Data,0,SEEK_SET);

    if (res)
        return BOOL_FALSE;

    size_t n = fread(&Hdr,sizeof(DataFileHdr),1,Data);

    if (n == 0)
        return BOOL_FALSE;

    n = fwrite(&Hdr,sizeof(DataFileHdr),1,newfile);

    if (n == 0)
        return BOOL_FALSE;
```

```
// read each record
for (;;)
    {
    IORecordHeader rechdr;
    DataFilePtr ptr;
    char * buf;

    // read record header
    n = fread(&rechdr,sizeof(IORecordHeader),1,Data);

    if (n == 0)
        break;

    if (rechdr.RecSig == SIG_DELETED)
        {
        // skip deleted records
        res = fseek(Data,rechdr.Size,SEEK_CUR);

        if (res)
            return BOOL_FALSE;
        }
    else
        {
        // allocate buffer to hold data
        buf = new char[rechdr.Size];

        if (buf == NULL)
            return BOOL_FALSE;

        // read data
        n = fread(buf,rechdr.Size,1,Data);

        if (n == 0)
            return BOOL_FALSE;

        // get output position in new file
        ptr = ftell(newfile);

        // write header to new file
        rechdr.Size = rechdr.RecSize;
```

```
        n = fwrite(&rechdr,sizeof(IORecordHeader),1,newfile);

        if (n == 0)
            return BOOL_FALSE;

        // write data to new file
        n = fwrite(buf,rechdr.Size,1,newfile);

        if (n == 0)
            return BOOL_FALSE;

        // call function
        if (func != NULL)
            func(ptr,DataBlock(rechdr.RecSig,
                                rechdr.Size,buf));

        // delete buffer
        delete buf;
        }
    }

// close files
fclose(newfile);
fclose(Data);

// delete old file
remove(FileName);

// rename new file
rename(tname,FileName);

// open newly compacted file
Data = fopen(FileName,DosMode);

if (Data == NULL)
    return BOOL_FALSE;

// read file header
n = fread(&Hdr,sizeof(DataFileHdr),1,Data);
```

```
    if (n == 0)
        return BOOL_FALSE;
    else
        return BOOL_TRUE;
    }
```

*Compact* begins by calling *Commit* to ensure that all data has been written to external storage. Then it generates a temporary file name using the current time. I don't use the ANSI-C *tmpnam* function here, because its file names are not guaranteed to be unique in a multi-user environment. Time-stamped temporary files prevent the creation of multiple files with the same name.

*Compact* opens the temporary file, and a header record containing a *FirstEmpty* value of *DFP_MARKER* is created. The *DataFile*'s current pointer is then set to its first record. Records are read sequentially from the *DataFile*; records that are not marked as deleted are written to the temporary file. For each record written, the function designated by the *func* parameter is called with the *DataBlock* and new file pointer. If *func* is *NULL*, no call is made. The function type of *func* is defined by *DFCompFunc*.

```
    typedef void (* DFCompFunc)(DataFilePtr ptr,
                                const DataBlock & db);
```

Once all the records have been written to the temporary file, the old *DataFile* is closed and deleted. The temporary file is then renamed and opened as the *DataFile*.

## 12.3 Using DataFiles

The following program demonstrates how a *DataFile* is used. It uses the *Object* class defined in Chapter 11.

```
    int main()
        {
        const size_t objCount = 20;

        Object obj[objCount] =
            {
```

```
        Object("Larry",        "Los Angeles"),
        Object("John",         "San Mateo"),
        Object("Karl",         "Boston"),
        Object("Fred",         "Philadelphia"),
        Object("Lucy",         "Seattle"),
        Object("Jerry",        "Newark"),
        Object("Adam",         "Houston"),
        Object("Carmichael",   "Lincoln"),
        Object("Scott",        "Colorado Springs"),
        Object("Maria",        "Colorado Springs"),
        Object("Rebecca",      "Colorado Springs"),
        Object("Elora",        "Colorado Springs"),
        Object("Rudolph",      "North Pole"),
        Object("Robert",       "Somerset"),
        Object("Mark",         "Phoenix"),
        Object("Abercrombie",  "Tucson"),
        Object("Ed",           "Salt Lake City"),
        Object("Theodore",     "Boise"),
        Object("Everett",      "Portland"),
        Object("Edwin",        "Cheyenne")
        };

const char * fn = "tsio2.dat";

size_t n;

//────────────────────────────────────
cout << "\nCreating file object\n";

DataFile * file = new DataFile(fn,FM_NEW);

if (file == NULL)
    {
    cout << fn << "\acould not be opened!\n";
    exit(EXIT_FAILURE);
    }

DataFilePtr ptr, ptr6, ptr19;

// write the objects
```

```cpp
for (n = 0; n < objCount; ++n)
    {
    ptr = file->Write(obj[n]);

    // show where objects were written
    cout << "Writing record #" << n << " @ " << ptr
        << " : " << obj[n] << endl;

    // save pointers to records 6 and 19
    switch (n)
        {
        case 6:
            ptr6 = ptr;
            break;

        case 19:
            ptr19 = ptr;
        }
    }

// close file
delete file;

//————————————————————————————
// open file
file = new DataFile(fn, FM_EXISTING, 5120);

if (file == NULL)
    {
    cout << fn << "\acould not be reopened!\n";
    exit(EXIT_FAILURE);
    }

Object * dataIn;

DataFilePtr result;

// delete record #6
file->Seek(ptr6);
file->Delete();
```

```
// delete record #19
file->Seek(ptr19);
file->Delete();

// write new records from objects #15 and #4
result = file->Write(obj[15]);
result = file->Write(obj[4]);

// rewind the file
file->Rewind();

n = 0;

DataBlock db;

// display records in file
for (;;)
    {
    db = file->Read();

    if (db.IsNull())
        {
        cout << "<< NULL BLOCK >>\n";
        break;
        }
    else
        {
        dataIn = new Object(db);

        if (dataIn == NULL)
            {
            cout << "unable to allocate dataIn\n";
            break;
            }

        cout << "Reading record #" << n
            << " : " << *dataIn << '\n';

        delete dataIn;
        }
```

```
            ++n;
            }

        // compact file to eliminate wasted space
        if (BOOL_FALSE == file->Compact())
            cout << "\a\acompact failed!\n";

        // close file
        delete file;
        }

void TestHashFile()
        {
        const size_t objCount = 20;

        Object obj[objCount] =
            {
            Object("Larry",        "Los Angeles"),
            Object("John",         "San Mateo"),
            Object("Karl",         "Boston"),
            Object("Fred",         "Philadelphia"),
            Object("Lucy",         "Seattle"),
            Object("Jerry",        "Newark"),
            Object("Adam",         "Houston"),
            Object("Carmichael",   "Lincoln"),
            Object("Scott",        "Colorado Springs"),
            Object("Maria",        "Colorado Springs"),
            Object("Rebecca",      "Colorado Springs"),
            Object("Elora",        "Colorado Springs"),
            Object("Rudolph",      "North Pole"),
            Object("Robert",       "Somerset"),
            Object("Mark",         "Phoenix"),
            Object("Abercrombie",  "Tucson"),
            Object("Ed",           "Salt Lake City"),
            Object("Theodore",     "Boise"),
            Object("Everett",      "Portland"),
            Object("Edwin",        "Cheyenne")
            };

        const char * fn = "hftest";
```

```
size_t n;

//———————————————————————
HashFile * file = new HashFile(23,fn);

cout << "OPENED\n";

if (file == NULL)
    {
    cout << "\acreate hash file failed!\n";
    return;
    }

delete file;

cout << "CLOSED\n";

//———————————————————————
file = new HashFile(fn);

cout << "OPENED\n";

// write objects
Boolean result;

for (n = 0; n < objCount; ++n)
    {
    result = file->Write(obj[n].MakeKey(),obj[n]);

    if (result == BOOL_FALSE)
        {
        cout << "\acouldn't write " << obj[n] << endl;
        return;
        }
    else
        cout << "WRITTEN: " << obj[n] << endl;
    }

KeyString key1(String("Edwin"));
KeyString key2("Elora");
```

```
DataBlock db = file->Read(key1);

if (db.IsNull())
    {
    cout << "\acould not find Edwin\n";
    return;
    }

Object obj1(db);

cout << "FOUND: " << obj1 << endl;

db = file->Read(key2);

if (db.IsNull())
    {
    cout << "\acould not find Elora\n";
    return;
    }

Object obj2(db);

cout << "FOUND: " << obj2 << endl;

// delete Elora and Edwin
result = file->Delete(key1);

if (result == BOOL_FALSE)
    {
    cout << "\acould not delete Edwin\n";
    return;
    }

cout << "DELETED: Edwin\n";

result = file->Delete(key2);

if (result == BOOL_FALSE)
    {
    cout << "\acould not delete Elora\n";
```

```
        return;
        }

    cout << "DELETED: Elora\n";


    // new objects
    Object newguy(String("Vincent"),  String("New York
City"));
    Object newgal(String("Samantha"), String("Pittsburg"));

    result = file->Write(newguy.MakeKey(),newguy);

    if (result == BOOL_FALSE)
        cout << "\acouldn't write " << newguy << endl;
    else
        cout << "WRITTEN: " << newguy << endl;

    // close file
    delete file;

    cout << "CLOSED\n";

    //————————————————————————————
    // open file
    file = new HashFile(fn);

    cout << "OPENED\n";

    db = file->Read(key1);

    if (db.IsNull())
        cout << "ALREADY DELETED: Edwin has been deleted\n";
    else
        {
        cout << "\aEdwin has been resurrected!\n";
        return;
        }

    result = file->Delete(String("Scott"));
```

```
    if (result == BOOL_FALSE)
        {
        cout << "\acould not delete Scott\n";
        return;
        }

    cout << "DELETED: " << obj[8] << endl;

    result = file->Write(newgal.MakeKey(),newgal);

    if (result == BOOL_FALSE)
        cout << "\acouldn't write " << newgal << endl;
    else
        cout << "WRITTEN: " << newgal << endl;

    delete file;

    cout << "CLOSED\n";
    }

void TestHashFile2()
    {
    cout << "\nDataFile to HashFile Conversion Test\n";

    const String iname = "tsio2.dat";
    const String oname = "newtsio2";

    DataFile * ifile = new DataFile(iname,FM_EXISTING);

    if (ifile == NULL)
        {
        cout << "can't open " << iname << endl;
        return;
        }

    HashFile * ofile = new
HashFile(29,*ifile,oname,GetObjectKey);

    if (ofile == NULL)
        {
```

```
            cout << "can't open " << oname << endl;
            return;
            }

        delete ifile;
        delete ofile;
        }

KeyString GetObjectKey(const DataBlock & db)
        {
        Object obj(db);

        cout << "GENERATING KEY FOR: " << obj << endl;

        return obj.MakeKey();
        }

Boolean ShowThem(const KeyString & key, const DataBlock & db)
        {
        Object obj(db);

        cout << "key = " << key.GetString() << "\tobj = " << obj
<< endl;

        return BOOL_TRUE;
        }
```

## 12.4 Hash Tables as Indexes

A random-access file is most useful when it is used in conjunction with an index that keeps track of which records reside at specific file pointers. An index based on a hash table is an excellent tool for manipulating a database of information

In designing my *HashFile* class, I decided that a *HashFile* would be both a *HashTable* and a *DataFile*. I could just as easily have created a *HashFile* class that included *HashTable* and *DataFile* objects; as I've said before, these design decisions are largely a matter of personal taste.

## 12.5 The HashFileEntry class

I began by defining a derivative of *HashEntryStr* that contained a file pointer.

```
struct HashFileEntry : public HashEntryStr,
                       public Persistent
    {
    DataFilePtr DataPtr;

    HashFileEntry(const KeyString & key,
                         DataFilePtr ptr);

    HashFileEntry(const DataBlock & db);

    virtual operator DataBlock() const;

    private:
        static const Signature Sig;
    };
```

The *DataPtr* member is a file pointer to the record associated with *KeyString* (which was inherited from *HashEntryStr*). Because the position of a record is known only when it has been written to a *DataFile*, *HashTableEntries* are created *after* a record is written.

The constructor is very simple, and I implemented it inline.

```
inline HashFileEntry::HashFileEntry(const KeyString & key,
                                             DataFilePtr ptr)
    : HashEntryStr(key)
    {
    DataPtr = ptr;
    }
```

*HashFileEntry* is also derived from *Persistent*. Because I want the hash table to be stored between different executions of a program, hash table entries need to be written to a file. As a derivative of *Persistent*, *HashFileEntry* defines conversions to and from *DataBlocks*.

```
HashFileEntry::HashFileEntry(const DataBlock & db)
    {
    // check sinature
    if (db.GetSignature() != Sig)
        ReportError(HE_BADTYPES);

    // get pointer to data
    const char * ptr = (const char *)db.GetBufferPtr();

    // get file pointer
    DataPtr = *((const DataFilePtr *)ptr);

    // move to beginning of string
    ptr += sizeof(DataFilePtr);

    // create key string
    Key = KeyString(String(ptr));
    }

HashFileEntry::operator DataBlock() const
    {
    // get reference to string
    const String & keystr = Key.GetString();

    // calculate size of block
    size_t sz = sizeof(DataFilePtr) + keystr.Length() + 1;

    // allocate memory
    char * buf = new char [sz];

    if (buf == NULL)
        ReportError(HE_ALLOC);

    // store data ptr
    *((DataFilePtr *)buf) = DataPtr;

    // store string
    strcpy(buf + sizeof(DataFilePtr),(const char *)keystr);

    // create data block
```

```
DataBlock db(Sig,sz,buf);

// delete buffer
delete buf;

return db;
}
```

The *DataBlock Signature* for a *HashFileEntry* is defined by the static *Sig* member.

```
const Signature HashFileEntry::Sig = SYS_SIG_BASE + 4;
```

*HashFileEntry* uses the virtual functions *KeyEquals*, *GetKeyType*, and *KeyEquals*, which it inherits from *HashEntryStr*.

## 12.6 The HashFileBucket class

A *HashFileBucket* is a *HashBucket* that knows how to store and retrieve entries from a file.

```
class HashFileBucket : public HashBucket
    {
    public:
        Boolean WriteEntries(DataFileOutput & file) const;

        Boolean ReadEntries(const DataFileInput & file);

    private:
        static const Signature Sig;
        static const DataBlock EntryEnd;
    };
```

The *Sig* static member is the signature of the header record for a list of entries.

```
const Signature HashFileBucket::Sig = SYS_SIG_BASE + 3;
```

The constant static member *EntryEnd* marks the end of a bucket's entries when they are stored in a file.

**382**

```
// a static variable used to construct EntryEnd
static const int DummyData = 0;

const DataBlock HashFileBucket::EntryEnd(HashFileBucket::Sig,
                                         sizeof(DummyData),
                                         &DummyData);
```

The *WriteEntries* function writes the entries in a *HashFileBucket* to the file specified by the *DataFileOutput* parameter file. A short header record is written, followed by the entries in sequential order, with the list being terminated by a *EntryEnd DataBlock*.

```
Boolean HashFileBucket::WriteEntries(DataFileOutput & file) const
    {
    HashFileEntry * e = (HashFileEntry *)First;

    while (e != NULL)
        {
        if (BOOL_FALSE == file.Write(*e))
            return BOOL_FALSE;

        e = (HashFileEntry *)(e->Next);
        }

    file.Write(EntryEnd);

    return BOOL_TRUE;
    }
```

The *ReadEntries* function assumes that it can begin reading a list of entries as formatted by *WriteEntries* from the file specified by its *DataFileInput* parameter.

```
Boolean HashFileBucket::ReadEntries(const DataFileInput & file)
    {
    HashFileEntry * e = NULL;
    DataBlock db;
```

```
for (;;)
    {
    db = file.Read();

    if (db.IsNull())
        return BOOL_FALSE;

    // NOTE: possibly store # of entries in size ?!?
    if ((Sig == db.GetSignature())
    && (sizeof(DummyData) == db.GetSizeOf()))
        break;

    e = new HashFileEntry(db);

    if (BOOL_FALSE == AddEntry(e))
        return BOOL_FALSE;
    }

return BOOL_TRUE;
}
```

Why didn't I derive *HashFileBucket* from *Persistent* and use the *DataBlock* conversion functions? My decision was based on simplicity and reliability; storing each entry as a *DataBlock* allowed me to control how the entries were written and read. I think of a *HashFileBucket* not as an object, but as a list of objects. So, the *WriteEntries* and *ReadEntries* function treat *HashFileBuckets* as a list of *HashFileEntries*.

When a *HashFile* is created, an empty hash file is created. If an existing *HashFile* is opened, the hash table is read from a *DataFileInput*. During the processing of a *HashFile*, the hash table is kept entirely in memory. When the *HashFile* object is destroyed, the buckets are written to a *DataFileOutput*. The actual data records are stored in a separate file.

By keeping the hash table resident in memory, program performance is improved. A *HashFile* does not need to perform any disk reads when looking up a key in the hash table. However, an in-memory hash table has two drawbacks. First, the table uses memory; second, the on-disk hash table may not be current if the program "crashes" and new records have been written to the data file.

The hash table does not use copious amounts of memory, and its presence should not significantly affect a program. The problem with mismatched data and hash files can be solved using some simple techniques shown later in the chapter.

## 12.7 The HashFileTable class

In Chapter 11, the *HashTableStrDB* class defined a type-specific version of the base *HashTableBase* class. The *HashFileTable* class provides a derivative of *HashTableBase* that works with *KeyStrings* and *DataFilePtrs*.

```
class HashFileTable : protected HashTableBase
    {
    public:
        // constructor
        HashFileTable(size_t buckets);

        // insert new object
        Boolean Insert(const KeyString & key, DataFilePtr ptr);

        // delete an object
        Boolean Delete(const KeyString & key);

        // check for duplicate key
        Boolean IsDupeKey(const KeyString & key);

        // look up object
        DataFilePtr LookUp(const KeyString & key);

        // list all objects
        Boolean Enumerate(HashFileEnumFunc func);

    protected:
        // callback functions for Enumerate
        virtual Boolean TravCallback
                            (const HashEntryBase * e)
    const;

        HashFileEnumFunc EnumCallback;
    };
```

The constructor merely calls the *HashTableBase* constructor, and it is implemented inline.

```
inline HashFileTable::HashFileTable(size_t buckets)
    : HashTableBase(buckets)
    {
    // void
    }
```

A new entry is inserted into the hash table using the *Insert* function.

```
Boolean HashFileTable::Insert(const KeyString & key,
DataFilePtr ptr)
    {
    // create new HashEntryStrDB
    HashFileEntry * entry = new HashFileEntry(key,ptr);

    if (entry == NULL)
        ReportError(HE_ALLOC);

    // insert into table
    return AddEntry(entry);
    }
```

The *Delete* function removes an entry identified by a *KeyString*.

```
Boolean HashFileTable::Delete(const KeyString & key)
    {
    // create new HashEntryStr
    HashEntryStr * entry = new HashEntryStr(key);

    if (entry == NULL)
        ReportError(HE_ALLOC);

    // insert into table
    return DelEntry(entry);
    }
```

*IsDupeKey* returns true if it finds an entry containing a specified *KeyString*.

```
Boolean HashFileTable::IsDupeKey(const KeyString & key)
    {
    // create new HashEntryStr
    HashEntryStr * entry = new HashEntryStr(key);

    if (entry == NULL)
        ReportError(HE_ALLOC);

    // insert into table
    return IsDupe(entry);
    }
```

*LookUp* returns the *DataFilePtr* associated with a given *KeyString*.

```
DataFilePtr HashFileTable::LookUp(const KeyString & key)
    {
    // create new HashEntryStr
    HashEntryStr * entry = new HashEntryStr(key);

    if (entry == NULL)
        ReportError(HE_ALLOC);

    const HashFileEntry * e = (const HashFileEntry
*)FindEntry(entry);

    if (e == NULL)
        return DFP_ERROR;
    else
        return e->DataPtr;
    }
```

*Enumerate* uses the *TravCallBack* function to perform calls to *func* for every entry in the hash table.

```
Boolean HashFileTable::Enumerate(HashFileEnumFunc func)
    {
```

```
if (func == NULL)
    return BOOL_FALSE;

EnumCallback = func;

return Traverse();
}

Boolean HashFileTable::TravCallback(const HashEntryBase * e)
const
    {
    if (e == NULL)
        return BOOL_FALSE;
    else
        {
        HashFileEntry * e2 = (HashFileEntry *)e;

        return EnumCallback(e2->Key, e2->DataPtr);
        }
    }
```

*HashFileEnumFunc* is defined as a function returning *Boolean* and accepting *KeyString* and *DataFilePtr* parameters.

```
typedef Boolean (* HashFileEnumFunc)(const KeyString & k,
                                     DataFilePtr ptr);
```

You can use the discussion of *HashTableStrDB* in Chapter 11 as a guide to understanding how *HashFileTable* is implemented and used.

## 12.8 The HashFile class

Now we get to the goal of this entire discussion — the creation of a *DataFile* that is indexed by a *HashTable*. The *HashFile* class is derived from two base classes: *DataFile* and *HashFileTable*.

```
class HashFile : private HashFileTable,
                 private DataFile
```

```
{
public:
    // constructors
    // existing hash file
    HashFile(const String & basename,
                    size_t   bufsize = 0);

    // new hash file
    HashFile(       size_t   buckets,
            const String & basename,
                    size_t   bufsize = 0);

    // has file from data file
    HashFile(       size_t       buckets,
                    DataFile & file,
            const String &   basename,
                    ReHashFunc getKey,
                    size_t       bufsize = 0);

    // copy constructor
    HashFile(const HashFile & hfile);

    // destructor
    ~HashFile();

    // write a record
    Boolean Write(const KeyString & key,
                    const DataBlock & db);

    // read a record
    DataBlock Read(const KeyString & key);

    // delete a record
    Boolean Delete(const KeyString & key);

    // commit data to disk
    Boolean Commit();

private:
    // name of hash file
```

```
        String HashFileName;

        // extensions for hash file and data file
        static const String HashFileExt;
        static const String DataFileExt;

        static const Signature HashHdrSig;

        // create file name from base and extension
        static String MakeFileName(const String & basename,
                                          const String & ext);

        // get buckets from hash file
        size_t GetBuckets(const String & hashname);
};
```

The base classes are private; I wanted all access to a *HashFile* to be through the functions it explicitly defines. Allowing a user to call the *DataFile* version of *Write*, for example, would result in a corrupted hash index.

I'll describe each member of *HashFile*, and then provide a complete example program to show you how to use *HashFile*s.

### 12.8.1 Data Members

*HashFile* objects generate two external files: one for the hash table, and the other for the data records. These two files have the same one-to-eight-character file name, but different extensions. The extensions for these files are defined by the *HashFileExt* and *DataFileExt* static class members.

```
    const String HashFile::HashFileExt(".HFH");
    const String HashFile::DataFileExt(".HFD");
```

The name of the file containing the hash index is generated when the *HashFile* object is created, and it is stored in the data member *HashFileName*.

The file containing the hash index has a header record that contains the number of buckets in the hash table. This header record has a *Signature* value of *HashHdrSig*.

```
const Signature HashFile::HashHdrSig = SYS_SIG_BASE + 5;
```

### 12.8.2 Constructors and Utility Functions

Base-class and object-member constructor calls occur between the time a constructor is called and the first line of constructor code that is executed. The only parameters that can be passed to base-class constructors are the arguments passed to the constructor. This presents a difficult problem when the constructor parameters need processing before the base classes are initialized.

The *HashFile* class defines three constructors. The first creates a new *HashFile* with an empty *DataFile* and *HashFileTable*. The second constructor creates a *HashFile* that uses an existing hash table (in an external file) and *DataFile*. The third constructor builds a *HashFile* from an existing *DataFile* by building a new *HashFileTable*. All three constructors must call constructors to initialize the base-class *DataFile* and *TableFile* objects, as well as to initialize the *HashFileName* data member.

The *DataFile* base class requires a file name; yet, the *HashFile* constructors are passed only the base-file name — without its extension. The actual *DataFile* name is constructed by appending *DataFileExt* to the base name. Similarly, the *HashFileName* data member also needs to be initialized with a file name made from concatenating the base name and the *HashFileExt*.

I created a private-utility function named *MakeFileName*, which returns the result of appending an extension to a base-file name. *MakeFileName* is called by the *DataFile* and *HashFileName* constructors to generate the appropriate names.

```
String HashFile::MakeFileName(const String & basename,
                              const String & ext)
  {
  String name;
```

```
if (basename.Length() < 8)
    name = basename;
else
    name = basename.CutHead(8);

name += ext;

return name;
}
```

The first constructor has only two paremeters: a number of buckets, and the base-file name. It uses *MakeFileName* to create names for the *DataFile* and *HashFileName*, and it creates an empty hash table by passing buckets to the *HashFileTable* constructor.

```
// new hash file
HashFile::HashFile(       size_t   buckets,
                    const String & basename,
                          size_t   bufsize)
    :
DataFile(MakeFileName(basename,DataFileExt),FM_NEW,bufsize),
    HashFileTable(buckets),
    HashFileName(MakeFileName(basename,HashFileExt))
    {
    // void
    }
```

The second constructor is more complicated. It opens an existing *HashFile*, and creates the internal hash file by reading data from the hash file stored in an external file.

Again, we have a minor problem: A *HashFileTable* must be told the number of buckets it contains when it is constructed. That information is stored in the header of the external hash table file. Therefore, we need to read the header of the external file and use the number of buckets stored to initialize the *HashFileTable*.

The only way I could figure doing this was to create another static-utility function, named *GetBuckets*, which reads the external hash file's header and returns the number of buckets stored. The constructor then calls *GetBuckets*.

```
size_t HashFile::GetBuckets(const String & hashname)
    {
    DataFileInput * file = new DataFileInput(hashname);

    size_t result = 0;

    if (file != NULL)
        {
        DataBlock db = file->Read();

        if ((db.GetSignature() == HashHdrSig)
        && (db.GetSizeOf() == sizeof(size_t)))
            result = *((size_t *)db.GetBufferPtr());
        }

    delete file;

    return result;
    }
```

Only static functions can be called within base-class and member-object constructors, because no object has been generated (yet) for use as this pointer in a member-function call.

Using *GetBuckets*, the second constructor is implemented like this:

```
// existing hash file
HashFile::HashFile(const String & basename,
                        size_t    bufsize)
    :
DataFile(MakeFileName(basename,DataFileExt),FM_EXISTING,bufsize),
   HashFileTable(GetBuckets(MakeFileName(basename,HashFileExt))),
     HashFileName(MakeFileName(basename,HashFileExt))
    {
    // read hash table
    DataFileInput * file = new DataFileInput(HashFileName);

    if (file == NULL)
        DataFileBase::ReportError("can't open input hash file");
```

```
        // ignore hash file header
        file->Skip();

        // get hash table entries
        Boolean result;

        for (size_t b = 0; b < NoOfBuckets; ++b)
            {
            // get bucket entries
            result =((HashFileBucket *)Table[b])->ReadEntries(*file);

            if (result == BOOL_FALSE)
                DataFileBase::ReportError
                                ("can't read bucket entries");
            }

        delete file;
        }
```

The external hash file is read from disk by calling *ReadEntries* for each *HashFileBucket* in the table.

The third constructor creates a *HashFile* from a *DataFile*. For each *DataBlock* in the *DataFile*, the constructor calls *func* to obtain a key value used to generate hash-table entries.

```
    HashFile::HashFile(      size_t     buckets,
                             DataFile & file,
                       const String &   basename,
                             ReHashFunc getKey,
                             size_t     bufsize)
        :
    DataFile(MakeFileName(basename,DataFileExt),FM_NEW,bufsize),
        HashFileTable(buckets),
        HashFileName(MakeFileName(basename,HashFileExt))
        {
        if (getKey == NULL)
            DataFile::ReportError("invalid rehash function");

        file.Rewind();
```

```
DataBlock db;

for (;;)
    {
    // read record from original file
    db = file.Read();

    // assume a NULL block indicates end of input
    if (db.IsNull())
        break;

    // write record to HashFile
    Write(getKey(db),db);

    // Note: Duplicate keys will be lost in the conversion!
    //       Also, no error checking is done on Write,
    //       because it returns an error on duplicate keys
    }
}
```

*func* returns a *KeyString* based on the *DataBlock* it was passed.

```
typedef KeyString (*ReHashFunc)(const DataBlock & db);
```

If the external hash file ceases to match its associated data file (such as when a program crashes before the external hash file is generated), this constructor can be used to generate a new hash table.

### 12.8.3 Destructor

The destructor writes the hash-table entries to the external hash table by calling *WriteEntries* for each *HashFileBucket* in the internal table.

```
HashFile::~HashFile()
    {
    // create hash output file
    DataFileOutput * file = new DataFileOutput(HashFileName);

    if (file == NULL)
```

```
                        DataFileBase::ReportError
                                ("can't create output hash file");

            // save hash table
            Boolean result;

            // store # of buckets
            file->Write(DataBlock(HashHdrSig,
                                    sizeof(size_t),
                                    &NoOfBuckets));

            for (size_t b = 0; b < NoOfBuckets; ++b)
                {
                // write bucket entries
                result = ((HashFileBucket *)
                                        Table[b])-
    >WriteEntries(*file);

                if (result == BOOL_FALSE)
                    DataFileBase::ReportError
                                    ("can't write bucket entries");
                }

            delete file;
            }
```

### 12.8.4  Writing Records

The *Write* function writes a DataBlock to disk and adds an associated *KeyString* to the hash table.

```
    Boolean HashFile::Write(const KeyString & key,
                            const DataBlock & db)
        {
        // check for (and delete) duplicate key
        if (IsDupeKey(key))
            {
            if (BOOL_FALSE == HashFile::Delete(key))
                return BOOL_FALSE;
            }
```

```
// store data
DataFilePtr ptr = DataFile::Write(db);

if (ptr == DFP_ERROR)
    return BOOL_FALSE;

// add key and pointer to hash table
Boolean result = Insert(key,ptr);

return result;
}
```

Because hash tables cannot contain duplicate records, the *Write* function must handle the situation where the *KeyString* already resides in the hash table. If the *KeyString* is a duplicate, *Write* calls the *Delete* function to remove the original record. This allows the new record to replace the existing one, and it is appropriate for applications where a modified record needs to overwrite a previous version of itself stored in the *HashFile*.

*Write* stores the *DataBlock* in the *DataFile*, obtaining the file pointer for the block. The file pointer and the *KeyString* are then added to the hash table.

### 12.8.5 Reading Records

The *Read* function looks up a key value in the hash table, receiving a file pointer that it uses to retrieve a *DataBlock* from the *DataFile*.

```
// read a record
DataBlock HashFile::Read(const KeyString & key)
    {
    // get pointer to record using key in hash table
    DataFilePtr ptr = LookUp(key);

    if (ptr == DFP_ERROR)
        return NULL_BLOCK;

    // set file pointer
    if (BOOL_FALSE == DataFile::Seek(ptr))
```

```
        return NULL_BLOCK;

    // read record at pointer
    DataBlock db(DataFile::Read());

    return db;
    }
```

### 12.8.6 Deleting Records

Assuming that a record identified by *KeyString* exists, the *Delete* function removes the *KeyString* entry from the hash table and deletes the associated record from the *DataFile*.

```
Boolean HashFile::Delete(const KeyString & key)
    {
    // get pointer to record using key lookup in hash table
    DataFilePtr ptr = LookUp(key);

    if (ptr == DFP_ERROR)
        return BOOL_FALSE;

    // set file pointer
    if (BOOL_FALSE == DataFile::Seek(ptr))
        return BOOL_FALSE;

    // delete record
    Boolean result = DataFile::Delete();

    if (result == BOOL_TRUE)
        {
        // delete key from hash table
        result = HashFileTable::Delete(key);
        }

    // done
    return result;
    }
```

### 12.8.7 Committing Data

Because the *DataFile* base class is private, the *DataFile::Commit* function cannot be called directly. Therefore, I created an inline *HashFile::Commit* function that simply calls the following:

```
inline Boolean HashFile::Commit()
    {
    return DataFile::Commit();
    }
```

I decided not to allow for the compaction of a hash file, because of the complexity of keeping the compacted *DataFile* and the *HashFileTable* in synch. A *HashFile* can be compacted simply by compacting its associated *DataFile* and regenerating the hash table using a constructor.

## 12.9 Using HashFiles

The following short program uses the *Object* class (from Chapters 10 and 11) and a *HashFile*.

```
KeyString GetObjectKey(const DataBlock & db);

int main()
    {
    const size_t objCount = 20;

    Object obj[objCount] =
        {
        Object("Larry",      "Los Angeles"),
        Object("John",       "San Mateo"),
        Object("Karl",       "Boston"),
        Object("Fred",       "Philadelphia"),
        Object("Lucy",       "Seattle"),
        Object("Jerry",      "Newark"),
        Object("Adam",       "Houston"),
        Object("Carmichael", "Lincoln"),
        Object("Scott",      "Colorado Springs"),
```

```
            Object("Maria",       "Colorado Springs"),
            Object("Rebecca",     "Colorado Springs"),
            Object("Elora",       "Colorado Springs"),
            Object("Rudolph",     "North Pole"),
            Object("Robert",      "Somerset"),
            Object("Mark",        "Phoenix"),
            Object("Abercrombie","Tucson"),
            Object("Ed",          "Salt Lake City"),
            Object("Theodore",    "Boise"),
            Object("Everett",     "Portland"),
            Object("Edwin",       "Cheyenne")
            };

    const char * fn = "hftest";

    size_t n;

    //————————————————————————————
    HashFile * file = new HashFile(23,fn);

    cout << "OPENED\n";

    if (file == NULL)
        {
        cout << "\acreate hash file failed!\n";
        return;
        }

    delete file;

    cout << "CLOSED\n";

    //————————————————————————————
    file = new HashFile(fn);

    cout << "OPENED\n";

    // write objects
    Boolean result;
```

```
for (n = 0; n < objCount; ++n)
    {
    result = file->Write(obj[n].MakeKey(),obj[n]);

    if (result == BOOL_FALSE)
        {
        cout << "\acouldn't write " << obj[n] << endl;
        return;
        }
    else
        cout << "WRITTEN: " << obj[n] << endl;
    }

KeyString key1(String("Edwin"));
KeyString key2("Elora");

DataBlock db = file->Read(key1);

if (db.IsNull())
    {
    cout << "\acould not find Edwin\n";
    return;
    }

Object obj1(db);

cout << "FOUND: " << obj1 << endl;

db = file->Read(key2);

if (db.IsNull())
    {
    cout << "\acould not find Elora\n";
    return;
    }

Object obj2(db);

cout << "FOUND: " << obj2 << endl;
```

```
// delete Elora and Edwin
result = file->Delete(key1);

if (result == BOOL_FALSE)
    {
    cout << "\acould not delete Edwin\n";
    return;
    }

cout << "DELETED: Edwin\n";

result = file->Delete(key2);

if (result == BOOL_FALSE)
    {
    cout << "\acould not delete Elora\n";
    return;
    }

cout << "DELETED: Elora\n";


// new objects
Object newguy(String("Vincent"),  String("New York City"));
Object newgal(String("Samantha"), String("Pittsburg"));

result = file->Write(newguy.MakeKey(),newguy);

if (result == BOOL_FALSE)
    cout << "\acouldn't write " << newguy << endl;
else
    cout << "WRITTEN: " << newguy << endl;

// close file
delete file;

cout << "CLOSED\n";
```

```
        //————————————————————————
        // open file
        file = new HashFile(fn);

        cout << "OPENED\n";

        db = file->Read(key1);

        if (db.IsNull())
            cout << "ALREADY DELETED: Edwin has been deleted\n";
        else
            {
            cout << "\aEdwin has been resurrected!\n";
            return;
            }

        result = file->Delete(String("Scott"));

        if (result == BOOL_FALSE)
            {
            cout << "\acould not delete Scott\n";
            return;
            }

        cout << "DELETED: " << obj[8] << endl;

        result = file->Write(newgal.MakeKey(),newgal);

        if (result == BOOL_FALSE)
            cout << "\acouldn't write " << newgal << endl;
        else
            cout << "WRITTEN: " << newgal << endl;

        delete file;

        cout << "CLOSED\n";
        }

KeyString GetObjectKey(const DataBlock & db)
```

```
{
Object obj(db);

cout << "GENERATING KEY FOR: " << obj << endl;

return obj.MakeKey();
}
```

The *HashFile* classes are defined in the file *hashfile.h* and *hashfile.cxx,* which are listed in their entirety in Appendix A. The *DataFile* classes are also listed in Appendix A, in the *datafile.h* and *datafile.cxx* files, which were introduced in Chapter 10.

# Tree Structures

A hash table is a tool that allows fast access to data through a key value. Hash tables, however, have a significant limitation: Keys are not stored in order. You can access a specific key or look at all the keys in a hash table, but you can't retrieve a list of the keys in sorted order.

A tree structure stores keys in sorted order. Using a tree index with a data file allows sorted access to the data without sorting the data.

## 13.1 Binary Trees

All trees consist of *nodes* that contain keys. Nodes have *links* to other nodes, and the type of tree being constructed defines the structure of the links between nodes. Links are unidirectional; they connect *parent* nodes to *child* nodes. All trees have a single *root* node, to which all other nodes are linked. Any node lacking links is known as a *leaf* node. These definitions will become clearer when you view the diagrams below.

A *binary tree* is the simplest type of tree structure. Each node in a binary tree contains a key and two links; one link connects to all nodes with lessor keys, and the other link connects to all nodes with greater keys. If there are no lessor or greater nodes, the link contains a sentinel value marking it as a *null link*.

### 13.1.1 Searching

I employ diagrams in which nodes are boxes containing their key value. For simplicity, the examples use single-letter keys. Links are represented by lines connecting the lower left- and right-hand corners of a parent node to the center top of a child node. Lessor nodes are linked on the left, greater nodes are linked on the right.

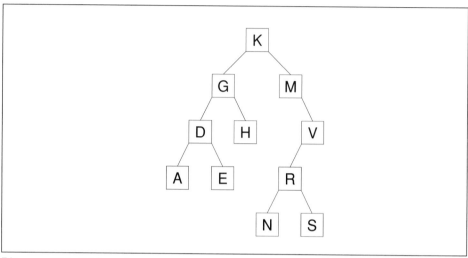

**Diagram 13-1. A binary tree.**

Diagram 13-1 shows an example of a binary tree. K is the root of the tree, and it is the parent of G and M. Notice that a node can be both a parent and a child; G is a child of K and the parent of D and H. The nodes containing the A, E, H, N, and S keys are leaf nodes.

The algorithm for finding a key in a binary tree begins by comparing the key to the key stored in the root node. If the key does not match, we move down the tree based on the relationship between the search key and the root key. If the search key is less than the root key, we follow the left link to the next node; if the search key is greater than the root key, we follow the right link. The newly selected node is now treated just as the root was, by comparing the search key against the node key and selecting the next search node. If the link to be followed does not connect to a child node, the search key is not in the tree.

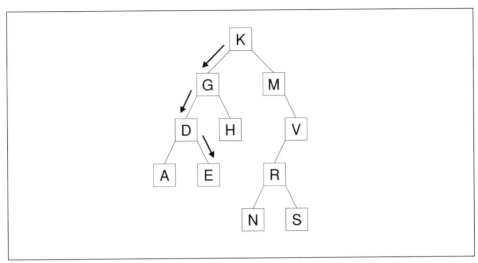

**Diagram 13-2. Searching for E in a binary tree.**

Diagram 13-2 uses arrows to show the links followed in searching for the key E in the example binary tree. E is less than the root node key K, so we follow the left link. E is less than G, so again we follow the left link. E is greater than D, and we follow the right link to the node that contains E.

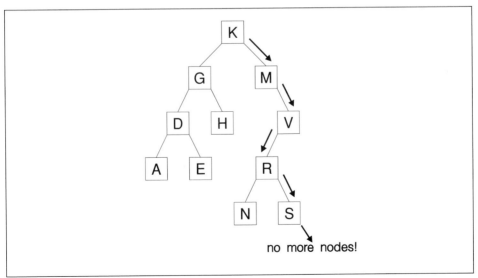

**Diagram 13-3. Searching for a key that is not in the tree.**

Diagram 13-3 shows the procedure followed when searching for the key T. The search begins at the root, and travels down through the tree until it reaches the S node. T would be connected to the right of S — if it were in the tree! When a null link is found, the search key is not resident in the tree.

You probably noticed that a binary tree search is recursive — it starts at the root node, compares keys, and selects another node. Again, it compares keys, and selects another node — and so on, until a null link is reached or the key is found.

### 13.1.2 Insertion

The first node inserted into a binary tree becomes the root node. Inserting subsequent nodes entails searching the tree for the proper location. If the key being inserted is not found, the search ends at a null link. When a null link is encountered, a new leaf node is constructed and linked to that part of the tree.

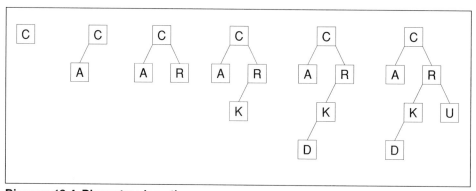

**Diagram 13-4. Binary tree insertion.**

Diagram 13-4 assumes that insertion begins with an empty tree, and it shows the results of inserting each of the keys C, A, R, K, D, and U.

The first key inserted, C, becomes the root node. A is less than C, so it is attached to the left of C; R is greater than C, so it links to C's right side. K is greater than C but less than R, which places it left of R. D is greater than C and less than R and K, so it is attached to K's left link. The U is greater than C and R, and it is linked to R's right side.

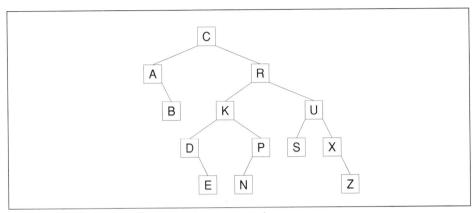

**Diagram 13-5a. The result of inserting more nodes.**

Diagram 13-5a shows the tree after adding the additional keys P, B, E, N, X, Z, and S. You may notice that more nodes are greater than the root, giving the tree a lopsided appearance. For now, we'll ignore this problem; I'll be addressing it later in the chapter.

### 13.1.3 Deletion

Deleting a node from a tree requires that we handle one of three situations. The node is either childless, or it has one or two links to child nodes.

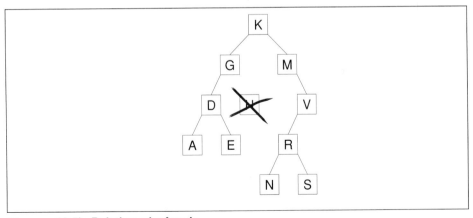

**Diagram 13-5b. Deleting a leaf node.**

Diagram 13-5b shows the deletion of the H node. Because H is a leaf node, it can be deleted simply by setting the link from its parent to null. Deleting a leaf node does not require that we change the organization of other nodes.

When a parent node is deleted from a binary tree, all of its child nodes must be relinked to the tree.

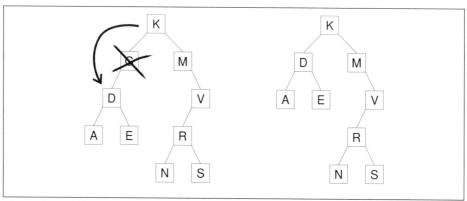

**Diagram 13-6. Deleting a parent node with one child.**

Diagram 13-6 shows how a parent with a single child is deleted from a binary tree. The deleted node is replaced by its child; in this case, G is replaced by D. All children of a node have the same relationship to the node's parent as does the node, so replacing a deleted node with its child maintains the integrity of the tree's organization.

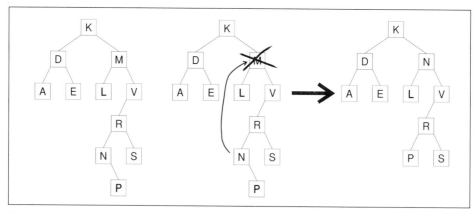

**Diagram 13-7. Deleting a parent node with two children.**

When deleting a two-child node from the tree, we need to use a more complicated algorithm, as shown in Diagram 13-7. The deleted node is replaced by its immediate successor, which is defined as the node that immediately follows the deleted node in sequence. In the diagram above, N immediately follows M and is therefore its successor. The data stored in N — such as the key value — is transferred to the deleted node, M. All of M's links remain intact. Once the successor node has replaced the deleted node, the algorithm deletes the original successor node from the tree. The relationship of the keys remains intact.

## 13.2 A Binary Tree Class

Implementing binary trees with a C++ class is not as complicated as one might expect. To keep the discussion simple, I've limited my binary tree to holding *DataBlocks* indexed by *KeyStrings*, as with the *HashTableStrDB* class described in Chapter 11.

### 13.2.1 Error Handling

I defined a static class named *TreeErrorBase* that provides a common error-handling facility for all of the binary-tree classes.

```
class TreeErrorBase
    {
    public:
        static void SetErrOut(const ErrReporter & er);

    protected:
        static ErrReporter * ErrOut;

        static void ReportError();
    };
```

The *TreeErrorBase* class serves the same purpose as the error-handling classes presented earlier in the book. Its functions are implemented as follows:

```
ErrReporter * TreeErrorBase::ErrOut = NULL;

void TreeErrorBase::ReportError()
```

```
    {
    if (ErrOut != NULL)
        ErrOut->Fatal("memory allocation failure in tree");
    }


void TreeErrorBase::SetErrOut(const ErrReporter & er)
    {
    if (ErrOut != NULL)
        delete ErrOut;

    ErrOut = new ErrReporter(er);
    }
```

### 13.2.2 The TreeNode structure

As are the buckets in a hash table, the nodes in a binary tree are defined by a structure.

```
struct TreeNode
    {
    // links
    TreeNode  * Less;
    TreeNode  * Greater;
    TreeNode  * Parent;

    // contents
    KeyString Key;
    DataBlock Data;

    // constructor
    TreeNode(const KeyString & k,
            const DataBlock & db);

    // copy constructor
    TreeNode(const TreeNode & node);

    // assignment operator
    void operator = (const TreeNode & node);
    };
```

The *Less* member points to a child node containing a lessor key; the *Greater* member points to a child node containing a greater key. Null nodes are indicated by *Less* or *Greater* pointers set to *NULL*.

The *Parent* pointer is a backward link to the node's parent. Deletion of nodes from the tree is greatly simplified when a link provides the address of the parent node.

*Key* contains the *KeyString* that identifies the information stored in the *DataBlock Data*. As with the hash table, *DataBlocks* are stored in the container to ensure data security.

The *TreeNode* constructors initialize a newly created node, and the assignment operator copies one *TreeNode* to another.

```
// constructor
TreeNode::TreeNode(const KeyString & k,
                   const DataBlock & db)
    : Key(k), Data(db)
    {
    Parent  = NULL;
    Less    = NULL;
    Greater = NULL;
    }

// copy constructor
TreeNode::TreeNode(const TreeNode & node)
    : Key(node.Key), Data(node.Data)
    {
    Parent  = node.Parent;
    Less    = node.Less;
    Greater = node.Greater;
    }

// assignment operator
void TreeNode::operator = (const TreeNode & node)
    {
    Parent  = node.Parent;
    Less    = node.Less;
    Greater = node.Greater;
```

```
        Key     = node.Key;
        Data    = node.Data;
        }
```

*TreeNodes* are dynamically allocated and freed by the binary-tree class.

### 13.2.3 The BinaryTree class

The *BinaryTree* class defines a binary tree data structure as defined in section 13.1. The class definition is:

```
    class BinaryTree : public TreeErrorBase
        {
    public:
        // constructor
        BinaryTree();

        // copy constructor
        BinaryTree(const BinaryTree & tree);

        // destructor
        ~BinaryTree();

        // assignment operator
        void operator = (const BinaryTree & tree);

        // store an item
        Boolean Insert(const KeyString & key,
                        const DataBlock & db);

        // delete an item
        Boolean Delete(const KeyString & key);

        // retrieve an item
        DataBlock LookUp(const KeyString & key) const;

        // traverse entire tree, calling a function for each node
        Boolean Enumerate(TreeEnumFunc func);
```

```
    protected:
        // data members
        TreeNode *   Root;     // root node
        TreeEnumFunc EnumFunc; // pointer to enumeration
function

        // recursive copy function
        void RecursiveCopy(TreeNode * node);

        // recursive traversal function
        void RecurseTraverse(TreeNode * node);

        // recursive deletion function
        void RecursiveDelete(TreeNode * node);
    };
```

The class defines two data members: the *Root* pointer to the root node, and a function pointer named *EnumFunc* used in listing the entries in a tree. The function pointer points to a function that has a *KeyString* and *DataBlock* parameters.

```
    typedef Boolean (* TreeEnumFunc)(const KeyString & str,
                                     const DataBlock & db);
```

### 13.2.4 Utility Functions

Three protected functions provide utility functions for a *BinaryTree*. These are recursive functions; they process all nodes in a given subtree by passing the *Less* and *Greater* pointers to themselves. To process the entire tree, pass these functions to the *Root* node.

```
    void BinaryTree::RecursiveCopy(TreeNode * node)
      {
      if (node != NULL)
        {
        Insert(node->Key,node->Data);

        RecursiveCopy(node->Less);
        RecursiveCopy(node->Greater);
        }
      }
```

*RecursiveCopy* duplicates a tree. The copy constructor and assignment operator call *RecursiveCopy* with the *Root* node of a tree which is being duplicated. Those nodes are then recursively added to the source tree's nodes to the destination tree.

```
Boolean BinaryTree::Enumerate(TreeEnumFunc func)
    {
    if (func == NULL)
        return BOOL_FALSE;

    EnumFunc = func;
    RecurseTraverse(Root);

    return BOOL_TRUE;
    }

void BinaryTree::RecurseTraverse(TreeNode * node)
    {
    if (node != NULL)
        {
        RecurseTraverse(node->Less);
        EnumFunc(node->Key,node->Data);
        RecurseTraverse(node->Greater);
        }
    }
```

*Enumerate* assigns the address of its parameter to the *EnumFunc* data member; then it calls *RecurseTraverse* with the *Root* node. *RecurseTraverse* first recursively processes the *Less* subtree, then it calls *EnumFunc* for the current node, and then it calls itself for the *Greater* subtree.

```
void BinaryTree::RecursiveDelete(TreeNode * node)
    {
    if (node != NULL)
        {
        RecursiveDelete(node->Less);
        RecursiveDelete(node->Greater);

        delete node;
```

```
        }
    }
```

The destructor calls *RecursiveDelete* with the *Root* node. *RecursiveDelete* recursively deletes the subtrees before deleting the node itself.

### 13.2.5 Constructors, Destructors, and Assignment Operators

The constructors, destructor, and assignment operator all are implemented as inline functions.

```
// constructor
inline BinaryTree::BinaryTree()
    {
    Root = NULL;
    }

// copy constructor
inline BinaryTree::BinaryTree(const BinaryTree & tree)
    {
    Root = NULL;

    RecursiveCopy(tree.Root);
    }

// destructor
inline BinaryTree::~BinaryTree()
    {
    RecursiveDelete(Root);
    }

// assignment operator
inline void BinaryTree::operator = (const BinaryTree & tree)
    {
    RecursiveDelete(Root);

    Root = NULL;

    RecursiveCopy(tree.Root);
    }
```

The constructor sets the *Root* node to NULL, indicating an empty *Tree*. The copy constructor sets *Root* to NULL, and then calls *RecursiveCopy* to duplicate the source tree. The destructor calls *RecursiveDelete* to delete all the nodes in the tree. The assignment operator deletes all the nodes in the tree with *RecursiveDelete*, sets the *Root* node to NULL, and calls *RecursiveCopy* to copy nodes from the source tree.

### 13.2.6 Insertion

The *Insert* function creates a *TreeNode* from the *KeyString* and *DataBlock* parameters.

```
Boolean BinaryTree::Insert(const KeyString & key,
                           const DataBlock & db)
    {
    Boolean result = BOOL_FALSE;

    TreeNode * newnode = new TreeNode(key,db);

    if (newnode == NULL)
        ReportError();

    if (Root == NULL)
        {
        Root   = newnode;
        result = BOOL_TRUE;
        }
    else
        {
        TreeNode * node = Root;

        while (node != NULL)
            {
            // replace a duplicate key
            if (newnode->Key == node->Key)
                {
                // copy links from old node
                newnode->Less    = node->Less;
                newnode->Greater = node->Greater;
```

```
        newnode->Parent  = node->Parent;

        // is node the root?
        if (node == Root)
            Root = newnode; // replace root node
        else
            {
            // replace node with newnode in parent
            if (node->Parent->Less == node)
                node->Parent->Less = newnode;
            else
                node->Parent->Greater = newnode;
            }

        // delete old node
        delete node;

        result = BOOL_TRUE;

        break;
        }

    if (newnode->Key < node->Key)
        {
        if (node->Less == NULL)
            {
            // insert node
            node->Less = newnode;
            newnode->Parent = node;
            result = BOOL_TRUE;
            break;
            }
        else // move to next node
            node = node->Less;
        }
    else
        {
        if (node->Greater == NULL)
            {
            // insert node
```

```
                        node->Greater = newnode;
                        newnode->Parent = node;
                        result = BOOL_TRUE;
                        break;
                        }
                else // move to next node
                    node = node->Greater;
                }
            }
        }

    return result;
    }
```

After the node is created, *Insert* searches the tree for the key value. If the key is found, the new node replaces the existing one using the original links and parent. Otherwise, the search ends at a null link where the new node is added.

### 13.2.7 Deletion

Deletion needs to handle the removal of nodes with zero, one, or two links. This algorithm is complicated by special handling requirements for deletion of the root node.

```
Boolean BinaryTree::Delete(const KeyString & key)
    {
    TreeNode * node = Root;

    while (node != NULL)
        {
        if (key == node->Key)
            break;

        if (key < node->Key)
            node = node->Less;
        else
            node = node->Greater;
        }
```

```
if (node == NULL)
    return BOOL_FALSE;

if (node->Greater == NULL)
    {
    if (node->Less == NULL)
        {
        if (node == Root)
            Root = NULL; // tree is now empty!
        else
            {
            // remove leaf node
            if (node->Parent->Less == node)
                node->Parent->Less = NULL;
            else
                node->Parent->Greater = NULL;
            }
        }
    else // node has a "lesser" subtree
        {
        if (node == Root)
            Root = node->Less;
        else
            {
            // splice "less" subtree
            if (node->Parent->Less == node)
                node->Parent->Less = node->Less;
            else
                node->Parent->Greater = node->Less;
            }
        }
    }
else // node has a "greater" subtree
    {
    if (node->Less == NULL)
        {
        if (node == Root)
            Root = node->Greater;  // new root node
        else
            {
```

```
                // splice "greater" subtree
                if (node->Parent->Less == node)
                    node->Parent->Less = node->Greater;
                else
                    node->Parent->Greater = node->Greater;
                }
            }
        else // deleted node has two descendants ugh!
            {
            // look for immediate successor
            TreeNode * successor = node->Greater;

            while (successor->Less != NULL)
                successor = successor->Less;

            // unlink successor from tree
            if (successor->Parent->Less == successor)
                successor->Parent->Less = successor->Greater;
            else
                successor->Parent->Greater = successor->Greater;

            // copy data from successor to deleted node
            node->Key  = successor->Key;
            node->Data = successor->Data;

            // update parent links in children
            if (successor->Greater != NULL)
                successor->Greater->Parent = node;

            // set successor to be deleted
            node = successor;
            }
        }

    // delete node that was removed
    delete node;

    return BOOL_TRUE;
    }
```

*Delete* begins by searching for the key. If the key isn't found, *Delete* returns *BOOL_FALSE*. Otherwise, node is deleted and the tree is adjusted. If the deleted node is the only node, *Delete* leaves an empty tree. If the node has only one child, that child replaces the deleted node — becoming the new root if the root node is being deleted. Otherwise, the node has two children, and it is swapped with its immediate successor.

### 13.2.8 Searches

The *LoopUp* function searches a tree for a given key.

```
DataBlock BinaryTree::LookUp(const KeyString & key) const
    {
    TreeNode * node = Root;

    while (node != NULL)
        {
        if (key == node->Key)
            break;

        if (key < node->Key)
            node = node->Less;
        else
            node = node->Greater;
        }

    if (node == NULL)
        return NULL_BLOCK;
    else
        return node->Data;
    }
```

If the key is found, *Lookup* returns the *DataBlock* stored in that key's node. If the key is not found, *LookUp* returns a *NULL_BLOCK*.

## 13.3 Using BinaryTrees

The following program uses a *BinaryTree* to manipulate several objects of the (by now) ubiquitous *Object* class.

```
int main()
    {
    // set error handlers
    TreeErrorBase::SetErrOut(ErrHandler);
    DataBlock::SetErrOut(ErrHandler);
    String::SetErrOut(ErrHandler);

    cout << "\n————————\nBinaryTree test #1\n————————\n";

    const size_t objCount = 20;

    Object obj[objCount] =
        {
        Object("Larry",        "Los Angeles"),
        Object("John",         "San Mateo"),
        Object("Karl",         "Boston"),
        Object("Fred",         "Philadelphia"),
        Object("Lucy",         "Seattle"),
        Object("Jerry",        "Newark"),
        Object("Adam",         "Houston"),
        Object("Carmichael",   "Lincoln"),
        Object("Scott",        "Colorado Springs"),
        Object("Maria",        "Colorado Springs"),
        Object("Rebecca",      "Colorado Springs"),
        Object("Elora",        "Colorado Springs"),
        Object("Rudolph",      "North Pole"),
        Object("Robert",       "Somerset"),
        Object("Mark",         "Phoenix"),
        Object("Abercrombie",  "Tucson"),
        Object("Ed",           "Salt Lake City"),
        Object("Theodore",     "Boise"),
        Object("Everett",      "Portland"),
        Object("Edwin",        "Cheyenne")
        };

    size_t n;

    BinaryTree tree;

    // insert records into tree
    for (n = 0; n < objCount; ++n)
```

```
        tree.Insert(obj[n].MakeKey(),obj[n]);

    // display all entries
    cout << "\nAll records inserted:\n————————\n";
    tree.Enumerate(ShowThem);

    // delete several nodes
    tree.Delete(obj[0].GetName());  // Larry (root!)
    tree.Delete(obj[3].GetName());  // Fred
    tree.Delete(obj[17].GetName()); // Theodore
    tree.Delete(obj[19].GetName()); // Edwin

    // display nodes again
    cout << "\nFour records deleted:\n————————\n";
    tree.Enumerate(ShowThem);

    // add in some new nodes
    tree.Insert(obj[0].MakeKey(),obj[0]);   // Larry;
    tree.Insert(obj[19].MakeKey(),obj[19]); // Edwin;

    // replace my node with new info
    Object Scott("Scott","Nowhere");

    tree.Insert(Scott.MakeKey(),Scott);

    // display nodes for third time
    cout << "\nThree records inserted:"
            "\n————————\n";
    tree.Enumerate(ShowThem);

    return 0;
    }

Boolean ShowThem(const KeyString & key, const DataBlock & db)
    {
    Object obj(db);

    cout << "key = " << key.GetString()
        << "\tobj = " << obj << endl;

    return BOOL_TRUE;
    }
```

## 13.4 Problems with Binary Trees

Binary trees sort information as it is inserted, making them very useful for applications where dynamic information must be organized. Binary trees, however, have deficiencies.

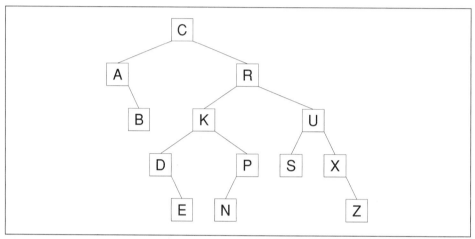

**Diagram 13-8. An unbalanced binary tree.**

Diagram 13-8 shows the tree constructed in section 13.1 from the keys C, A, R, K, D, U, P, B, E, N, X, Z, and S — in that order. The tree has two nodes left of the root and 10 nodes to its right. Searching for a key greater than C can require up to five comparisons.

A tree is balanced when it has equal numbers of nodes on both sides of its root. For example, inserting the same set of keys in a different order results in a perfectly balanced tree.

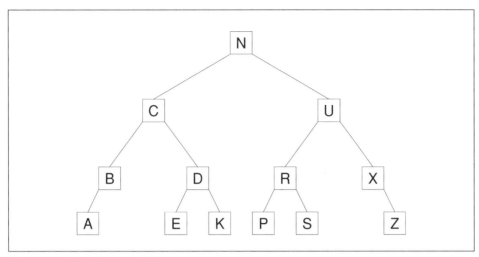

**Diagram 13-9. A balanced binary tree**

Diagram 13-9 shows the keys inserted in the order NCUBADEKRPSXZ. N is a good root value, because it is near the median value of all keys. C was a bad root value, because it tended toward one end of the range of values.

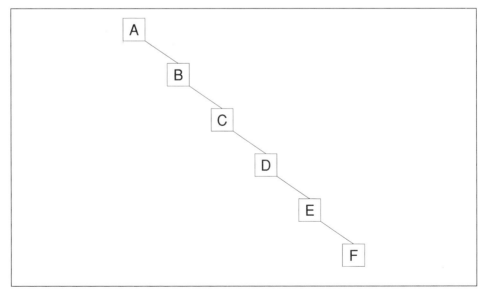

**Diagram 13-10. A degenerate binary tree.**

Diagram 13-10 shows a binary tree generated from the keys A, B, C, D, E, and F. Because each subsequent node is greater than its predecessor, the binary tree degenerates into a linked list. A search on a linked list is very inefficient, and all benefits of a binary tree are lost.

Sorted and almost-sorted data is common, and, as with QuickSort, computer scientists have developed several schemes for lessening the impact of sorted data. Balancing and nearly-balancing binary trees requires sophisticated rearrangement of the tree as nodes are added and deleted. AVL-Tree uses rotations to adjust the tree after insertions and deletions; red-black trees use a marking technique to ensure that portions of the tree do not become massively imbalanced with other parts of the tree. All of these tree-balancing algorithms build upon the basic binary-tree structure.

The goal of this chapter is to introduce tree structures for file handling. In this context, binary trees are not a good choice because they include too many levels. The number of times data must be read from an external file determines the efficiency of any file-indexing scheme. The goal is to minimize the number of records which must be read from the index file while searching for a key.

A balanced binary tree containing a thousand keys has ten levels; a tree containing ten thousand nodes contains fourteen levels. Unbalanced trees are still "deeper." Nodes could be stored as individual records, but several records would need to be read during a key search. Paging schemes that store more than one node per record work well — until you change the tree and need to move nodes between pages.

Keeping the binary tree in memory eliminates the need to read key data from an external file; this was the solution I used with the hash-file classes in the last chapter. The drawback to keeping the tree in memory is just that: it uses memory. In an ideal situation, an index should be stored in a file on disk, where it avoids using internal memory. The file would be organized such that reading would be kept to a minimum.

When using a tree as an index, what is needed is a structure that keeps itself balanced, holds more than one key per page, and is easy to reorganize. A brilliant algorithm for manipulating just this type of tree was invented in 1972 by R. Bayer and E. McCreight. These structures are known as B-trees, and they have become the foundation of nearly every database product on the market today. This book culminates with Chapter 14's discussion of BTrees as they apply to file indexing.

# Indexing Files with BTrees

Binary trees, which were the subject matter of the previous chapter, are very useful in many contexts. However, they fail to provide a solution to indexing files. Binary trees can easily become unbalanced, and even a balanced binary tree is too "high" for practical use on large files. Balancing techniques and paged binary files improve the situation, but only slightly.

What we need is a tree structure that stores many keys in a few records, and which automatically maintains its balance. That type of tree is known as a BTree.

## 14.1 Properties of BTrees

BTrees were invented and introduced by R. Bayer and E. McCreight in a 1972 paper named "Organization and Maintenance of Larger Order Indexes." Within a very few years, BTrees were synonymous with file handling; nearly every major database system, from ISAM to dBASE, now uses BTrees.

As I discussed at the end of Chapter 13, a binary tree's problems stem from the way in which it is constructed. We begin with a root and build downward from there; if the root key is a bad one, such that most subsequent keys are greater or less than the root, the tree becomes unbalanced. Various algorithms can then come into play to rebalance the tree — in other words, fixing the problem after it's occurred.

Bayer and McCreight solved the binary tree's problems by looking at the problem from a new perspective. They decided to build a tree structure from the bottom up, letting the root emerge as keys are added. To reduce the number of nodes in the tree, they decided to store more than one key per node. Apparently, Bayer and McCreight named their creation a BTree because it sounded appropriate.

| C | | | |
|---|---|---|---|

a new root containing one key

**Diagram 14-1. A BTree page.**

Diagram 14-1 shows a BTree node, known as a *page*. Each page contains a set of keys and a set of pointers (also called links) to other pages. The keys are stored in an ordered sequential list. There is always one more pointer than there are keys, and the maximum number of pointers in a page is known as the BTree's *order*. Diagram 14-2 shows a BTree page of order 5. The pointer to the left of a key points to a subtree that contains all lessor keys. The key to the right points to a subtree containing all greater keys.

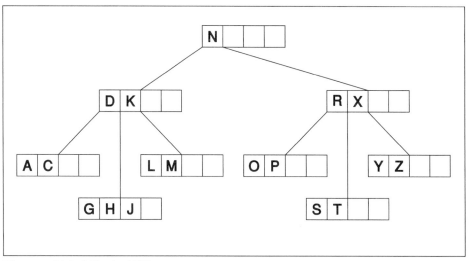

**Diagram 14-2. A Typical BTree.**

Diagram 14-2 shows a BTree of order 5, in which the single-letter keys CAKRMGOTDXSLJZNPW have been inserted.

BTrees follow these rules:

1. A BTree consists of pages that contain *order* links and *order - 1* keys.
2. The keys are stored in sequential lists.
3. Every page has a maximum number of *order* descendants.
4. All leaf pages are the same number of links away from the root.
5. With the exception of the root and leaf pages, every page has at least *order / 2* links.
6. The root has at least one key and two links, unless it is also a leaf page.
7. A leaf page has at least *order / 2 - 1* keys.
8. New keys are added only to leaf pages.

The construction of this tree is described in section 14.1.2; however, let's first look at searching a BTree for a given key.

### 14.1.1 Searching

To describe searching, I'll use these terms: the s*earch key* is the key being sought, and the *page key* is a key in a page. The search key is compared against page keys until a match is found or the end of the tree is reached.

Searching a page entails sequentially comparing page keys with the search key. The algorithm's action depends upon the relationship of the search key and the page key.

1. If a match is found, the search has been successful.
2. If the page key is less than the search key, we move to the next key in the page. If the algorithm has reached the last key in the page, it follows the rightmost link to a page that contains greater keys.
3. If the page key is greater than the search key, we can move to a new page by following the link to a page containing keys less than the page key.
4. In cases 2 and 3, the algorithm may find that the link it wishes to follow does not connect to another page, indicating that the search is in a leaf page. When this happens, the algorithm has failed to find the search key, because there are no more pages to search.

To search the entire tree, begin by examining the first key in the root page. The search routine can be called recursively when the algorithm moves to a new page.

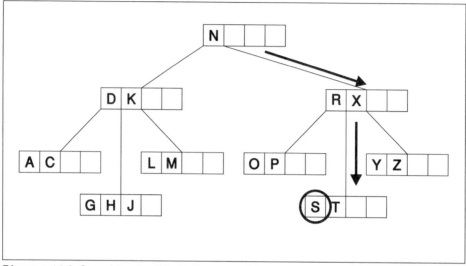

**Diagram 14-3. Searching for S (which succeeds).**

Diagram 14-3 shows the process followed in looking for some keys in the BTree shown in Diagram 14-2. Here are the steps involved in looking for the key S:

1.  We begin at the root page. S is greater than the first root key, N. N is the only key in the root page, so we follow the link to the pages which contain keys greater than N.
2.  The next page contains the keys R and X. S is between R and X, so we follow the middle link to the next page.
3.  The first key in the page matches S — and we're done!

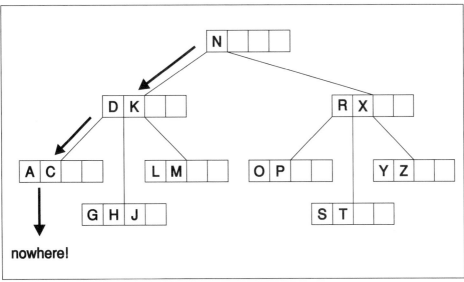

**Diagram 14-4. Searching for B (which fails).**

Diagram 14-4 shows how looking for the B leads us down a different path:

1. B is less than the root key N, so we move to the page that contains keys less than N.
2. B is less than D, so we move to a new page.
3. B is between A and C, but this is a leaf page, so we can't go any farther. B was not found.

### 14.1.2 Insertion

To demonstrate key insertion, I'll use an order-5 BTree. Each page can contain up to five links and four keys.

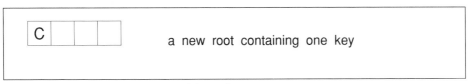

**Diagram 14-5 . A new root page, with one key.**

Inserting the first key into a BTree is simple; it becomes the only key in a new root page. Note that the root page begins existence as a leaf page. Diagram 14-5 shows a new root containing a single key, C.

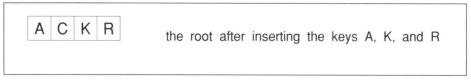

the root after inserting the keys A, K, and R

**Diagram 14-6 . A full root page.**

The root page is full after inserting the three keys AKR. Diagram 14-6 shows the full root page.

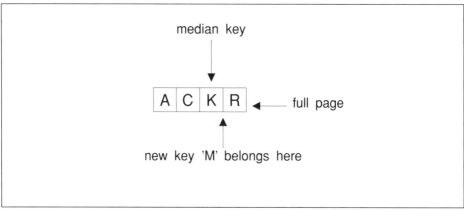

**Diagram 14-7. Identifying the components when a page splits.**

Inserting the next key, M, forces changes in the tree structure. Were there enough key slots in the page, M would be inserted between K and R. Because there isn't an open slot, we need to add pages to the tree.

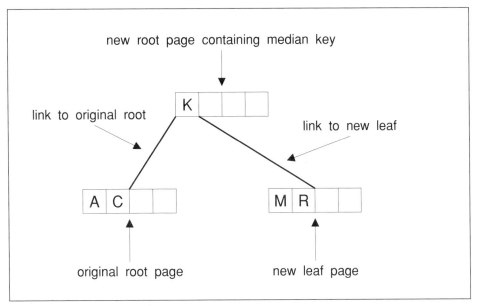

**Diagram 14-8. Splitting and Promotion.**

For the purpose of making the algorithm simpler, let's assume that we can "squeeze" M in between K and R. We then *split* the page by creating a new page and distributing the keys between it and the original page. The keys A and C remain in the original page, and the keys M and R move into the new page. The median (middle) key K is then *promoted* to separate the original page and its new sibling. Because the original page was the root, K becomes the sole key in a new root, increasing the height of the tree by one level. Diagram 14-8 shows the result of this process.

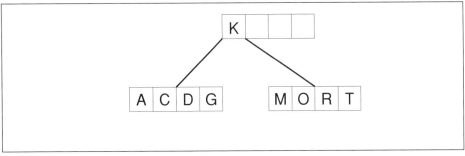

**Diagram 14-9. Adding a few more keys.**

After adding the keys MGDT, both leaf pages are full. Diagram 14-9 shows the tree just before the key H is inserted.

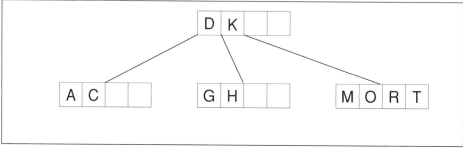

**Diagram 14-10. Splitting and promoting a key into a parent page.**

When a non-root page is split, it promotes its median key into its parent. Thus, the page containing ACDG splits, creating two pages with the keys AC and GH, respectively. The median key D is promoted into the parent page (which is also the root). Diagram 14-10 shows the result of this split and promotion.

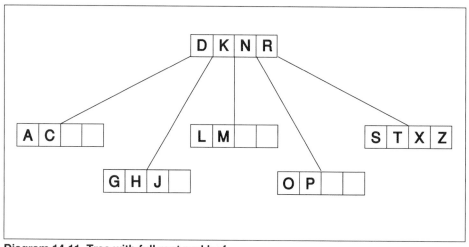

**Diagram 14-11. Tree with full root and leaf.**

When a key is promoted, it will cause a full parent page to split and promote, too. This chain reaction broadens the base of the tree by splitting, and it pushes the root up by promotion. Diagram 14-11 shows that, after adding the keys OXSLJZNP to the tree, the root page has become full through promotions.

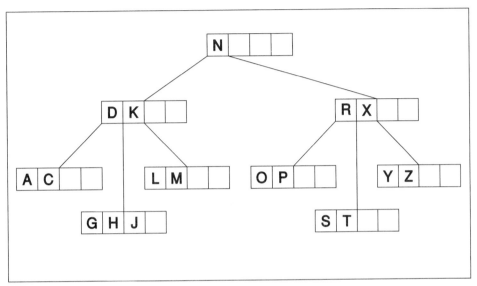

**Diagram 14-12. The tree after inserting Y.**

Adding the key Z splits a leaf node and promotes the key X into the root. Because the root is full, it too splits. A new root is generated, and the height of the tree is uniformly increased by one level.

This algorithm guarantees that insertions do not cause the tree to become unbalanced, and that the internal nodes always have at least *order/2* keys. In the tree above, 17 keys were stored in 9 pages. Assuming that each page is stored as a record in a file, no more than three records must be read from the file to find any key.

### 14.1.3 Deletion

When I embarked upon creating my own BTree class library, I encountered a significant problem: A general lack of documentation on the *deletion* of keys! Most references explain insertion and searching in depth, but when they come to deletion they give vague excuses about complexity. The implementation of BTree key deletion is often given as a "reader exercise."

Deleting a key isn't very difficult, once you realize that it involves three major actions that are implemented for a variety of tree configurations. When deleting a key, one must maintain the rules of a BTree as set forth above. This involves the following process:

1.  Search the tree for the key to be deleted. We'll presume that the key is found.
2.  If the key is in the root or an internal page, replace the key with its immediate successor, deleting the successor from the leaf. If the key is found in a leaf page, simply remove it.
3.  A page has now shrunk by one key entry. This may reduce the number of keys in the page below *order / 2*. If so, we must reorganize the tree.
4.  If the leaf page has a sibling with more that *order / 2* keys, we simply redistribute keys among the sibling, its parent, and the leaf page.
5.  If the page's siblings have only *order /2 keys*, then we concatenate the page and a sibling. The key in the parent page that separates the deletion page and its sibling is demoted into the combined page. If demoting a key from the parent reduces the parent below *order / 2* keys, we process the parent page beginning at step 4. This recursive process continues until we reach a parent node that has more than *order / 2* keys, or we can redistribute rather than concatenate.

It is possible that the concatenations and demotions will remove the only key from a single-key node, thus reducing the height of the tree by one level.

In essence, deleting a key from the tree involves the reverse of an insertion. Where insertion splits nodes and promotes keys, deletion concatenates nodes and demotes keys. Where insertions can increase the height of the tree by splitting the root page, deletion can reduce the height of the tree by concatenating two sibling pages and demoting the only key out of the root page.

I couldn't draw any diagrams that made the deletion process easier to visualize. Review the code that follows; it should clarify how the deletion process works.

### 14.1.4 Implementation

A compromise must be struck between the size of a tree's pages and its height. The larger the order, the shorter the tree — which reduces the number of pages that must be read to find a key. However, larger pages require longer sequential searches for keys in each page. A tree with order 500, for example, will store a million keys in three levels, while a tree with order 10 will require six levels of pages. In general, because reading data from disk is vastly slower than sequentially searching a list of in-memory keys, the page size should be made as large as possible.

To use a BTree as an index, each key must be associated with a pointer to a data record. In my implementation, I decided to implement a BTree-indexed file using two physical disk files. One file contains the BTree pages, and the other contains the data records. After I write a record to the data file, I pass its key and its file pointer to the routine that inserts the information into the BTree.

Until now, the file types described in this book have stored variable-length records. A list of deleted records is kept, and when a new record is written to the file, the empty records are scanned to see if any of them are large enough to contain the new record. When a variable-length record is changed, it may become larger, and it may not be written into the same position it originally occupied. This scheme works well for data records, because they often vary a great deal in length.

A file that contains BTree pages has different requirements. Because pages have links to other pages, it makes algorithms simpler to implement if pages are treated as fixed-length records stored in a fixed location. This requires a file that contains a fixed-length record, and which stores a modified record in the same location from which it was read. Because pages are sometimes deleted from the tree when keys are deleted, the page file needs to keep a list of deleted records for use by newly generated pages.

I decided to use *Strings* as keys. Although other data types are often used to identify data records, most indexing is performed on databases where we need to look up a record using a text string. It should not be difficult to implement a broader-based key type based on the code below; in fact, my personal library implements a system whereby almost any data type can be a key. However, to maintain simplicity, I've limited this book to *String* keys.

In implementing BTrees, I created five classes. The *BTreeErrorBase* class implements the same system of error reporting that I introduced in earlier chapters. A fixed-length string data type is needed for the pages, to keep the pages fixed in length. Because *Strings* and *KeyString* classes do not control the length of text data,

I created the *PageKey* class specifically for string BTree keys. The *Page* class defines a page, and the *PageFile* class implements a file type specific to storing pages. The *BTreeFile* class contains a *PageFile* that stores pages which index the records in a *DataFile*.

## 14.2 The BTreeErrorBase Class

Yes, here it is again — yet another base class that provides a common error-reporting mechanism for a group of related classes.

```
enum BTreeError
    {
    BTE_ALLOC,      // fatal: memory allocation failure
    BTE_TOOSMALL,   // fatal: created bucket w/ zero buckets
    BTE_CORRUPTED   // fatal: table / list has been corrupted
    };

class BTreeErrorBase
    {
    public:
        static void SetErrOut(const ErrReporter & er);

    protected:
        static ErrReporter * ErrOut;

        static void ReportError(BTreeError err);
    };
```

The BTreeErrorBase functions are implemented as follows:

```
ErrReporter * BTreeErrorBase::ErrOut = NULL;

void BTreeErrorBase::ReportError(BTreeError err)
    {
    if (ErrOut != NULL)
        {
        switch (err)
            {
            case BTE_ALLOC:
```

```
                ErrOut->Fatal("memory allocation failure");
                break;

            case BTE_TOOSMALL:
                ErrOut->Fatal("cannot create zero-size
table");
                break;

            case BTE_CORRUPTED:
                ErrOut->Fatal("corrupted");
                break;

            default:
                ErrOut->Fatal("unknown");
                break;
            }
        }
    }

void BTreeErrorBase::SetErrOut(const ErrReporter & er)
    {
    if (ErrOut != NULL)
        delete ErrOut;

    ErrOut = new ErrReporter(er);
    }
```

## 14.3 The PageKey Class

Pages contain string keys, and those strings must have a fixed maximum length
in order for the pages to have a fixed size. I created the *PageKey* class to implement
this type of string. While I could have derived *PageKey* from *String*, that would have
endowed *PageKey* with an overhead for capabilities that it simply doesn't need.

```
    class PageKey : public BTreeErrorBase
        {
        public:
            // constructors
            PageKey();
            PageKey(size_t maxlen, const char * str);
```

```
        PageKey(size_t maxlen, const String & str);
        PageKey(const PageKey & pgkey);

        // destructor
        ~PageKey();

        // assignment
        void operator = (const PageKey & pgkey);

        // interrogation
        size_t GetMax() const;
        size_t GetLen() const;

        // get pointer
        operator const char * () const;

        // is this an "empty" key?
        Boolean IsEmpty() const;

        // compare two keys
        int Compare(const PageKey & pgkey);
    private:
        char * Txt; // pointer to buffer containing text
        size_t Len; // number of characters in Txt
        size_t Max; // maximum # of characters in Txt
    };
```

The *Txt* data member points to a dynamically allocated buffer containing the string. *Len* is the number of characters in the string, and *Max* contains the maximum number of characters in *Len*.

*PageKey* does not implement functions for manipulating, searching, or otherwise changing text. A key's value is set when it is created; a manipulable string can be created from it, but the key itself cannot be changed. A key identifies a specific piece of data, and that identification should not require editing.

The *String* and *const char* * constructors create a new *PageKey* object. The maximum length must be supplied so that *Max* can be set and the incoming text can be truncated if it is too long.

```
PageKey::PageKey(size_t maxlen, const char * str)
    {
    Max = maxlen;

    // allocate buffer
    Txt = new char [Max];

    if (Txt == NULL)
        ReportError(BTE_ALLOC);

    // copy string
    strncpy(Txt,str,Max);

    // make sure there's a terminating NULL
    Txt[Max - 1] = 0;

    Len = strlen(Txt);
    }

PageKey::PageKey(size_t maxlen, const String & str)
    {
    Max = maxlen;

    // allocate buffer
    Txt = new char [Max];

    if (Txt == NULL)
        ReportError(BTE_ALLOC);

    // copy string
    strncpy(Txt,(const char *)str,Max);

    // make sure there's a terminating NULL
    Txt[Max - 1] = 0;

    Len = strlen(Txt);
    }
```

The copy constructor creates a new *PageKey* from an existing one.

**443**

```
PageKey::PageKey(const PageKey & pgkey)
    {
    Max = pgkey.Max;
    Len = pgkey.Len;

    if (pgkey.Txt == NULL)
        Txt = NULL;
    else
        {
        // allocate buffer
        Txt = new char [Max];

        if (Txt == NULL)
            ReportError(BTE_ALLOC);

        // copy string
        strcpy(Txt,pgkey.Txt);
        }
    }
```

The default constructor creates an empty *String*; I created this constructor to simplify some algorithms, where a duplicate of an existing key needs to be made.

```
// constructors
PageKey::PageKey()
    {
    Max = 0;
    Len = 0;
    Txt = NULL;
    }
```

The destructor deletes the buffer pointed to by *Txt*.

```
// destructor
PageKey::~PageKey()
    {
    if (Txt != NULL)
        delete [] Txt;
    }
```

To assign the value of one key to another, use the assignment operator.

```
// assignment
void PageKey::operator = (const PageKey & pgkey)
    {
    // delete existing buffer
    if (Txt != NULL)
        delete [] Txt;

    // assign values
    Max = pgkey.Max;
    Len = pgkey.Len;

    if (pgkey.Txt == NULL)
        Txt = NULL;
    else
        {
        // allocate buffer
        Txt = new char [Max];

        if (Txt == NULL)
            ReportError(BTE_ALLOC);

        // copy string
        strcpy(Txt,pgkey.Txt);
        }
    }
```

The *const char* * conversion returns a constant pointer to *Txt*. The *GetMax* and *GetLen* function interrogate a *PageKey* for its *Max* and *Len* members, respectively. *IsEmpty* returns *BOOL_FALSE* if the *PageKey* contains text, and *BOOL_TRUE* if the *Txt* member is *NULL*.

```
// interrogation
inline size_t PageKey::GetMax() const
    {
    return Max;
    }
```

**445**

```
inline size_t PageKey::GetLen() const
    {
    return Len;
    }

// get pointer
inline PageKey::operator const char * () const
    {
    return Txt;
    }

// is this an "empty" key?
inline Boolean PageKey::IsEmpty() const
    {
    if (Txt == NULL)
        return BOOL_TRUE;
    else
        return BOOL_FALSE;
    }
```

In the *String* class, the *Compare* function was implemented to return an enumerated value that indicated the relationship of two strings. The *PageKey::Compare* function was implemented to return the result of a call to the ANSI function *strcmp*. As you'll see later in the chapter, this simplified the *BTreeFile::Search* function.

```
// compare two keys
inline int PageKey::Compare(const PageKey & pgkey)
    {
    return strcmp(Txt,pgkey.Txt);
    }
```

## 14.4 The Page Class

The *Page* structure defines a single page in a BTree. I defined it as a structure to simplify manipulation of its contents. Implementing *Page* as a class, with its data members private, would have required a mass of function that allowed changes to those members — eliminating any value in making them private in the first place!

```
struct Page : private BTreeErrorBase
    {
    PageHeader    Hdr; // header information
    PageKey     * Key; // key array [MaxKeys]
    DataFilePtr * Ptr; // rec  index array [MaxKeys]
    PageFilePtr * Lnk; // page index array [Order]

    // construct a new, empty page
    Page(size_t ord, size_t ksize);

    // construct a copy of a page
    Page(const Page & p);

    // destructor
    ~Page();

    // assignment operator
    void operator = (const Page & page);
    };
```

The parameters defining the *Page* are contained in a header. The *Hdr* record simplifies writing the page to a file, as you'll see in the implementation of the *PageFile* class.

```
struct PageHeader
    {
    PageFilePtr FilePtr;   // ptr to location in PageFile
    PageFilePtr ParentPtr; // ptr to parent in PageFile

    size_t      Order;     // maximum # of page links in page
    size_t      MaxKeys;   // maximum # of keys in page
    size_t      MinKeys;   // minimum # of keys in page
    size_t      NoOfKeys;  // actual  # of keys in page
    size_t      KeySize;   // maximum # of characters in a key
    };
```

In the header, *Order* is the order of the tree, *KeySize* is the maximum length of the keys it contains, *NoOfKeys* is the number of keys currently stored in a *Page*,

*MaxKeys* is the maximum number of keys the *Page* can hold, and *MinKeys* is the minimum number of keys allowed in an internal *Page*. The file pointer of a *Page*'s parent is stored in its *ParentPtr* member, and *FilePtr* contains the location in the *PageFile* where a *Page* is stored.

The *PageFilePtr* type defines a file pointer that locates a position within a *PageFile*. It serves the same function with *PageFiles* that *DataFilePtr* serves for *DataFiles*.

```
typedef long PageFilePtr;
```

The *Key*, *Ptr*, and *Lnk* members point to dynamically allocated arrays of *PageKeys*, *DataFilePtrs*, and *PageFilePtrs*.

The constructor's parameters define the order and key size for a new *Page*. Other header values are calculated from the order. A new *Page* is always empty; it has no parent, no children, and it does not contain any keys or links.

```
// create a new page
Page::Page(size_t ord, size_t ksize)
    {
    size_t n;

    Hdr.FilePtr   = PFP_NULL;
    Hdr.ParentPtr = PFP_NULL;
    Hdr.Order     = ord;
    Hdr.MaxKeys   = ord - 1;
    Hdr.MinKeys   = ord / 2;
    Hdr.NoOfKeys  = 0;
    Hdr.KeySize   = ksize;

    if (Hdr.Order == 0)
        {
        Key = NULL;
        Ptr = NULL;
        Lnk = NULL;

        return;
        }
```

```
// allocate key array
Key = new PageKey [Hdr.MaxKeys];

if (Key == NULL)
    ReportError(BTE_ALLOC);

// allocate record pointer array
Ptr = new DataFilePtr [Hdr.MaxKeys];

if (Ptr == NULL)
    ReportError(BTE_ALLOC);

// set pointers to nothing
for (n = 0; n < Hdr.MaxKeys; ++n)
    Ptr[n] = DFP_ERROR;

// allocate page pointer array
Lnk = new PageFilePtr [Hdr.Order];

if (Lnk == NULL)
    ReportError(BTE_ALLOC);

/// fill page indexes with "empty" values
for (n = 0; n < Hdr.Order; ++n)
    Lnk[n] = PFP_NULL;
}
```

The copy constructor creates a new page from an existing one.

```
Page::Page(const Page & pg)
    {
    Hdr = pg.Hdr;

    // allocate key array
    Key = new PageKey [Hdr.MaxKeys];

    if (Key == NULL)
        ReportError(BTE_ALLOC);

    for (size_t n = 0; n < Hdr.MaxKeys; ++n)
```

```
        Key[n] = pg.Key[n];

    // allocate record pointer array
    Ptr = new DataFilePtr [Hdr.MaxKeys];

    if (Ptr == NULL)
        ReportError(BTE_ALLOC);

    memcpy(Ptr,pg.Ptr,
            Hdr.MaxKeys * sizeof(DataFilePtr));

    // allocate page pointer array
    Lnk = new PageFilePtr [Hdr.Order];

    if (Lnk == NULL)
        ReportError(BTE_ALLOC);

    // fill page indexes with source values
    memcpy(Lnk,pg.Lnk,
            Hdr.Order * sizeof(PageFilePtr));
    }
```

The destructor deletes the *Key*, *Ptr*, and *Lnk* arrays when a *Page* object is destroyed.

```
    Page::~Page()
        {
        // delete old buffers
        delete [] Key;
        delete [] Ptr;
        delete [] Lnk;
        }
```

The assignment operator copies the contents of one *Page* to another. It copies the source *Page*'s header, deletes the existing buffers (if they have been allocated), allocates new buffers, and copies the contents of the source buffers.

```
void Page::operator = (const Page & pg)
    {
    Hdr = pg.Hdr;

    // allocate key array
    if (Key != NULL)
        delete [] Key;

    Key = new PageKey [Hdr.MaxKeys];

    if (Key == NULL)
        ReportError(BTE_ALLOC);

    for (size_t n = 0; n < Hdr.MaxKeys; ++n)
        Key[n] = pg.Key[n];

    // allocate record pointer array
    if (Ptr != NULL)
        delete [] Ptr;

    Ptr = new DataFilePtr [Hdr.MaxKeys];

    if (Ptr == NULL)
        ReportError(BTE_ALLOC);

    memcpy(Ptr,pg.Ptr,
           Hdr.MaxKeys * sizeof(DataFilePtr));

    // allocate page pointer array
    if (Lnk != NULL)
        delete [] Lnk;

    Lnk = new PageFilePtr [Hdr.Order];

    if (Lnk == NULL)
        ReportError(BTE_ALLOC);

    // fill page indexes with source values
    memcpy(Lnk,pg.Lnk,
           Hdr.Order * sizeof(PageFilePtr));
    }
```

## 14.5 The PageFile Class

A *PageFile* is a file type specifically optimized for storing BTree *Page* objects. *PageFile* is based on the the *DataFileBase* class, and it has some similarities to the *DataFile* class (see Chapter 12).

```
class PageFile : public DataFileBase
    {
    public:
        // use existing page file
        PageFile(const String & name);

        // create new page file
        PageFile(const String & name,
                        size_t   ord,
                        size_t   ksize);

        // destructor
        ~PageFile();

        // get root page
        Boolean ReadRoot(Page & pg);

        // write a page
        Boolean Write(Page & pg, Boolean root = BOOL_FALSE);

        // read a page
        Boolean Read(PageFilePtr ptr, Page & pg);

        // delete a page
        Boolean Delete(PageFilePtr ptr);

        // commit data & header
        Boolean Flush();

    private:
        // header record
        PageFileHdr Hdr;
    };
```

A *PageFile* defines a single data member, *Hdr*, which is a file header containing format information. *Hdr* is a *PageFileHdr* structure.

```
struct PageFileHdr
    {
    size_t KeySize;
    size_t Order;

    PageFilePtr RootPtr;
    PageFilePtr FirstDead;
    };
```

The *PageFile* header stores the order of pages stored in the file, the maximum size of a key, a file pointer to the root page, and a file pointer to the first deleted record. All pages stored in a given *PageFile* have the same order and page size, allowing a *PageFile* to treat *Pages* as fixed-length records.

*PageFiles* maintain a list of deleted records, using the techniques demonstrated by the *DataFile* class in Chapter 12. When a *Page* is deleted, it is placed at the head of the list by storing the current *Hdr.FirstDead* value in the record and placing the file pointer of the deleted record in *Hdr.FirstDead*.

A new *PageFile* is constructed by providing a filename, order, and maximum key size.

```
PageFile::PageFile(const String & name,
                         size_t   ord,
                         size_t   ksize)
    : DataFileBase(name,FM_NEW)
    {
    Hdr.Order     = ord;
    Hdr.KeySize   = ksize;
    Hdr.RootPtr   = PFP_NULL;
    Hdr.FirstDead = PFP_NULL;

    size_t n = fwrite(&Hdr,sizeof(PageFileHdr),1,Data);

    if (n == 0)
```

```
        ReportError("unable to create header in new page file");

// create Root page
Page root(Hdr.Order,Hdr.KeySize);

// store root
Write(root);

// save root address
Hdr.RootPtr = root.Hdr.FilePtr;
}
```

An existing *PageFile* can be opened by simply constructing a *PageFile* object with a name. The order and key-size information are retrieved from the file header.

```
PageFile::PageFile(const String & name)
    : DataFileBase(name,FM_EXISTING)
    {
    size_t n;

    n = fread(&Hdr,sizeof(PageFileHdr),1,Data);

    if (n == 0)
        ReportError("unable to create header in new page file");
    }
```

The destructor simply calls *Flush* to make certain that the header record has been updated before the *PageFile* is closed.

```
inline PageFile::~PageFile()
    {
    Flush();
    }
```

A *Page* is the only type of data that can be stored in a *PageFile*. The *Write* function has two parameters: *pg*, a reference to a page being written, and *root*, a *Boolean* value indicating that a new root page is being written. The default value of *root* is *BOOL_FALSE*; a program does not generate new roots as often as it creates internal and leaf pages.

```
Boolean PageFile::Write(Page & pg, Boolean root)
    {
    size_t n;
    int res;

    // confirm that this page belongs in this file
    if ((Hdr.Order    != pg.Hdr.Order)
    || (Hdr.KeySize != pg.Hdr.KeySize))
        return BOOL_FALSE;

    // if this page has never been written
    // find a spot to write it
    if (pg.Hdr.FilePtr == PFP_NULL)
        {
        if (Hdr.FirstDead != PFP_NULL)
            {
            // write this record to first dead one in list
            pg.Hdr.FilePtr = Hdr.FirstDead;

            // find record where the new page will be written
            res = fseek(Data,Hdr.FirstDead,SEEK_SET);

            if (res)
                return BOOL_FALSE;

            // set first dead to next dead record in list
            n = fread(&Hdr.FirstDead,sizeof(PageFilePtr),1,Data);

            if (n == 0)
                return BOOL_FALSE;
            }
        else // append to end of file!
            {
            // look for end of file
            res = fseek(Data,0,SEEK_END);

            if (res)
```

```
                    return BOOL_FALSE;

            // and get a pointer to it
            pg.Hdr.FilePtr = ftell(Data);
            }
        }

    // construct block of memory
    size_t keysize = (pg.Hdr.MaxKeys * Hdr.KeySize);
    size_t ptrsize = (pg.Hdr.MaxKeys * sizeof(DataFilePtr));
    size_t lnksize = (pg.Hdr.Order   * sizeof(PageFilePtr));

    size_t bufsize = sizeof(PageHeader)
                        + keysize + ptrsize + lnksize;

    char * buffer = new char [bufsize];

    if (buffer == NULL)
        return BOOL_FALSE;

    char * bufptr = buffer;

    // copy page header to buffer
    memcpy(bufptr,&pg.Hdr,sizeof(PageHeader));

    bufptr += sizeof(PageHeader);

    memset(bufptr,0,keysize);

    // copy keys to buffer
    for (n = 0; n < pg.Hdr.MaxKeys; ++n)
        {
        if (!pg.Key[n].IsEmpty())
            strcpy(bufptr,(const char *)(pg.Key[n]));

        bufptr += Hdr.KeySize;
        }

    // copy data record pointers
    memcpy(bufptr,pg.Ptr,ptrsize);
```

```
    bufptr += ptrsize;

    // copy page links
    memcpy(bufptr,pg.Lnk,lnksize);

    // write buffer to file
    res = fseek(Data,pg.Hdr.FilePtr,SEEK_SET);

    if (res)
        return BOOL_FALSE;

    n = fwrite(buffer,bufsize,1,Data);

    if (n == 0)
        return BOOL_FALSE;

    // delete buffer
    delete [] buffer;

    // update root pointer in header, if this is a new root
    if (root)
        Hdr.RootPtr = pg.Hdr.FilePtr;

    // make sure header is current
    Flush();

    return BOOL_TRUE;
    }
```

*Write* begins by comparing the order and key size stored in its header with the order and key size of the page being written. If these values don't match, the page is rejected and *Write* returns *BOOL_FALSE*. This ensures that the *PageFile* contains only pages with identical orders and key sizes.

If the *Page* being written has an assigned file pointer in its *Hdr.FilePtr* member, *Write* stores the *Page* in its original location. If *Hdr.FilePtr* is empty (indicated by a *PFP_NULL* value), *Write* checks the deleted list to see if any "dead" records are available. If the deleted record list contains an entry, the new *Page* is written into the first deleted record. Otherwise, the new *Page* is appended to the file. If the *Page* has a *Hdr.FilePtr* value of *PFP_NULL*, *Hdr.FilePtr* is set to the location where the *Page* was written before it is stored.

*Pages* are written using a simple technique. The *Page Hdr* value is written first. Next, the keys are written as a fixed-length block, with NUL characters filling the trailing space in each key. Then, the arrays pointed to by *Ptr* and *Lnk* are written.

The *Read* function differs in many respects from the *Read* function in *DataFile*. Where *DataFile::Read* reads a *DataBlock* from the current position in a file, the *PageFile::Read* function obtains a *Page* from a file location specified by the parameter *ptr*. *PageFile* does not implement a *Seek* function. Each page contains explicit links to other pages, and pages are directly accessed using those links.

*DataFile::Delete* returns a *DataBlock*; if an error occurs, it returns a null *DataBlock*. *PageFile::Read* returns a *Boolean* success value, and it stores the retrieved data in a *Page* referenced by the parameter *pg*.

```
Boolean PageFile::Read(PageFilePtr ptr, Page & pg)
    {
    size_t n;
    int    res;

    // locate requested record
    res = fseek(Data,ptr,SEEK_SET);

    if (res)
        return BOOL_FALSE;

    // create a blank page
    Page temp(Hdr.Order,Hdr.KeySize);

    n = fread(&temp.Hdr,sizeof(PageHeader),1,Data);

    // be sure that this header matches the expected values
    if ((n == 0)
    || (temp.Hdr.Order   != Hdr.Order)
    || (temp.Hdr.KeySize != Hdr.KeySize)
    || (temp.Hdr.FilePtr != ptr))
        return BOOL_FALSE;
```

```
// allocate a buffer to hold incoming keys
size_t bufsize = temp.Hdr.KeySize * temp.Hdr.MaxKeys;

char * buffer = new char [bufsize];

if (buffer == NULL)
    return BOOL_FALSE;

// read keys from file
n = fread(buffer,bufsize,1,Data);

if (n == 0)
    return BOOL_FALSE;

char * bufptr = buffer;

// move keys into page
for (n = 0; n < temp.Hdr.MaxKeys; ++n)
    {
    if (*bufptr == 0)
        temp.Key[n] = PageKey();
    else
        temp.Key[n] = PageKey(temp.Hdr.KeySize,bufptr);

    bufptr += temp.Hdr.KeySize;
    }

// read data record pointers
n = fread(temp.Ptr,temp.Hdr.MaxKeys *
                        sizeof(DataFilePtr),1,Data);

if (n == 0)
    return BOOL_FALSE;

// read page links
n = fread(temp.Lnk,temp.Hdr.Order *
                        sizeof(PageFilePtr),1,Data);

if (n == 0)
    return BOOL_FALSE;
```

```
pg = temp;

return BOOL_TRUE;
}
```

*Read* checks the data read from the file to be sure that the *Order* and *KeySize* values in the *Page*'s header match the corresponding values in the *PageFile*'s header

To read the root record, use the *ReadRoot* function. It is a simple inline function that returns the result of calling *Read* with an argument of *Hdr.RootPtr*.

```
inline Boolean PageFile::ReadRoot(Page & pg)
    {
    return Read(Hdr.RootPtr, pg);
    }
```

*Delete* removes a *Page* from a *PageFile* by marking its record as deleted. The newly deleted record's location in the file becomes the *FirstDead* value in the header, and the previous value of *FirstDead* is stored in the first few bytes of the deleted record. This maintains a linked list of deleted records that can be reused by the *Write* function.

```
Boolean PageFile::Delete(PageFilePtr ptr)
    {
    // locate record to be deleted
    int res = fseek(Data,ptr,SEEK_SET);

    if (res)
        return BOOL_FALSE;

    // stored the previous head of the deleted list
    size_t n = fwrite(&Hdr.FirstDead,sizeof(PageFilePtr),1,Data);

    if (n == 0)
        return BOOL_FALSE;

    // update header
    Hdr.FirstDead = ptr;
```

```
Flush();

return BOOL_TRUE;
}
```

*Flush* updates the file header on disk from the *Hdr* data member.

```
Boolean PageFile::Flush()
    {
    // rewrite header
    rewind(Data);

    size_t n = fwrite(&Hdr,sizeof(PageFileHdr),1,Data);

    if (n == 0)
        return BOOL_FALSE;

    // empty any internal buffers (which there shouldn't be!)
    fflush(Data);

    return BOOL_TRUE;
    }
```

## 14.6 BTreeFile class

Now we get to the meat: the *BTreeFile* class. A *BTreeFile* has a *PageFile* object for storing *Pages* and a *DataFile* object for storing *DataBlocks*. When a *DataBlock* is stored in a *BTreeFile*, it is associated with a key in the *PageFile*. To find a record, a key is used to retrieve the *DataFilePtr* of its *DataBlock* from a *Page* in the *PageFile*.

```
class BTreeFile : private BTreeErrorBase
    {
    public:
        // constructors
        // use existing files
        BTreeFile(const String & basename);
```

```
        // create new files
        BTreeFile(const String & basename,
                          size_t ord,
                          size_t ksize);

        // copy constructor
        BTreeFile(const BTreeFile & btfile);

        // destructor
        ~BTreeFile();

        // write a record
        Boolean Write(const PageKey & key,
                    const DataBlock & db);

        // read a record
        DataBlock Read(const PageKey & key);

        // delete a record
        Boolean Delete(const PageKey & key);

        // enumerate all records
        void InOrder(BTreeEnumFunc func);

    private:
        // data members
        DataFile * Data; // file containing DataBlocks
        PageFile * Tree; // file containing tree pages

        Page        Root; // root page (always in memory)

        String      DataFileName; // name of data file
        String      TreeFileName; // name of tree file

        BTreeEnumFunc EnumFunc; // function called by Traverse

        // search for a node
        Boolean Search(const     Page & pg,
                    const PageKey & searchkey,
                            Page & keypage,
                        size_t & pos);
```

```
          // insert node into leaf
          Boolean InsertKey(const PageKey & inskey,
                                  DataFilePtr dataptr);

          Boolean PromoteInternal(        Page & pg,
                                const PageKey & inskey,
                                    DataFilePtr dataptr,
                                    PageFilePtr pagelnk);

          Boolean PromoteRoot(const PageKey & inskey,
                                  DataFilePtr dataptr,
                                  PageFilePtr lesslnk,
                                  PageFilePtr grtrlnk);

          void RecurseTraverse(const Page & pg);

          // extensions for hash file and data file
          static const String TreeFileExt;
          static const String DataFileExt;

          // create file name from base and extension
          static String MakeFileName(const String & basename,
                                     const String & ext);
      };
```

The data members *Data* and *Tree* are the files that contain the BTree's *DataBlocks* and *Pages*, respectively. I implemented these as pointers and allocated *DataFile* and *PageFile* objects during *BTreeFile* construction. I could have derived *BTreeFile* from *DataFile* and *PageFile*, as I derived *HashFile* from *HashFileTable* and *DataFile*; the difference in designs serves to illustrate different approaches to solving similar problems. *HashFile* isn't implemented any better than *BTreeFile* — or vice versa.

The members *DataFileExt* and *HashFileExt* provide extensions that are appended to the base-file name by the private *MakeFileName* function. The *HashFile* class used a similar convention.

```
const String BTreeFile::TreeFileExt(".BFT");
const String BTreeFile::DataFileExt(".BFD");



// create file name from base and extension
String BTreeFile::MakeFileName(const String & basename,
                               const String & ext)
    {
    String name;

    if (basename.Length() < 8)
        name = basename;
    else
        name = basename.CutHead(8);

    name += ext;

    return name;
    }
```

The *Locked* value is set to *BOOL_TRUE* when the *InOrder* function is called; otherwise, it is *BOOL_FALSE*. When *Locked* is *BOOL_TRUE*, the *Write* and *Delete* functions return *BOOL_FALSE*. This prevents changes from being made to the files while the *InOrder* function is enumerating their contents.

*Root* contains the current root *Page* of the BTree; it speeds up operations if the root is resident in memory.

A new *BTreeFile* is constructed by providing a base-file name, an order, and a maximum key size. It begins by calling constructors to assign values to the file names *DataFileName* and *PageFileName*. Then, it creates *DataFile* and *PageFile* objects that generate new files on disk. The constructor finishes by reading the blank root page from *Page*.

```
BTreeFile::BTreeFile(const String & basename,
                     size_t ord,
                     size_t ksize)
    : DataFileName(MakeFileName(basename,DataFileExt)),
```

```
      TreeFileName(MakeFileName(basename,TreeFileExt)),
      Root(0,0)
   {
   // create data file object
   Data = new DataFile(DataFileName,FM_NEW);

   if (Data == NULL)
       ReportError(BTE_ALLOC);

   // create tree file object
   Tree = new PageFile(TreeFileName,ord,ksize);

   if (Tree == NULL)
       ReportError(BTE_ALLOC);

   // create root page
   Boolean result = Tree->ReadRoot(Root);

   if (result == NULL)
       ReportError(BTE_ALLOC);
   }
```

To open an existing *BTreeFile*, only the base file name is specified. The file names are constructed, *DataFile* and *PageFile* objects are created to open and access the existing information, and the root page is read.

```
   BTreeFile::BTreeFile(const String & basename)
      : DataFileName(MakeFileName(basename,DataFileExt)),
        TreeFileName(MakeFileName(basename,TreeFileExt)),
        Root(0,0)
      {
      // create data file object
      Data = new DataFile(DataFileName,FM_EXISTING);

      if (Data == NULL)
          ReportError(BTE_ALLOC);

      // create tree file object
      Tree = new PageFile(TreeFileName);
```

```
if (Tree == NULL)
    ReportError(BTE_ALLOC);

// create root page
Boolean result = Tree->ReadRoot(Root);

if (result == NULL)
    ReportError(BTE_ALLOC);
    }
```

The destructor automatically deletes the allocated file objects when a *BTreeFile* object is destroyed. The data and pages, of course, remain in the files on disk.

```
// destructor
BTreeFile::~BTreeFile()
    {
    // delete files
    delete Data;
    delete Tree;
    }
```

To write a record in a *BTreeFile*, a key and a *DataBlock* must be provided. The *DataBlock* is written to the *Data* file object, which returns a *DataFilePtr* indicating the location of the *DataBlock* in the file. That pointer and the key are then passed to the *InsertKey* function, which updates the *BTree*.

```
Boolean BTreeFile::Write(const PageKey & key,
                         const DataBlock & db)
    {
    // write the data record
    DataFilePtr dataptr = Data->Write(db);

    if (dataptr == DFP_ERROR)
        return BOOL_FALSE;

    // store the key in a page
    return InsertKey(key,dataptr);
    }
```

The *Search* function is a private-member function. *Search* is recursive; it is called initially with the root page of the tree, and it moves down the tree, following links, by calling itself. If *Search* finds the search key, *keypage* is assigned the page in which the key was found and *pos* is set to the key's location within that page. If the key is not found, *Search* returns *BOOL_FALSE*, sets *keypage* to the leaf page where the search key should be inserted, and sets *pos* to the position in that page where the key belongs. *The Read, Write,* and *Delete* functions use *Search* to find keys or the leaf into which a key should be inserted.

```
Boolean BTreeFile::Search(const    Page & pg,
                          const PageKey & searchkey,
                                  Page & keypage,
                              size_t & pos)
    {
    Boolean result;

    pos = 0;

    int comp;

    for (;;)
        {
        if (pos == pg.Hdr.NoOfKeys)
            {
            result = BOOL_FALSE;
            goto getpage;
            }

        comp = pg.Key[pos].Compare(searchkey);

        if (comp == 0)
            {
            keypage = pg;
            result  = BOOL_TRUE;
            break;
            }
        else
            {
```

```
                        if (comp < 0)
                            {
                            ++pos;
                            }
                    else
                            {
                            // I know this is a label — so shoot me!
                            getpage:

                            // if we're in a leaf page, key wasn't found
                            if (pg.Lnk[pos] == PFP_NULL)
                                {
                                keypage = pg;
                                result  = BOOL_FALSE;
                                }
                            else
                                {
                                // dynamically allocate to save stack space
                                Page nextpg(pg.Hdr.Order,
                                            pg.Hdr.KeySize);

                                Tree->Read(pg.Lnk[pos],nextpg);

                                // recursively search new page
                                result =
                                    Search(nextpg,searchkey,keypage,pos);
                                }

                            break;
                            }
                        }
                }

        return result;
        }
```

*InsertKey* is a private-member function; it is called only by the *Write* function. *InsertKey* begins by calling the *Search* function. If the key is found, *InsertKey* deletes the data record associated with its entry in the *Page*, and then it sets the *Page* to point

**468**

to the new record referenced by *dataptr*. Thus, duplicate keys cause a new data record to replace the old data associated with a key.

```
Boolean BTreeFile::InsertKey(const PageKey & inskey,
                                DataFilePtr dataptr)
    {
    // refresh root in memory
    Tree->ReadRoot(Root);

    Page   inspage(Root.Hdr.Order,Root.Hdr.KeySize);
    size_t inspos;

    Boolean found = Search(Root,inskey,inspage,inspos);

    if (found)
        {
        // delete old data record
        Data->Seek(inspage.Ptr[inspos]);

        Data->Delete();

        // store new data record pointer
        inspage.Ptr[inspos] = dataptr;

        // rewrite modified page
        Tree->Write(inspage);
        }
    else
        {
        if (inspage.Hdr.NoOfKeys == inspage.Hdr.MaxKeys)
            {
            // temporary arrays
            PageKey    * tempkeys = new
                        PageKey[inspage.Hdr.MaxKeys + 1];
            DataFilePtr * tempptrs = new
                        DataFilePtr[inspage.Hdr.MaxKeys + 1];

            // copy entries from inspage to temporaries
            size_t nt = 0; // index into temporaries
```

```
size_t ni = 0; // index into inspage

tempkeys[inspos] = PageKey(inskey);
tempptrs[inspos] = dataptr;

while (ni < inspage.Hdr.MaxKeys)
    {
    if (ni == inspos)
        ++nt;

    tempkeys[nt] = inspage.Key[ni];
    tempptrs[nt] = inspage.Ptr[ni];

    ++ni;
    ++nt;
    }

// generate a new leaf node
Page sibpage(inspage.Hdr.Order,
             inspage.Hdr.KeySize);

sibpage.Hdr.ParentPtr = inspage.Hdr.ParentPtr;

// clear # of keys in pages
inspage.Hdr.NoOfKeys = 0;
sibpage.Hdr.NoOfKeys = 0;

// copy appropriate keys from temp to pages
for (ni = 0; ni < inspage.Hdr.MinKeys; ++ni)
    {
    inspage.Key[ni] = tempkeys[ni];
    inspage.Ptr[ni] = tempptrs[ni];

    ++inspage.Hdr.NoOfKeys;
    }

for (ni = inspage.Hdr.MinKeys + 1;
     ni <= inspage.Hdr.MaxKeys; ++ni)
    {
```

```
    sibpage.Key[ni - 1 - inspage.Hdr.MinKeys] =
                                    tempkeys[ni];
    sibpage.Ptr[ni - 1 - inspage.Hdr.MinKeys] =
                                    tempptrs[ni];

    ++sibpage.Hdr.NoOfKeys;
    }

// Fill any remaining entries in inspage with null.
// Note that sibpage is initialized to null values
// by the constructor.

for (ni = inspage.Hdr.MinKeys; ni <
                    inspage.Hdr.MaxKeys; ++ni)
    {
    inspage.Key[ni] = PageKey();
    inspage.Ptr[ni] = DFP_MARKER;
    }

// write pages
Tree->Write(inspage);
Tree->Write(sibpage);

// promote key and pointer
if (inspage.Hdr.ParentPtr == PFP_NULL)
    {
    // we need to create a new root
    PromoteRoot(tempkeys[inspage.Hdr.MinKeys],
                tempptrs[inspage.Hdr.MinKeys],
                inspage.Hdr.FilePtr,
                sibpage.Hdr.FilePtr);

    inspage.Hdr.ParentPtr = Root.Hdr.FilePtr;
    sibpage.Hdr.ParentPtr = Root.Hdr.FilePtr;

    // rewrite pages
    Tree->Write(inspage);
    Tree->Write(sibpage);
    }
```

```
                        else
                            {
                            Page parpage(inspage.Hdr.Order,
                                        inspage.Hdr.KeySize);

                            Tree->Read(inspage.Hdr.ParentPtr,parpage);

                            // promote into parent
                            PromoteInternal(parpage,
                                        tempkeys[inspage.Hdr.MinKeys],
                                        tempptrs[inspage.Hdr.MinKeys],
                                        sibpage.Hdr.FilePtr);
                            }

                    delete [] tempkeys;
                    delete [] tempptrs;
                    }
                else // simply insert new key and data ptr
                    {
                    for (size_t n = inspage.Hdr.NoOfKeys; n > inspos; —n)
                        {
                        inspage.Key[n] = inspage.Key[n - 1];
                        inspage.Ptr[n] = inspage.Ptr[n - 1];
                        }

                    inspage.Key[inspos] = inskey;
                    inspage.Ptr[inspos] = dataptr;

                    ++inspage.Hdr.NoOfKeys;

                    Tree->Write(inspage);
                    }
                }

        return BOOL_TRUE;
        }
```

If the key was not found, *Search* returns the leaf page in *inspage* where the key should be inserted at *inspos*. If *inspage* is not full, the key is inserted by shifting keys to the left and placing the new key and its data-record pointer in the opened position.

When *inspage* is full, it needs to be split and the median key promoted. The split is accomplished by creating a temporary list of keys and data-record pointers, in which the new key and its data pointer are located in their correct relationship to other keys. The first half of these keys is copied back into *inspage*, and the second half is copied into the sibling page. The median key is then promoted. If inspage has a parent, *InsertKey* calls *PromoteKey* to promote the median key into the parent page; otherwise, *PromoteRoot* is called to generate a new root page.

The private *PromoteInternal* function inserts a key promoted by splitting into a parent page.

```
Boolean BTreeFile::PromoteInternal(        Page & inspage,
                                    const PageKey & inskey,
                                        DataFilePtr dataptr,
                                        PageFilePtr pagelnk)
    {
    if (inspage.Hdr.NoOfKeys == inspage.Hdr.MaxKeys)
        {
        // temporary arrays
        PageKey     * tempkeys = new
                        PageKey[inspage.Hdr.MaxKeys + 1];
        DataFilePtr * tempptrs = new
                        DataFilePtr[inspage.Hdr.MaxKeys + 1];
        PageFilePtr * templnks = new
                        PageFilePtr[inspage.Hdr.Order   + 1];

        // copy entries from inspage to temporaries
        size_t nt = 0; // index into temporaries
        size_t ni = 0; // index into inspage

        templnks[0] = inspage.Lnk[0];

        size_t inspos = 0;

        // find insertion position
        while ((inspos < inspage.Hdr.MaxKeys)
          && (inspage.Key[inspos].Compare(inskey) < 0))
            {
            ++inspos;
            }
```

```
// store new info
tempkeys[inspos]     = PageKey(inskey);
tempptrs[inspos]     = dataptr;
templnks[inspos + 1] = pagelnk;

// copy existing keys
while (ni < inspage.Hdr.MaxKeys)
    {
    if (ni == inspos)
        ++nt;

    tempkeys[nt]     = inspage.Key[ni];
    tempptrs[nt]     = inspage.Ptr[ni];
    templnks[nt + 1] = inspage.Lnk[ni + 1];

    ++ni;
    ++nt;
    }

// generate a new leaf node
Page sibpage(inspage.Hdr.Order,
             inspage.Hdr.KeySize);

sibpage.Hdr.ParentPtr = inspage.Hdr.ParentPtr;

// clear # of keys in pages
inspage.Hdr.NoOfKeys = 0;
sibpage.Hdr.NoOfKeys = 0;

inspage.Lnk[0] = templnks[0];

// copy appropriate keys from temp to pages
for (ni = 0; ni < inspage.Hdr.MinKeys; ++ni)
    {
    inspage.Key[ni]     = tempkeys[ni];
    inspage.Ptr[ni]     = tempptrs[ni];
    inspage.Lnk[ni + 1] = templnks[ni + 1];

    ++inspage.Hdr.NoOfKeys;
    }
```

```
sibpage.Lnk[0] = templnks[inspage.Hdr.MinKeys + 1];

for (ni = inspage.Hdr.MinKeys + 1; ni <=
 inspage.Hdr.MaxKeys; ++ni)
    {
    sibpage.Key[ni - 1 - inspage.Hdr.MinKeys] =
                                    tempkeys[ni];
    sibpage.Ptr[ni - 1 - inspage.Hdr.MinKeys] =
                                    tempptrs[ni];
    sibpage.Lnk[ni - inspage.Hdr.MinKeys]      =
                                    templnks[ni + 1];


    ++sibpage.Hdr.NoOfKeys;
    }

// Fill any remaining entries in inspage with null.
// Note that sibpage is initialized to null values
// by the constructor.

for (ni = inspage.Hdr.MinKeys; ni <
                            inspage.Hdr.MaxKeys; ++ni)
    {
    inspage.Key[ni]      = PageKey();
    inspage.Ptr[ni]      = DFP_MARKER;
    inspage.Lnk[ni + 1] = PFP_NULL;
    }

// write pages
Tree->Write(inspage);
Tree->Write(sibpage);

// update child parent links
Page child(sibpage.Hdr.Order,sibpage.Hdr.KeySize);

for (ni = 0; ni <= sibpage.Hdr.NoOfKeys; ++ni)
    {
    Tree->Read(sibpage.Lnk[ni],child);

    child.Hdr.ParentPtr = sibpage.Hdr.FilePtr;
```

```
                        Tree->Write(child);
                        }

            // promote key and pointer
            if (inspage.Hdr.ParentPtr == PFP_NULL)
                {
                // we need to create a new root
                PromoteRoot(tempkeys[inspage.Hdr.MinKeys],
                            tempptrs[inspage.Hdr.MinKeys],
                            inspage.Hdr.FilePtr,
                            sibpage.Hdr.FilePtr);

                inspage.Hdr.ParentPtr = Root.Hdr.FilePtr;
                sibpage.Hdr.ParentPtr = Root.Hdr.FilePtr;

                // rewrite pages
                Tree->Write(inspage);
                Tree->Write(sibpage);
                }
            else
                {
                Page parpage(inspage.Hdr.Order,
                             inspage.Hdr.KeySize);

                Tree->Read(inspage.Hdr.ParentPtr,parpage);

                // promote into parent
                PromoteInternal(parpage,
                                tempkeys[inspage.Hdr.MinKeys],
                                tempptrs[inspage.Hdr.MinKeys],
                                sibpage.Hdr.FilePtr);
                }

        delete [] tempkeys;
        delete [] tempptrs;
        delete [] templnks;
        }
    else // simply insert new key and data ptr
        {
        size_t inspos = 0;
```

```
// find insertion position
while ((inspos < inspage.Hdr.NoOfKeys)
  && (inspage.Key[inspos].Compare(inskey) < 0))
    {
    ++inspos;
    }

// shift any keys right
for (size_t n = inspage.Hdr.NoOfKeys; n > inspos; --n)
    {
    inspage.Key[n]     = inspage.Key[n - 1];
    inspage.Ptr[n]     = inspage.Ptr[n - 1];
    inspage.Lnk[n + 1] = inspage.Lnk[n];
    }

// store new info
inspage.Key[inspos]     = PageKey(inskey);
inspage.Ptr[inspos]     = dataptr;
inspage.Lnk[inspos + 1] = pagelnk;

++inspage.Hdr.NoOfKeys;

Tree->Write(inspage);
    }

return BOOL_TRUE;
}
```

When the root node is split by *InsertKey* or *PromoteKey*, they call the *PromoteRoot* function to generate a new root that contains a single key.

```
Boolean BTreeFile::PromoteRoot(const PageKey & inskey,
                              DataFilePtr dataptr,
                              PageFilePtr lesslnk,
                              PageFilePtr grtrlnk)
{
// create new root page
Page newroot(Root.Hdr.Order,Root.Hdr.KeySize);

// insert key into new root
```

```
newroot.Key[0] = inskey;
newroot.Ptr[0] = dataptr;

newroot.Lnk[0] = lesslnk;
newroot.Lnk[1] = grtrlnk;

newroot.Hdr.NoOfKeys = 1;

// write new root to tree file
Boolean result = Tree->Write(newroot,BOOL_TRUE);

// store pointer to new root
Tree->ReadRoot(Root);

return result;
}
```

Reading a record from the file is very simple: *Search* for the key in the BTree, and if it is found, read the *DataFile* record identified by that key's *Ptr* value.

```
DataBlock BTreeFile::Read(const PageKey & key)
    {
    Page   inspage(Root.Hdr.Order,Root.Hdr.KeySize);
    size_t inspos;

    Boolean result = Search(Root,key,inspage,inspos);

    if (result == BOOL_TRUE)
        {
        // seek data record
        Data->Seek(inspage.Ptr[inspos]);

        // read data record
        return Data->Read();
        }
    else
        return NULL_BLOCK;
    }
```

And now we come to deletion. The *Delete* function performs the first stage of deletion, which involves removing a key from a leaf page.

```
Boolean BTreeFile::Delete(const PageKey & delkey)
    {
    if (Locked)
        return BOOL_FALSE;

    if (BOOL_FALSE == Tree->ReadRoot(Root))
        return BOOL_FALSE;

    Page   delpage(0,0);
    size_t delpos;

    Boolean found = Search(Root,delkey,delpage,delpos);

    if (!found)
        return BOOL_FALSE;

    // delete data record associated with deleted key
    Data->Seek(delpage.Ptr[delpos]);

    Data->Delete();

    if (delpage.Lnk[0] == PFP_NULL) // is this a leaf page?
        {
        // remove key from leaf
        —delpage.Hdr.NoOfKeys;

        for (size_t n = delpos; n < delpage.Hdr.NoOfKeys; ++n)
            {
            delpage.Key[n] = delpage.Key[n + 1];
            delpage.Ptr[n] = delpage.Ptr[n + 1];
            }

        delpage.Key[delpage.Hdr.NoOfKeys] = PageKey();
        delpage.Ptr[delpage.Hdr.NoOfKeys] = DFP_MARKER;

        // write page to disk
        if (BOOL_FALSE == Tree->Write(delpage))
```

**479**

```
                return BOOL_FALSE;

        // adjust tree
        if (delpage.Hdr.NoOfKeys < delpage.Hdr.MinKeys)
            return AdjustTree(delpage);
        }
    else // delpage is internal
        {
        // replace deleted key with immediate successor
        Page sucpage(0,0);

        // find successor
        if (BOOL_FALSE == Tree->Read(delpage.Lnk[delpos +
                                        1],sucpage))
            return BOOL_FALSE;

        while (sucpage.Lnk[0] != PFP_NULL)
            {
            if (BOOL_FALSE == Tree->Read(sucpage.Lnk[0],sucpage))
                return BOOL_FALSE;
            }

        // first key is the "swappee"
        delpage.Key[delpos] = sucpage.Key[0];
        delpage.Ptr[delpos] = sucpage.Ptr[0];

        // deleted swapped key from sucpage
        -sucpage.Hdr.NoOfKeys;

        for (size_t n = 0; n < sucpage.Hdr.NoOfKeys; ++n)
            {
            sucpage.Key[n] = sucpage.Key[n + 1];
            sucpage.Ptr[n] = sucpage.Ptr[n + 1];
            sucpage.Lnk[n + 1] = sucpage.Lnk[n + 2];
            }

        sucpage.Key[sucpage.Hdr.NoOfKeys] = PageKey();
        sucpage.Ptr[sucpage.Hdr.NoOfKeys] = DFP_MARKER;
        sucpage.Lnk[sucpage.Hdr.NoOfKeys + 1] = PFP_NULL;
```

```
        // write pages to disk
        if (BOOL_FALSE == Tree->Write(delpage))
            return BOOL_FALSE;

        if (BOOL_FALSE == Tree->Write(sucpage))
            return BOOL_FALSE;

        // adjust tree for leaf node
        if (sucpage.Hdr.NoOfKeys < sucpage.Hdr.MinKeys)
            return AdjustTree(sucpage);
        }

    return BOOL_TRUE;
    }
```

The *Delete* function begins by calling search to find the key in the tree. If the key was not found, the function returns *BOOL_FALSE*, since it can't delete a key that isn't there!

*Delete* checks the page where the key was found; if the page is a leaf, it simply removes the key. If the pages has children, it is an internal (possibly root) page. For an internal node, *Delete* searches through the tree, finding the key which immediately succeeds the deleted key. The successor key is found by looking at the subtree containing keys greater than the deleted key, travelling down the tree until a leaf is found. The first key in that leaf is the successor, and its values replace those of the deleted key. Then the successor key is deleted from the leaf. If the leaf contains less than *Hdr.MinKeys* keys, the *AdjustTree* function is called.

```
    Boolean BTreeFile::AdjustTree(Page & pg)
        {
        if (pg.Hdr.ParentPtr == PFP_NULL)
            return BOOL_TRUE;

        Page parpage(0,0);
        Page sibless(0,0);
        Page sibgrtr(0,0);
```

```
    // get parent page
    if (BOOL_FALSE == Tree->Read(pg.Hdr.ParentPtr,parpage))
        return BOOL_FALSE;

    // find pointer to pg in parent
    for (size_t n = 0; parpage.Lnk[n] != pg.Hdr.FilePtr; ++n)
        ;

    // read sibling pages
    if (n < parpage.Hdr.NoOfKeys)
        {
        if (BOOL_FALSE == Tree->Read(parpage.Lnk[n +
1],sibgrtr))
            return BOOL_FALSE;
        }

    if (n > 0)
        {
        if (BOOL_FALSE == Tree->Read(parpage.Lnk[n -
1],sibless))
            return BOOL_FALSE;
        }

    // decide to redistribute or concatenate
    if (sibless.Hdr.NoOfKeys > sibgrtr.Hdr.NoOfKeys)
        {
        -n;

        if (sibless.Hdr.NoOfKeys > sibless.Hdr.MinKeys)
            return Redistribute(n,sibless,parpage,pg);
        else
            return Concatenate(n,sibless,parpage,pg);
        }
    else
        {
        if (sibgrtr.Hdr.NoOfKeys > sibgrtr.Hdr.MinKeys)
            return Redistribute(n,pg,parpage,sibgrtr);
        else
            return Concatenate(n,pg,parpage,sibgrtr);
        }
    }
```

The parameter *pg* references a page which contains *order / 2 - 1* keys; when *AdjustTree* is called by *Delete*, *pg* will reference the leaf page from which a key was deleted. *AdjustTree* find the the sibling nodes of *pg*. Note that *pg* will have at least one sibling, and it may have two. If a *pg* has only one sibling, the other (non-existent) sibling is assumed to contain zero keys for comparison purposes. *AdjustTree* also reads *pg*'s parent page.

*AdjustTree* calls the *Concatenate* function to combine *pg* with a sibling, or the *Redistribute* function to redistribute keys between *pg*, its parent page, and a sibling page. *Redistribute* is called if one of *pg*'s siblings has more than *MinKeys* keys; otherwise, *Concatenate* is called. A comparison is made to redistribute or concatenate with the sibling that has the most keys; thus, *pg* may be the page to the right of the parent's separation key, or it may be to the left, depending on the number of keys in the sibling with which it is processed. Both *Concatenate* and *Redistribute* are passed the index of the key in the parent page that separates *pg* and its sibling; this key is hereafter called the separation key.

```
Boolean BTreeFile::Redistribute(size_t keypos,
                                Page & lesspage,
                                Page & parpage,
                                Page & grtrpage)
    {
    // note: this function is ONLY called for leaf nodes!
    size_t n;

    if (lesspage.Lnk[0] == PFP_NULL) // working with leaves
        {
        if (lesspage.Hdr.NoOfKeys > grtrpage.Hdr.NoOfKeys)
            {
            // slide a key from lesser to greater
            // move keys in greater to the left by one
            for (n = grtrpage.Hdr.NoOfKeys; n > 0; --n)
                {
                grtrpage.Key[n] = grtrpage.Key[n - 1];
                grtrpage.Ptr[n] = grtrpage.Ptr[n - 1];
                }
```

```
                // store parent separator key in greater page
                grtrpage.Key[0] = parpage.Key[keypos];
                grtrpage.Ptr[0] = parpage.Ptr[keypos];

                // increment greater page's key count
                ++grtrpage.Hdr.NoOfKeys;

                // decrement lessor page's key count
                -lesspage.Hdr.NoOfKeys;

                // move last key in less page to parent as separator
                parpage.Key[keypos]
                    = lesspage.Key[lesspage.Hdr.NoOfKeys];
                parpage.Ptr[keypos]
                    = lesspage.Ptr[lesspage.Hdr.NoOfKeys];

                // clear last key in less page
                lesspage.Key[lesspage.Hdr.NoOfKeys] = PageKey();
                lesspage.Ptr[lesspage.Hdr.NoOfKeys] = DFP_MARKER;
                }
            else
                {
                // slide a key from greater to lessor
                // add parent key to lessor page
                lesspage.Key[lesspage.Hdr.NoOfKeys]
                    = parpage.Key[keypos];
                lesspage.Ptr[lesspage.Hdr.NoOfKeys]
                    = parpage.Ptr[keypos];

                // increment lessor page's key count
                ++lesspage.Hdr.NoOfKeys;

                // insert in parent the lowest key in greater page
                parpage.Key[keypos] = grtrpage.Key[0];
                parpage.Ptr[keypos] = grtrpage.Ptr[0];

                // decrement # of keys in greater page
                -grtrpage.Hdr.NoOfKeys;

                // move keys in greater page to left
                for (n = 0; n < grtrpage.Hdr.NoOfKeys; ++n)
```

```
                        {
                        grtrpage.Key[n] = grtrpage.Key[n + 1];
                        grtrpage.Ptr[n] = grtrpage.Ptr[n + 1];
                        }

                  // make last key blank
                  grtrpage.Key[n]    = PageKey();
                  grtrpage.Ptr[n]    = DFP_MARKER;
                  }
            }
      else
            {
            if (lesspage.Hdr.NoOfKeys > grtrpage.Hdr.NoOfKeys)
                  {
                  // slide a key from lesser to greater
                  // move keys in greater to the left by one
                  for (n = grtrpage.Hdr.NoOfKeys; n > 0; -n)
                        {
                        grtrpage.Key[n] = grtrpage.Key[n - 1];
                        grtrpage.Ptr[n] = grtrpage.Ptr[n - 1];
                        grtrpage.Lnk[n + 1] = grtrpage.Lnk[n];
                        }

                  grtrpage.Lnk[1] = grtrpage.Lnk[0];

                  // store parent separator key in greater page
                  grtrpage.Key[0] = parpage.Key[keypos];
                  grtrpage.Ptr[0] = parpage.Ptr[keypos];
                  grtrpage.Lnk[0] =lesspage.Lnk[lesspage.Hdr.NoOfKeys];

                  // update child link
                  Page child(0,0);

                  if (BOOL_FALSE == Tree-
>Read(grtrpage.Lnk[0],child))
                        return BOOL_FALSE;

                  child.Hdr.ParentPtr = grtrpage.Hdr.FilePtr;

                  if (BOOL_FALSE == Tree->Write(child))
                        return BOOL_FALSE;
```

**485**

```
        // increment greater page's key count
        ++grtrpage.Hdr.NoOfKeys;

        // decrement lessor page's key count
        -lesspage.Hdr.NoOfKeys;

        // move last key in less page to parent as separator
        parpage.Key[keypos]
                = lesspage.Key[lesspage.Hdr.NoOfKeys];
        parpage.Ptr[keypos]
                = lesspage.Ptr[lesspage.Hdr.NoOfKeys];

        // clear last key in less page
        lesspage.Key[lesspage.Hdr.NoOfKeys] = PageKey();
        lesspage.Ptr[lesspage.Hdr.NoOfKeys] = DFP_MARKER;
        lesspage.Lnk[lesspage.Hdr.NoOfKeys + 1] = PFP_NULL;
        }
    else
        {
        // slide a key from greater to lessor
        // add parent key to lessor page
        lesspage.Key[lesspage.Hdr.NoOfKeys]
                                = parpage.Key[keypos];
        lesspage.Ptr[lesspage.Hdr.NoOfKeys]
                                = parpage.Ptr[keypos];
        lesspage.Lnk[lesspage.Hdr.NoOfKeys + 1]
                                = grtrpage.Lnk[0];

        // update child link
        Page child(0,0);

        if (BOOL_FALSE == Tree->Read(grtrpage.Lnk[0],child))
            return BOOL_FALSE;

        child.Hdr.ParentPtr = lesspage.Hdr.FilePtr;

        if (BOOL_FALSE == Tree->Write(child))
            return BOOL_FALSE;
```

```
        // increment lessor page's key count
        ++lesspage.Hdr.NoOfKeys;

        // insert in parent the lowest key in greater page
        parpage.Key[keypos] = grtrpage.Key[0];
        parpage.Ptr[keypos] = grtrpage.Ptr[0];

        // decrement # of keys in greater page
        —grtrpage.Hdr.NoOfKeys;

        // move keys in greater page to left
        for (n = 0; n < grtrpage.Hdr.NoOfKeys; ++n)
            {
            grtrpage.Key[n] = grtrpage.Key[n + 1];
            grtrpage.Ptr[n] = grtrpage.Ptr[n + 1];
            grtrpage.Lnk[n] = grtrpage.Lnk[n + 1];
            }

        grtrpage.Lnk[n] = grtrpage.Lnk[n + 1];

        // make last key blank
        grtrpage.Key[n]     = PageKey();
        grtrpage.Ptr[n]     = DFP_MARKER;
        grtrpage.Lnk[n + 1] = PFP_NULL;
        }
    }

// write pages
if (Tree->Write(lesspage))
    {
    if (Tree->Write(parpage))
        {
        if (Tree->Write(grtrpage))
            return BOOL_TRUE;
        }
    }

return BOOL_FALSE;
}
```

*Redistribute* looks long and complicated, but it is actually one process implemented for special cases. Redistribution will either occur from *lesspage* to *grtrpage*, or from *grtrpage* to *lesspage*; when redistributing keys among internal nodes, links will have to be changed as well, while leaf nodes can have their keys redistributed without worrying about links. This gives us four cases. In each case, the separator key is moved from the parent into the page which is short a key. The page that has extra keys provides a new separator key. No further adjustments in the tree are required, since no page is reduced below *MinKeys* keys.

*Concatenate* begins by appending the separation key to *lesspage*; the separation key is them removed from the parent page. The keys from the *grtrpage* are sequentially added to *lesspage*, and *grtrpage* is deleted. *Concatenate* updates the parent links in all moved nodes so that they point back to *lesspage*. If the parent page now contains zero keys, it is deleted and *lesspage* becomes the new root. And, if the parent page has been reduced to fewer than *MinKeys*, *Concatenate* calls *AdjustTree*. This is, of course, recursive, since *AdjustTree* calls *Concatenate*.

```
Boolean BTreeFile::Concatenate(size_t keypos,
                               Page & lesspage,
                               Page & parpage,
                               Page & grtrpage)
    {
    size_t n, ng;

    // move separator key from parent into lesspage
    lesspage.Key[lesspage.Hdr.NoOfKeys] = parpage.Key[keypos];
    lesspage.Ptr[lesspage.Hdr.NoOfKeys] = parpage.Ptr[keypos];
    lesspage.Lnk[lesspage.Hdr.NoOfKeys + 1] = grtrpage.Lnk[0];

    ++lesspage.Hdr.NoOfKeys;

    // delete separator from parent
    —parpage.Hdr.NoOfKeys;

    for (n = keypos; n < parpage.Hdr.NoOfKeys; ++n)
        {
        parpage.Key[n] = parpage.Key[n + 1];
```

```
    parpage.Ptr[n] = parpage.Ptr[n + 1];
    parpage.Lnk[n + 1] = parpage.Lnk[n + 2];
    }

// clear unused key in parent
parpage.Key[n]     = PageKey();
parpage.Ptr[n]     = DFP_MARKER;
parpage.Lnk[n + 1] = PFP_NULL;

// copy keys from grtrpage to lesspage
ng = 0;
n  = lesspage.Hdr.NoOfKeys;

while (ng < grtrpage.Hdr.NoOfKeys)
    {
    ++lesspage.Hdr.NoOfKeys;

    lesspage.Key[n] = grtrpage.Key[ng];
    lesspage.Ptr[n] = grtrpage.Ptr[ng];
    lesspage.Lnk[n + 1] = grtrpage.Lnk[ng + 1];

    ++ng;
    ++n;
    }

// delete greater page
Tree->Delete(grtrpage.Hdr.FilePtr);

// is this a leaf page?
if (lesspage.Lnk[0] != PFP_NULL)
    {
    // adjust child pointers to point to less page
    Page child(0,0);

    for (n = 0; n <= lesspage.Hdr.NoOfKeys; ++n)
        {
        if (BOOL_FALSE == Tree->Read(lesspage.Lnk[n],child))
            return BOOL_FALSE;

        child.Hdr.ParentPtr = lesspage.Hdr.FilePtr;
```

```
                    if (BOOL_FALSE == Tree->Write(child))
                        return BOOL_FALSE;
                    }
                }

        // write less page and parent
        if (parpage.Hdr.NoOfKeys == 0)
            {
            // note: only the root page can ever be deleted to 0 keys
            Tree->Delete(parpage.Hdr.FilePtr);

            lesspage.Hdr.ParentPtr = PFP_NULL;

            if (BOOL_FALSE == Tree->Write(lesspage,BOOL_TRUE))
                return BOOL_FALSE;
            }
        else
            {
            if (BOOL_FALSE == Tree->Write(lesspage))
                return BOOL_FALSE;

            if (BOOL_FALSE == Tree->Write(parpage))
                return BOOL_FALSE;

            // if parent is too small, adjust tree!
            if (parpage.Hdr.NoOfKeys < parpage.Hdr.MinKeys)
                return AdjustTree(parpage);
            }

        return BOOL_TRUE;
        }
```

The greatest advantage of BTree indexes over hash indexes is that BTrees allow sequential access to the data records. To examine all the records in a *BTreeFile*, in alphabetical order, call the *InOrder* member.

```
    void BTreeFile::InOrder(BTreeEnumFunc func)
        {
        Tree->ReadRoot(Root);
```

```
EnumFunc = func;

RecurseTraverse(Root);
}
```

The *BTreeEnumFunc* parameter is defined as a *void* function that accepts a *PageKey* and a *DataBlock* as parameters.

```
typedef void (* BTreeEnumFunc)(const   PageKey & str,
                                const DataBlock & db);
```

*InOrder* stores the *func* value in the data member *EnumFunc*, and calls the private recursive function *RecurseTraverse*. *RecurseTraverse* alternates between calling itself for page links and calling *EnumFunc* with keys and *DataBlocks*.

```
void BTreeFile::RecurseTraverse(const Page & pg)
    {
    size_t n;
    Page * p = new Page(pg.Hdr.Order,pg.Hdr.KeySize);
    DataBlock * db = new DataBlock;

    for (n = 0; n < pg.Hdr.NoOfKeys; ++n)
        {
        if (pg.Lnk[n] != PFP_NULL)
            {
            Tree->Read(pg.Lnk[n],*p);

            RecurseTraverse(*p);
            }

        Data->Seek(pg.Ptr[n]);

        *db = Data->Read();

        EnumFunc(pg.Key[n],*db);
        }

    if (pg.Lnk[n] != PFP_NULL)
```

```
                  {
                  Tree->Read(pg.Lnk[n],*p);

                  RecurseTraverse(*p);
                  }

          delete db;
          delete p;
          }
```

## 14.6 Using BTree Files

The following program illustrates the use of a *BTree* file. A hundred records are written to a *BTreeFile*, a record is changed, and *InOrder* is called to display all the records in alphabetical order.

```cpp
#include "btree.h"
#include "iostream.h"
#include "iomanip.h"
#include "stdlib.h"
#include "string.h"

#define B_ORDER    7
#define B_KEYSIZE 16
#define BASENAME  "btreetst"

String ErrLead("PAGETEST");

DosErrReporter ErrExit(&ErrLead);

void TestPageFile();
void TestBTreeFile();
void ShowThem(const PageKey & str, const DataBlock & db);

const Signature InputSig = 666999666;

struct NameCity : public Persistent
    {
    char * Name;
```

```
    char * City;

    Boolean Allocated;

    ~NameCity();

    NameCity(char * n, char * c);

    NameCity(const DataBlock & db);

    virtual operator DataBlock () const;
    };

NameCity::~NameCity()
    {
    if (Allocated)
        {
        delete Name;
        delete City;
        }
    }

NameCity::NameCity(char * n, char * c)
    {
    Name = n;
    City = c;

    Allocated = BOOL_FALSE;
    }

NameCity::NameCity(const DataBlock & db)
    {
    if (db.GetSignature() != InputSig)
        {
        cout << "\a\ainvalid input object signature!!!\n";
        exit(EXIT_FAILURE);
        }

    char * buffer = (char *)db.GetBufferPtr();
```

```cpp
        Name = strdup(buffer);

        buffer += strlen(Name) + 1;

        City = strdup(buffer);

        Allocated = BOOL_TRUE;
        }

NameCity::operator DataBlock () const
        {
        size_t bufsize = strlen(Name) + strlen(City) + 2;

        char * buffer = new char[bufsize];

        strcpy(buffer,Name);
        strcpy(buffer + strlen(Name) + 1,City);

        DataBlock db(InputSig,bufsize,buffer);

        delete [] buffer;

        return db;
        }

size_t InputSize;

int main(int argc, char * argv[])
        {
        if (argc < 2)
            InputSize = 100;
        else
            InputSize = (size_t)atoi(argv[1]);

        TestBTreeFile();

        return 0;
        }

void TestBTreeFile()
        {
```

```
NameCity InputList [100] =
        {
        { NameCity("John","Burbank")                },
        { NameCity("Karyn","Bombay")                 },
        { NameCity("Aynn","San Diego")               },
        { NameCity("David","Pueblo")                 },
        { NameCity("Jim","London")                   },
        { NameCity("Gerald","Moscow")                },
        { NameCity("Toni","Sacramento")              },
        { NameCity("William","Nome")                 },
        { NameCity("Wesley","Auckland")              },
        { NameCity("Antoinette","Hamburg")           },
        { NameCity("Greg","New York")                },
        { NameCity("Robert","Los Angeles")           },
        { NameCity("Ernest","Denver")                },
        { NameCity("Paulette","Montrose")            },
        { NameCity("Lynette","Tin Cup")              },
        { NameCity("Ethel","Boulder")                },
        { NameCity("Glen","Fort Collins")            },
        { NameCity("George","Georgetown")            },
        { NameCity("Ray","Alamosa")                  },
        { NameCity("Anthony","Kansas City")          },
        { NameCity("Jean","Raleigh")                 },
        { NameCity("Irvin","San Francisco")          },
        { NameCity("Hazel","Blythville")             },
        { NameCity("Cherry","El Paso")               },
        { NameCity("Jane","Miami")                   },
        { NameCity("Kirk","Des Moines")              },
        { NameCity("Ranee","Merced")                 },
        { NameCity("Margaret","Pittsburg")           },
        { NameCity("Lisa","Levenworth")              },
        { NameCity("Dennis","Parkville")             },
        { NameCity("Matt","Biscayne")                },
        { NameCity("Ashley","Portland")              },
        { NameCity("Randy","Sterling")               },
        { NameCity("Jerry","Simla")                  },
        { NameCity("Hugh","Paonia")                  },
        { NameCity("Peter","Petersburg")             },
        { NameCity("Eric","Oslo")                    },
        { NameCity("Mimi","Paris")                   },
```

```
{ NameCity("Gertrude","Berlin")          },
{ NameCity("Vanna","Burbank")             },
{ NameCity("Evelyn","Liverpool")         },
{ NameCity("Bonnie","Glasgow")           },
{ NameCity("Gabriel","Tel Aviv")         },
{ NameCity("Regina","Rome")              },
{ NameCity("Edna","Milan")               },
{ NameCity("Gregorio","Venice")          },
{ NameCity("April","San Diego")          },
{ NameCity("Carl","Boston")              },
{ NameCity("Sharon","Avon")              },
{ NameCity("Bruce","Woodland Park")      },
{ NameCity("Tom","Fort Morgan")          },
{ NameCity("Theodora","Ankara")          },
{ NameCity("Sara","Istanbul")            },
{ NameCity("Heidi","Geneva")             },
{ NameCity("Ron","Crested Butte")        },
{ NameCity("Miriam","Haifa")             },
{ NameCity("Felix","Manila")             },
{ NameCity("Jesse","Reno")               },
{ NameCity("Rebecca","Las Vegas")        },
{ NameCity("Eldon","Gunnison")           },
{ NameCity("Scott","Dublin")             },
{ NameCity("Bud","Rush")                 },
{ NameCity("Sidney","Bedford")           },
{ NameCity("Charles","Crescent City")    },
{ NameCity("Rae","Macon")                },
{ NameCity("Patricia","Roswell")         },
{ NameCity("Mary","Raton")               },
{ NameCity("Anjelica","Mexico City")     },
{ NameCity("Raphael","Cuernavaca")       },
{ NameCity("Joyce","Durango")            },
{ NameCity("Zeba","Tehran")              },
{ NameCity("Norman","Brest")             },
{ NameCity("Elora","Athens")             },
{ NameCity("Marnie","Brush")             },
{ NameCity("Heather","Edinburgh")        },
{ NameCity("Maria","Orlando")            },
{ NameCity("Hope","Charleston")          },
{ NameCity("Edward","Tallin")            },
```

```
        { NameCity("Emil","San Salvador")     },
        { NameCity("Wanda","Brooklyn")        },
        { NameCity("Emily","Chicago")         },
        { NameCity("Yoko","Tokyo")            },
        { NameCity("Kurt","Bonn")             },
        { NameCity("Aino","Helsinki")         },
        { NameCity("Olu","Lagos")             },
        { NameCity("Geordi","Port-au-Prince") },
        { NameCity("Rea","Bandung")           },
        { NameCity("Thomas","Cheyenne")       },
        { NameCity("Lynn","Butte")            },
        { NameCity("Cody","Marble")           },
        { NameCity("Jeff","Livingston")       },
        { NameCity("Cora","Sault Ste. Marie") },
        { NameCity("Ida","Quebec")            },
        { NameCity("Marie","Edmonton")        },
        { NameCity("Vanessa","Houston")       },
        { NameCity("Dean","Pensacola")        },
        { NameCity("Allen","Toronto")         },
        { NameCity("Eve","Cleveland")         },
        { NameCity("Suzanne","Calgary")       },
        { NameCity("Joseph","Detroit")        }
        };

// create a BTree file
BTreeFile btfile(BASENAME,B_ORDER,B_KEYSIZE);

Boolean result;

// store the records
for (size_t n = 0; n < InputSize; ++n)
    {
    cout << "inserting # " << n << flush;

    result =
        btfile.Write(PageKey(B_KEYSIZE,InputList[n].Name),
                        InputList[n]);

    if (result == BOOL_FALSE)
        {
```

```
                    cout << " \a\aERROR!\n";
                    exit(EXIT_FAILURE);
                    }

            cout << " done!" << endl;
            }

    // show all the records, in order
    btfile.InOrder(ShowThem);

    // create a page key
    PageKey pk(B_KEYSIZE,"Scott");

    // find a record
    DataBlock db = btfile.Read(pk);

    // create an object
    NameCity nc(db);

    // display record data
    cout << "found " << nc.Name
        << ", who lives in " << nc.City << endl;

    // create a new record with the same name and a different
                                                    city
    NameCity newnc(nc.Name,"Walla Walla");

    // write the new record
    result = btfile.Write(pk,newnc);

    if (result == BOOL_FALSE)
        {
        cout << " \a\aERROR!\n";
        exit(EXIT_FAILURE);
        }

    cout << newnc.Name << " has been changed" << endl;

    // read changed record and display it
    db = btfile.Read(pk);
```

```
        NameCity nc2(db);

        cout << "found " << nc2.Name
             << ", who lives in " << nc2.City << endl;

        // list the records again, in order
        btfile.InOrder(ShowThem);
        }

void ShowThem(const PageKey & key, const DataBlock & db)
        {
        NameCity nc(db);

        cout << "key = " << setw(16) << key
             << "\t rec = " << nc.Name
             << " of " << nc.City << endl;
        }
```

## 14.7 Farewell

This book has been fun to write. I was able to take working code from my personal library and present it for others to use. I hope that you've enjoyed what you've found here, and that the code will aid you in your work. Good luck!

# PART IV

# Appendices

# Appendix A: Code Listings

## Chapter 2:  A Library of Tools

**Listing 2-1. boolean.h.**

```
//==========================================
//   UTILITY LIBRARY
//       boolean.h
//
//       Copyright 1992 by Scott Robert Ladd
//       All rights reserved
//==========================================

#ifndef BOOLEAN_H
#define BOOLEAN_H

enum Boolean
    {
    BOOL_FALSE = 0,
    BOOL_TRUE  = 1
    };

#endif
```

**Listing 2-2. switch.h.**

```
//==========================================
//   MATHEMATICAL CLASS LIBRARY
//       switch.h
//
//       Copyright 1991 by Scott Robert Ladd
//       All rights reserved
//==========================================

#ifndef SWITCH_H
#define SWITCH_H

enum Switch
    {
    OFF = 0,
    ON  = 1
    };

#endif
```

**Listing 2-3. err_rptr.h.**

```
//================================================================
//   MATHEMATICAL LIBRARY
//       err_rptr.h
//
//       A class defining an object for reporting warnings and
//       errors
//
//       Copyright 1992 by Scott Robert Ladd
//       All rights reserved
//================================================================

#ifndef ERR_RPTR_H
#define ERR_RPTR_H

class ErrReporter;

#include "stddef.h"
#include "iostream.h"
#include "str.h"

//─────────────────────────────
// ErrReporter
//      Base class for error reporting
//─────────────────────────────

class ErrReporter
    {
    public:
        ErrReporter(const String * lead);

        ~ErrReporter();

        virtual void Warning(const String & msg);
        virtual void Fatal(const String & msg);

    protected:
        virtual void MsgOut(const String & msg);

        String * Leader;
    };


//─────────────────────────────
// DosErrReporter
//      Class for reporting objects in DOS text-based program
//─────────────────────────────

class DosErrReporter : public ErrReporter
```

**502**

```
    {
    public:
        DosErrReporter(const String * lead = NULL,
                            ostream * strm = NULL);

        virtual void Warning(const String & msg);
        virtual void Fatal(const String & msg);

    protected:
        virtual void MsgOut(const String & msg);

    private:
        ostream * Destination;
    };

#endif
```

**Listing 2-4. err_rptr.cxx.**

```
//==============================================================
//   MATHEMATICAL LIBRARY
//       err_rptr.cxx
//
//       A class defining an object for reporting warnings and
//       errors
//
//       Copyright 1992 by Scott Robert Ladd
//       All rights reserved
//==============================================================

#include "err_rptr.h"
#include "stdlib.h"
#include "string.h"

ErrReporter::ErrReporter(const String * lead)
    {
    if (lead == NULL)
        Leader = NULL;
    else
        Leader = new String(*lead);
    }

ErrReporter::~ErrReporter()
    {
    // delete leader if it was allocated
    if (Leader != NULL)
        delete Leader;
    }
```

**503**

```
void ErrReporter::Warning(const String & msg)
    {
    // does nothing!
    }

void ErrReporter::Fatal(const String & msg)
    {
    // does nothing!
    }

void ErrReporter::MsgOut(const String & msg)
    {
    // does nothing!
    }

DosErrReporter::DosErrReporter(const String * lead,
                                        ostream * strm)
    : ErrReporter(lead)
    {
    if (strm == NULL)
        Destination = &cerr;
    else
        Destination = strm;
    }

void DosErrReporter::Warning(const String & msg)
    {
    *Destination << "\nWARNING - ";

    MsgOut(msg);
    }

void DosErrReporter::Fatal(const String & msg)
    {
    *Destination << "\nFATAL ERROR - ";

    MsgOut(msg);

    exit(EXIT_FAILURE);
    }

void DosErrReporter::MsgOut(const String & msg)
    {
    if (Leader == NULL)
        *Destination << msg << endl;
    else
        *Destination << *Leader << ": " << msg << endl;
    }
```

**Listing 2-5. randgen.h.**

```
//================================================================
//   MATHEMATICAL CLASS LIBRARY
//       Random Number Generator (randgen.h)
//
//       The RandGen class defines a pseudo-random number
//       generator that uses the linear congruential method.
//
//
//       _____
//       08-Jan-1992  1.00  Original version
//       _____
//
//
//       Copyright 1992 by Scott Robert Ladd
//       All rights reserved
//================================================================

#ifndef _RANDGEN_H
#define _RANDGEN_H

#include "stddef.h"
#include "time.h"

//_____
// class definition
//_____

class RandGen
    {
    public:
        // constructor
        RandGen(unsigned long initSeed = (unsigned long)time(NULL));

        // set seed value
        void SetSeed(unsigned long newSeed = (unsigned long)time(NULL));

        // get a psuedo-random number from 0 to (lim - 1)
        unsigned short operator () (unsigned short lim);

    private:
        unsigned long Seed;
    };

//_____
// inline function definitions
//_____

inline RandGen::RandGen(unsigned long initSeed)
    {
```

```
    Seed = initSeed;
    }

inline void RandGen::SetSeed(unsigned long newSeed)
    {
    Seed = newSeed;
    }

#endif
```

**Listing 2-6. randgen.cxx.**

```
//==============================================================
//   MATHEMATICAL CLASS LIBRARY
//       Random Number Generator (randgen.cxx)
//
//       The RandGen class defines a pseudo-random number
//       generator that uses the linear congruential method.
//
//       ————————————————————————
//
//       08-Jan-1992  1.00  Original version
//       ————————————————————————
//
//
//       Copyright 1992 by Scott Robert Ladd
//       All rights reserved
//==============================================================

#include "randgen.h"

//————————————————————————
// NOTE:
//       This generator depends upon overflow. It will NOT
//       work correctly in an environment where shorteger
//       arithmetic can generate an overflow exception.
//————————————————————————

unsigned short RandGen::operator () (unsigned short lim)
    {
    // get next seed value
    Seed = Seed * 5709421UL + 1UL;

    // return value from 0 to (lim - 1)
    return (unsigned short)((Seed >> 16UL) % lim);
    }
```

# Chapter 3: A String Class

**Listing 3-1. str.h.**

```
//===========================================================
//   DYNAMIC STRING CLASS
//        str.h
//
//        Provides a general dynamic string class.
//
//        Copyright 1991, 1992 Scott Robert Ladd
//        All Rights Reserved
//===========================================================

#ifndef STR_H
#define STR_H

class String;
class BoyerMoore;

#include "stddef.h"
#include "iostream.h"
#include "err_rptr.h"
#include "boolean.h"

//———————————————————————————
// String class
//———————————————————————————

enum StrCompVal
    {
    SC_LESS,
    SC_EQUAL,
    SC_GREATER,
    SC_ERROR
    };

enum StrCompMode
    {
    SM_SENSITIVE,
    SM_IGNORE
    };

enum StrError
    {
    SE_ALLOC,
    SE_TOO_LONG,
    SE_INVALID
```

```
        };

class String
      {
    public:
        // constructor
        String();
        String(const String & str);
        String(const char * cstr);
        String(size_t count,   char fillCh = '\0');
        String(size_t maxsize, const char * format, ... );

        // destructor
        ~String();

        // version number
        static int Version();

        // value return methods
        size_t Length() const;
        size_t Size() const;

        // Assign an exception handler
        static void SetErrOut(const ErrReporter & er);

        // create a c-string from String method
        operator const char * () const;

        // assignment method
        String operator = (const String & str);

        // concatenation methods
        friend String operator + (const String & str1,
                                  const String & str2);

        friend String operator + (const String & str1, char ch);

        void operator += (const String & str);
        void operator += (char ch);

        // comparison methods
        int operator <  (const String & str) const;
        int operator >  (const String & str) const;
        int operator <= (const String & str) const;
        int operator >= (const String & str) const;
        int operator == (const String & str) const;
        int operator != (const String & str) const;
```

```
    StrCompVal Compare(const String & str,
                       StrCompMode caseChk = SM_IGNORE) const;

    // substring search methods
    Boolean Find(const BoyerMoore & bm, size_t & pos) const;

    Boolean Find(const String & str,
                 size_t & pos,
                 StrCompMode caseChk = SM_IGNORE) const;

    // substring deletion method
    void Delete(size_t pos, size_t count);

    // substring insertion methods
    void Insert(size_t pos, char ch);
    void Insert(size_t pos, const String & str);

    // substring retrieval method
    String Cut(size_t start, size_t count) const;
    String CutHead(size_t count) const;
    String CutTail(size_t count) const;

    // character retrieval method
    char operator [] (size_t pos) const;

    // case-modification methods
    void ToUpper();
    void ToLower();

    String AsUpper() const;
    String AsLower() const;

    // stream input/output methods
    friend ostream & operator << (ostream & strm,
                                  const String & str);

    friend istream & operator >> (istream & strm,
                                  String & str);

private:
    // instance variables
    size_t Siz; // allocated size
    size_t Len; // current length
    char * Txt; // pointer to text

    // error display object
    static ErrReporter * ErrOut;
```

```
        // class constant
        static size_t AllocIncr;

        // pointer to error handler
        static void ErrorHandler(StrError err);

        // calc alloc size for needed bytes
        static size_t CalcSiz(size_t needed);
    };

// obtain version number
inline int String::Version()
    {
    return 0x0500;
    }

// value return methods
inline size_t String::Length() const
    {
    return Len;
    }

inline size_t String::Size() const
    {
    return Siz;
    }

// add-assignment operator
inline void String::operator += (const String & str)
    {
    *this = *this + str;
    }

inline void String::operator += (char ch)
    {
    *this = *this + ch;
    }

// create a c-string from String method
inline String::operator const char * () const
    {
    return Txt;
    }

// comparison methods
inline int String::operator <  (const String & str) const
    {
    return (Compare(str) == SC_LESS);
    }
```

```
inline int String::operator >  (const String & str) const
    {
    return (Compare(str) == SC_GREATER);
    }

inline int String::operator <= (const String & str) const
    {
    return (Compare(str) != SC_GREATER);
    }

inline int String::operator >= (const String & str) const
    {
    return (Compare(str) != SC_LESS);
    }

inline int String::operator == (const String & str) const
    {
    return (Compare(str) == SC_EQUAL);
    }

inline int String::operator != (const String & str) const
    {
    return (Compare(str) != SC_EQUAL);
    }

// character retrieval method
inline char String::operator [] (size_t pos) const
    {
    if (pos >= Len)
        return '\x00';
    else
        return Txt[pos];
    }

// stream I/O functions

inline ostream & operator << (ostream & strm, const String & str)
    {
    strm << str.Txt;

    return strm;
    }

//────────────────────────────
//  BoyerMoore class
//────────────────────────────

class BoyerMoore
    {
```

```
    public:
        // constructors
        BoyerMoore(const String & pattern);
        BoyerMoore(const BoyerMoore & bm);

        // destructor
        ~BoyerMoore();

        // assignment operator
        void operator = (const BoyerMoore & bm);

        // get charactre from pattern string
        char operator [] (size_t index) const;

        // get delta value from table
        size_t GetDelta(char ch) const;

        // get length of pattern used to create table
        size_t GetPatternLen() const;

        // Assign an exception handler
        static void SetErrOut(const ErrReporter & er);

    private:

        // error display object
        static ErrReporter * ErrOut;

        // pointer to error handler
        static void ReportError();

        // size of delta table
        static const size_t DeltaSize;

        // pointer to delta table
        size_t * Delta;
        String Pattern;
    };

// destructor
inline BoyerMoore::~BoyerMoore()
    {
    delete Delta;
    }

// get delta value for a given character
inline size_t BoyerMoore::GetDelta(char ch) const
    {
```

```
    return Delta[size_t(ch)];
    }

// get length of pattern used to create table
inline size_t BoyerMoore::GetPatternLen() const
    {
    return Pattern.Length();
    }

inline char BoyerMoore::operator [] (size_t index) const
    {
    return Pattern[index];
    };

#endif
```

**Listing 3-2. str.cxx.**

```
//===============================================================
//   DYNAMIC STRING CLASS
//       str.cxx
//
//       Provides a general dynamic string class.
//
//       Copyright 1991, 1992 Scott Robert Ladd
//       All Rights Reserved
//===============================================================

#include "str.h"
#include "iomanip.h"
#include "string.h"
#include "stdlib.h"
#include "stdio.h"
#include "stdarg.h"
#include "ctype.h"
#include "limits.h"


//————————————————————————————
//   String class
//————————————————————————————

// class-global constant initialization
size_t String::AllocIncr = 8;

ErrReporter * String::ErrOut = NULL;

// error reporting function
void String::ErrorHandler(StrError err)
    {
```

```cpp
    if (ErrOut != NULL)
        {
        switch (err)
            {
            case SE_ALLOC :
                ErrOut->Fatal("String allocation failure");
                break;

            case SE_TOO_LONG :
                ErrOut->Fatal("String exceeded character limit");
                break;

            case SE_INVALID :
                ErrOut->Fatal("String invalid parameters");
            }
        }
    }

// Assign an exception handler
void String::SetErrOut(const ErrReporter & er)
    {
    if (ErrOut != NULL)
        delete ErrOut;

    ErrOut = new ErrReporter(er);
    }

// calculate the allocation size for a string
inline size_t String::CalcSiz(size_t needed)
    {
    size_t x;

    x = ((needed + AllocIncr) / AllocIncr) * AllocIncr;

    return x;
    }

// constructor
String::String()
    {
    Len = 0;
    Siz = 0;
    Txt = NULL;
    }

String::String(const String & str)
    {
    Len = str.Len;
```

```
    Siz = str.Siz;

    if (str.Txt == NULL)
        Txt = NULL;
    else
        {
        Txt = new char[Siz];

        if (Txt == NULL)
            ErrorHandler(SE_ALLOC);

        memcpy(Txt,str.Txt,Len + 1);
        }
    }

String::String(const char * cstr)
    {
    if ((cstr == NULL) || (cstr[0] == '\x00'))
        {
        Len = 0;
        Siz = 0;
        Txt = NULL;
        }
    else
        {
        Len = strlen(cstr);
        Siz = CalcSiz(Len);

        Txt = new char [Siz];

        if (Txt == NULL)
            ErrorHandler(SE_ALLOC);

        memcpy(Txt,cstr,Len + 1);
        }
    }

String::String(size_t count, char fillCh)
    {
    if (count == 0)
        ErrorHandler(SE_INVALID);

    Siz = CalcSiz(count);
    Len = count;

    Txt = new char[Siz];

    if (Txt == NULL)
```

```
            ErrorHandler(SE_ALLOC);

        memset(Txt,fillCh,count);

        Txt[count] = '\x00';
        }

String::String(size_t maxsize, const char * format, ... )
        {
        // allocate temporary buffer
        char * buffer = new char[maxsize];

        if (buffer == NULL)
            ErrorHandler(SE_ALLOC);

        // initialize argument list
        va_list args;

        va_start(args,format);

        // format items into buffer based on format
        Len = vsprintf(buffer,format,args);

        // end argument list processing
        va_end(args);

        // calculate require Txt length
        Siz = CalcSiz(Len);

        // allocate Txt
        Txt = new char[Siz];

        if (Txt == NULL)
            ErrorHandler(SE_ALLOC);

        // duplicate data from buffer
        strcpy(Txt,buffer);

        // delete buffer
        delete buffer;
        }

// destructor
String::~String()
        {
        if (Txt != NULL)
            delete Txt;
        }
```

```
// assignment method
String String::operator = (const String & str)
    {
    Len = str.Len;
    Siz = str.Siz;

    if (Txt != NULL)
        delete Txt;

    if (Siz == 0)
        Txt = NULL;
    else
        {
        Txt = new char[Siz];

        if (Txt == NULL)
            ErrorHandler(SE_ALLOC);

        memcpy(Txt,str.Txt,Len + 1);
        }

    return *this;
    }

// concatenation methods
String operator + (const String & str1,
                   const String & str2)
    {
    String temp;

    unsigned long totalLen = str1.Len + str2.Len;

    if (totalLen == 0)
        return temp;

    if (totalLen > UINT_MAX)
        String::ErrorHandler(SE_TOO_LONG);

    temp.Len = 0;
    temp.Siz = String::CalcSiz((size_t)totalLen);
    temp.Txt = new char[temp.Siz];

    if (temp.Txt == NULL)
        String::ErrorHandler(SE_ALLOC);

    temp.Txt[0] = '\000';

    if (str1.Txt != NULL)
```

```
        {
        memcpy(temp.Txt,str1.Txt,str1.Len);
        temp.Len = str1.Len;
        }

    if (str2.Txt != NULL)
        {
        memcpy(&temp.Txt[temp.Len],str2.Txt,str2.Len + 1);
        temp.Len += str2.Len;
        }

    return temp;
    }

// concatenation methods
String operator + (const String & str, char ch)
    {
    String temp;

    if (str.Txt == NULL)
        {
        temp.Len = 1;
        temp.Siz = String::AllocIncr;
        temp.Txt = new char [temp.Siz];

        if (temp.Txt == NULL)
            String::ErrorHandler(SE_ALLOC);

        temp.Txt[0] = ch;
        temp.Txt[1] = '\000';
        }
    else
        {
        if (str.Len == UINT_MAX)
            String::ErrorHandler(SE_TOO_LONG);

        temp.Len = str.Len + 1;

        if (temp.Len == str.Siz)
            temp.Siz = str.Siz + String::AllocIncr;
        else
            temp.Siz = str.Siz;

        temp.Txt = new char[temp.Siz];

        if (temp.Txt == NULL)
            String::ErrorHandler(SE_ALLOC);
```

```
        memcpy(temp.Txt,str.Txt,str.Len);

        temp.Txt[str.Len]  = ch;
        temp.Txt[temp.Len] = '\000';
        }

    return temp;
    }

StrCompVal String::Compare(const String & str,
                           StrCompMode caseChk) const
    {
    // handle special cases where one string is empty
    if (Txt == NULL)
        if (str.Txt == NULL)
            return SC_EQUAL;
        else
            return SC_LESS;

    if (str.Txt == NULL)
        return SC_GREATER;

    // compare the # of characters in the shorter string
    size_t count;

    if (str.Len < Len)
        count = str.Len;
    else
        count = Len;

    // working variables
    char    c1, c2;
    size_t i;

    if (caseChk == SM_IGNORE)
        {
        // case insensitive comparison
        for (i = 0; i < count; ++i)
            {
            c1 = (char)tolower(Txt[i]);
            c2 = (char)tolower(str.Txt[i]);

            // if characters differ
            if (c1 != c2)
                {
                // select appropriate result
                if (c1 < c2)
                    return SC_LESS;
```

```
                        else
                            return SC_GREATER;
                        }
                    }
                }
        else
            {
            for (i = 0; i < count; ++i)
                {
                c1 = Txt[i];
                c2 = str.Txt[i];

                // if characters differ
                if (c1 != c2)
                    {
                    // select appropriate result
                    if (c1 < c2)
                        return SC_LESS;
                    else
                        return SC_GREATER;
                    }
                }
            }

        // at this point, no differences were found
        if (Len == str.Len)
            return SC_EQUAL;
        else
            {
            // is lengths differ, shorter string < longer one
            if (Len < str.Len)
                return SC_LESS;
            else
                return SC_GREATER;
            }
        }

// substring search methods
Boolean String::Find(const BoyerMoore & bm, size_t & pos) const
    {
    size_t i, j, patlen;

    // store pattern length locally (it gets used a lot)
    patlen = bm.GetPatternLen();

    // i is the index into the target
    i = patlen;
```

```
    while (i <= Len)
        {
        // j is an index into pattern
        j = patlen;

        // while corresponding characters match
        while (bm[j - 1] == Txt[i - 1])
            {
            if (j > 1)
                {
                // move left one character for next comparison
                -j;
                -i;
                }
            else
                {
                // we've reached the beginning of the pattern
                // pattern found!
                pos = i - 1;
                return BOOL_TRUE;
                }
            }

        // move target index by delta value of
        // mismatched character
        i += bm.GetDelta(Txt[i - 1]);
        }

    return BOOL_FALSE;
    }

Boolean String::Find(const String & str,
                     size_t & pos,
                     StrCompMode caseChk) const
    {
    // uses the brute force method
    if (Len < str.Len)
        return BOOL_FALSE;

    // duplicate buffers
    char * target = new char[Len + 1];

    if (target == NULL)
        ErrorHandler(SE_ALLOC);

    strcpy(target,Txt);

    char * pattern = new char[str.Len + 1];
```

```
if (pattern == NULL)
    ErrorHandler(SE_ALLOC);

strcpy(pattern,str.Txt);

// create return value variable
Boolean result;

// convert to all lowercase if case-insensitive search
if (caseChk == SM_IGNORE)
    {
    strlwr(target);
    strlwr(pattern);
    }

// calculate last position in *this where str could be
size_t end = Len - str.Len;
size_t p, t;

// start at the beginning of ttarget
pos = 0;

for (;;)
    {
    p = 0;   // beginning of pattern
    t = pos; // beginning of search position in target

    // while characters match
    // and we're not at the end of the strings

    while ((pattern[p] == target[t])
        && (pattern[p] != 0)
        && (target[t]  != 0))
        {
        // move to next character
        ++t;
        ++p;
        }

    // if we've reached the end of pattern
    //     we've found pattern in target

    if (pattern[p] == 0)
        {
        result = BOOL_TRUE;
        break;
        }

    // if we've reached the end of target
```

```
        // or we've searched far enough
        //      pattern has not been found

        if ((target[t] == 0) || (pos >= end))
            {
            result = BOOL_FALSE;
            break;
            }

        // keep looking, starting at the mismatch

        ++pos;
        }

    // delete temporary buffers
    delete target;
    delete pattern;

    // outa here
    return result;
    }

// substring deletion method
void String::Delete(size_t pos, size_t count)
    {
    if (Txt == NULL)
        return;

    size_t newLen, i;

    // error if deleting outside of string
    if ((pos + count - 1) > Len)
        ErrorHandler(SE_INVALID);

    // length of new string
    newLen = Len - count;

    if ((Siz - newLen) > AllocIncr)
        {
        // allocation size has changed
        // calculate new size

        Siz = CalcSiz(newLen);

        // create new buffer

        char * temp = new char[Siz];
```

```
        if (temp == NULL)
            ErrorHandler(SE_ALLOC);

        // copy characters into new buffer
        char * tptr = temp;

        for (i = 0; i <= Len; ++i)
            {
            // when count is reached, skip deleted characters
            if (i == pos)
                i += count;

            *tptr = Txt[i];
            ++tptr;
            }

        // delete old buffer
        delete Txt;

        // assign new buffer
        Txt = temp;
        }
    else
        {
        // just "slide" characters down
        for (i = pos + count; i <= Len; ++i)
            Txt[i] = Txt[i + count];
        }

    Len = newLen;
    }

// substring insertion methods
void String::Insert(size_t pos, char ch)
    {
    if (pos > Len)
        ErrorHandler(SE_INVALID);

    if (Txt == NULL)
        {
        // an empty string == ch
        Len = 1;
        Siz = AllocIncr;

        Txt = new char [Siz];

        if (Txt == NULL)
            String::ErrorHandler(SE_ALLOC);
```

```
    Txt[0] = ch;
    Txt[1] = '\000';
    }
else
    {
    size_t newLen = Len + 1;
    size_t i;

    if (newLen == Siz)
        {
        // need a larger buffer
        Siz += AllocIncr;

        // create temporary buffer
        char * temp = new char[Siz];
        char * tptr = temp;

        if (temp == NULL)
            ErrorHandler(SE_ALLOC);

        // copy in old buffer, inserting ch when needed
        for (i = 0; i <= Len; ++i)
            {
            if (i == pos)
                {
                *tptr = ch;
                ++tptr;
                }

            *tptr = Txt[i];
            ++tptr;
            }

        // delete old buffer
        delete Txt;

        // assign new buffer and length
        Txt = temp;
        Len = newLen;
        }
    else
        {
        // slide characters right
        for (i = newLen; i > pos; --i)
            Txt[i] = Txt[i-1];

        // insert character
        Txt[pos] = ch;
```

```
                // adjust length
                Len = newLen;
                }
            }
        }

void String::Insert(size_t pos, const String & str)
    {
    if (str.Txt == NULL)
        return;

    if (pos > Len)
        ErrorHandler(SE_INVALID);

    if (Txt == NULL)
        {
        // empty string = str
        *this = str;
        }
    else
        {
        // calculate new length
        unsigned long totalLen = str.Len + Len;

        if (totalLen > UINT_MAX)
            ErrorHandler(SE_TOO_LONG);

        size_t i, j;

        // if new  length > current size
        if (totalLen > Siz)
            {
            // allocate new buffer
            Siz = CalcSiz((size_t)totalLen);

            char * temp = new char [Siz];
            char * tptr = temp;

            // copy buffers from source strings
            for (i = 0; i <= Len; ++i)
                {
                if (i == pos)
                    {
                    for (j = 0; j < str.Len; ++j)
                        {
                        *tptr = str.Txt[j];
                        ++tptr;
                        }
```

```
                            }

                        *tptr = Txt[i];
                        ++tptr;
                        }

                // delete old buffer
                delete Txt;

                // assign new buffer
                Txt = temp;
                }
            else
                {
                // slide section old buffer to right
                for (i = Len + str.Len; i > pos + str.Len; —i)
                    Txt[i] = Txt[i - str.Len];

                // insert new string
                for (i = 0; i < str.Len; ++i)
                    Txt[pos + i] = str.Txt[i];
                }

        Len = (size_t)totalLen;
        }
    }

// substring retrieval method
String String::Cut(size_t start, size_t count) const
    {
    if ((start + count) > Len)
        ErrorHandler(SE_INVALID);

    String temp;

    if ((start < Len) && (count > 0))
        {
        temp.Len = count;
        temp.Siz = CalcSiz(count);
        temp.Txt = new char[temp.Siz];

        if (temp.Txt == NULL)
            ErrorHandler(SE_ALLOC);

        memcpy(temp.Txt,&Txt[start],count);

        temp.Txt[count] = '\000';
        }
```

```
    return temp;
    }

String String::CutHead(size_t count) const
    {
    if (count > Len)
        ErrorHandler(SE_INVALID);

    String temp;

    if (count > 0)
        {
        temp.Len = count;
        temp.Siz = CalcSiz(count);
        temp.Txt = new char[temp.Siz];

        if (temp.Txt == NULL)
            ErrorHandler(SE_ALLOC);

        memcpy(temp.Txt,Txt,count);

        temp.Txt[count] = '\000';
        }

    return temp;
    }

String String::CutTail(size_t count) const
    {
    if (count > Len)
        ErrorHandler(SE_INVALID);

    String temp;

    if (count > 0)
        {
        temp.Len = count;
        temp.Siz = CalcSiz(count);
        temp.Txt = new char[temp.Siz];

        if (temp.Txt == NULL)
            ErrorHandler(SE_ALLOC);

        memcpy(temp.Txt,&Txt[Len - count - 1],count);

        temp.Txt[count] = '\000';
        }
```

```
    return temp;
    }

// case-modification methods
void String::ToUpper()
    {
    if (Txt != NULL)
        strupr(Txt);
    }

void String::ToLower()
    {
    if (Txt != NULL)
        strlwr(Txt);
    }

String String::AsUpper() const
    {
    String temp = *this;

    if (temp.Txt != NULL)
        strupr(temp.Txt);

    return temp;
    }

String String::AsLower() const
    {
    String temp = *this;

    if (temp.Txt != NULL)
        strlwr(temp.Txt);

    return temp;
    }

// stream I/O functions

istream & operator >> (istream & strm, String & str)
    {
    static char buf[128];

    if ((str.Txt == NULL) || (str.Len == 0))
        {
        strm >> setw(128) >> buf;

        #ifdef __ZTC__
            str = (const char *)buf;
```

```
        #else
            str = buf;
        #endif
        }
    else
        strm >> setw(str.Len) >> str.Txt;


    return strm;
    }


//————————————————————————————
//  BoyerMoore class
//————————————————————————————

const size_t BoyerMoore::DeltaSize = 256;

ErrReporter * BoyerMoore::ErrOut = NULL;

// report an error
void BoyerMoore::ReportError()
    {
    if (ErrOut != NULL)
        ErrOut->Fatal("Boyer-Moore allocation failure");
    }

// Assign an exception handler
void BoyerMoore::SetErrOut(const ErrReporter & er)
    {
    if (ErrOut != NULL)
        delete ErrOut;

    ErrOut = new ErrReporter(er);
    }

BoyerMoore::BoyerMoore(const String & pat)
    : Pattern(pat)
    {
    // allocate delta table
    Delta = new size_t [DeltaSize];

    if (Delta == NULL)
        ReportError();

    // clear table
    size_t i;

    // get length of pattern
```

```
    size_t patlen = Pattern.Length();

    for (i = 0; i < DeltaSize; ++i)
        Delta[i] = patlen;

    // set table values
    for (i = 1; i < patlen; ++i)
        Delta[(size_t)Pattern[i - 1]] = patlen - i;

    // set value for last pattern character
    Delta[(size_t)Pattern[patlen - 1]] = 1;
    }

BoyerMoore::BoyerMoore(const BoyerMoore & bm)
    : Pattern(bm.Pattern)
    {
    // allocate delta table
    Delta = new size_t [DeltaSize];

    if (Delta == NULL)
        ReportError();

    // copy contents of source
    memcpy(Delta,bm.Delta,DeltaSize * sizeof(char));
    }

void BoyerMoore::operator = (const BoyerMoore & bm)
    {
    Delta = bm.Delta;
    }
```

# Chapter 4: Ranges and Indexes

**Listing 4-1. range.h.**
```
//======================================================
//   MATHEMATICAL LIBRARY
//      range.h
//
//      A class that defines a subrange of int values.
//      Defining the preprocessor symbol RANGE_CHK_OFF
//      will remove all range checking code.
//
//      Copyright 1992 by Scott Robert Ladd
//      All rights reserved
//======================================================

#ifndef RANGE_H
```

```
#define RANGE_H

#include "limits.h"
#include "err_rptr.h"
#include "switch.h"

class Range
    {
    public:
        //———————
        // constructors
        //———————

        Range(int rmin, int rmax);
        Range(int rmax);
        Range(const Range & r);

        //———————————
        // assignment operator
        //———————————

        Range & operator = (const Range & r);

        #ifndef RANGE_CHK_OFF
        //———————————————
        // set error reporter object
        //———————————————

        static void SetErrOut(const ErrReporter & er);
        #endif

        //———————
        // add ranges
        //———————

        friend Range operator + (const Range & r1, const Range & r2);

        //———————————
        // comparison operator
        //———————————

        int operator == (const Range & r) const;
        int operator != (const Range & r) const;

        //———————————————
        // information retrieval functions
        //———————————————
```

```
    int GetMin() const;
    int GetMax() const;
    unsigned int GetMagnitude() const;

    //————————————
    // report error if 'n' is invalid
    //————————————

    void Check(int n) const;

    //————————————
    // check for 'n' or range within bounds
    //————————————

    int Includes(int n) const;
    int Includes(const Range & r) const;

    int Excludes(int n) const;
    int Excludes(const Range & r) const;

    //————————————
    // range checking functions
    //————————————

    static void CheckOn();
    static void CheckOff();

    static Switch GetCheck();

protected:
    //————————————
    // minimum and maximum values
    //————————————

    int Minimum;
    int Maximum;

    //————————————
    // number of values in range
    //————————————

    unsigned int Magnitude;

    #ifndef RANGE_CHK_OFF
    //————————————
    // error output object
    //————————————
```

```
        static ErrReporter * ErrOut;

        static void ReportError(const String & msg);

        //—————
        // range-checking switch
        //—————

        static Switch RangeCheck;
        #endif
    };

//———
// constructors
//———

inline Range::Range(const Range & r)
    {
    Minimum   = r.Minimum;
    Maximum   = r.Maximum;
    Magnitude = r.Magnitude;
    }

//—————
// assignment operator
//—————

inline Range & Range::operator = (const Range & r)
    {
    Minimum   = r.Minimum;
    Maximum   = r.Maximum;
    Magnitude = r.Magnitude;

    return *this;
    }

//—————
// comparison operator
//—————

inline int Range::operator == (const Range & r) const
    {
    return ((Minimum == r.Minimum) && (r.Maximum == r.Maximum));
    }

inline int Range::operator != (const Range & r) const
    {
    return ((Minimum != r.Minimum) || (r.Maximum != r.Maximum));
```

```
    }

//————————————
// information retrieval functions
//————————————

inline int Range::GetMin() const
    {
    return Minimum;
    }

inline int Range::GetMax() const
    {
    return Maximum;
    }

inline unsigned int Range::GetMagnitude() const
    {
    return Magnitude;
    }

//————————————————
// check for 'n' or range within bounds
//————————————————

inline int Range::Includes(int n) const
    {
    return ((n >= Minimum) && (n <= Maximum));
    }

inline int Range::Includes(const Range & r) const
    {
    return ((Minimum <= r.Minimum) && (Maximum >= r.Maximum));
    }

inline int Range::Excludes(int n) const
    {
    return ((n < Minimum) || (n > Maximum));
    }

inline int Range::Excludes(const Range & r) const
    {
    return ((Minimum > r.Minimum) || (Maximum < r.Maximum));
    }

//——————————
// range checking functions
//——————————
```

```
inline void Range::CheckOn()
    {
    #ifndef RANGE_CHK_OFF
        RangeCheck = ON;
    #endif
    }

inline void Range::CheckOff()
    {
    #ifndef RANGE_CHK_OFF
        RangeCheck = OFF;
    #endif
    }

inline Switch Range::GetCheck()
    {
    #ifndef RANGE_CHK_OFF
        return RangeCheck;
    #else
        return OFF;
    #endif
    }

#endif
```

**Listing 4-2. range.cxx.**

```
//============================================================
// MATHEMATICAL LIBRARY
//      range.cxx
//
//      A class that defines a subrange of int values.
//      Defining the preprocessor symbol RANGE_CHK_OFF
//      will remove all range checking code.
//
//      Copyright 1992 by Scott Robert Ladd
//      All rights reserved
//============================================================

#include "range.h"
#include "limits.h"

#ifndef RANGE_CHK_OFF
    #include "stdlib.h"

    //————————
    // error output object
    //————————
```

```
    static const String ErrMsg("Range");

    ErrReporter * Range::ErrOut = new DosErrReporter(&ErrMsg);

    //——————
    // range-checking switch
    //——————

    Switch Range::RangeCheck = OFF;

    //——————
    // function to call ErrOut
    //——————

    void Range::ReportError(const String & msg)
        {
        if (ErrOut != NULL)
            ErrOut->Fatal(msg);
        }

    //————————
    // function to create a new ErrOut
    //————————

    void Range::SetErrOut(const ErrReporter & er)
        {
        if (ErrOut != NULL)
            delete ErrOut;

        ErrOut = new ErrReporter(er);

        if (ErrOut == NULL)
            exit(EXIT_FAILURE);
        }
#endif

//——
// constructors
//——

Range::Range(int rmin, int rmax)
    {
    #ifndef RANGE_CHK_OFF
        if (RangeCheck == ON)
            {
            if (rmax < rmin)
                ReportError("maximum < minimum");
            }
```

```
    #endif

    Minimum = rmin;
    Maximum = rmax;

    if (Minimum < 0)
        {
        if (Maximum < 0)
            Magnitude = (unsigned int)(Minimum - Maximum);
        else
            Magnitude = (unsigned int)(-Minimum) + (unsigned int)Maximum;
        }
    else
        Magnitude = Maximum - Minimum;

    ++Magnitude;
    }

Range::Range(int rmax)
    {
    #ifndef RANGE_CHK_OFF
        if (RangeCheck == ON)
            {
            if (rmax <= 1)
                ReportError("invalid construction");
            }
    #endif

    Minimum   = 1;
    Maximum   = rmax;
    Magnitude = rmax + 1;
    }

//———
// add ranges
//———

Range operator + (const Range & r1, const Range & r2)
    {
    #ifndef RANGE_CHK_OFF
        if (Range::RangeCheck == ON)
            {
            if ((unsigned int)(INT_MAX - r1.Maximum) < r2.Magnitude)
                Range::ReportError("addition out-of-range");
            }
    #endif

    Range result(r1.Minimum,r1.Maximum + r2.Magnitude);
```

```
    return result;
    }

//————————
// report error if 'n' is invalid
//————————

void Range::Check(int n) const
    {
    #ifndef RANGE_CHK_OFF
        if ((RangeCheck == ON)
        && ((n < Minimum) || (n > Maximum)))
            ReportError("value out-of-bounds");
    #endif
    }
```

**Listing 4-3. index.h.**
```
//===============================================================
//  MATHEMATICAL LIBRARY
//      index.h
//
//      Defines a data type used for indexing arrays
//
//      Copyright 1992 by Scott Robert Ladd
//      All rights reserved
//===============================================================

#ifndef INDEX_H
#define INDEX_H

#include "range.h"

class Index : public Range
    {
    public:

        //————
        // constructors
        //————

        Index(int imin, int imax);
        Index(const Range & r);
        Index(const Range & r, int i);
        Index(const Index & i);

        //————
        // conversions
        //————
```

```
operator int() const;          // returns exact value
operator unsigned int() const; // returns zero-based value

//———
// value checks
//———

int IsMin() const;
int IsMax() const;

//————
// explicit assignments
//————

void SetMin();
void SetMax();

//————
// assignment operators
//————

Index & operator = (int n);
Index & operator = (const Index & i);

//———
// math operators
//———

Index operator + (const Index & i);
Index operator - (const Index & i);

Index operator + (int i);
Index operator - (int i);

//————
// shorthand operators
//————

Index & operator += (const Index & i);
Index & operator -= (const Index & i);

Index & operator += (int n);
Index & operator -= (int n);

//————
// increment and decrement
//————
```

```
        Index & operator ++ ();
        Index & operator - ();

        //—————
        // comparison operators
        //—————

        int operator >  (const Index & i) const;
        int operator >= (const Index & i) const;
        int operator == (const Index & i) const;
        int operator != (const Index & i) const;
        int operator <= (const Index & i) const;
        int operator <  (const Index & i) const;

        int operator >  (int i) const;
        int operator >= (int i) const;
        int operator == (int i) const;
        int operator != (int i) const;
        int operator <= (int i) const;
        int operator <  (int i) const;

    protected:

        //—————
        // current index value
        //—————

        int Value;
    };

//———
// constructors
//———

inline Index::Index(int imin, int imax)
    : Range(imin,imax)
    {
    Value = Minimum;
    }

inline Index::Index(const Range & r)
    : Range(r)
    {
    Value = Minimum;
    }

inline Index::Index(const Index & i)
    : Range(i)
```

```
    {
    Value = i.Value;
    }

//———
// conversions
//———

inline Index::operator int () const
    {
    return Value;
    }

//———
// value checks
//———

inline int Index::IsMin() const
    {
    return (Value == Minimum);
    }

inline int Index::IsMax() const
    {
    return (Value == Maximum);
    }

//————
// explicit assignments
//————

inline void Index::SetMin()
    {
    Value = Minimum;
    }

inline void Index::SetMax()
    {
    Value = Maximum;
    }

//———
// math operators
//———

inline Index Index::operator + (const Index & i)
    {
    return *this + i.Value;
```

```
    }

inline Index Index::operator - (const Index & i)
    {
    return *this - i.Value;
    }

//——————
// shorthand operators
//——————

inline Index & Index::operator += (const Index & i)
    {
    return *this += i.Value;
    }

inline Index & Index::operator -= (const Index & i)
    {
    return *this -= i.Value;
    }

inline Index & Index::operator += (int i)
    {
    return *this = *this + i;
    }

inline Index & Index::operator -= (int i)
    {
    return *this = *this - i;
    }

//——————
// comparison operators
//——————

inline int Index::operator > (const Index & i) const
    {
    return (Value > i.Value);
    }

inline int Index::operator >= (const Index & i) const
    {
    return (Value >= i.Value);
    }

inline int Index::operator == (const Index & i) const
    {
    return (Value == i.Value);
```

```
    }

inline int Index::operator != (const Index & i) const
    {
    return (Value != i.Value);
    }

inline int Index::operator <= (const Index & i) const
    {
    return (Value <= i.Value);
    }

inline int Index::operator < (const Index & i) const
    {
    return (Value < i.Value);
    }

inline int Index::operator > (int i) const
    {
    return (Value > i);
    }

inline int Index::operator >= (int i) const
    {
    return (Value >= i);
    }

inline int Index::operator == (int i) const
    {
    return (Value == i);
    }

inline int Index::operator != (int i) const
    {
    return (Value != i);
    }

inline int Index::operator <= (int i) const
    {
    return (Value <= i);
    }

inline int Index::operator < (int i) const
    {
    return (Value < i);
    }

#endif
```

**Listing 4-4. index.cxx.**

```
//================================================================
//   MATHEMATICAL LIBRARY
//       index.cxx
//
//       Defines a data type used for indexing arrays
//
//       Copyright 1992 by Scott Robert Ladd
//       All rights reserved
//================================================================

#include "index.h"

//————
// constructors
//————

Index::Index(const Range & r, int i)
    : Range(r)
    {
    #ifndef RANGE_CHK_OFF
        if (RangeCheck == ON)
            {
            if ((i < Minimum) || (i > Maximum))
                ReportError("assignment out of range");
            }
    #endif

    Value = i;
    }

//————
// conversions
//————

Index::operator unsigned int () const
    {
    unsigned long result;

    if (Minimum < 0)
        {
        result = (unsigned int)(-Minimum);

        if (Value < 0)
            result -= (unsigned int)(-Value);
        else
            result += (unsigned int)Value;
        }
```

```
        else
            result = (unsigned long)Value - (unsigned long)Minimum;

        return (unsigned int)result;
        }

//————————
// assignment operators
//————————

Index & Index::operator = (int i)
        {
        #ifndef RANGE_CHK_OFF
            if (RangeCheck == ON)
                {
                if ((i < Minimum) || (i > Maximum))
                    ReportError("assignment out of range");
                }
        #endif

        Value = i;

        return *this;
        }

Index & Index::operator = (const Index & i)
        {
        this->Range::operator = (i);

        Value = i.Value;

        return *this;
        }

//————————
// math operators
//————————

Index Index::operator + (int i)
        {
        #ifndef RANGE_CHK_OFF
            if (RangeCheck == ON)
                {
                if (i < 0)
                    {
                    if ((Value - Minimum) < -i)
                        ReportError("underflow in addition");
                    }
```

```
            else
                {
                if ((Maximum - Value) < i)
                    ReportError("overflow in addition");
                }
            }
    #endif

    Index result(*this);

    result.Value += i;

    return result;
    }

Index Index::operator - (int i)
    {
    #ifndef RANGE_CHK_OFF
        if (RangeCheck == ON)
            {
            if (i > 0)
                {
                if ((Value - Minimum) < i)
                    ReportError("underflow in subtraction");
                }
            else
                {
                if ((Maximum - Value) < -i)
                    ReportError("overflow in subtraction");
                }
            }
    #endif

    Index result(*this);

    result.Value -= i;

    return result;
    }

//—————————
// increment and decrement
//—————————

Index & Index::operator ++ ()
    {
    #ifndef RANGE_CHK_OFF
        if (RangeCheck == ON)
```

```
                {
                if (Value == Maximum)
                    ReportError("overflow on increment");
                }
        #endif

        ++Value;

        return *this;
        }

Index & Index::operator - ()
        {
        #ifndef RANGE_CHK_OFF
            if (RangeCheck == ON)
                {
                if (Value == Minimum)
                    ReportError("underflow on decrement");
                }
        #endif

        -Value;

        return *this;
        }
```

# Chapter 5: Building Blocks for Arrays

**Listing 5-1. array.h.**

```
//=================================================================
//   MATHEMATICAL CLASS LIBRARY
//        array.h
//
//        Defines the base class upon which all array classes
//        are based. Also defined is the array pointer type
//        that provides efficient access to elements in array
//        objects.
//
//        Copyright 1992 by Scott Robert Ladd
//        All rights reserved
//=================================================================

#ifndef ARRAY_H
#define ARRAY_H

#include "index.h"
#include "stddef.h"
```

```
//————————————
// type definitions for function types
//————————————

typedef void * (* ElemCreate)(void *);
typedef void * (* ElemDestroy)(void *);

//-=-=-=-=-=-=-=-=-=-=-=-=-=-=-=-=-=-=-=-=-=-=-=-=-=-=-=
//
//  Array class
//
//-=-=-=-=-=-=-=-=-=-=-=-=-=-=-=-=-=-=-=-=-=-=-=-=-=-=-=

class Array
    {
    public:

        //————————————
        // assign a new error reporter
        //————————————

        static void SetErrOut(const ErrReporter & er);

        //————————————
        // create an appropriate index
        //————————————

        Index MakeIndex() const;

        //————————
        // get the range
        //————————

        Range GetRange() const;

        //————————————
        // get number of elements
        //————————————

        unsigned int GetCount() const;

        //————————————
        // get size of an element
        //————————————

        size_t GetElemSize() const;

        //————————————————
```

```
    // get address of destroy function
    //————————————

    ElemDestroy GetDestroyFunc() const;

protected:

    //————
    // constructors
    //————

    // original
    Array(const Range & r,
          size_t elemsize,
          ElemCreate  create  = NULL,
          ElemDestroy destroy = NULL);

    // copy
    Array(const Array & a);

    // concatenate
    Array(const Array & a1, const Array & a2);

    // subrange
    Array(const Array & a, const Index & first, const Index & last);

    //————
    // destructor
    //————

    ~Array();

    //——————
    // assignment operator
    //——————

    Array & operator = (const Array & r);

    //——————
    // element access functions
    //——————

    const void * ReadElement(const Index & i) const;
    const void * ReadElement(int i) const;

    void * GetElement(const Index & i);
    void * GetElement(int i);
```

```
        //————
        // data members
        //————

        Range   IndexRange;
        char * Buffer;
        size_t ElementSize;
        size_t BufferSize;

        unsigned int Count;

        //————————————————————
        // pointer to function that destroys an element
        //————————————————————

        ElemDestroy DestroyFunc;

        //——————————
        // error handler object
        //——————————

        static ErrReporter * ErrOut;

        static void ReportError(const String & msg);

    private:
        //————————————
        // function to delete all elements
        //————————————

        void Kill();

        //——————————
        // copies elements from "a"
        //——————————

        void Copy(const Array & a);
    };

//————
// constructors
//————

inline Array::Array(const Array & a)
    : IndexRange(a.IndexRange)
    {
    Copy(a);
    }
```

```
//———
// destructor
//———

inline Array::~Array()
    {
    Kill();
    }

//—————————
// create an appropriate index
//—————————

inline Index Array::MakeIndex() const
    {
    return Index(IndexRange);
    }

//————
// get the range
//————

inline Range Array::GetRange() const
    {
    return IndexRange;
    }

//—————————
// get size of an element
//—————————

inline size_t Array::GetElemSize() const
    {
    return ElementSize;
    }

//——————————
// get address of destroy function
//——————————

inline ElemDestroy Array::GetDestroyFunc() const
    {
    return DestroyFunc;
    }

//—————
// get number of elements
//—————
```

```
inline unsigned int Array::GetCount() const
    {
    return Count;
    }

//————————
// element access functions
//————————

inline void * Array::GetElement(int i)
    {
    return GetElement(Index(IndexRange,i));
    }

inline const void * Array::ReadElement(int i) const
    {
    return ReadElement(Index(IndexRange,i));
    }

//-=-=-=-=-=-=-=-=-=-=-=-=-=-=-=-=-=-=-=-=-=-=-=-=-=-=-=
//
//   ArrayPtr class
//
//-=-=-=-=-=-=-=-=-=-=-=-=-=-=-=-=-=-=-=-=-=-=-=-=-=-=-=

class ArrayPtr
    {
    public:

        //————
        // copy constructor
        //————

        ArrayPtr(const ArrayPtr & aptr);

        //————————
        // assignment operators
        //————

        ArrayPtr & operator = (const ArrayPtr & aptr);
        ArrayPtr & operator = (const Index & i);
        ArrayPtr & operator = (int i);

        //————————
        // increment and decrement
        //————————

        ArrayPtr & operator ++ ();          // prefix
```

```
    ArrayPtr operator ++ (int dummy); // postfix

    ArrayPtr & operator - ();          // prefix
    ArrayPtr operator - (int dummy); // postfix

    //——————————
    // set to first or last element
    //——————————

    void SetFirst();
    void SetLast();

    //—————————
    // value check functions
    //—————————

    int IsFirst();
    int IsLast();

    //—————————
    // comparison operators
    //—————————

    int operator == (const ArrayPtr & aptr);
    int operator != (const ArrayPtr & aptr);

protected:

    //———————
    // constructor
    //———————

    ArrayPtr(char * base, size_t esize, const Range & r);

    //———————
    // data elements
    //———————

    size_t ElemSize;    // bytes per element
    Range  ElemRange;   // range of pointer

    char * ElemFirst;   // address of first element
    char * ElemLast;    // address of last  element

    char * ElemPtr;     // pointer to element
};
```

```
//—————————
// increment and decrement
//—————————

inline ArrayPtr & ArrayPtr::operator ++ ()
    {
    // prefix
    if (ElemPtr != ElemLast)
        ElemPtr += ElemSize;

    return *this;
    }

inline ArrayPtr ArrayPtr::operator ++ (int dummy)
    {
    // postfix

    // save current state
    ArrayPtr result(*this);

    // move to next element
    if (ElemPtr != ElemLast)
        ElemPtr += ElemSize;

    // return previous state
    return result;
    }

inline ArrayPtr & ArrayPtr::operator - ()
    {
    // prefix
    if (ElemPtr != ElemFirst)
        ElemPtr -= ElemSize;

    return *this;
    }

inline ArrayPtr ArrayPtr::operator - (int dummy)
    {
    // postfix

    // save current state
    ArrayPtr result(*this);

    // move to next element
    if (ElemPtr != ElemFirst)
        ElemPtr -= ElemSize;
```

```
    // return previous state
    return result;
    }

//————————————
// set to first or last element
//————————————

inline void ArrayPtr::SetFirst()
    {
    ElemPtr = ElemFirst;
    }

inline void ArrayPtr::SetLast()
    {
    ElemPtr = ElemLast;
    }

//————————
// value check functions
//————————

inline int ArrayPtr::IsFirst()
    {
    return (ElemPtr == ElemFirst);
    }

inline int ArrayPtr::IsLast()
    {
    return (ElemPtr == ElemLast);
    }

//————————
// comparison operators
//————————

inline int ArrayPtr::operator == (const ArrayPtr & aptr)
    {
    return (ElemPtr == aptr.ElemPtr);
    }

inline int ArrayPtr::operator != (const ArrayPtr & aptr)
    {
    return (ElemPtr != aptr.ElemPtr);
    }

#endif
```

**Listing 5-2. array.cxx.**

```
//=============================================================
//   MATHEMATICAL CLASS LIBRARY
//       array.cxx
//
//       Defines the base class upon which all array classes
//       are based. Also defined is the array pointer type
//       that provides efficient access to elements in array
//       objects.
//
//       Copyright 1992 by Scott Robert Ladd
//       All rights reserved
//=============================================================

#include "array.h"
#include "string.h"

#ifdef __ZTC__
#include "iostream.hpp"
#else
#include "iostream.h"
#endif


//-=-=-=-=-=-=-=-=-=-=-=-=-=-=-=-=-=-=-=-=-=-=-=-=-=-=-=-=-=-=
//
//   Array class
//
//-=-=-=-=-=-=-=-=-=-=-=-=-=-=-=-=-=-=-=-=-=-=-=-=-=-=-=-=-=-=

//------------
// error handler object
//------------

static const String ErrMsg("Array");

ErrReporter * Array::ErrOut = new DosErrReporter(&ErrMsg);

//---------------
// function to call ErrOut
//---------------

void Array::ReportError(const String & msg)
    {
    if (ErrOut != NULL)
        ErrOut->Fatal(msg);
    }

//-----------------
```

```
// assign a new error reporter
//————————

void Array::SetErrOut(const ErrReporter & er)
    {
    if (ErrOut != NULL)
        delete ErrOut;

    ErrOut = new ErrReporter(er);
    }

//————
// constructors
//————

Array::Array(const Range & r,
             size_t       elemSize,
             ElemCreate   create,
             ElemDestroy  destroy)
    : IndexRange(r)
    {
    if (r.GetMagnitude() > UINT_MAX / elemSize)
        ReportError("capacity exceeded in construction");

    BufferSize = elemSize * r.GetMagnitude();

    Buffer = (char *)new char[BufferSize];

    if (Buffer == NULL)
        ReportError("unable to allocate buffer");

    ElementSize = elemSize;
    DestroyFunc = destroy;

    if (create != NULL)
        {
        for (size_t n = 0; n < r.GetMagnitude(); ++n)
            create((void *)(Buffer + n * elemSize));
        }

    Count = IndexRange.GetMagnitude();
    }

Array::Array(const Array & a1, const Array & a2)
    : IndexRange(a1.IndexRange + a2.IndexRange)
    {
    if (a1.ElementSize != a2.ElementSize)
        ReportError("construction using incompatible array types");
```

```
    BufferSize = a1.ElementSize * IndexRange.GetMagnitude();

    Buffer = (char *)new char[BufferSize];

    if (Buffer == NULL)
        ReportError("unable to allocate buffer");

    ElementSize = a1.ElementSize;
    DestroyFunc = a1.DestroyFunc;

    memcpy(Buffer,
           a1.Buffer,
           a1.BufferSize);

    memcpy(Buffer + a1.BufferSize,
           a2.Buffer,
           a2.BufferSize);
    }

Array::Array(const Array & a, const Index & first, const Index & last)
    : IndexRange((int)first,(int)last)
    {
    if ((Range(first) == a.IndexRange)
    && (Range(last)  == a.IndexRange))
        {
        BufferSize = a.ElementSize * IndexRange.GetMagnitude();

        Buffer = (char *)new char[BufferSize];

        if (Buffer == NULL)
            ReportError("unable to allocate buffer");

        ElementSize = a.ElementSize;
        DestroyFunc = a.DestroyFunc;

        memcpy(Buffer,
               a.Buffer + (unsigned int)first * ElementSize,
               ((unsigned int)last - (unsigned int)first) * ElementSize);
        }
    else
        ReportError("construction with incompatible indexes");
    }

//————
// assignment operator
//————

Array & Array::operator = (const Array & a)
```

```
    {
    Kill();
    IndexRange = a.IndexRange;

    Copy(a);
    return *this;
    }

//——————————
// element access functions
//——————————

void * Array::GetElement(const Index & i)
    {
    void * result;

    if (IndexRange == Range(i))
        result = (void *)(Buffer + ElementSize * (unsigned int)i);
    else
        ReportError("invalid index");

    return result;
    }

const void * Array::ReadElement(const Index & i) const
    {
    const void * result;

    if (IndexRange == Range(i))
        result = (const void *)(Buffer + ElementSize * (unsigned int)i);
    else
        ReportError("invalid index");

    return result;
    }

//——————————
// function to delete all elements
//——————————

void Array::Kill()
    {
    if (DestroyFunc != NULL)
        {
        for (size_t n = 0; n < IndexRange.GetMagnitude(); ++n)
            DestroyFunc((void *)(Buffer + n * ElementSize));
        }
```

```
    delete [BufferSize] Buffer;
    }

//————————
// copies elements from "a"
//————————

void Array::Copy(const Array & a)
    {
    BufferSize = a.BufferSize;

    Buffer = (char *)new char[BufferSize];

    if (Buffer == NULL)
        ReportError("unable to allocate buffer");

    memcpy(Buffer, a.Buffer, BufferSize);

    IndexRange  = a.IndexRange;
    ElementSize = a.ElementSize;
    DestroyFunc = a.DestroyFunc;
    Count       = a.Count;
    }

//-=-=-=-=-=-=-=-=-=-=-=-=-=-=-=-=-=-=-=-=-=-=-=-=-=-=-=-=
//
//   ArrayPtr class
//
//-=-=-=-=-=-=-=-=-=-=-=-=-=-=-=-=-=-=-=-=-=-=-=-=-=-=-=-=

//————
// constructor
//————

ArrayPtr::ArrayPtr(char * base, size_t esize, const Range & r)
    : ElemRange(r)
    {
    ElemSize  = esize;
    ElemFirst = base;
    ElemLast  = ElemFirst + ElemSize * (ElemRange.GetMagnitude() - 1);
    ElemPtr   = ElemFirst;
    }

//————
// copy constructor
//————

ArrayPtr::ArrayPtr(const ArrayPtr & aptr)
```

```
    : ElemRange(aptr.ElemRange)
    {
    ElemSize  = aptr.ElemSize;
    ElemFirst = aptr.ElemFirst;
    ElemLast  = aptr.ElemLast;
    ElemPtr   = aptr.ElemPtr;
    }


//————————
// assignment operators
//————————

ArrayPtr & ArrayPtr::operator = (const ArrayPtr & aptr)
    {
    ElemSize  = aptr.ElemSize;
    ElemRange = aptr.ElemRange;
    ElemFirst = aptr.ElemFirst;
    ElemLast  = aptr.ElemLast;
    ElemPtr   = aptr.ElemPtr;

    return *this;
    }

ArrayPtr & ArrayPtr::operator = (const Index & i)
    {
    if (ElemRange == Range(i))
        ElemPtr = ElemFirst + ElemSize * (unsigned int)i;

    return *this;
    }

ArrayPtr & ArrayPtr::operator = (int i)
    {
    ElemRange.Check(i);

    ElemPtr = ElemFirst + ElemSize * i;

    return *this;
    }
```

# Chapter 6: Sortable Arrays

**Listing 6-1. srtarray.h.**

```
//=============================================================
//  MATHEMATICAL LIBRARY
//      srtarray.h
//
//      A variant of the Array class that supports sorting
//
//      Copyright 1992 by Scott Robert Ladd
//      All rights reserved
//=============================================================

#ifndef SRTARRAY_H
#define SRTARRAY_H

#include "array.h"

class SortableArray : public Array
    {
    public:
        //————
        // sorting function
        //————

        void Sort();

    protected:
        //————
        // constructors
        //————

        SortableArray(const Range & r,
                      size_t elemsize,
                      ElemCreate  create  = NULL,
                      ElemDestroy destroy = NULL);

        SortableArray(const SortableArray & a);

        // concatenate
        SortableArray(const SortableArray & a1,
                      const SortableArray & a2);

        // subrange
        SortableArray(const SortableArray & a,
                      const Index & first,
                      const Index & last);
```

```
        //————————
        // assignment operator
        //————————

        SortableArray & operator = (const SortableArray & a);

    private:

        //————————————————
        // is the first element before the second?
        //————————————————

        virtual int  IsBefore(const Index & i1, const Index & i2) = 0;

        //————————
        // exchange two elements
        //————————

        virtual void Exchange(const Index & i1, const Index & i2) = 0;
    };

//————
// constructors
//————

inline SortableArray::SortableArray(const Range & r,
                                    size_t elemsize,
                                    ElemCreate  create,
                                    ElemDestroy destroy)
    : Array(r,elemsize,create,destroy)
    {
    // does nothing else
    }

inline SortableArray::SortableArray(const SortableArray & a)
    : Array(a)
    {
    // does nothing else
    }

inline SortableArray::SortableArray(const SortableArray & a1,
                                    const SortableArray & a2)
    : Array(a1,a2)
    {
    // does nothing else
    }
```

```
inline SortableArray::SortableArray(const SortableArray & a,
                                    const Index & first,
                                    const Index & last)

    : Array(a,first,last)
    {
    // does nothing else
    }

//—————————
// assignment operator
//—————————

inline SortableArray & SortableArray::operator = (const SortableArray & a)
    {
    this->Array::operator = (a);

    return *this;
    }

#endif
```

**Listing 6-2. srtarray.cxx.**

```
//===============================================================
//   MATHEMATICAL LIBRARY
//       srtarray.cxx
//
//       A variant of the Array class that supports sorting
//
//       Copyright 1992 by Scott Robert Ladd
//       All rights reserved
//===============================================================

#include "srtarray.h"

//—————————————————
// The stackItem class defines a list of left
// and right index values used in iteration.
//—————————————————

//—————————
// a structure used by Sort
//—————————

struct stackItem
    {
    Index left;
    Index right;
```

```
    static Range lrRange;

    stackItem();
    };

Range stackItem::lrRange(0,1);

stackItem::stackItem()
    : left(lrRange), right(lrRange)
    {
    // empty
    }

//————
// sorting function
//————

void SortableArray::Sort()
    {
    //———
    // create stack
    //———

    stackItem::lrRange = IndexRange;

    const size_t stackSize = CHAR_BIT * sizeof(int);

    stackItem * stack = new stackItem [stackSize];

    if (stack == NULL)
        ReportError("cannot allocate stack for sorting");

    size_t stackPtr = 0;

    //————————————
    // size of minimum partition to median-of-three
    //————————————

    const int Threshold = 7;

    //—————————
    // sizes of left and right partitions
    //—————————

    int lsize, rsize;

    //————————
    // create working indexes
```

```
//——————

Index l(IndexRange),       // left    partition index
      r(IndexRange),       // right   partition index
      mid(IndexRange),     // middle  partition index
      scanl(IndexRange),   // index scanning from left
      scanr(IndexRange),   // index scanning from right
      pivot(IndexRange);   // pivot element index

//—————
// set initial values
//—————

l.SetMin();
r.SetMax();

//——————
// main loop
//——————

for (;;)
    {
    while (r > l)
        {
        if (((int)r - (int)l) > Threshold)
            {
            //———————————
            // "median-of-three" partitioning
            //———————————

            mid = ((int)l + (int)r) / 2;

            //————————————————
            // three-sort left, middle, and right elements
            //————————————————

            if (IsBefore(mid,l))
                Exchange(mid,l);

            if (IsBefore(r,l))
                Exchange(r,l);

            if (IsBefore(r,mid))
                Exchange(r,mid);

            //——————————
            // set-up for partitioning
            //——————————
```

```
        pivot = r - 1;

        Exchange(mid,pivot);

        scanl = l + 1;
        scanr = r - 2;
        }
else
        {
        //————————
        // set-up for partitioning
        //————————

        pivot = r;
        scanl = l;
        scanr = r - 1;
        }

for (;;)
        {
        //————————————
        // scan from left for element >= to pivot
        //————————————

        while (IsBefore(scanl,pivot) && (scanl < r))
            ++scanl;

        //————————————
        // scan from right for element <= to pivot
        //————————————

        while (IsBefore(pivot,scanr) && (scanr > l))
            --scanr;

        //————————————
        // if scans have met, exit inner loop
        //————————————

        if (scanl >= scanr)
            break;

        //————————
        // exchange elements
        //————————
        Exchange(scanl,scanr);

        if (scanl < r)
            ++scanl;
```

```
    if (scanr > l)
        —scanr;
    }


//——————————
// exchange final element
//——————————

Exchange(pivot,scanl);

//——————————————
// place largest partition on stack
//——————————————

lsize = (int)scanl - (int)l;
rsize = (int)r - (int)scanl;

if (lsize > rsize)
    {
    if (lsize != 1)
        {
        ++stackPtr;

        if (stackPtr == stackSize)
            ReportError("stack overflow (left)");

        stack[stackPtr].left  = l;
        stack[stackPtr].right = scanl - 1;
        }

    if (rsize != 0)
        l = scanl + 1;
    else
        break;
    }
else
    {
    if (rsize != 1)
        {
        ++stackPtr;

        if (stackPtr == stackSize)
            ReportError("stack overflow (right)");

        stack[stackPtr].left  = scanl + 1;
        stack[stackPtr].right = r;
        }
```

```
                    if (lsize != 0)
                        r = scanl - 1;
                    else
                        break;
                    }
                }

        //————————————
        // iterate with values from stack
        //————————————

        if (stackPtr)
            {
            l = stack[stackPtr].left;
            r = stack[stackPtr].right;

            —stackPtr;
            }
        else
            break;
        }

    delete [stackSize] stack;
    }
```

# Chapter 7: Integer Arrays

**Listing 7-1. iarray.h.**
```
//==============================================================
//   MATHEMATICAL LIBRARY
//       iarray.h
//
//       An array of integers
//
//       Copyright 1992 by Scott Robert Ladd
//       All rights reserved
//==============================================================

#ifndef IARRAY_H
#define IARRAY_H

#include "srtarray.h"
#include "randgen.h"


//-=-=-=-=-=-=-=-=-=-=-=-=-=-=-=-=-=-=-=-=-=-=-=-=-=-=-=-=-=-=
//
//   IntArrayPtr class
```

```
//
//-=-=-=-=-=-=-=-=-=-=-=-=-=-=-=-=-=-=-=-=-=-=-=-=-=-=-=-=-=

class IntArrayPtr : public ArrayPtr
    {
    friend class IntArray;

    public:

        //————————
        // copy constructor
        //————————

        IntArrayPtr(const IntArrayPtr & aptr);
        IntArrayPtr(const ArrayPtr & aptr);

        //————————
        // assignment operators
        //————————

        IntArrayPtr & operator = (const IntArrayPtr & aptr);
        IntArrayPtr & operator = (const Index & i);
        IntArrayPtr & operator = (int i);

        //————————
        // increment and decrement
        //————————

        IntArrayPtr & operator ++ ();
        IntArrayPtr & operator - ();

        //————————
        // get pointer value
        //————————

        operator int * () const;

        //————————
        // dereference
        //————————

        int & operator * ();

    protected:

        //————————
        // constructor
        //————————
```

```
        IntArrayPtr(char * base, size_t esize, const Range & r);
    };

//————
// constructor
//————

inline IntArrayPtr::IntArrayPtr(char * base,
                                size_t esize,
                                const Range & r)
    : ArrayPtr(base,esize,r)
    {
    // empty
    }

//————
// copy constructor
//————

inline IntArrayPtr::IntArrayPtr(const IntArrayPtr & aptr)
    : ArrayPtr(aptr)
    {
    // empty
    }

inline IntArrayPtr::IntArrayPtr(const ArrayPtr & aptr)
    : ArrayPtr(aptr)
    {
    // empty
    }

//————
// assignment operators
//————

inline IntArrayPtr & IntArrayPtr::operator = (const IntArrayPtr & aptr)
    {
    this->ArrayPtr::operator = (aptr);

    return *this;
    }

inline IntArrayPtr & IntArrayPtr::operator = (const Index & i)
    {
    this->ArrayPtr::operator = (i);

    return *this;
    }
```

```
inline IntArrayPtr & IntArrayPtr::operator = (int i)
    {
    this->ArrayPtr::operator = (i);

    return *this;
    }

//——————————
// increment and decrement
//——————————

inline IntArrayPtr & IntArrayPtr::operator ++ ()
    {
    this->ArrayPtr::operator ++ ();

    return *this;
    }

inline IntArrayPtr & IntArrayPtr::operator − ()
    {
    this->ArrayPtr::operator − ();

    return *this;
    }

//—————————
// get pointer value
//—————————

inline IntArrayPtr::operator int * () const
    {
    return (int *)ElemPtr;
    }

//———————
// dereference
//———————

inline int & IntArrayPtr::operator * ()
    {
    return *((int *)ElemPtr);
    }

//-=-=-=-=-=-=-=-=-=-=-=-=-=-=-=-=-=-=-=-=-=-=-=-=-=-=-=-=
//
//   IntArrayPtr class
//
//-=-=-=-=-=-=-=-=-=-=-=-=-=-=-=-=-=-=-=-=-=-=-=-=-=-=-=-=
```

# C++ COMPONENTS AND ALGORITHMS

```
class IntArrayConstPtr : public ArrayPtr
    {
    friend class IntArray;

    public:

        //————
        // copy constructor
        //————

        IntArrayConstPtr(const IntArrayConstPtr & aptr);
        IntArrayConstPtr(const ArrayPtr & aptr);

        //————
        // assignment operators
        //————

        IntArrayConstPtr & operator = (const IntArrayConstPtr & aptr);
        IntArrayConstPtr & operator = (const Index & i);
        IntArrayConstPtr & operator = (int i);

        //————
        // increment and decrement
        //————

        IntArrayConstPtr & operator ++ ();
        IntArrayConstPtr & operator — ();

        //————
        // get pointer value
        //————

        operator const int * () const;

        //————
        // dereference
        //————

        const int & operator * ();

    protected:
        IntArrayConstPtr(char * base, size_t esize, const Range & r);
    };

//————
// constructor
//————
```

**574**

```
inline IntArrayConstPtr::IntArrayConstPtr(char * base,
                                          size_t esize,
                                          const Range & r)
    : ArrayPtr(base,esize,r)
    {
    // empty
    }

//————
// copy constructor
//————

inline IntArrayConstPtr::IntArrayConstPtr(const IntArrayConstPtr & aptr)
    : ArrayPtr(aptr)
    {
    // empty
    }

inline IntArrayConstPtr::IntArrayConstPtr(const ArrayPtr & aptr)
    : ArrayPtr(aptr)
    {
    // empty
    }

//————
// assignment operators
//————

inline IntArrayConstPtr & IntArrayConstPtr::operator = (const
IntArrayConstPtr & aptr)
    {
    this->ArrayPtr::operator = (aptr);

    return *this;
    }

inline IntArrayConstPtr & IntArrayConstPtr::operator = (const Index & i)
    {
    this->ArrayPtr::operator = (i);

    return *this;
    }

inline IntArrayConstPtr & IntArrayConstPtr::operator = (int i)
    {
    this->ArrayPtr::operator = (i);

    return *this;
```

```
    }

//——————————
// increment and decrement
//——————————

inline IntArrayConstPtr & IntArrayConstPtr::operator ++ ()
    {
    this->ArrayPtr::operator ++ ();

    return *this;
    }

inline IntArrayConstPtr & IntArrayConstPtr::operator — ()
    {
    this->ArrayPtr::operator — ();

    return *this;
    }

//—————————
// get pointer value
//—————————

inline IntArrayConstPtr::operator const int * () const
    {
    return (const int *)ElemPtr;
    }

//———————
// dereference
//———————

inline const int & IntArrayConstPtr::operátor * ()
    {
    return *((const int *)ElemPtr);
    }

//-=-=-=-=-=-=-=-=-=-=-=-=-=-=-=-=-=-=-=-=-=-=-=-=-=-=-=-=
//
//   IntArray class
//
//-=-=-=-=-=-=-=-=-=-=-=-=-=-=-=-=-=-=-=-=-=-=-=-=-=-=-=-=

class IntArray : public SortableArray
    {
    protected:
```

```
    //————————————
    // default value assigned to array members
    //————————————

    static int InitValue;

public:

    //————
    // constructors
    //————

    IntArray(const Range & r);
    IntArray(const IntArray & ia);

    IntArray(const int * a, int len);

    // concatenate
    IntArray(const IntArray & a1,
             const IntArray & a2);

    // subrange
    IntArray(const IntArray & a,
             const Index & first,
             const Index & last);

    //————
    // conversions
    //————

    operator int * ();

    //————————
    // assignment operator
    //————————

    IntArray & operator = (const IntArray & ia);

    //————————
    // create an approprite ArrayPtr
    //————————

    IntArrayPtr MakePtr();

    IntArrayConstPtr MakeConstPtr() const;

    //————————
    // element access operators
```

```
//—————————

int & operator [] (const Index & i);
int & operator [] (int i);

//———————————
// functions for reading elements
//———————————

const int & Read(const Index & i) const;
const int & Read(int i) const;

//————————
// unary operators
//————————

IntArray operator + ();
IntArray operator - ();

IntArray operator ~ ();
IntArray operator ! ();

//————————
// basic operators
//————————

IntArray operator + (const IntArray & ia);
IntArray operator + (int n);

IntArray operator - (const IntArray & ia);
IntArray operator - (int n);

IntArray operator * (const IntArray & ia);
IntArray operator * (int n);

IntArray operator / (const IntArray & ia);
IntArray operator / (int n);

IntArray operator % (const IntArray & ia);
IntArray operator % (int n);

//————————
// shift operators
//————————

IntArray operator << (const IntArray & ia);
IntArray operator << (int n);
```

```
IntArray operator >> (const IntArray & ia);
IntArray operator >> (int n);

//————————
// bit-level operators
//————————

IntArray operator & (const IntArray & ia);
IntArray operator & (int n);

IntArray operator | (const IntArray & ia);
IntArray operator | (int n);

IntArray operator ^ (const IntArray & ia);
IntArray operator ^ (int n);

//————————
// shorthand operators
//————————

IntArray & operator += (const IntArray & ia);
IntArray & operator += (int n);

IntArray & operator -= (const IntArray & ia);
IntArray & operator -= (int n);

IntArray & operator *= (const IntArray & ia);
IntArray & operator *= (int n);

IntArray & operator /= (const IntArray & ia);
IntArray & operator /= (int n);

IntArray & operator %= (const IntArray & ia);
IntArray & operator %= (int n);

//————————
// shorthand shift operators
//————————

IntArray & operator <<= (const IntArray & ia);
IntArray & operator <<= (int n);

IntArray & operator >>= (const IntArray & ia);
IntArray & operator >>= (int n);

//————————
// shorthand bit-level operators
//————————
```

```
        IntArray & operator &= (const IntArray & ia);
        IntArray & operator &= (int n);

        IntArray & operator |= (const IntArray & ia);
        IntArray & operator |= (int n);

        IntArray & operator ^= (const IntArray & ia);
        IntArray & operator ^= (int n);

        //—————————
        // comparison functions
        //—————————

        // compare complete array contents for equality

        int Equals(const IntArray & ia) const;

        // compare array elements

        friend IntArray operator <  (const IntArray &ia1,
                                     const IntArray &ia2);

        friend IntArray operator <= (const IntArray &ia1,
                                     const IntArray &ia2);

        friend IntArray operator == (const IntArray &ia1,
                                     const IntArray &ia2);

        friend IntArray operator != (const IntArray &ia1,
                                     const IntArray &ia2);

        friend IntArray operator >= (const IntArray &ia1,
                                     const IntArray &ia2);

        friend IntArray operator >  (const IntArray &ia1,
                                     const IntArray &ia2);

        //—————————
        // fill functions
        //—————————

        typedef int (* IA_FillRecFunc)(int);
        typedef int (* IA_FillByFunc)(const Index & i);

        static void SetInit(int i);

        void Fill(int i = InitValue);
```

```
        void FillArithmetic(int first, int incr);
        void FillGeometric(int first,  int mult);
        void FillRecursive(int first,  IA_FillRecFunc func);

        void FillRandom(RandGen & rg);
        void FillRandomBounded(int low, int high, RandGen & rg);

        void FillBy(IA_FillByFunc func);

        //——————————
        // absolute value function
        //——————————

        IntArray & abs();

        friend IntArray abs(const IntArray & ia);

        //—————————————————
        // functions required by Sortable base class
        //—————————————————

        virtual int  IsBefore(const Index & i1, const Index & i2);
        virtual void Exchange(const Index & i1, const Index & i2);

    private:

        //—————————————
        // sets the initial value of an element
        //—————————————

        static void Set(int * i);

        //————————————
        // err exit function for friend functions
        //————————————

        static void FriendErrExit(const char * msg);
    };

//————
// constructors
//————

inline IntArray::IntArray(const Range & r)
    : SortableArray(r,sizeof(int),(ElemCreate)IntArray::Set)
    {
    // does nothing
    }
```

```
inline IntArray::IntArray(const IntArray & ia)
    : SortableArray(ia)
    {
    // does nothing
    }

inline IntArray::IntArray(const IntArray & a1,
                          const IntArray & a2)
    : SortableArray(a1,a2)
    {
    // does nothing else
    }

inline IntArray::IntArray(const IntArray & a,
                          const Index & first,
                          const Index & last)
    : SortableArray(a,first,last)
    {
    // does nothing else
    }

//——————————
// assignment operator
//——————————

inline IntArray & IntArray::operator = (const IntArray & ia)
    {
    this->SortableArray::operator = (ia);

    return *this;
    }

//————————————————
// create an approprite ArrayPtr
//————————————————

inline IntArrayPtr IntArray::MakePtr()
    {
    return IntArrayPtr(Buffer,ElementSize,IndexRange);
    }

inline IntArrayConstPtr IntArray::MakeConstPtr() const
    {
    return IntArrayConstPtr(Buffer,ElementSize,IndexRange);
    }

//——————————
// element access operators
//——————————
```

```
inline int & IntArray::operator [] (const Index & i)
    {
    return *((int *)(GetElement(i)));
    }

inline int & IntArray::operator [] (int i)
    {
    return *((int *)(GetElement(i)));
    }

//————————————
// functions for reading elements
//————————————

inline const int & IntArray::Read(const Index & i) const
    {
    return *((const int *)(ReadElement(i)));
    }

inline const int & IntArray::Read(int i) const
    {
    return *((const int *)(ReadElement(i)));
    }

//—————
// unary operators
//—————

inline IntArray IntArray::operator + ()
    {
    return *this;
    }

//—————
// fill functions
//—————

inline void IntArray::SetInit(int d)
    {
    InitValue = d;
    }

//————————————
// err exit function for friend functions
//————————————

inline void IntArray::FriendErrExit(const char * msg)
```

```
        {
    ReportError(msg);
        }

#endif
```

## Listing 7-2. iarray.cxx.

```
//================================================================
//   MATHEMATICAL LIBRARY
//       iarray.cxx
//
//       An array of integers
//
//       Copyright 1992 by Scott Robert Ladd
//       All rights reserved
//================================================================

#include "iarray.h"
#include "string.h"
#include "stdlib.h"

//————————————————
// default value assigned to array members
//————————————————

int IntArray::InitValue = 0;

//———————
// constructors
//———————

IntArray::IntArray(const int * a, int len)
    : SortableArray(Range(0,len - 1),sizeof(int))
    {
    memcpy(Buffer,a,BufferSize);
    }

//——————————
// conversion operators
//——————————

IntArray::operator int * ()
    {
    int * result;

    result = new int[BufferSize];

    if (result == NULL)
```

```
        ReportError("cannot allocate memory for int []");

    memcpy(result,Buffer,BufferSize);

    return result;
    }

//————————
// unary operators
//————————

IntArray IntArray::operator - ()
    {
    IntArray result(*this);

    IntArrayPtr ptr = result.MakePtr();

    for (;;)
        {
        *ptr = -(*ptr);

        if (ptr.IsLast())
            break;

        ++ptr;
        }

    return result;
    }

IntArray IntArray::operator ~ ()
    {
    IntArray result(*this);

    IntArrayPtr ptr = result.MakePtr();

    for (;;)
        {
        *ptr = ~(*ptr);

        if (ptr.IsLast())
            break;

        ++ptr;
        }

    return result;
    }
```

```
IntArray IntArray::operator ! ()
    {
    IntArray result(*this);

    IntArrayPtr ptr = result.MakePtr();

    for (;;)
        {
        *ptr = !(*ptr);

        if (ptr.IsLast())
            break;

        ++ptr;
        }

    return result;
    }

//————
// basic operators
//————

IntArray IntArray::operator + (const IntArray & ia)
    {
    if (IndexRange != ia.IndexRange)
        ReportError("incompatible arrays: +");

    IntArray result(*this);

    IntArrayPtr dest = result.MakePtr();

    IntArrayConstPtr src = ia.MakeConstPtr();

    for (;;)
        {
        *dest += *src;

        if (dest.IsLast())
            break;

        ++dest;
        ++src;
        }

    return result;
    }
```

```
IntArray IntArray::operator + (int n)
    {
    IntArray result(*this);

    IntArrayPtr ptr = result.MakePtr();

    for (;;)
        {
        *ptr += n;

        if (ptr.IsLast())
            break;

        ++ptr;
        }

    return result;
    }

IntArray IntArray::operator - (const IntArray & ia)
    {
    if (IndexRange != ia.IndexRange)
        ReportError("incompatible arrays: -");

    IntArray result(*this);

    IntArrayPtr dest = result.MakePtr();

    IntArrayConstPtr src = ia.MakeConstPtr();

    for (;;)
        {
        *dest -= *src;

        if (dest.IsLast())
            break;

        ++dest;
        ++src;
        }

    return result;
    }

IntArray IntArray::operator - (int n)
    {
    IntArray result(*this);
```

```
    IntArrayPtr ptr = result.MakePtr();

    for (;;)
        {
        *ptr -= n;

        if (ptr.IsLast())
            break;

        ++ptr;
        }

    return result;
    }

IntArray IntArray::operator * (const IntArray & ia)
    {
    if (IndexRange != ia.IndexRange)
        ReportError("incompatible arrays: *");

    IntArray result(*this);

    IntArrayPtr dest = result.MakePtr();

    IntArrayConstPtr src = ia.MakeConstPtr();

    for (;;)
        {
        *dest *= *src;

        if (dest.IsLast())
            break;

        ++dest;
        ++src;
        }

    return result;
    }

IntArray IntArray::operator * (int n)
    {
    IntArray result(*this);

    IntArrayPtr ptr = result.MakePtr();

    for (;;)
        {
```

```
        *ptr *= n;

        if (ptr.IsLast())
            break;

        ++ptr;
        }

    return result;
    }

IntArray IntArray::operator / (const IntArray & ia)
    {
    if (IndexRange != ia.IndexRange)
        ReportError("incompatible arrays: /");

    IntArray result(*this);

    IntArrayPtr dest = result.MakePtr();

    IntArrayConstPtr src = ia.MakeConstPtr();

    for (;;)
        {
        *dest /= *src;

        if (dest.IsLast())
            break;

        ++dest;
        ++src;
        }

    return result;
    }

IntArray IntArray::operator / (int n)
    {
    IntArray result(*this);

    IntArrayPtr ptr = result.MakePtr();

    for (;;)
        {
        *ptr /= n;

        if (ptr.IsLast())
            break;
```

```
        ++ptr;
        }

    return result;
    }

IntArray IntArray::operator % (const IntArray & ia)
    {
    if (IndexRange != ia.IndexRange)
        ReportError("incompatible arrays: %");

    IntArray result(*this);

    IntArrayPtr dest = result.MakePtr();

    IntArrayConstPtr src = ia.MakeConstPtr();

    for (;;)
        {
        *dest %= *src;

        if (dest.IsLast())
            break;

        ++dest;
        ++src;
        }

    return result;
    }

IntArray IntArray::operator % (int n)
    {
    IntArray result(*this);

    IntArrayPtr ptr = result.MakePtr();

    for (;;)
        {
        *ptr %= n;

        if (ptr.IsLast())
            break;

        ++ptr;
        }

    return result;
```

```
    }

//————
// shift operators
//————

IntArray IntArray::operator << (const IntArray & ia)
    {
    if (IndexRange != ia.IndexRange)
        ReportError("incompatible arrays: <<");

    IntArray result(*this);

    IntArrayPtr dest = result.MakePtr();

    IntArrayConstPtr src = ia.MakeConstPtr();

    for (;;)
        {
        *dest <<= *src;

        if (dest.IsLast())
            break;

        ++dest;
        ++src;
        }

    return result;
    }

IntArray IntArray::operator << (int n)
    {
    IntArray result(*this);

    IntArrayPtr ptr = result.MakePtr();

    for (;;)
        {
        *ptr <<= n;

        if (ptr.IsLast())
            break;

        ++ptr;
        }

    return result;
```

```
        }

IntArray IntArray::operator >> (const IntArray & ia)
    {
    if (IndexRange != ia.IndexRange)
        ReportError("incompatible arrays: >>");

    IntArray result(*this);

    IntArrayPtr dest = result.MakePtr();

    IntArrayConstPtr src = ia.MakeConstPtr();

    for (;;)
        {
        *dest >>= *src;

        if (dest.IsLast())
            break;

        ++dest;
        ++src;
        }

    return result;
    }

IntArray IntArray::operator >> (int n)
    {
    IntArray result(*this);

    IntArrayPtr ptr = result.MakePtr();

    for (;;)
        {
        *ptr >>= n;

        if (ptr.IsLast())
            break;

        ++ptr;
        }

    return result;
    }

//————————
// bit-level operators
//————————
```

```
IntArray IntArray::operator & (const IntArray & ia)
    {
    if (IndexRange != ia.IndexRange)
        ReportError("incompatible arrays: &");

    IntArray result(*this);

    IntArrayPtr dest = result.MakePtr();

    IntArrayConstPtr src = ia.MakeConstPtr();

    for (;;)
        {
        *dest &= *src;

        if (dest.IsLast())
            break;

        ++dest;
        ++src;
        }

    return result;
    }

IntArray IntArray::operator & (int n)
    {
    IntArray result(*this);

    IntArrayPtr ptr = result.MakePtr();

    for (;;)
        {
        *ptr &= n;

        if (ptr.IsLast())
            break;

        ++ptr;
        }

    return result;
    }

IntArray IntArray::operator | (const IntArray & ia)
    {
    if (IndexRange != ia.IndexRange)
        ReportError("incompatible arrays: |");
```

```
    IntArray result(*this);

    IntArrayPtr dest = result.MakePtr();

    IntArrayConstPtr src = ia.MakeConstPtr();

    for (;;)
        {
        *dest |= *src;

        if (dest.IsLast())
            break;

        ++dest;
        ++src;
        }

    return result;
    }

IntArray IntArray::operator | (int n)
    {
    IntArray result(*this);

    IntArrayPtr ptr = result.MakePtr();

    for (;;)
        {
        *ptr |= n;

        if (ptr.IsLast())
            break;

        ++ptr;
        }

    return result;
    }

IntArray IntArray::operator ^ (const IntArray & ia)
    {
    if (IndexRange != ia.IndexRange)
        ReportError("incompatible arrays: ^");

    IntArray result(*this);

    IntArrayPtr dest = result.MakePtr();
```

```
    IntArrayConstPtr src = ia.MakeConstPtr();

    for (;;)
        {
        *dest ^= *src;

        if (dest.IsLast())
            break;

        ++dest;
        ++src;
        }

    return result;
    }

IntArray IntArray::operator ^ (int n)
    {
    IntArray result(*this);

    IntArrayPtr ptr = result.MakePtr();

    for (;;)
        {
        *ptr ^= n;

        if (ptr.IsLast())
            break;

        ++ptr;
        }

    return result;
    }

//————————
// shorthand operators
//————————

IntArray & IntArray::operator += (const IntArray & ia)
    {
    if (IndexRange != ia.IndexRange)
        ReportError("incompatible arrays: +=");

    IntArrayPtr      dest = MakePtr();
    IntArrayConstPtr src  = ia.MakeConstPtr();

    for (;;)
```

```
        {
        *dest += *src;

        if (dest.IsLast())
            break;

        ++dest;
        ++src;
        }

    return *this;
    }

IntArray & IntArray::operator += (int n)
    {
    IntArrayPtr dest = MakePtr();

    for (;;)
        {
        *dest += n;

        if (dest.IsLast())
            break;

        ++dest;
        }

    return *this;
    }

IntArray & IntArray::operator -= (const IntArray & ia)
    {
    if (IndexRange != ia.IndexRange)
        ReportError("incompatible arrays: -=");

    IntArrayPtr      dest = MakePtr();
    IntArrayConstPtr src  = ia.MakeConstPtr();

    for (;;)
        {
        *dest -= *src;

        if (dest.IsLast())
            break;

        ++dest;
        ++src;
        }
```

```
    return *this;
    }

IntArray & IntArray::operator -= (int n)
    {
    IntArrayPtr dest = MakePtr();

    for (;;)
        {
        *dest -= n;

        if (dest.IsLast())
            break;

        ++dest;
        }

    return *this;
    }

IntArray & IntArray::operator *= (const IntArray & ia)
    {
    if (IndexRange != ia.IndexRange)
        ReportError("incompatible arrays: *=");

    IntArrayPtr      dest = MakePtr();
    IntArrayConstPtr src  = ia.MakeConstPtr();

    for (;;)
        {
        *dest *= *src;

        if (dest.IsLast())
            break;

        ++dest;
        ++src;
        }

    return *this;
    }

IntArray & IntArray::operator *= (int n)
    {
    IntArrayPtr dest = MakePtr();

    for (;;)
        {
```

```
        *dest *= n;

        if (dest.IsLast())
            break;

        ++dest;
        }

    return *this;
    }

IntArray & IntArray::operator /= (const IntArray & ia)
    {
    if (IndexRange != ia.IndexRange)
        ReportError("incompatible arrays: /=");

    IntArrayPtr      dest = MakePtr();
    IntArrayConstPtr src  = ia.MakeConstPtr();

    for (;;)
        {
        *dest /= *src;

        if (dest.IsLast())
            break;

        ++dest;
        ++src;
        }

    return *this;
    }

IntArray & IntArray::operator /= (int n)
    {
    IntArrayPtr dest = MakePtr();

    for (;;)
        {
        *dest /= n;

        if (dest.IsLast())
            break;

        ++dest;
        }

    return *this;
    }
```

```
IntArray & IntArray::operator %= (const IntArray & ia)
    {
    if (IndexRange != ia.IndexRange)
        ReportError("incompatible arrays: %=");

    IntArrayPtr      dest = MakePtr();
    IntArrayConstPtr src  = ia.MakeConstPtr();

    for (;;)
        {
        *dest %= *src;

        if (dest.IsLast())
            break;

        ++dest;
        ++src;
        }

    return *this;
    }

IntArray & IntArray::operator %= (int n)
    {
    IntArrayPtr dest = MakePtr();

    for (;;)
        {
        *dest %= n;

        if (dest.IsLast())
            break;

        ++dest;
        }

    return *this;
    }


//————————
// shorthand shift operators
//————————

IntArray & IntArray::operator <<= (const IntArray & ia)
    {
    if (IndexRange != ia.IndexRange)
        ReportError("incompatible arrays: <<=");
```

```
    IntArrayPtr      dest = MakePtr();
    IntArrayConstPtr src  = ia.MakeConstPtr();

    for (;;)
        {
        *dest <<= *src;

        if (dest.IsLast())
            break;

        ++dest;
        ++src;
        }

    return *this;
    }

IntArray & IntArray::operator <<= (int n)
    {
    IntArrayPtr dest = MakePtr();

    for (;;)
        {
        *dest <<= n;

        if (dest.IsLast())
            break;

        ++dest;
        }

    return *this;
    }

IntArray & IntArray::operator >>= (const IntArray & ia)
    {
    if (IndexRange != ia.IndexRange)
        ReportError("incompatible arrays: >>=");

    IntArrayPtr      dest = MakePtr();
    IntArrayConstPtr src  = ia.MakeConstPtr();

    for (;;)
        {
        *dest >>= *src;

        if (dest.IsLast())
            break;
```

```
            ++dest;
            ++src;
            }

        return *this;
        }

IntArray & IntArray::operator >>= (int n)
        {
        IntArrayPtr dest = MakePtr();

        for (;;)
            {
            *dest >>= n;

            if (dest.IsLast())
                break;

            ++dest;
            }

        return *this;
        }

//————————————
// shorthand bit-level operators
//————————————

IntArray & IntArray::operator &= (const IntArray & ia)
        {
        if (IndexRange != ia.IndexRange)
            ReportError("incompatible arrays: &=");

        IntArrayPtr      dest = MakePtr();
        IntArrayConstPtr src  = ia.MakeConstPtr();

        for (;;)
            {
            *dest &= *src;

            if (dest.IsLast())
                break;

            ++dest;
            ++src;
            }

        return *this;
```

```
    }

IntArray & IntArray::operator &= (int n)
    {
    IntArrayPtr dest = MakePtr();

    for (;;)
        {
        *dest &= n;

        if (dest.IsLast())
            break;

        ++dest;
        }

    return *this;
    }

IntArray & IntArray::operator |= (const IntArray & ia)
    {
    if (IndexRange != ia.IndexRange)
        ReportError("incompatible arrays: |=");

    IntArrayPtr      dest = MakePtr();
    IntArrayConstPtr src  = ia.MakeConstPtr();

    for (;;)
        {
        *dest |= *src;

        if (dest.IsLast())
            break;

        ++dest;
        ++src;
        }

    return *this;
    }

IntArray & IntArray::operator |= (int n)
    {
    IntArrayPtr dest = MakePtr();

    for (;;)
        {
        *dest |= n;
```

```
        if (dest.IsLast())
            break;

        ++dest;
        }

    return *this;
    }

IntArray & IntArray::operator ^= (const IntArray & ia)
    {
    if (IndexRange != ia.IndexRange)
        ReportError("incompatible arrays: ^=");

    IntArrayPtr      dest = MakePtr();
    IntArrayConstPtr src  = ia.MakeConstPtr();

    for (;;)
        {
        *dest ^= *src;

        if (dest.IsLast())
            break;

        ++dest;
        ++src;
        }

    return *this;
    }

 IntArray & IntArray::operator ^= (int n)
    {
    IntArrayPtr dest = MakePtr();

    for (;;)
        {
        *dest ^= n;

        if (dest.IsLast())
            break;

        ++dest;
        }

    return *this;
    }
```

C++ COMPONENTS AND ALGORITHMS

```
//————————
// comparison functions
//————————

int IntArray::Equals(const IntArray & ia) const
    {
    int result = 1;

    if (IndexRange == ia.IndexRange)
        {
        IntArrayConstPtr left  = MakeConstPtr();
        IntArrayConstPtr right = ia.MakeConstPtr();

        for (;;)
            {
            if (*left != *right)
                {
                result = 0;
                break;
                }

            if (left.IsLast())
                break;

            ++left;
            ++right;
            }
        }
    else
        result = 0;

    return result;
    }

IntArray operator < (const IntArray & ia1,
                     const IntArray & ia2)
    {
    if (ia1.IndexRange != ia2.IndexRange)
        IntArray::FriendErrExit("incompatible arrays: <");

    IntArray result(ia1.IndexRange);

    IntArrayPtr      dest  = result.MakePtr();
    IntArrayConstPtr left  = ia1.MakeConstPtr();
    IntArrayConstPtr right = ia2.MakeConstPtr();

    for (;;)
        {
```

**604**

```
        *dest = *left < *right;

        if (dest.IsLast())
            break;

        ++dest;
        ++left;
        ++right;
        }

    return result;
    }

IntArray operator <= (const IntArray & ia1,
                      const IntArray & ia2)
    {
    if (ia1.IndexRange != ia2.IndexRange)
        IntArray::FriendErrExit("incompatible arrays: <=");

    IntArray result(ia1.IndexRange);

    IntArrayPtr      dest  = result.MakePtr();
    IntArrayConstPtr left  = ia1.MakeConstPtr();
    IntArrayConstPtr right = ia2.MakeConstPtr();

    for (;;)
        {
        *dest = *left <= *right;

        if (dest.IsLast())
            break;

        ++dest;
        ++left;
        ++right;
        }

    return result;
    }

IntArray operator == (const IntArray & ia1,
                      const IntArray & ia2)
    {
    if (ia1.IndexRange != ia2.IndexRange)
        IntArray::FriendErrExit("incompatible arrays: ==");

    IntArray result(ia1.IndexRange);
```

```
    IntArrayPtr      dest  = result.MakePtr();
    IntArrayConstPtr left  = ia1.MakeConstPtr();
    IntArrayConstPtr right = ia2.MakeConstPtr();

    for (;;)
        {
        *dest = *left == *right;

        if (dest.IsLast())
            break;

        ++dest;
        ++left;
        ++right;
        }

    return result;
    }

IntArray operator != (const IntArray & ia1,
                      const IntArray & ia2)
    {
    if (ia1.IndexRange != ia2.IndexRange)
        IntArray::FriendErrExit("incompatible arrays: !=");

    IntArray result(ia1.IndexRange);

    IntArrayPtr      dest  = result.MakePtr();
    IntArrayConstPtr left  = ia1.MakeConstPtr();
    IntArrayConstPtr right = ia2.MakeConstPtr();

    for (;;)
        {
        *dest = *left != *right;

        if (dest.IsLast())
            break;

        ++dest;
        ++left;
        ++right;
        }

    return result;
    }

IntArray operator >= (const IntArray & ia1,
                      const IntArray & ia2)
```

```
    {
    if (ia1.IndexRange != ia2.IndexRange)
        IntArray::FriendErrExit("incompatible arrays: >=");

    IntArray result(ia1.IndexRange);

    IntArrayPtr      dest  = result.MakePtr();
    IntArrayConstPtr left  = ia1.MakeConstPtr();
    IntArrayConstPtr right = ia2.MakeConstPtr();

    for (;;)
        {
        *dest = *left >= *right;

        if (dest.IsLast())
            break;

        ++dest;
        ++left;
        ++right;
        }

    return result;
    }

IntArray operator > (const IntArray & ia1,
                     const IntArray & ia2)
    {
    if (ia1.IndexRange != ia2.IndexRange)
        IntArray::FriendErrExit("incompatible arrays: >");

    IntArray result(ia1.IndexRange);

    IntArrayPtr      dest  = result.MakePtr();
    IntArrayConstPtr left  = ia1.MakeConstPtr();
    IntArrayConstPtr right = ia2.MakeConstPtr();

    for (;;)
        {
        *dest = *left > *right;

        if (dest.IsLast())
            break;

        ++dest;
        ++left;
        ++right;
        }
```

```
    return result;
    }

//————
// fill functions
//————

void IntArray::Fill(int n)
    {
    IntArrayPtr ptr = MakePtr();

    for (;;)
        {
        *ptr = n;

        if (ptr.IsLast())
            break;

        ++ptr;
        }
    }

void IntArray::FillArithmetic(int first, int incr)
    {
    int value;

    IntArrayPtr ptr = MakePtr();

    value = first;

    *ptr = value;

    if (!ptr.IsLast())
        {
        ++ptr;

        for (;;)
            {
            value += incr;

            *ptr = value;

            if (ptr.IsLast())
                break;

            ++ptr;
            }
        }
```

```
    }

void IntArray::FillGeometric(int first,  int mult)
    {
    int value;

    IntArrayPtr ptr = MakePtr();

    value = first;

    *ptr = value;

    if (!ptr.IsLast())
        {
        ++ptr;

        for (;;)
            {
            value *= mult;

            *ptr = value;

            if (ptr.IsLast())
                break;

            ++ptr;
            }
        }
    }

void IntArray::FillRecursive(int first, IA_FillRecFunc func)
    {
    int value;

    IntArrayPtr ptr = MakePtr();

    value = first;

    *ptr = value;

    if (!ptr.IsLast())
        {
        ++ptr;

        for (;;)
            {
            value = func(value);
```

```
            *ptr = value;

            if (ptr.IsLast())
                break;

            ++ptr;
            }
        }
    }

void IntArray::FillRandom(RandGen & rg)
    {
    IntArrayPtr ptr = MakePtr();

    for (;;)
        {
        *ptr = (int)rg(INT_MAX);

        if (ptr.IsLast())
            break;

        ++ptr;
        }
    }

void IntArray::FillRandomBounded(int low, int high,
                                 RandGen & rg)
    {
    if (high <= low)
        ReportError("high bound <= low bound");

    int x = high - low + 1;

    IntArrayPtr ptr = MakePtr();

    for (;;)
        {
        *ptr = (int)(rg(x)) + low;

        if (ptr.IsLast())
            break;

        ++ptr;
        }
    }

void IntArray::FillBy(IA_FillByFunc func)
    {
```

**610**

```
    Index i(IndexRange);

    for (;;)
        {
        (*this)[i] = func(i);

        if (i.IsMax())
            break;

        ++i;
        }
    }

//————————
// absolute value functions
//————————

IntArray & IntArray::abs()
    {
    IntArrayPtr ptr = MakePtr();

    for (;;)
        {
        *ptr = ::abs(*ptr);

        if (ptr.IsLast())
            break;

        ++ptr;
        }

    return *this;
    }

IntArray abs(const IntArray & ia)
    {
    IntArray result(ia);

    IntArrayPtr ptr = result.MakePtr();

    for (;;)
        {
        *ptr = ::abs(*ptr);

        if (ptr.IsLast())
            break;

        ++ptr;
        }
```

```
    return result;
    }

//——————————————————
// functions required by Sortable base class
//——————————————————

int IntArray::IsBefore(const Index & i1, const Index & i2)
    {
    return ((*this)[i1] < (*this)[i2]);
    }

void IntArray::Exchange(const Index & i1, const Index & i2)
    {
    int temp = (*this)[i1];

    (*this)[i1] = (*this)[i2];
    (*this)[i2] = temp;
    }

//——————————————
// set new array elements
//——————————————

void IntArray::Set(int * i)
    {
    *i = 0;
    }
```

# Chapter 8: Floating-Point Arrays

**Listing 8-1. darray.h.**

```
//============================================================
//  MATHEMATICAL LIBRARY
//      darray.h
//
//      An array of doubles
//
//      Copyright 1992 by Scott Robert Ladd
//      All rights reserved
//============================================================

#ifndef DARRAY_H
#define DARRAY_H

#include "srtarray.h"
#include "randgen.h"
```

```
class IntArray;

//-=-=-=-=-=-=-=-=-=-=-=-=-=-=-=-=-=-=-=-=-=-=-=-=-=-=-=-=-=
//
//   DblArrayPtr class
//
//-=-=-=-=-=-=-=-=-=-=-=-=-=-=-=-=-=-=-=-=-=-=-=-=-=-=-=-=-=

class DblArrayPtr : public ArrayPtr
    {
    friend class DblArray;

    public:

        //————
        // copy constructor
        //————

        DblArrayPtr(const DblArrayPtr & aptr);
        DblArrayPtr(const ArrayPtr & aptr);

        //—————
        // assignment operators
        //—————

        DblArrayPtr & operator = (const DblArrayPtr & aptr);
        DblArrayPtr & operator = (const Index & i);
        DblArrayPtr & operator = (int i);

        //——————
        // increment and decrement
        //——————

        DblArrayPtr & operator ++ ();
        DblArrayPtr & operator - ();

        //—————
        // get pointer value
        //—————

        operator double * () const;

        //————
        // dereference
        //————

        double & operator * ();
```

```
    protected:

        //————
        // constructor
        //————

        DblArrayPtr(char * base, size_t esize, const Range & r);
    };

//————
// constructor
//————

inline DblArrayPtr::DblArrayPtr(char * base,
                                size_t esize,
                                const Range & r)
    : ArrayPtr(base,esize,r)
    {
    // empty
    }

//————
// copy constructor
//————

inline DblArrayPtr::DblArrayPtr(const DblArrayPtr & aptr)
    : ArrayPtr(aptr)
    {
    // empty
    }

inline DblArrayPtr::DblArrayPtr(const ArrayPtr & aptr)
    : ArrayPtr(aptr)
    {
    // empty
    }

//————
// assignment operators
//————

inline DblArrayPtr & DblArrayPtr::operator = (const DblArrayPtr & aptr)
    {
    this->ArrayPtr::operator = (aptr);

    return *this;
    }
```

```
inline DblArrayPtr & DblArrayPtr::operator = (const Index & i)
    {
    this->ArrayPtr::operator = (i);

    return *this;
    }

inline DblArrayPtr & DblArrayPtr::operator = (int i)
    {
    this->ArrayPtr::operator = (i);

    return *this;
    }

//———————————
// increment and decrement
//———————————

inline DblArrayPtr & DblArrayPtr::operator ++ ()
    {
    this->ArrayPtr::operator ++ ();

    return *this;
    }

inline DblArrayPtr & DblArrayPtr::operator — ()
    {
    this->ArrayPtr::operator — ();

    return *this;
    }

//—————————
// get pointer value
//—————————

inline DblArrayPtr::operator double * () const
    {
    return (double *)ElemPtr;
    }

//———————
// dereference
//———————

inline double & DblArrayPtr::operator * ()
    {
    return *((double *)ElemPtr);
    }
```

```
//-=-=-=-=-=-=-=-=-=-=-=-=-=-=-=-=-=-=-=-=-=-=-=-=-=-=-=-=-=-=
//
//  DblArrayConstPtr class
//
//-=-=-=-=-=-=-=-=-=-=-=-=-=-=-=-=-=-=-=-=-=-=-=-=-=-=-=-=-=-=

class DblArrayConstPtr : public ArrayPtr
    {
    friend class DblArray;

    public:

        //————
        // copy constructor
        //————

        DblArrayConstPtr(const DblArrayConstPtr & aptr);
        DblArrayConstPtr(const ArrayPtr & aptr);

        //————
        // assignment operators
        //————

        DblArrayConstPtr & operator = (const DblArrayConstPtr & aptr);
        DblArrayConstPtr & operator = (const Index & i);
        DblArrayConstPtr & operator = (int i);

        //————
        // increment and decrement
        //————

        DblArrayConstPtr & operator ++ ();
        DblArrayConstPtr & operator - ();

        //————
        // get pointer value
        //————

        operator const double * () const;

        //————
        // dereference
        //————

        const double & operator * ();

    protected:
        DblArrayConstPtr(char * base, size_t esize, const Range & r);
    };
```

**616**

```
//————
// constructor
//————

inline DblArrayConstPtr::DblArrayConstPtr(char * base,
                                          size_t esize,
                                          const Range & r)
    : ArrayPtr(base,esize,r)
    {
    // empty
    }

//————
// copy constructor
//————

inline DblArrayConstPtr::DblArrayConstPtr(const DblArrayConstPtr & aptr)
    : ArrayPtr(aptr)
    {
    // empty
    }

inline DblArrayConstPtr::DblArrayConstPtr(const ArrayPtr & aptr)
    : ArrayPtr(aptr)
    {
    // empty
    }

//————
// assignment operators
//————

inline DblArrayConstPtr & DblArrayConstPtr::operator = (const
DblArrayConstPtr & aptr)
    {
    this->ArrayPtr::operator = (aptr);

    return *this;
    }

inline DblArrayConstPtr & DblArrayConstPtr::operator = (const Index & i)
    {
    this->ArrayPtr::operator = (i);

    return *this;
    }

inline DblArrayConstPtr & DblArrayConstPtr::operator = (int i)
```

```
    {
    this->ArrayPtr::operator = (i);

    return *this;
    }

//————————
// increment and decrement
//————————

inline DblArrayConstPtr & DblArrayConstPtr::operator ++ ()
    {
    this->ArrayPtr::operator ++ ();

    return *this;
    }

inline DblArrayConstPtr & DblArrayConstPtr::operator - ()
    {
    this->ArrayPtr::operator - ();

    return *this;
    }

//————————
// get pointer value
//————————

inline DblArrayConstPtr::operator const double * () const
    {
    return (const double *)ElemPtr;
    }

//————
// dereference
//————

inline const double & DblArrayConstPtr::operator * ()
    {
    return *((const double *)ElemPtr);
    }

//-=-=-=-=-=-=-=-=-=-=-=-=-=-=-=-=-=-=-=-=-=-=-=-=-=-=-=-=
//
//   DblArray class
//
//-=-=-=-=-=-=-=-=-=-=-=-=-=-=-=-=-=-=-=-=-=-=-=-=-=-=-=-=
```

```
class DblArray : public SortableArray
    {
    protected:

        //——————————————————
        // default value assigned to array members
        //——————————————————

        static double InitValue;

    public:

        //———————
        // constructors
        //———————

        DblArray(const Range & r);
        DblArray(const DblArray & da);
        DblArray(const IntArray & ia);
        DblArray(const double * a, int len);

        // concatenate
        DblArray(const DblArray & a1,
                const DblArray & a2);

        // subrange
        DblArray(const DblArray & a,
                const Index & first,
                const Index & last);

        //——————————
        // conversion operators
        //——————————

        operator double * ();

        //——————————
        // assignment operator
        //——————————

        DblArray & operator = (const DblArray & da);

        //——————————————
        // create an approprite ArrayPtr
        //——————————————

        DblArrayPtr MakePtr();
```

```
DblArrayConstPtr MakeConstPtr() const;

//——————————
// reference array elements
//——————————

double & operator [] (const Index & i);
double & operator [] (int i);

//——————————
// read array elements
//——————————

const double & Read(const Index & i) const;
const double & Read(int i) const;

//——————————
// unary operators
//——————————

DblArray operator + ();
DblArray operator - ();

//——————————
// basic operators
//——————————

DblArray operator + (const DblArray & da);
DblArray operator + (double n);

DblArray operator - (const DblArray & da);
DblArray operator - (double n);

DblArray operator * (const DblArray & da);
DblArray operator * (double n);

DblArray operator / (const DblArray & da);
DblArray operator / (double n);

//——————————————
// short-hand assignment operators
//——————————————

DblArray & operator += (const DblArray & da);
DblArray & operator += (double n);

DblArray & operator -= (const DblArray & da);
DblArray & operator -= (double n);
```

```
DblArray & operator *= (const DblArray & da);
DblArray & operator *= (double n);

DblArray & operator /= (const DblArray & da);
DblArray & operator /= (double n);

//————————
// comparison operators
//————————

// compare complete array contents for equality

int Equals(const DblArray & da) const;

// compare array elements

friend IntArray operator <  (const DblArray &da1,
                             const DblArray &da2);

friend IntArray operator <= (const DblArray &da1,
                             const DblArray &da2);

friend IntArray operator == (const DblArray &da1,
                             const DblArray &da2);

friend IntArray operator != (const DblArray &da1,
                             const DblArray &da2);

friend IntArray operator >= (const DblArray &da1,
                             const DblArray &da2);

friend IntArray operator >  (const DblArray &da1,
                             const DblArray &da2);

//————————
// fill functions and types
//————————

typedef double (* DA_FillRecFunc)(double);
typedef double (* DA_FillByFunc)(const Index & i);

static void SetInit(double d);

void Fill(double d = InitValue);

void FillArithmetic(double first, double incr);
void FillGeometric(double first,  double mult);
void FillRecursive(double first,  DA_FillRecFunc func);
```

```
void FillRandom(RandGen & rg);
void FillRandomBounded(double low, double high,
                       RandGen & rg);

void FillBy(DA_FillByFunc func);

//————————
// trigonometric functions
//————————

// cosine

DblArray & cos();
friend DblArray cos(const DblArray & da);

DblArray & cosh();
friend DblArray cosh(const DblArray & da);

DblArray & acos();
friend DblArray acos(const DblArray & da);

// sine

DblArray & sin();
friend DblArray sin(const DblArray & da);

DblArray & sinh();
friend DblArray sinh(const DblArray & da);

DblArray & asin();
friend DblArray asin(const DblArray & da);

// tangent

DblArray & tan();
friend DblArray tan(const DblArray & da);

DblArray & tanh();
friend DblArray tanh(const DblArray & da);

DblArray & atan();
friend DblArray atan(const DblArray & da);

DblArray & atan2(const DblArray & den);

friend DblArray atan2(const DblArray & num,
                      const DblArray & den);
```

```
//——————
// logarithmic functions
//——————

// natural logarithm

DblArray & log();
friend DblArray log(const DblArray & da);

// natural exponentiation

DblArray & exp();
friend DblArray exp(const DblArray & da);

// base-10 logarithm

DblArray & log10();
friend DblArray log10(const DblArray & da);

// exponentiation

friend DblArray pow(const DblArray & da,
                    double p);

DblArray & pow(double p);

DblArray & pow(const DblArray & p);

friend DblArray pow(const DblArray & da,
                    const DblArray & p);

// square root

DblArray & sqroot();
friend DblArray sqroot(const DblArray & da);

//————
// sign functions
//————

// absolute value

DblArray & abs();
friend DblArray abs(const DblArray & da);

//——————
// power of 2 functions
//——————
```

```
// multiply by power of 2

friend DblArray ldexp(const DblArray & da,
                      int p);

DblArray & ldexp(int p);

DblArray & ldexp(const IntArray & p);

friend DblArray ldexp(const DblArray & da,
                      const IntArray & p);

// get fraction and power of 2

DblArray & frexp(IntArray & pow2);

friend DblArray frexp(const DblArray & da,
                      IntArray & pow2);

//————
// rounding functions
//————

// round toward negative infinity

DblArray & floor();
friend DblArray floor(const DblArray & da);

// round toward positive infinity

DblArray & ceil();
friend DblArray ceil(const DblArray & da);

//————
// miscellaneous functions
//————

// compute remainder

friend DblArray fmod(const DblArray & da,
                     double div);

DblArray & fmod(double div);

DblArray & fmod(const DblArray & div);

friend DblArray fmod(const DblArray & da,
                     const DblArray & div);
```

**624**

```
        // get frantional and integer parts

        DblArray & modf(DblArray & ipart);

        friend DblArray modf(const DblArray & da,
                             DblArray & ipart);

        //—————————————————————
        // functions required by Sortable base class
        //—————————————————————

        virtual int  IsBefore(const Index & i1, const Index & i2);
        virtual void Exchange(const Index & i1, const Index & i2);

    protected:

        //——————————
        // set new array elements
        //——————————

        static void Set(double * d);

        //————————————————
        // err exit function for friend functions
        //————————————————

        static void FriendErrExit(const char * msg);
    };

//———————
// constructors
//———————

inline DblArray::DblArray(const Range & r)
    : SortableArray(r,sizeof(double),(ElemCreate)DblArray::Set)
    {
    // empty
    }

inline DblArray::DblArray(const DblArray & da)
    : SortableArray(da)
    {
    // does nothing else
    }

inline DblArray::DblArray(const DblArray & a1,
                                const DblArray & a2)
    : SortableArray(a1,a2)
```

```
    {
    // does nothing else
    }

inline DblArray::DblArray(const DblArray & a,
                                const Index & first,
                                const Index & last)
    : SortableArray(a,first,last)
    {
    // does nothing else
    }

//————————
// assignment operator
//————————

inline DblArray & DblArray::operator = (const DblArray & da)
    {
    this->Array::operator = (da);

    return *this;
    }

//————————————
// create an approprite ArrayPtr
//————————————

inline DblArrayPtr DblArray::MakePtr()
    {
    return DblArrayPtr(Buffer,ElementSize,IndexRange);
    }

inline DblArrayConstPtr DblArray::MakeConstPtr() const
    {
    return DblArrayConstPtr(Buffer,ElementSize,IndexRange);
    }

//————————
// reference array elements
//————————

inline double & DblArray::operator [] (const Index & i)
    {
    return *((double *)(GetElement(i)));
    }

inline double & DblArray::operator [] (int i)
    {
```

```
    return *((double *)(GetElement(i)));
    }

//————
// read array elements
//————

inline const double & DblArray::Read(const Index & i) const
    {
    return *((const double *)(ReadElement(i)));
    }

inline const double & DblArray::Read(int i) const
    {
    return *((const double *)(ReadElement(i)));
    }

//————
// unary operators
//————

inline DblArray DblArray::operator + ()
    {
    return *this;
    }

//————
// fill functions
//————

inline void DblArray::SetInit(double d)
    {
    InitValue = d;
    }

//————
// err exit function for friend functions
//————

inline void DblArray::FriendErrExit(const char * msg)
    {
    ReportError(msg);
    }

#endif
```

**Listing 8-2. darray.cxx.**

```
//===============================================================
//   MATHEMATICAL LIBRARY
//      darray.cxx
//
//      An array of doubles
//
//      Copyright 1992 by Scott Robert Ladd
//      All rights reserved
//===============================================================

#include "darray.h"
#include "iarray.h"
#include "string.h"
#include "stdlib.h"
#include "limits.h"
#include "math.h"


//————————————————————
// default value assigned to array members
//————————————————————

double DblArray::InitValue = 0.0;

//————————
// constructors
//————————

DblArray::DblArray(const IntArray & ia)
    : SortableArray(ia.GetRange(),
                    sizeof(double),
                    (ElemCreate)NULL)
    {
    Index i(IndexRange);

    for (;;)
        {
        (*this)[i] = (double)ia.Read(i);

        if (i.IsMax())
            break;

        ++i;
        }
    }

DblArray::DblArray(const double * a, int len)
    : SortableArray(Range(0,len - 1),
```

```
                    sizeof(double),
                    (ElemCreate)NULL)
        {
        memcpy(Buffer,a,BufferSize);
        }


//————————
// conversion operators
//————————

DblArray::operator double * ()
        {
        double * result;

        result = new double[BufferSize];

        if (result == NULL)
            ReportError("unable to allocate memory for double []");

        memcpy(result,Buffer,BufferSize);

        return result;
        }


//————————
// unary operators
//————————

DblArray DblArray::operator - ()
        {
        DblArray result(*this);

        DblArrayPtr ptr = result.MakePtr();

        for (;;)
            {
            *ptr = -(*ptr);

            if (ptr.IsLast())
                break;

            ++ptr;
            }

        return result;
        }
```

```
//————
// basic operators
//————

DblArray DblArray::operator + (const DblArray & da)
    {
    if (IndexRange != da.IndexRange)
        ReportError("incompatible arrays: +");

    DblArray result(*this);

    DblArrayPtr      dest = result.MakePtr();
    DblArrayConstPtr src  = da.MakeConstPtr();

    for (;;)
        {
        *dest += *src;

        if (dest.IsLast())
            break;

        ++dest;
        ++src;
        }

    return result;
    }

DblArray DblArray::operator + (double n)
    {
    DblArray result(*this);

    DblArrayPtr ptr = result.MakePtr();

    for (;;)
        {
        *ptr += n;

        if (ptr.IsLast())
            break;

        ++ptr;
        }

    return result;
    }

DblArray DblArray::operator - (const DblArray & da)
    {
```

```
    if (IndexRange != da.IndexRange)
        ReportError("incompatible arrays: -");

    DblArray result(*this);

    DblArrayPtr      dest = result.MakePtr();
    DblArrayConstPtr src  = da.MakeConstPtr();

    for (;;)
        {
        *dest -= *src;

        if (dest.IsLast())
            break;

        ++dest;
        ++src;
        }

    return result;
    }

DblArray DblArray::operator - (double n)
    {
    DblArray result(*this);

    DblArrayPtr ptr = result.MakePtr();

    for (;;)
        {
        *ptr -= n;

        if (ptr.IsLast())
            break;

        ++ptr;
        }

    return result;
    }

DblArray DblArray::operator * (const DblArray & da)
    {
    if (IndexRange != da.IndexRange)
        ReportError("incompatible arrays: *");

    DblArray result(*this);

    DblArrayPtr      dest = result.MakePtr();
```

```
    DblArrayConstPtr src  = da.MakeConstPtr();

    for (;;)
        {
        *dest *= *src;

        if (dest.IsLast())
            break;

        ++dest;
        ++src;
        }

    return result;
    }

DblArray DblArray::operator * (double n)
    {
    DblArray result(*this);

    DblArrayPtr ptr = result.MakePtr();

    for (;;)
        {
        *ptr *= n;

        if (ptr.IsLast())
            break;

        ++ptr;
        }

    return result;
    }

DblArray DblArray::operator / (const DblArray & da)
    {
    if (IndexRange != da.IndexRange)
        ReportError("incompatible arrays: /");

    DblArray result(*this);

    DblArrayPtr     dest = result.MakePtr();
    DblArrayConstPtr src  = da.MakeConstPtr();

    for (;;)
        {
        *dest /= *src;
```

```
        if (dest.IsLast())
            break;

        ++dest;
        ++src;
        }

    return result;
    }

DblArray DblArray::operator / (double n)
    {
    DblArray result(*this);

    DblArrayPtr ptr = result.MakePtr();

    for (;;)
        {
        *ptr /= n;

        if (ptr.IsLast())
            break;

        ++ptr;
        }

    return result;
    }

//————————————
// short-hand assignment operators
//————————————

DblArray & DblArray::operator += (const DblArray & da)
    {
    if (IndexRange != da.IndexRange)
        ReportError("incompatible arrays: +=");

    DblArrayPtr      dest = MakePtr();
    DblArrayConstPtr src  = da.MakeConstPtr();

    for (;;)
        {
        *dest += *src;

        if (dest.IsLast())
            break;
```

```
            ++dest;
            ++src;
            }

        return *this;
        }

DblArray & DblArray::operator += (double n)
        {
        DblArrayPtr ptr = MakePtr();

        for (;;)
            {
            *ptr += n;

            if (ptr.IsLast())
                break;

            ++ptr;
            }

        return *this;
        }

DblArray & DblArray::operator -= (const DblArray & da)
        {
        if (IndexRange != da.IndexRange)
            ReportError("incompatible arrays: -=");

        DblArrayPtr      dest = MakePtr();
        DblArrayConstPtr src  = da.MakeConstPtr();

        for (;;)
            {
            *dest -= *src;

            if (dest.IsLast())
                break;

            ++dest;
            ++src;
            }

        return *this;
        }

DblArray & DblArray::operator -= (double n)
        {
        DblArrayPtr ptr = MakePtr();
```

```
    for (;;)
        {
        *ptr -= n;

        if (ptr.IsLast())
            break;

        ++ptr;
        }

    return *this;
    }

DblArray & DblArray::operator *= (const DblArray & da)
    {
    if (IndexRange != da.IndexRange)
        ReportError("incompatible arrays: *=");

    DblArrayPtr      dest = MakePtr();
    DblArrayConstPtr src  = da.MakeConstPtr();

    for (;;)
        {
        *dest *= *src;

        if (dest.IsLast())
            break;

        ++dest;
        ++src;
        }

    return *this;
    }

DblArray & DblArray::operator *= (double n)
    {
    DblArrayPtr ptr = MakePtr();

    for (;;)
        {
        *ptr *= n;

        if (ptr.IsLast())
            break;

        ++ptr;
        }
```

```
        return *this;
        }

DblArray & DblArray::operator /= (const DblArray & da)
        {
        if (IndexRange != da.IndexRange)
            ReportError("incompatible arrays: /=");

        DblArrayPtr      dest = MakePtr();
        DblArrayConstPtr src  = da.MakeConstPtr();

        for (;;)
            {
            *dest /= *src;

            if (dest.IsLast())
                break;

            ++dest;
            ++src;
            }

        return *this;
        }

DblArray & DblArray::operator /= (double n)
        {
        DblArrayPtr ptr = MakePtr();

        for (;;)
            {
            *ptr /= n;

            if (ptr.IsLast())
                break;

            ++ptr;
            }

        return *this;
        }

//————————
// comparison operators
//————————

// compare complete array contents for equality
```

```
int DblArray::Equals(const DblArray & da) const
    {
    int result = 1;

    if (IndexRange == da.IndexRange)
        {
        DblArrayConstPtr ptr1 = MakeConstPtr();
        DblArrayConstPtr ptr2 = da.MakeConstPtr();

        for (;;)
            {
            if (*ptr1 != *ptr2)
                {
                result = 0;
                break;
                }

            if (ptr1.IsLast())
                break;

            ++ptr1;
            ++ptr2;
            }
        }
    else
        result = 0;

    return result;
    }

// compare array elements

IntArray operator < (const DblArray & da1,
                     const DblArray & da2)
    {
    if (da1.IndexRange != da2.IndexRange)
        DblArray::FriendErrExit("incompatible arrays: <");

    IntArray result(da1.IndexRange);

    IntArrayPtr      dest  = result.MakePtr();
    DblArrayConstPtr left  = da1.MakeConstPtr();
    DblArrayConstPtr right = da2.MakeConstPtr();

    for (;;)
        {
        *dest = *left < *right;
```

```
            if (dest.IsLast())
                break;

            ++dest;
            ++left;
            ++right;
            }

    return result;
    }

IntArray operator <= (const DblArray & da1,
                      const DblArray & da2)
    {
    if (da1.IndexRange != da2.IndexRange)
        DblArray::FriendErrExit("incompatible arrays: <=");

    IntArray result(da1.IndexRange);

    IntArrayPtr      dest  = result.MakePtr();
    DblArrayConstPtr left  = da1.MakeConstPtr();
    DblArrayConstPtr right = da2.MakeConstPtr();

    for (;;)
        {
        *dest = *left <= *right;

        if (dest.IsLast())
            break;

        ++dest;
        ++left;
        ++right;
        }

    return result;
    }

IntArray operator == (const DblArray & da1,
                      const DblArray & da2)
    {
    if (da1.IndexRange != da2.IndexRange)
        DblArray::FriendErrExit("incompatible arrays: ==");

    IntArray result(da1.IndexRange);

    IntArrayPtr      dest  = result.MakePtr();
    DblArrayConstPtr left  = da1.MakeConstPtr();
```

```
    DblArrayConstPtr right = da2.MakeConstPtr();

    for (;;)
        {
        *dest = *left == *right;

        if (dest.IsLast())
            break;

        ++dest;
        ++left;
        ++right;
        }

    return result;
    }

IntArray operator != (const DblArray & da1,
                      const DblArray & da2)
    {
    if (da1.IndexRange != da2.IndexRange)
        DblArray::FriendErrExit("incompatible arrays: !=");

    IntArray result(da1.IndexRange);

    IntArrayPtr      dest  = result.MakePtr();
    DblArrayConstPtr left  = da1.MakeConstPtr();
    DblArrayConstPtr right = da2.MakeConstPtr();

    for (;;)
        {
        *dest = *left != *right;

        if (dest.IsLast())
            break;

        ++dest;
        ++left;
        ++right;
        }

    return result;
    }

IntArray operator >= (const DblArray & da1,
                      const DblArray & da2)
    {
    if (da1.IndexRange != da2.IndexRange)
```

```
            DblArray::FriendErrExit("incompatible arrays: >=");

        IntArray result(da1.IndexRange);

        IntArrayPtr      dest  = result.MakePtr();
        DblArrayConstPtr left  = da1.MakeConstPtr();
        DblArrayConstPtr right = da2.MakeConstPtr();

        for (;;)
            {
            *dest = *left >= *right;

            if (dest.IsLast())
                break;

            ++dest;
            ++left;
            ++right;
            }

        return result;
        }

IntArray operator > (const DblArray & da1,
                     const DblArray & da2)
        {
        if (da1.IndexRange != da2.IndexRange)
            DblArray::FriendErrExit("incompatible arrays: >");

        IntArray result(da1.IndexRange);

        IntArrayPtr      dest  = result.MakePtr();
        DblArrayConstPtr left  = da1.MakeConstPtr();
        DblArrayConstPtr right = da2.MakeConstPtr();

        for (;;)
            {
            *dest = *left > *right;

            if (dest.IsLast())
                break;

            ++dest;
            ++left;
            ++right;
            }

        return result;
        }
```

```
//————
// fill functions
//————

void DblArray::Fill(double d)
    {
    DblArrayPtr dest = MakePtr();

    for (;;)
        {
        *dest = d;

        if (dest.IsLast())
            break;

        ++dest;
        }
    }

void DblArray::FillArithmetic(double first, double incr)
    {
    double value;

    DblArrayPtr dest = MakePtr();

    value = first;

    *dest = value;

    if (!dest.IsLast())
        {
        ++dest;

        for (;;)
            {
            value += incr;

            *dest = value;

            if (dest.IsLast())
                break;

            ++dest;
            }
        }
    }

void DblArray::FillGeometric(double first,  double mult)
    {
```

```
    double value;

    DblArrayPtr dest = MakePtr();

    value = first;

    *dest = value;

    if (!dest.IsLast())
        {
        ++dest;

        for (;;)
            {
            value *= mult;

            *dest = value;

            if (dest.IsLast())
                break;

            ++dest;
            }
        }
    }

void DblArray::FillRecursive(double first, DA_FillRecFunc func)
    {
    double value;

    DblArrayPtr dest = MakePtr();

    value = first;

    *dest = value;

    if (!dest.IsLast())
        {
        ++dest;

        for (;;)
            {
            value = func(value);

            *dest = value;

            if (dest.IsLast())
                break;
```

```
                ++dest;
                }
            }
        }

void DblArray::FillRandom(RandGen & rg)
    {
    DblArrayPtr dest = MakePtr();

    for (;;)
        {
        *dest = double(rg(UINT_MAX)) / double(UINT_MAX);

        if (dest.IsLast())
            break;

        ++dest;
        }
    }

void DblArray::FillRandomBounded(double low, double high, RandGen & rg)
    {
    if (high <= low)
        ReportError("high bound <= low bound");

    double range = high - low;

    DblArrayPtr dest = MakePtr();

    for (;;)
        {
        *dest = double(rg(UINT_MAX)) / double(UINT_MAX) * range + low;

        if (dest.IsLast())
            break;

        ++dest;
        }
    }

void DblArray::FillBy(DA_FillByFunc func)
    {
    Index i(IndexRange);

    for (;;)
        {
        (*this)[i] = func(i);
```

```
        if (i.IsMax())
            break;

        ++i;
        }
    }


//————————————————
// functions required by Sortable base class
//————————————————

int DblArray::IsBefore(const Index & i1, const Index & i2)
    {
    return ((*this)[i1] < (*this)[i2]);
    }

void DblArray::Exchange(const Index & i1, const Index & i2)
    {
    double temp = (*this)[i1];

    (*this)[i1] = (*this)[i2];
    (*this)[i2] = temp;
    }

//————————
// set new array elements
//————————

void DblArray::Set(double * d)
    {
    *d = InitValue;
    }

//——————————
// trigonometric functions
//——————————

// cosine

DblArray & DblArray::cos()
    {
    DblArrayPtr ptr = MakePtr();

    for (;;)
        {
        *ptr = ::cos(*ptr);

        if (ptr.IsLast())
            break;
```

```
            ++ptr;
            }

        return *this;
        }

DblArray cos(const DblArray & da)
        {
        DblArray result(da);

        DblArrayPtr        dest = result.MakePtr();
        DblArrayConstPtr   src = da.MakeConstPtr();

        for (;;)
            {
            *dest = ::cos(*src);

            if (dest.IsLast())
                break;

            ++dest;
            ++src;
            }

        return result;
        }

DblArray & DblArray::cosh()
        {
        DblArrayPtr ptr = MakePtr();

        for (;;)
            {
            *ptr = ::cosh(*ptr);

            if (ptr.IsLast())
                break;

            ++ptr;
            }

        return *this;
        }

DblArray cosh(const DblArray & da)
        {
        DblArray result(da);
```

```
    DblArrayPtr      dest = result.MakePtr();
    DblArrayConstPtr  src = da.MakeConstPtr();

    for (;;)
        {
        *dest = ::cosh(*src);

        if (dest.IsLast())
            break;

        ++dest;
        ++src;
        }

    return result;
    }

DblArray & DblArray::acos()
    {
    DblArrayPtr ptr = MakePtr();

    for (;;)
        {
        *ptr = ::acos(*ptr);

        if (ptr.IsLast())
            break;

        ++ptr;
        }

    return *this;
    }

DblArray acos(const DblArray & da)
    {
    DblArray result(da);

    DblArrayPtr      dest = result.MakePtr();
    DblArrayConstPtr  src = da.MakeConstPtr();

    for (;;)
        {
        *dest = ::acos(*src);

        if (dest.IsLast())
            break;
```

```
        ++dest;
        ++src;
        }

    return result;
    }

// sine

DblArray & DblArray::sin()
    {
    DblArrayPtr ptr = MakePtr();

    for (;;)
        {
        *ptr = ::sin(*ptr);

        if (ptr.IsLast())
            break;

        ++ptr;
        }

    return *this;
    }

DblArray sin(const DblArray & da)
    {
    DblArray result(da);

    DblArrayPtr      dest = result.MakePtr();
    DblArrayConstPtr  src = da.MakeConstPtr();

    for (;;)
        {
        *dest = ::sin(*src);

        if (dest.IsLast())
            break;

        ++dest;
        ++src;
        }

    return result;
    }

DblArray & DblArray::sinh()
    {
```

```
    DblArrayPtr ptr = MakePtr();

    for (;;)
        {
        *ptr = ::sinh(*ptr);

        if (ptr.IsLast())
            break;

        ++ptr;
        }

    return *this;
    }

DblArray sinh(const DblArray & da)
    {
    DblArray result(da);

    DblArrayPtr      dest = result.MakePtr();
    DblArrayConstPtr  src = da.MakeConstPtr();

    for (;;)
        {
        *dest = ::sinh(*src);

        if (dest.IsLast())
            break;

        ++dest;
        ++src;
        }

    return result;
    }

DblArray & DblArray::asin()
    {
    DblArrayPtr ptr = MakePtr();

    for (;;)
        {
        *ptr = ::asin(*ptr);

        if (ptr.IsLast())
            break;

        ++ptr;
        }
```

```
    return *this;
    }

DblArray asin(const DblArray & da)
    {
    DblArray result(da);

    DblArrayPtr      dest = result.MakePtr();
    DblArrayConstPtr  src = da.MakeConstPtr();

    for (;;)
        {
        *dest = ::asin(*src);

        if (dest.IsLast())
            break;

        ++dest;
        ++src;
        }

    return result;
    }

// tangent

DblArray & DblArray::tan()
    {
    DblArrayPtr ptr = MakePtr();

    for (;;)
        {
        *ptr = ::tan(*ptr);

        if (ptr.IsLast())
            break;

        ++ptr;
        }

    return *this;
    }

DblArray tan(const DblArray & da)
    {
    DblArray result(da);

    DblArrayPtr      dest = result.MakePtr();
```

```
    DblArrayConstPtr  src = da.MakeConstPtr();

    for (;;)
        {
        *dest = ::tan(*src);

        if (dest.IsLast())
            break;

        ++dest;
        ++src;
        }

    return result;
    }

DblArray & DblArray::tanh()
    {
    DblArrayPtr ptr = MakePtr();

    for (;;)
        {
        *ptr = ::tanh(*ptr);

        if (ptr.IsLast())
            break;

        ++ptr;
        }

    return *this;
    }

DblArray tanh(const DblArray & da)
    {
    DblArray result(da);

    DblArrayPtr      dest = result.MakePtr();
    DblArrayConstPtr  src = da.MakeConstPtr();

    for (;;)
        {
        *dest = ::tanh(*src);

        if (dest.IsLast())
            break;

        ++dest;
```

```
        ++src;
        }

    return result;
    }

DblArray & DblArray::atan()
    {
    DblArrayPtr ptr = MakePtr();

    for (;;)
        {
        *ptr = ::atan(*ptr);

        if (ptr.IsLast())
            break;

        ++ptr;
        }

    return *this;
    }

DblArray atan(const DblArray & da)
    {
    DblArray result(da);

    DblArrayPtr      dest = result.MakePtr();
    DblArrayConstPtr  src = da.MakeConstPtr();

    for (;;)
        {
        *dest = ::atan(*src);

        if (dest.IsLast())
            break;

        ++dest;
        ++src;
        }

    return result;
    }

DblArray & DblArray::atan2(const DblArray & den)
    {
    if (IndexRange != den.IndexRange)
        ReportError("incompatible arrays: atan2(1)");
```

```
    DblArrayPtr      nptr = MakePtr();
    DblArrayConstPtr dptr = den.MakeConstPtr();

    for (;;)
        {
        *nptr = ::atan2(*nptr,*dptr);

        if (nptr.IsLast())
            break;

        ++nptr;
        ++dptr;
        }

    return *this;
    }

DblArray atan2(const DblArray & num,const DblArray & den)
    {
    if (num.IndexRange != den.IndexRange)
        DblArray::FriendErrExit("incompatible arrays: atan2(2)");

    DblArray result(num.IndexRange);

    DblArrayPtr      dest = result.MakePtr();
    DblArrayConstPtr nptr = num.MakeConstPtr();
    DblArrayConstPtr dptr = den.MakeConstPtr();

    for (;;)
        {
        *dest = ::atan2(*nptr,*dptr);

        if (dest.IsLast())
            break;

        ++dest;
        ++nptr;
        ++dptr;
        }

    return result;
    }

//—————————
// logarithmic functions
//—————————

// natural logarithm
```

```
DblArray & DblArray::log()
    {
    DblArrayPtr ptr = MakePtr();

    for (;;)
        {
        *ptr = ::log(*ptr);

        if (ptr.IsLast())
            break;

        ++ptr;
        }

    return *this;
    }

DblArray log(const DblArray & da)
    {
    DblArray result(da);

    DblArrayPtr      dest = result.MakePtr();
    DblArrayConstPtr  src = da.MakeConstPtr();

    for (;;)
        {
        *dest = ::log(*src);

        if (dest.IsLast())
            break;

        ++dest;
        ++src;
        }

    return result;
    }

// natural exponentiation

DblArray & DblArray::exp()
    {
    DblArrayPtr ptr = MakePtr();

    for (;;)
        {
        *ptr = ::exp(*ptr);

        if (ptr.IsLast())
```

```
            break;
        ++ptr;
        }

    return *this;
    }

DblArray exp(const DblArray & da)
    {
    DblArray result(da);

    DblArrayPtr      dest = result.MakePtr();
    DblArrayConstPtr  src = da.MakeConstPtr();

    for (;;)
        {
        *dest = ::exp(*src);

        if (dest.IsLast())
            break;

        ++dest;
        ++src;
        }

    return result;
    }

// base-10 logarithm

DblArray & DblArray::log10()
    {
    DblArrayPtr ptr = MakePtr();

    for (;;)
        {
        *ptr = ::log10(*ptr);

        if (ptr.IsLast())
            break;

        ++ptr;
        }

    return *this;
    }

DblArray log10(const DblArray & da)
```

```
    {
    DblArray result(da);

    DblArrayPtr      dest = result.MakePtr();
    DblArrayConstPtr src = da.MakeConstPtr();

    for (;;)
        {
        *dest = ::log10(*src);

        if (dest.IsLast())
            break;

        ++dest;
        ++src;
        }

    return result;
    }

// exponentiation

DblArray & DblArray::pow(double p)
    {
    DblArrayPtr ptr = MakePtr();

    for (;;)
        {
        *ptr = ::pow(*ptr,p);

        if (ptr.IsLast())
            break;

        ++ptr;
        }

    return *this;
    }

DblArray pow(const DblArray & da, double p)
    {
    DblArray result(da.IndexRange);

    DblArrayPtr      dest = result.MakePtr();
    DblArrayConstPtr src = da.MakeConstPtr();

    for (;;)
        {
```

```
        *dest = ::pow(*src,p);

        if (dest.IsLast())
            break;

        ++dest;
        ++src;
        }

    return result;
    }

DblArray & DblArray::pow(const DblArray & p)
    {
    if (IndexRange != p.IndexRange)
        ReportError("incompatible arrays: pow(1)");

    DblArrayPtr      base = MakePtr();
    DblArrayConstPtr pwr  = p.MakeConstPtr();

    for (;;)
        {
        *base = ::pow(*base,*pwr);

        if (base.IsLast())
            break;

        ++base;
        ++pwr;
        }

    return *this;
    }

DblArray pow(const DblArray & da, const DblArray & p)
    {
    if (da.IndexRange != p.IndexRange)
        DblArray::FriendErrExit("incompatible arrays: pow(2)");

    DblArray result(da.IndexRange);

    DblArrayPtr      dest = result.MakePtr();
    DblArrayConstPtr base = da.MakeConstPtr();
    DblArrayConstPtr  pwr = p.MakeConstPtr();

    for (;;)
        {
        *dest = ::pow(*base,*pwr);
```

```
        if (dest.IsLast())
            break;

        ++dest;
        ++base;
        ++pwr;
        }

    return result;
    }

// square root

DblArray & DblArray::sqroot()
    {
    DblArrayPtr ptr = MakePtr();

    for (;;)
        {
        *ptr = ::sqrt(*ptr);

        if (ptr.IsLast())
            break;

        ++ptr;
        }

    return *this;
    }

DblArray sqroot(const DblArray & da)
    {
    DblArray result(da);

    DblArrayPtr      dest = result.MakePtr();
    DblArrayConstPtr src = da.MakeConstPtr();

    for (;;)
        {
        *dest = ::sqrt(*src);

        if (dest.IsLast())
            break;

        ++dest;
        ++src;
        }
```

```
    return result;
    }

//————
// sign functions
//————

// absolute value

DblArray & DblArray::abs()
    {
    DblArrayPtr ptr = MakePtr();

    for (;;)
        {
        *ptr = ::fabs(*ptr);

        if (ptr.IsLast())
            break;

        ++ptr;
        }

    return *this;
    }

DblArray abs(const DblArray & da)
    {
    DblArray result(da);

    DblArrayPtr      dest = result.MakePtr();
    DblArrayConstPtr  src = da.MakeConstPtr();

    for (;;)
        {
        *dest = ::fabs(*src);

        if (dest.IsLast())
            break;

        ++dest;
        ++src;
        }

    return result;
    }
```

```
//————
// power of 2 functions
//————

// multiply by power of 2

DblArray & DblArray::ldexp(int p)
    {
    DblArrayPtr ptr = MakePtr();

    for (;;)
        {
        *ptr = ::ldexp(*ptr,p);

        if (ptr.IsLast())
            break;

        ++ptr;
        }

    return *this;
    }

DblArray ldexp(const DblArray & da, int p)
    {
    DblArray result(da.IndexRange);

    DblArrayPtr      dest = result.MakePtr();
    DblArrayConstPtr src = da.MakeConstPtr();

    for (;;)
        {
        *dest = ::ldexp(*src,p);

        if (dest.IsLast())
            break;

        ++dest;
        ++src;
        }

    return result;
    }

DblArray & DblArray::ldexp(const IntArray & p)
    {
    if (IndexRange != p.GetRange())
        ReportError("incompatible arrays: ldexp(1)");
```

```
    DblArrayPtr      base = MakePtr();
    IntArrayConstPtr pptr = p.MakeConstPtr();

    for (;;)
        {
        *base = ::ldexp(*base,*pptr);

        if (base.IsLast())
            break;

        ++base;
        ++pptr;
        }

    return *this;
    }

DblArray ldexp(const DblArray & da,const IntArray & p)
    {
    if (da.IndexRange != p.GetRange())
        DblArray::FriendErrExit("incompatible arrays: ldexp(2)");

    DblArray result(da.IndexRange);

    DblArrayPtr      dest = result.MakePtr();
    DblArrayConstPtr base = da.MakeConstPtr();
    IntArrayConstPtr pptr = p.MakeConstPtr();

    for (;;)
        {
        *dest = ::ldexp(*base,*pptr);

        if (dest.IsLast())
            break;

        ++dest;
        ++base;
        ++pptr;
        }

    return result;
    }

DblArray & DblArray::frexp(IntArray & pow2)
    {
    if (IndexRange != pow2.GetRange())
        DblArray::FriendErrExit("incompatible arrays: frexp(1)");
```

```
    DblArrayPtr base = MakePtr();

    Index i = pow2.MakeIndex();

    for (;;)
        {
        *base = ::frexp(*base,&(pow2[i]));

        if (base.IsLast())
            break;

        ++base;
        ++i;
        }

    return *this;
    }

DblArray frexp(const DblArray & da, IntArray & pow2)
    {
    if (da.IndexRange != pow2.GetRange())
        DblArray::FriendErrExit("incompatible arrays: frexp(2)");

    DblArray result(da.IndexRange);

    DblArrayPtr      dest = result.MakePtr();
    DblArrayConstPtr base = da.MakeConstPtr();

    Index i = pow2.MakeIndex();

    for (;;)
        {
        *dest = ::frexp(*base,&(pow2[i]));

        if (dest.IsLast())
            break;

        ++dest;
        ++base;
        ++i;
        }

    return result;
    }

//—————
// rounding functions
//—————
```

```
// round toward negative infinity

DblArray & DblArray::floor()
    {
    DblArrayPtr ptr = MakePtr();

    for (;;)
        {
        *ptr = ::floor(*ptr);

        if (ptr.IsLast())
            break;

        ++ptr;
        }

    return *this;
    }

DblArray floor(const DblArray & da)
    {
    DblArray result(da);

    DblArrayPtr      dest = result.MakePtr();
    DblArrayConstPtr src = da.MakeConstPtr();

    for (;;)
        {
        *dest = ::floor(*src);

        if (dest.IsLast())
            break;

        ++dest;
        ++src;
        }

    return result;
    }

// round toward positive infinity

DblArray & DblArray::ceil()
    {
    DblArrayPtr ptr = MakePtr();

    for (;;)
        {
```

```
        *ptr = ::ceil(*ptr);

        if (ptr.IsLast())
            break;

        ++ptr;
        }

    return *this;
    }

DblArray ceil(const DblArray & da)
    {
    DblArray result(da);

    DblArrayPtr      dest = result.MakePtr();
    DblArrayConstPtr src = da.MakeConstPtr();

    for (;;)
        {
        *dest = ::ceil(*src);

        if (dest.IsLast())
            break;

        ++dest;
        ++src;
        }

    return result;
    }

//————————
// miscellaneous functions
//————————

// compute remainder

DblArray & DblArray::fmod(double div)
    {
    DblArrayPtr ptr = MakePtr();

    for (;;)
        {
        *ptr = ::fmod(*ptr,div);

        if (ptr.IsLast())
            break;
```

```
        ++ptr;
        }

    return *this;
    }

DblArray fmod(const DblArray & da, double div)
    {
    DblArray result(da.IndexRange);

    DblArrayPtr      dest = result.MakePtr();
    DblArrayConstPtr  src = da.MakeConstPtr();

    for (;;)
        {
        *dest = ::fmod(*src,div);

        if (dest.IsLast())
            break;

        ++dest;
        ++src;
        }

    return result;
    }

DblArray & DblArray::fmod(const DblArray & div)
    {
    if (IndexRange != div.GetRange())
        DblArray::FriendErrExit("incompatible arrays: fmod(1)");

    DblArrayPtr      dest = MakePtr();
    DblArrayConstPtr dptr = div.MakeConstPtr();

    for (;;)
        {
        *dest = ::fmod(*dest,*dptr);

        if (dest.IsLast())
            break;

        ++dest;
        ++dptr;
        }

    return *this;
    }
```

```
DblArray fmod(const DblArray & da,
            const DblArray & div)
    {
    if (da.IndexRange != div.GetRange())
        DblArray::FriendErrExit("incompatible arrays: fmod(2)");

    DblArray result(da.IndexRange);

    DblArrayPtr      dest = result.MakePtr();
    DblArrayConstPtr  src = da.MakeConstPtr();
    DblArrayConstPtr dptr = div.MakeConstPtr();

    for (;;)
        {
        *dest = ::fmod(*src,*dptr);

        if (dest.IsLast())
            break;

        ++dest;
        ++src;
        ++dptr;
        }

    return result;
    }

// get fractional and integer parts

DblArray & DblArray::modf(DblArray & ipart)
    {
    if (IndexRange != ipart.GetRange())
        DblArray::FriendErrExit("incompatible arrays: modf(1)");

    DblArrayPtr fptr = MakePtr();
    DblArrayPtr iptr = ipart.MakePtr();

    for (;;)
        {
        *fptr = ::modf(*fptr,&(*iptr));

        if (fptr.IsLast())
            break;

        ++fptr;
        ++iptr;
        }
```

```
        return *this;
        }

DblArray modf(const DblArray & da,DblArray & ipart)
        {
        if (da.IndexRange != ipart.GetRange())
            DblArray::FriendErrExit("incompatible arrays: modf(2)");

        DblArray result(da.IndexRange);

        DblArrayPtr       fptr = result.MakePtr();
        DblArrayConstPtr  src = da.MakeConstPtr();
        DblArrayPtr       iptr = ipart.MakePtr();

        for (;;)
            {
            *fptr = ::modf(*src,&(*iptr));

            if (fptr.IsLast())
                break;

            ++fptr;
            ++src;
            ++iptr;
            }

        return result;
        }
```

# Chapter 9: Statistical Arrays

**Listing 9-1. dsarray.h.**
```
//=========================================================
//   MATHEMATICAL LIBRARY
//       dsarray.h
//
//       A variation of the DblArray used for rudimentary
//       statistical analysis.
//
//       Copyright 1992 by Scott Robert Ladd
//       All rights reserved
//=========================================================

#ifndef DSARRAY_H
#define DSARRAY_H

#include "darray.h"
#include "math.h"
```

```
//-=-=-=-=-=-=-=-=-=-=-=-=-=-=-=-=-=-=-=-=-=-=-=-=-=-=-=-=-=
//
//  DblStatArray class
//
//-=-=-=-=-=-=-=-=-=-=-=-=-=-=-=-=-=-=-=-=-=-=-=-=-=-=-=-=-=

class DblStatArray : public DblArray
    {
    public:

        //————
        // constructors
        //————

        DblStatArray(const Range & r);
        DblStatArray(const DblArray & da);
        DblStatArray(const DblStatArray & dsa);
        DblStatArray(const IntArray & ia);

        // concatenate
        DblStatArray(const DblStatArray & a1,
                     const DblStatArray & a2);

        // subrange
        DblStatArray(const DblStatArray & a,
                     const Index & first,
                     const Index & last);

        //——————
        // assignment operator
        //——————

        DblStatArray & operator = (const DblStatArray & da);

        //——————————————
        // mathematical and statistical functions
        //——————————————

        // minimum, maximum, and range determination
        double Min() const;
        double Max() const;

        void MinMax(double & minimum, double & maximum) const;

        double RangeOf() const;

        // series calculations
        double Sum() const;
```

```
        double Product() const;

        // calculate moments of distribution
        double Mean() const;
        double Median() const;
        double MedianSort();

        double Variance() const;

        double StdDeviation() const;
        double AvgDeviation() const;

        double Skew() const;
        double Kurt() const;

        // calculate several values at once
        void Moment(double & mean,
                    double & avgdev,
                    double & stddev,
                    double & var,
                    double & skew,
                    double & kurt) const;

        // calculate standardized scores (z-scores)
        double ZScore(const Index & i) const;
        double ZScore(int i) const;

        DblStatArray ZScore() const;

        // calculate Pearson's coefficient of correlation
        // for a pair of arrays
        double Correlation(const DblStatArray & dsa);
    };

//————
// constructors
//————

inline DblStatArray::DblStatArray(const Range & r)
    : DblArray(r)
    {
    // empty
    }

inline DblStatArray::DblStatArray(const DblArray & da)
    : DblArray(da)
    {
    // empty
    }
```

```
inline DblStatArray::DblStatArray(const DblStatArray & dsa)
    : DblArray(dsa)
    {
    // empty
    }

inline DblStatArray::DblStatArray(const IntArray & ia)
    : DblArray(ia)
    {
    // empty
    }

inline DblStatArray::DblStatArray(const DblStatArray & a1,
                                  const DblStatArray & a2)
    : DblArray(a1,a2)
    {
    // does nothing else
    }

inline DblStatArray::DblStatArray(const DblStatArray & a,
                                  const Index & first,
                                  const Index & last)
    : DblArray(a,first,last)
    {
    // does nothing else
    }

//—————
// assignment operator
//—————

inline DblStatArray & DblStatArray::operator = (const DblStatArray & da)
    {
    this->DblArray::operator = (da);

    return *this;
    }

//—————
// standard deviation
//—————

inline double DblStatArray::StdDeviation() const
    {
    return sqrt(Variance());
    }

#endif
```

**Listing 9-2. dsarray.cxx.**

```
//=====================================================
//   MATHEMATICAL LIBRARY
//       dsarray.cxx
//
//       A variation of the DblArray used for rudimentary
//       statistical analysis.
//
//       Copyright 1992 by Scott Robert Ladd
//       All rights reserved
//=====================================================

#include "dsarray.h"
#include "math.h"
#include "float.h"

double DblStatArray::Min() const
    {
    DblArrayConstPtr ptr = MakeConstPtr();

    double result = *ptr;

    for (;;)
        {
        if (ptr.IsLast())
            break;

        ++ptr;

        if (*ptr < result)
            result = *ptr;
        }

    return result;
    }

double DblStatArray::Max() const
    {
    DblArrayConstPtr ptr = MakeConstPtr();

    double result = *ptr;

    for (;;)
        {
        if (ptr.IsLast())
            break;

        ++ptr;
```

```
            if (*ptr > result)
                result = *ptr;
            }

    return result;
    }

void DblStatArray::MinMax(double & minimum, double & maximum) const
    {
    DblArrayConstPtr ptr = MakeConstPtr();

    maximum = *ptr;
    minimum = *ptr;

    for (;;)
        {
        if (ptr.IsLast())
            break;

        ++ptr;

        if (*ptr < minimum)
            minimum = *ptr;

        if (*ptr > maximum)
            maximum = *ptr;
        }
    }

double DblStatArray::RangeOf() const
    {
    double minimum, maximum;

    MinMax(minimum,maximum);

    return ::fabs(maximum - minimum);
    }

double DblStatArray::Sum() const
    {
    double result = 0.0;

    DblArrayConstPtr ptr = MakeConstPtr();

    for (;;)
        {
        result += *ptr;
```

```
        if (ptr.IsLast())
            break;

        ++ptr;
        }

    return result;
    }

double DblStatArray::Product() const
    {
    double result = 1.0;

    DblArrayConstPtr ptr = MakeConstPtr();

    for (;;)
        {
        result *= *ptr;

        if (ptr.IsLast())
            break;

        ++ptr;
        }

    return result;
    }

double DblStatArray::Mean() const
    {
    return Sum() / (double)Count;
    }

double DblStatArray::Median() const
    {
    DblStatArray temp(*this);

    int middle = (IndexRange.GetMin() + IndexRange.GetMax()) / 2;

    temp.Sort();

    return temp[middle];
    }

double DblStatArray::MedianSort()
    {
    int middle = (IndexRange.GetMin() + IndexRange.GetMax()) / 2;
```

```
    Sort();

    return Read(middle);
    }

double DblStatArray::Variance() const
    {
    double temp, result = 0.0;

    double m = Mean();

    DblArrayConstPtr ptr = MakeConstPtr();

    for (;;)
        {
        temp = *ptr - m;

        result += temp * temp;

        if (ptr.IsLast())
            break;

        ++ptr;
        }

    result /= ((double)(Count - 1));

    return result;
    }

double DblStatArray::AvgDeviation() const
    {
    double result = 0.0;
    double m = Mean();

    DblArrayConstPtr ptr = MakeConstPtr();

    for (;;)
        {
        result += fabs(*ptr - m);

        if (ptr.IsLast())
            break;

        ++ptr;
        }

    result /= (double)Count;
```

```
    return result;
    }

double DblStatArray::Skew() const
    {
    double result;
    double sd = StdDeviation();

    if (sd == 0.0)
        result = 0.0;
    else
        {
        double temp;
        double m  = Mean();

        DblArrayConstPtr ptr = MakeConstPtr();

        for (;;)
            {
            temp = (*ptr - m) / sd;

            result += (temp * temp * temp);

            if (ptr.IsLast())
                break;

            ++ptr;
            }

        result /= ((double)(Count - 1));
        }

    return result;
    }

double DblStatArray::Kurt() const
    {
    double result = 0.0;
    double sd = StdDeviation();

    if (sd == 0.0)
        result = 0.0;
    else
        {
        double temp;
        double m  = Mean();

        DblArrayConstPtr ptr = MakeConstPtr();
```

```
        for (;;)
            {
            temp = (*ptr - m) / sd;
            result += (temp * temp * temp * temp);

            if (ptr.IsLast())
                break;

            ++ptr;
            }

        result /= (double)Count;
        result -= 3.0;
        }

    return result;
    }

void DblStatArray::Moment(double & mean,
                          double & avgdev,
                          double & stddev,
                          double & var,
                          double & skew,
                          double & kurt) const
    {
    double temp, tempsqr, cnt;

    cnt  = (double)Count;
    mean = Mean();

    var    = 0.0;
    avgdev = 0.0;

    DblArrayConstPtr ptr = MakeConstPtr();

    for (;;)
        {
        temp = *ptr - mean;

        var    += temp * temp;
        avgdev += fabs(temp);

        if (ptr.IsLast())
            break;

        ++ptr;
        }
```

```
    var     /= cnt - 1.0;
    avgdev /= cnt;
    stddev  = sqrt(var);

    if (stddev == 0.0)
        {
        skew = 0.0;
        kurt = 0.0;
        }
    else
        {
        ptr.SetFirst();

        skew = 0.0;
        kurt = 0.0;

        for (;;)
            {
            temp = (*ptr - mean) / stddev;

            tempsqr = temp * temp;

            kurt += (tempsqr * tempsqr);
            skew += (tempsqr * temp);

            if (ptr.IsLast())
                break;

            ++ptr;
            }

        skew /= cnt - 1.0;
        kurt /= cnt;
        kurt -= 3.0;
        }
    }

double DblStatArray::ZScore(const Index & i) const
    {
    double result = 0.0;

    double sd = StdDeviation();

    if (sd == 0.0)
        result = 0.0;
    else
        result = (Read(i) - Mean()) / sd;
```

```
    return result;
    }

double DblStatArray::ZScore(int i) const
    {
    double result = 0.0;

    double sd = StdDeviation();

    if (sd == 0.0)
        result = 0.0;
    else
        result = (Read(i) - Mean()) / sd;

    return result;
    }

DblStatArray DblStatArray::ZScore() const
    {
    DblStatArray result(IndexRange);

    double sd = StdDeviation();

    if (sd == 0.0)
        result.Fill(0.0);
    else
        {
        DblArrayConstPtr  src = MakeConstPtr();
        DblArrayPtr       dest = result.MakePtr();

        double m  = Mean();

        for (;;)
            {
            *dest = (*src - m) / sd;

            if (src.IsLast())
                break;

            ++src;
            ++dest;
            }
        }

    return result;
    }

double DblStatArray::Correlation(const DblStatArray & dsa)
```

```
    {
    if (IndexRange != dsa.IndexRange)
        ReportError("Incompatible arrays in Correlation");

    DblArrayConstPtr ptr1 = MakeConstPtr();
    DblArrayConstPtr ptr2 = dsa.MakeConstPtr();

    double result = 0.0;

    double  m1 = Mean();
    double  m2 = dsa.Mean();
    double sd1 = StdDeviation();
    double sd2 = dsa.StdDeviation();

    if ((sd1 == 0.0) || (sd2 == 0.0))
        {
        if (sd1 == sd2)
            result = 1.0;
        else
            result = 0.0;
        }
    else
        {
        for (;;)
            {
            result += ((*ptr1 - m1) / sd1) * ((*ptr2 - m2) / sd2);

            if (ptr1.IsLast())
                break;

            ++ptr1;
            ++ptr2;
            }

        result /= Count;
        }

    return result;
    }
```

**Listing 9-3. rain.cxx.**

```
//===============================================================
//      rain.cxx
//
//      Performs statistical analysis on rainfall amounts for
//      Sagecliff, Colorado.
//===============================================================
```

```
#include "iostream.h"
#include "dsarray.h"

const Range DataRange(1970,1991);

double RainValues[] =
    {
    1.5, 2.3, 2.1, 7.5, 3.0, 2.4, 1.9, 1.8, 2.0, 2.5, 2.3,
    2.4, 3.0, 0.2, 1.9, 2.5, 2.1, 2.6, 3.5, 1.8, 2.1, 6.0
    };

double TempValues[] =
    {
    91, 81, 84, 75, 79, 81, 81, 88, 87, 80, 83,
    81, 79, 94, 77, 79, 78, 82, 90, 73, 77, 76
    };

DblStatArray RainData(DataRange);
DblStatArray TempData(DataRange);

int main()
    {
    // fill arrays with data
    DblArrayPtr rainPtr = RainData.MakePtr();
    DblArrayPtr tempPtr = TempData.MakePtr();

    int n = 0;

    for (;;)
        {
        *rainPtr = RainValues[n];
        *tempPtr = TempValues[n];

        if (rainPtr.IsLast())
            break;

        ++rainPtr;
        ++tempPtr;
        ++n;
        }

    double mean, var, sd, ad, skew, kurt, z;

    RainData.Moment(mean,ad,sd,var,skew,kurt);

    cout << "\nRainData has a mean of " << mean
        << " and a standard deviation of " << sd << "\n\n";
```

```
    z = RainData.ZScore(1973);

    cout << "In 1973: "
         << RainData[1973]
         << " inches of rain represents a z-score of "
         << z << '\n';

    z = RainData.ZScore(1977);

    cout << "In 1977: "
         << RainData[1977]
         << " inches of rain represents a z-score of "
         << z << '\n';

    z = RainData.ZScore(1983);

    cout << "In 1983: "
         << RainData[1983]
         << " inches of rain represents a z-score of "
         << z << '\n';

    z = RainData.ZScore(1988);

    cout << "In 1988: "
         << RainData[1988]
         << " inches of rain represents a z-score of "
         << z << '\n';

    z = RainData.ZScore(1991);

    cout << "In 1991: "
         << RainData[1991]
         << " inches of rain represents a z-score of "
         << z << "\n\n";

    TempData.Moment(mean,ad,sd,var,skew,kurt);

    cout << "\nTempData has a mean of " << mean
         << " and a standard deviation of " << sd << "\n\n";

    double cor = RainData.Correlation(TempData);

    cout << "The correlation between rain and temp data is: "
         << cor << "\n";

    return 0;
}
```

# Chapter 10: Persistent Objects

**Listing 10-1. persist.h.**

```
//////////////////////////////////////////////////////////////
//  PERSISTENCE LIBRARY
//      persist.h
//
//      Defines a class for handling type-independent data.
//
//      Copyright 1992 Scott Robert Ladd
//      All rights reserved
//////////////////////////////////////////////////////////////

#ifndef DATABLK_H
#define DATABLK_H

#include "err_rptr.h"
#include "str.h"
#include "boolean.h"
#include "stddef.h"


//————————————————————————
//  Signature
//      The data type used as an identification code for
//      blocks of data. This should be a unique value for
//      each object type.
//————————————————————————

typedef unsigned long Signature;

const Signature USER_SIG_BASE = 0x00000000;
const Signature SYS_SIG_BASE  = 0x80000000;
const Signature USER_SIG_MAX  = SYS_SIG_BASE - 1;


//————————————————————————
//  DataBlock
//      Containers store these; objects are created from them
//————————————————————————

class DataBlock
    {
    public:
        // constructors
        DataBlock();

        DataBlock(Signature sig,
                  size_t sz,
```

```
                const void * data);

        DataBlock(const DataBlock & db);

        // destructor
        ~DataBlock();

        // assignment
        void operator = (const DataBlock & db);

        // interrogation
        Signature    GetSignature() const;
        size_t       GetSizeOf() const;
        const void * GetBufferPtr() const;

        // check for NULL block
        Boolean IsNull() const;

        // change error reporter
        static void SetErrOut(const ErrReporter & er);

    protected:
        Signature BlockSig;
        size_t    BufferSize;
        void *    BufferPtr;

        static ErrReporter * ErrOut;

        static void ReportError();
    };

inline DataBlock::DataBlock()
    {
    BufferSize = 0;
    BufferPtr  = NULL;
    BlockSig   = 0;
    }

inline DataBlock::~DataBlock()
    {
    if (BufferPtr != NULL)
        delete BufferPtr;
    }

inline Signature DataBlock::GetSignature() const
    {
    return BlockSig;
    }
```

```
inline size_t DataBlock::GetSizeOf() const
    {
    return BufferSize;
    }

inline const void * DataBlock::GetBufferPtr() const
    {
    return BufferPtr;
    }

inline Boolean DataBlock::IsNull() const
    {
    if (BufferSize == 0)
        return BOOL_TRUE;
    else
        return BOOL_FALSE;
    }

extern const DataBlock NULL_BLOCK;

//————————————————————————
// Persistent
//      A characteristic class for persistent objects
//————————————————————————

class Persistent
    {
    public:
        //*****************************************
        // all persistent classes should define a
        // a constructor that converts a DataBlock
        // to an object:
        //
        // Persistent(const DataBlock & db);
        //*****************************************

        virtual operator DataBlock() const = 0;
    };

//————————————————————————————
// KeyString
//      A key firdl that uses a String
//————————————————————————————

class KeyString : public Persistent
    {
    public:
        KeyString();
```

```
        KeyString(const String & str);
        KeyString(const char * str);
        KeyString(const DataBlock & db);
        KeyString(const KeyString & key);

        const String & GetString() const;

        virtual operator DataBlock() const;

        StrCompVal Compare(const KeyString & key,
                           StrCompMode chkCase = SM_SENSITIVE);

        int operator <  (const KeyString & key) const;
        int operator <= (const KeyString & key) const;
        int operator == (const KeyString & key) const;
        int operator != (const KeyString & key) const;
        int operator >= (const KeyString & key) const;
        int operator >  (const KeyString & key) const;

    protected:
        static const Signature Sig;

    private:
        String KStr;
    };

inline KeyString::KeyString()
    {
    // void
    }

inline KeyString::KeyString(const String & str)
    : KStr(str)
    {
    // void
    }

inline KeyString::KeyString(const char * str)
    : KStr(str)
    {
    // void
    }

inline KeyString::KeyString(const DataBlock & db)
    : KStr((const char *)(db.GetBufferPtr()))
    {
    // void
    }
```

```
inline KeyString::KeyString(const KeyString & keystr)
    : KStr(keystr.KStr)
    {
    // void
    }

inline const String & KeyString::GetString() const
    {
    return KStr;
    }

inline StrCompVal KeyString::Compare(const KeyString & key,
                                     StrCompMode chkCase)
    {
    return KStr.Compare(key.KStr,chkCase);
    }

inline int KeyString::operator <  (const KeyString & key) const
    {
    return (KStr < key.KStr);
    }

inline int KeyString::operator <= (const KeyString & key) const
    {
    return (KStr <= key.KStr);
    }

inline int KeyString::operator == (const KeyString & key) const
    {
    return (KStr == key.KStr);
    }

inline int KeyString::operator != (const KeyString & key) const
    {
    return (KStr != key.KStr);
    }

inline int KeyString::operator >= (const KeyString & key) const
    {
    return (KStr >= key.KStr);
    }

inline int KeyString::operator >  (const KeyString & key) const
    {
    return (KStr > key.KStr);
    }
```

```
//————————————————————
//  KeyByString
//      Identifies an object that can be key-identified
//      by a string
//————————————————————

class KeyByString
    {
    public:
        virtual KeyString MakeKey() const = 0;
    };

#endif
```

**Listing 10-2. persist.cxx.**

```
//////////////////////////////////////////////////////////////
//  PERSISTENCE LIBRARY
//      persist.cxx
//
//      Defines a class for handling type-independent data.
//
//      Copyright 1992 Scott Robert Ladd
//      All rights reserved
//////////////////////////////////////////////////////////////

#include "persist.h"
#include "string.h"

ErrReporter * DataBlock::ErrOut = NULL;

const DataBlock NULL_BLOCK;

//————————————————————————
//  DataBlock
//      A dynamically-allocated piece of memory
//————————————————————————

void DataBlock::ReportError()
    {
    if (ErrOut != NULL)
        ErrOut->Fatal("memory allocation failure");
    }

void DataBlock::SetErrOut(const ErrReporter & er)
    {
    if (ErrOut != NULL)
        delete ErrOut;
```

```
    ErrOut = new ErrReporter(er);
    }

DataBlock::DataBlock(Signature sig, size_t sz, const void * data)
    {
    BufferSize = sz;
    BlockSig   = sig;

    BufferPtr = (void *)new char[sz];

    if (BufferPtr == NULL)
        ReportError();

    if (data == NULL)
        memset(BufferPtr,0,sz);
    else
        memcpy(BufferPtr,data,sz);
    }

DataBlock::DataBlock(const DataBlock & db)
    {
    BufferSize = db.BufferSize;
    BlockSig   = db.BlockSig;

    BufferPtr  = (void *)new char[BufferSize];

    if (BufferPtr == NULL)
        ReportError();

    memcpy(BufferPtr,db.BufferPtr,BufferSize);
    }

void DataBlock::operator = (const DataBlock & db)
    {
    BufferSize = db.BufferSize;
    BlockSig   = db.BlockSig;

    if (BufferPtr != NULL)
        delete BufferPtr;

    BufferPtr = (void *)new char[BufferSize];

    if (BufferPtr == NULL)
        ReportError();

    memcpy(BufferPtr,db.BufferPtr,BufferSize);
    }
```

```
//————————————————————
//  KeyString
//      A KeyBlock that uses a String
//————————————————————

const Signature KeyString::Sig = SYS_SIG_BASE + 1;

KeyString::operator DataBlock() const
    {
    return DataBlock(Sig,(size_t)(KStr.Length() + 1),
                    ((const void *)((const char *)KStr)));
    }
```

Listing 10-3  datafile.h

```
////////////////////////////////////////////////////////////
//  PERSISTENCE LIBRARY
//      datafile.h
//
//      Defines a file type for disk-based data files
//
//      Copyright 1992 Scott Robert Ladd
//      All rights reserved
////////////////////////////////////////////////////////////

#ifndef DATAFILE_H
#define DATAFILE_H

#include "persist.h"
#include "stdio.h"

//————————————————————————
//  DataFile
//      The base class for binary data files
//————————————————————————

enum FileMode
    {
    FM_NEW,
    FM_EXISTING,
    FM_APPEND,
    FM_TEMPORARY
    };

struct RecordHeader
    {
    size_t RecSize;
    Signature RecSig;
    };
```

```
class DataFileBase
    {
    public:
        // constructor
        DataFileBase(const char * name = NULL,
                     FileMode m        = FM_TEMPORARY,
                     size_t bufsiz     = 0);

        // destructor
        ~DataFileBase();

        // set error reporting object
        static Boolean SetErrOut(const ErrReporter & er);

    protected:
        // data members
        FileMode Mode;
        char *   FileName;
        FILE *   Data;
        char *   Buffer;
        size_t   BufferSize;
        char     DosMode[4];

        // error reporting mechanisms
        static ErrReporter * ErrOut;

        static void ReportError(const String & msg);
    };

//————————————————————————————
//  DataFileInput
//      A file for the sequential input of information
//————————————————————————————

class DataFileInput : virtual public DataFileBase
    {
    public:
        DataFileInput(const char * name = NULL,
                      size_t bufsiz     = 0);

        DataBlock Read() const;

        Boolean Rewind();
        Boolean Skip();
    };

inline DataFileInput::DataFileInput(const char * name,
                                    size_t bufsiz)
```

```
        : DataFileBase(name,FM_EXISTING,bufsiz)
        {
        // a shell for calling the base class constructor
        }


//————————————————————————
//  DataFileOutput
//      A file for the sequential output of information
//————————————————————————

class DataFileOutput : virtual public DataFileBase
    {
    public:
        DataFileOutput(const char * name = NULL,
                       size_t bufsiz     = 0,
                       FileMode m        = FM_NEW);

        Boolean Write(const DataBlock & db);
    };

inline DataFileOutput::DataFileOutput(const char * name,
                                      size_t bufsiz,
                                      FileMode m)
    : DataFileBase(name,m,bufsiz)
    {
    // void
    }


//————————————————————————
//  DataFilePtr
//      A type used to locate information in a data file
//————————————————————————

// type of a data file ptr
typedef long DataFilePtr;

// constants
extern const DataFilePtr DFP_MARKER;
#define DFP_ERROR DFP_MARKER

extern const Signature SIG_DELETED;


//————————————————————————
//  DataFile
//      Defines a random access, I/O file
//————————————————————————

struct DataFileHdr
    {
```

```
    DataFilePtr FirstEmpty;
    };

struct IORecordHeader : public RecordHeader
    {
    size_t Size;
    DataFilePtr NextDeleted;
    };

typedef void (* DFCompFunc)(DataFilePtr ptr, const DataBlock & db);

class DataFile : public DataFileBase
    {
    public:
        // constructor
        DataFile(const char * name,
                 FileMode m     = FM_EXISTING,
                 size_t bufsiz = 0);

        // write a record
        DataFilePtr Write(const DataBlock & db);

        // read a record
        DataBlock Read() const;

        // commit data to disk
        Boolean Commit();

        // delete a record
        Boolean Delete();

        // move to next record
        Boolean Skip();

        // return to beginning of file
        Boolean Rewind();

        // remove blanks and wasted space
        Boolean Compact(DFCompFunc func = NULL);

        // go to  position in file
        DataFilePtr Seek(DataFilePtr pos) const;

        // get current file position
        DataFilePtr CurrentPtr() const;

    protected:
        DataFileHdr Hdr;
    };
```

```
// get current file position
inline DataFilePtr DataFile::CurrentPtr() const
    {
    return ftell(Data);
    }


#endif
```

**Listing 10-4. datafile.cxx.**

```
//////////////////////////////////////////////////////////////////
//    PERSISTENCE LIBRARY
//        datafile.cxx
//
//        Defines a file type for disk-based data files
//
//        Copyright 1992 Scott Robert Ladd
//        All rights reserved
//////////////////////////////////////////////////////////////////

#include "datafile.h"
#include "string.h"
#include "time.h"


//————————————————————————————————
//    DataFileBase
//        The base class for binary data files
//————————————————————————————————

ErrReporter * DataFileBase::ErrOut = NULL;

Boolean DataFileBase::SetErrOut(const ErrReporter & er)
    {
    if (ErrOut != NULL)
        delete ErrOut;

    ErrOut = new ErrReporter(er);

    if (ErrOut == NULL)
        return BOOL_FALSE;
    else
        return BOOL_TRUE;
    }

void DataFileBase::ReportError(const String & msg)
    {
    if (ErrOut != NULL)
        ErrOut->Fatal(msg);
    }
```

```
DataFileBase::DataFileBase(const char * name,
                           FileMode m,
                           size_t bufsize)
    {
    // store file name
    if (name == NULL)
        FileName = new char[64];
    else
        FileName = new char[strlen(name) + 1];

    if (FileName == NULL)
        ReportError("cannot allocate memory for file name");

    if (name == NULL)
        {
        if (NULL == tmpnam(FileName))
            ReportError("cannot generate temp file name");
        }
    else
        strcpy(FileName,name);

    // generate DosMode string
    Mode = m;

    DosMode[1] = 'b';
    DosMode[2] = 0;

    switch (Mode)
        {
        case FM_NEW:
        case FM_TEMPORARY:
            DosMode[0] = 'w';
            DosMode[2] = '+';
            DosMode[3] = 0;
            break;

        case FM_EXISTING:
            DosMode[0] = 'r';
            DosMode[2] = '+';
            DosMode[3] = 0;
            break;

        case FM_APPEND:
            DosMode[0] = 'a';
            break;

        default:
            ReportError("invalid file mode");
```

```
            }

    BufferSize = bufsize;

    int failed;

    // open file
    Data = fopen(FileName,DosMode);

    if (Data == NULL)
        ReportError("cannot open file");

    // create buffer (if needed)
    if (BufferSize == 0)
        {
        // unbuffered file
        Buffer = NULL;

        failed = setvbuf(Data,NULL,_IONBF,0);
        }
    else
        {
        // buffered file
        Buffer = new char[BufferSize];

        if (Buffer == NULL)
            failed = 1;
        else
            failed = setvbuf(Data,Buffer,_IOFBF,BufferSize);
        }

    if (failed)
        ReportError("cannot set file buffer");
    }

DataFileBase::~DataFileBase()
    {
    // close up!
    fclose(Data);

    // delete buffer if allocated
    if (Buffer != NULL)
        delete Buffer;

    // if temp file, delete it!
    if (Mode == FM_TEMPORARY)
        remove(FileName);
```

```
        // delete file name buffer (if any)
        if (FileName != NULL)
            delete FileName;
        }

//────────────────────────────────
//  DataFileInput
//       A file for the sequential input of information
//────────────────────────────────

DataBlock DataFileInput::Read() const
        {
        if (feof(Data))
            return NULL_BLOCK;

        RecordHeader hdr;
        size_t res;

        // read record header
        res = fread(&hdr,sizeof(RecordHeader),1,Data);

        if (res == 0)
            return NULL_BLOCK;

        // allocate buffer to hold data
        void * buf = (void *)new char[hdr.RecSize];

        if (buf == NULL)
            return NULL_BLOCK;

        // read data
        res = fread(buf,hdr.RecSize,1,Data);

        if (res == 0)
            return NULL_BLOCK;

        // create an DataBlock
        DataBlock result(hdr.RecSig,hdr.RecSize,buf);

        // delete the data buffer
        delete buf;

        // outa here
        return result;
        }

Boolean DataFileInput::Rewind()
        {
```

```
    rewind(Data);

    return BOOL_TRUE;
    }

Boolean DataFileInput::Skip()
    {
    RecordHeader hdr;
    size_t res;

    // read record header
    res = fread(&hdr,sizeof(RecordHeader),1,Data);

    if (res == 0)
        return BOOL_FALSE;

    // skip data
    if (0 != fseek(Data,hdr.RecSize,SEEK_CUR))
        return BOOL_FALSE;

    return BOOL_TRUE;
    }

//————————————--————————————
//  DataFileOutput
//      A file for the sequential output of information
//————————————————————————

Boolean DataFileOutput::Write(const DataBlock & db)
    {
    RecordHeader hdr;

    hdr.RecSig  = db.GetSignature();
    hdr.RecSize = db.GetSizeOf();

    // store record header
    size_t n = fwrite(&hdr,sizeof(RecordHeader),1,Data);

    if (n == 0)
        return BOOL_FALSE;

    // store data
    n = fwrite(db.GetBufferPtr(),hdr.RecSize,1,Data);

    if (n == 0)
        return BOOL_FALSE;

    return BOOL_TRUE;
    }
```

**696**

```
//————————————————————————
//  DataFile
//      Defines a random access, I/O file
//————————————————————————

const DataFilePtr DFP_MARKER  = -1;
const Signature   SIG_DELETED = 0xFFFFFFFF;

// constructor
DataFile::DataFile(const char * name,
                   FileMode m,
                   size_t bufsiz)
    : DataFileBase(name,m,bufsiz)
    {
    size_t n;

    if ((m == FM_NEW) || (m == FM_TEMPORARY))
        {
        Hdr.FirstEmpty = DFP_MARKER;

        n = fwrite(&Hdr,sizeof(DataFileHdr),1,Data);

        if (n == 0)
            ReportError("cannot create file header");
        }
    else
        {
        n = fread(&Hdr,sizeof(DataFileHdr),1,Data);

        if (n == 0)
            ReportError("cannot read file header");
        }
    }

// write a record
DataFilePtr DataFile::Write(const DataBlock & db)
    {
    // search for first open record that can hold this one
    IORecordHeader rechdr;
    DataFilePtr ptr;
    int res;
    size_t n;

    if (Hdr.FirstEmpty == DFP_MARKER)
        {
        // append new data to end of file
        res = fseek(Data,0,SEEK_END);
```

```
        if (res)
            return DFP_ERROR;

        ptr = ftell(Data);

        rechdr.Size = db.GetSizeOf();
        }
    else
        {
        // start with first empty record
        DataFilePtr prev = DFP_MARKER;

        ptr = Hdr.FirstEmpty;

        for (;;)
            {
            // set file pointer
            res = fseek(Data,ptr,SEEK_SET);

            if (res)
                return DFP_ERROR;

            // read record header
            n = fread(&rechdr,sizeof(IORecordHeader),1,Data);

            if ((n == 0) || (rechdr.RecSig != SIG_DELETED))
                return DFP_ERROR;

            // is it big enough?
            if (rechdr.Size >= db.GetSizeOf())
                {
                // go to previous record
                if (prev == DFP_MARKER)
                    {
                    // change entry in header
                    Hdr.FirstEmpty = rechdr.NextDeleted;

                    // go to beginning of file
                    fseek(Data,0,SEEK_SET);

                    // write new header
                    n = fwrite(&Hdr,sizeof(DataFileHdr),1,Data);

                    if (n == 0)
                        return DFP_ERROR;
                    }
                else
                    {
```

```
        // adjust chain by putting next in prev
        res = fseek(Data,prev,SEEK_SET);

        if (res)
            return DFP_ERROR;

        // read previous record's header
        IORecordHeader prevhdr;

        n = fread(&prevhdr,sizeof(IORecordHeader),1,Data);

        if (n == 0)
            return DFP_ERROR;

        // change next deleted reference
        prevhdr.NextDeleted = rechdr.NextDeleted;

        // rewrite prev. header
        res = fseek(Data,prev,SEEK_SET);

        if (res)
            return DFP_ERROR;

        // read previous record's header
        n = fwrite(&prevhdr,sizeof(IORecordHeader),1,Data);

        if (n == 0)
            return DFP_ERROR;
        }

    // set pointer to beginning of ptr record
    fseek(Data,ptr,SEEK_SET);
    break;
    }

// save pointer
prev = ptr;

if (rechdr.NextDeleted == DFP_MARKER)
    {
    // append new data to end of file
    res = fseek(Data,0,SEEK_END);

    if (res)
        return DFP_ERROR;

    ptr = ftell(Data);
```

```
                    rechdr.Size = db.GetSizeOf();

                    break;
                    }
                else
                    ptr = rechdr.NextDeleted;
                }
            }

    rechdr.RecSig      = db.GetSignature();
    rechdr.RecSize     = db.GetSizeOf();
    rechdr.NextDeleted = DFP_MARKER;

    // store signature
    n = fwrite(&rechdr,sizeof(IORecordHeader),1,Data);

    if (n == 0)
        return DFP_ERROR;

    // store data
    n = fwrite(db.GetBufferPtr(),rechdr.RecSize,1,Data);

    if (n == 0)
        return DFP_ERROR;

    // return location data was written to
    return ptr;
    }

// read a record
DataBlock DataFile::Read() const
    {
    if (feof(Data))
        return NULL_BLOCK;

    size_t n;

    IORecordHeader rechdr;

    for (;;)
        {
        // read record header
        n = fread(&rechdr,sizeof(IORecordHeader),1,Data);

        // this may indicate end-of-file
        if (n == 0)
            return NULL_BLOCK;
```

```
        // return null for deleted record
        if (rechdr.RecSig == SIG_DELETED)
            fseek(Data,rechdr.Size,SEEK_CUR);
        else
            break;
        }

    // allocate buffer to hold data
    void * buf = (void *)new char[rechdr.RecSize];

    if (buf == NULL)
        return NULL_BLOCK;

    // read data
    n = fread(buf,rechdr.RecSize,1,Data);

    if (n == 0)
        return NULL_BLOCK;

    // create an DataBlock
    DataBlock result(rechdr.RecSig,rechdr.RecSize,buf);

    // skip over any "waste" characters
    if (rechdr.RecSize < rechdr.Size)
        fseek(Data,rechdr.Size - rechdr.RecSize, SEEK_CUR);

    // delete the data buffer
    delete buf;

    // outa here
    return result;
    }

// force file data to disk
Boolean DataFile::Commit()
    {
    if (Buffer != NULL)
        {
        int res = fflush(Data);

        if (res)
            return BOOL_FALSE;
        }

    return BOOL_TRUE;
    }

// delete a record
```

```
Boolean DataFile::Delete()
    {
    size_t n;
    int res;
    IORecordHeader rechdr;

    // save this position
    DataFilePtr curptr = ftell(Data);

    // make sure we're not in the header
    if (curptr < sizeof(DataFileHdr))
        return BOOL_FALSE;

    // read header
    n = fread(&rechdr,sizeof(IORecordHeader),1,Data);

    if (n == 0)
        return BOOL_FALSE;

    // mark as deleted
    if (rechdr.RecSig != SIG_DELETED)
        {
        // update record header
        rechdr.RecSig      = SIG_DELETED;
        rechdr.NextDeleted = Hdr.FirstEmpty;

        // write record header
        res = fseek(Data,curptr,SEEK_SET);

        if (res)
            return BOOL_FALSE;

        n = fwrite(&rechdr,sizeof(IORecordHeader),1,Data);

        if (n == 0)
            return BOOL_FALSE;

        // modify header
        Hdr.FirstEmpty = curptr;

        res = fseek(Data,0,SEEK_SET);

        if (res)
            return BOOL_FALSE;

        n = fwrite(&Hdr,sizeof(DataFileHdr),1,Data);

        if (n == 0)
```

```
            return BOOL_FALSE;
        }

    // move back to start of deleted record
    res = fseek(Data,curptr,SEEK_SET);

    if (res)
        return BOOL_FALSE;
    else
        return BOOL_TRUE;
    }

// remove blanks and wasted space
Boolean DataFile::Compact(DFCompFunc func)
    {
    if (BOOL_FALSE == Commit())
        return BOOL_FALSE;

    // generate temporary file name
    char tname[32];

    sprintf(tname,"%lx.TMP",time(NULL));

    // open temporary file
    FILE * newfile = fopen(tname,"wb");

    if (newfile == NULL)
        return BOOL_FALSE;

    // read and copy header
    int res = fseek(Data,0,SEEK_SET);

    if (res)
        return BOOL_FALSE;

    size_t n = fread(&Hdr,sizeof(DataFileHdr),1,Data);

    if (n == 0)
        return BOOL_FALSE;

    n = fwrite(&Hdr,sizeof(DataFileHdr),1,newfile);

    if (n == 0)
        return BOOL_FALSE;

    // read each record
    for (;;)
        {
        IORecordHeader rechdr;
```

```
DataFilePtr ptr;
char * buf;

// read record header
n = fread(&rechdr,sizeof(IORecordHeader),1,Data);

if (n == 0)
    break;

if (rechdr.RecSig == SIG_DELETED)
    {
    // skip deleted records
    res = fseek(Data,rechdr.Size,SEEK_CUR);

    if (res)
        return BOOL_FALSE;
    }
else
    {
    // allocate buffer to hold data
    buf = new char[rechdr.Size];

    if (buf == NULL)
        return BOOL_FALSE;

    // read data
    n = fread(buf,rechdr.Size,1,Data);

    if (n == 0)
        return BOOL_FALSE;

    // get output position in new file
    ptr = ftell(newfile);

    // write header to new file
    rechdr.Size = rechdr.RecSize;

    n = fwrite(&rechdr,sizeof(IORecordHeader),1,newfile);

    if (n == 0)
        return BOOL_FALSE;

    // write data to new file
    n = fwrite(buf,rechdr.Size,1,newfile);

    if (n == 0)
        return BOOL_FALSE;
```

```
            // call function
            if (func != NULL)
                func(ptr,DataBlock(rechdr.RecSig,rechdr.Size,buf));

            // delete buffer
            delete buf;
            }
        }

    // close files
    fclose(newfile);
    fclose(Data);

    // delete old file
    remove(FileName);

    // rename new file
    rename(tname,FileName);

    // open newly-compacted file
    Data = fopen(FileName,DosMode);

    if (Data == NULL)
        return BOOL_FALSE;

    // read file header
    n = fread(&Hdr,sizeof(DataFileHdr),1,Data);

    if (n == 0)
        return BOOL_FALSE;
    else
        return BOOL_TRUE;
    }

// go to  position in file
DataFilePtr DataFile::Seek(DataFilePtr pos) const
    {
    // make sure position is outside of header
    if (pos < sizeof(DataFileHdr))
        return DFP_ERROR;

    // get current position
    DataFilePtr ptr = ftell(Data);

    // move to new position
    int res = fseek(Data,pos,SEEK_SET);

    // check for error
```

```
    if (res)
        {
        // try to restore previous position
        fseek(Data,ptr,SEEK_SET);

        ptr = DFP_ERROR;
        }

    // done
    return ptr;
    }

// move to next record
Boolean DataFile::Skip()
    {
    IORecordHeader rechdr;
    int res;
    size_t n;

    // read record header
    n = fread(&rechdr,sizeof(IORecordHeader),1,Data);

    if (n == 0)
        return BOOL_FALSE;

    // skip data
    res = fseek(Data,rechdr.Size,SEEK_CUR);

    if (res)
        return BOOL_FALSE;
    else
        return BOOL_TRUE;
    }

// return to beginning of file
Boolean DataFile::Rewind()
    {
    int res = fseek(Data,sizeof(DataFileHdr),SEEK_SET);

    if (res)
        return BOOL_FALSE;
    else
        return BOOL_TRUE;
    }
```

# Chapter 11: Hash Tables

**Listing 11-1. hash.h**

```
/////////////////////////////////////////////////////////////
//  HASH TABLE LIBRARY
//      hash.h
//
//      Defines the abstract base class for implementing a
//      hash table.
//
//      Copyright 1992 Scott Robert Ladd
//      All rights reserved
/////////////////////////////////////////////////////////////

#ifndef HASH_H
#define HASH_H

#include "persist.h"

//─────────────────────────────
// HashErrorBase
//      Base class providing error reporting for hash classes
//─────────────────────────────

enum HashError
    {
    HE_ALLOC,     // fatal:   memory allocation failure
    HE_ZEROSIZE,  // fatal:   created bucket w/ zero buckets
    HE_CORRUPTED, // fatal:   table / list has been corrupted
    HE_BADTYPES,  // fatal:   mismatched data types
    HW_TOOSMALL,  // warning: about very small table sizes
    HW_DUPEKEY    // warning: about duplicate keys
    };

class HashErrorBase
    {
    public:
        static void SetErrOut(const ErrReporter & er);

    protected:
        static ErrReporter * ErrOut;

        static void ReportError(HashError herr);
    };
```

# C++ COMPONENTS AND ALGORITHMS

```
//————————————————————
//  HashEntryBase
//      Base class for entries in buckets (linked lists)
//————————————————————

enum HashKeyType
    {
    KEY_STRING,
    KEY_LONG,
    KEY_OTHER1,
    KEY_OTHER2
    };

struct HashEntryBase : public HashErrorBase
    {
    HashEntryBase * Prev;
    HashEntryBase * Next;

    HashEntryBase();

    virtual HashKeyType GetKeyType() const = 0;

    virtual size_t Hash(size_t buckets) const = 0;

    virtual int KeyEquals(const HashEntryBase * entry) const = 0;
    };

inline HashEntryBase::HashEntryBase()
    {
    Prev = NULL;
    Next = NULL;
    }


//————————————————————
//  HashEntryStr
//      A HashEntry containing a KeyString
//————————————————————

struct HashEntryStr : public HashEntryBase
    {
    KeyString Key;

    HashEntryStr(const KeyString & k);
    HashEntryStr(const HashEntryStr & e);

    virtual HashKeyType GetKeyType() const;

    virtual size_t Hash(size_t buckets) const;
```

```
    virtual int KeyEquals(const HashEntryBase * entry) const;

    protected:
        HashEntryStr();
    };

inline HashEntryStr::HashEntryStr()
    {
    // void
    }

inline HashEntryStr::HashEntryStr(const KeyString & k)
    : Key(k)
    {
    // void
    }

inline HashEntryStr::HashEntryStr(const HashEntryStr & e)
    : Key(e.Key)
    {
    // void
    }

//————————————————————————
//  HashEntryStrDB
//      A HashEntry containing a KeyString and a DataBlock
//————————————————————————

struct HashEntryStrDB : public HashEntryStr
    {
    DataBlock Data;

    HashEntryStrDB(const KeyString & k, const DataBlock & db);
    };

inline HashEntryStrDB::HashEntryStrDB(const KeyString & k,
                                     const DataBlock & db)
    : HashEntryStr(k)
    {
    Data = db;
    }

//————————————————————————
//  HashTableBase
//      Base class for all hash tables
//————————————————————————

class HashBucket;
```

```
class HashTableBase : public HashErrorBase
    {
    public:
        HashTableBase(size_t buckets);
        ~HashTableBase();

    protected:
        Boolean AddEntry(HashEntryBase * newe);
        Boolean DelEntry(const HashEntryBase * dele);
        Boolean IsDupe(const HashEntryBase * dupe);

        const HashEntryBase * FindEntry(const HashEntryBase * finde);

        Boolean Traverse();

        virtual Boolean TravCallback(const HashEntryBase * e) const = 0;

        // data elements
        size_t NoOfBuckets;

        HashBucket * * Table;
    };
//————————————————————————
//  HashTravFunc
//      Function type used when traversing hash table entries
//————————————————————————

typedef Boolean (HashTableBase::*HashTravFunc)(const HashEntryBase * e)
const;

//————————————————————————
//  HashBucket
//      Base class for buckets
//——— -————————————————————

class HashBucket : virtual public HashErrorBase
    {
    public:
        HashBucket();
        ~HashBucket();

        Boolean AddEntry(HashEntryBase * newe);
        Boolean DelEntry(const HashEntryBase * dele);
        Boolean IsDupe(const HashEntryBase * dupe);

        const HashEntryBase * FindEntry(const HashEntryBase * finde);
```

```
        Boolean Traverse(const HashTableBase & table,
                         HashTravFunc func);

    protected:
        HashEntryBase * First;
    };

inline HashBucket::HashBucket()
    {
    First = NULL;
    }


//————————————————————————————
// HashEnumFuncStrDB
//      Function to retrieve all records in table
//————————————————————————————

typedef Boolean (* HashEnumFuncStrDB)(const KeyString & k,
                                      const DataBlock & db);


//————————————————————————————
// HashTableStrDB
//      A HashTable indexed by Strings
//————————————————————————————

class HashTableStrDB : private HashTableBase
    {
    public:
        HashTableStrDB(size_t buckets);

        Boolean Insert(const KeyString & key, const DataBlock & db);
        Boolean Delete(const KeyString & key);

        DataBlock LookUp(const KeyString & key);

        Boolean Enumerate(HashEnumFuncStrDB func);

    protected:
        virtual Boolean TravCallback(const HashEntryBase * e) const;

        HashEnumFuncStrDB EnumCallback;
    };

inline HashTableStrDB::HashTableStrDB(size_t buckets)
    : HashTableBase(buckets)
    {
    // void
    }

#endif
```

**Listing 11-2. hash.cxx.**

```
//////////////////////////////////////////////////////////
//  HASH TABLE LIBRARY
//      hash.cxx
//
//      Defines the abstract base class for implementing a
//      hash table.
//
//      Copyright 1992 Scott Robert Ladd
//      All rights reserved
//////////////////////////////////////////////////////////

#include "hash.h"
#include "iostream.h"
#include "iomanip.h"
#include "stdlib.h"


//————————————————————————————
//  HashErrorBase
//      Base class providing error reporting for hash classes
//————————————————————————————

ErrReporter * HashErrorBase::ErrOut = NULL;

void HashErrorBase::ReportError(HashError herr)
    {
    if (ErrOut != NULL)
        {
        switch (herr)
            {
            case HE_ALLOC:
                ErrOut->Fatal("memory allocation failure");
                break;

            case HE_ZEROSIZE:
                ErrOut->Fatal("cannot create zero-size table");
                break;

            case HE_CORRUPTED:
                ErrOut->Fatal("corrupted");
                break;

            case HE_BADTYPES:
                ErrOut->Fatal("mismatched types");
                break;

            case HW_TOOSMALL:
                ErrOut->Warning("# buckets is very small");
                break;
```

**712**

```
            case HW_DUPEKEY:
                ErrOut->Warning("duplicate key ignored");
                break;

            default:
                ErrOut->Fatal("unknown");
                break;
            }
        }
    }

void HashErrorBase::SetErrOut(const ErrReporter & er)
    {
    if (ErrOut != NULL)
        delete ErrOut;

    ErrOut = new ErrReporter(er);
    }


//————————————————————————————
// HashEntryStr
//     A HashEntry containing a KeyString
//————————————————————————————

HashKeyType HashEntryStr::GetKeyType() const
    {
    return KEY_STRING;
    }

size_t HashEntryStr::Hash(size_t buckets) const
    {
    unsigned long n = 0;
    const String & str = Key.GetString();
    size_t len = str.Length();

    for (size_t i = 0; i < len; ++i)
        {
        n <<= 1;
        n += str[i];
        }

    return size_t(n % (unsigned long)buckets);
    }

int HashEntryStr::KeyEquals(const HashEntryBase * e) const
    {
    if (KEY_STRING != e->GetKeyType())
        ReportError(HE_BADTYPES);
```

```
    return (Key == ((const HashEntryStr *)e)->Key);
    }


//————————————————————————————
// HashTableBase
//     Base class for all hash tables
//————————————————————————————

HashTableBase::HashTableBase(size_t buckets)
    {
    // verify number of buckets
    if (buckets == 0)
        ReportError(HE_ZEROSIZE);

    if (buckets < 9)
        ReportError(HW_TOOSMALL);

    // store number of buckets
    NoOfBuckets = buckets;

    // allocate Table
    Table = new HashBucket * [NoOfBuckets];

    if (Table == NULL)
        ReportError(HE_ALLOC);

    // assign empty buckets to table
    for (size_t b = 0; b < NoOfBuckets; ++b)
        {
        Table[b] = new HashBucket;

        if (Table[b] == NULL)
            ReportError(HE_ALLOC);
        }
    }

HashTableBase::~HashTableBase()
    {
    // delete buckets
    for (size_t b = 0; b < NoOfBuckets; ++b)
        delete Table[b];

    // delete table
    delete[] Table;
    }

Boolean HashTableBase::AddEntry(HashEntryBase * newe)
    {
```

```
    if (newe == NULL)
        return BOOL_FALSE;

    size_t bucket = newe->Hash(NoOfBuckets);

    return Table[bucket]->AddEntry(newe);
    }

Boolean HashTableBase::DelEntry(const HashEntryBase * dele)
    {
    if (dele == NULL)
        return BOOL_FALSE;

    size_t bucket = dele->Hash(NoOfBuckets);

    return Table[bucket]->DelEntry(dele);
    }

Boolean HashTableBase::IsDupe(const HashEntryBase * dupe)
    {
    if (dupe == NULL)
        return BOOL_FALSE;

    size_t bucket = dupe->Hash(NoOfBuckets);

    return Table[bucket]->IsDupe(dupe);
    }

const HashEntryBase * HashTableBase::FindEntry(const HashEntryBase * finde)
    {
    if (finde == NULL)
        return NULL;

    size_t bucket = finde->Hash(NoOfBuckets);

    return Table[bucket]->FindEntry(finde);
    }

Boolean HashTableBase::Traverse()
    {
    Boolean result;

    for (size_t n = 0; n < NoOfBuckets; ++n)
        {
        result = Table[n]->Traverse(*this,&HashTableBase::TravCallback);

        if (result == BOOL_FALSE)
            break;
```

```
        }

    return result;
    }


//————————————————————————————
//  HashBucket
//      Base class for buckets
//————————————————————————————

HashBucket::~HashBucket()
    {
    if (First != NULL)
        {
        HashEntryBase * e, * enext;

        e = First;

        while (e != NULL)
            {
            enext = e->Next;

            delete e;

            e = enext;
            }
        }
    }

Boolean HashBucket::AddEntry(HashEntryBase * newe)
    {
    if (newe == NULL)
        return BOOL_FALSE;

    if (First == NULL)
        First = newe;
    else
        {
        HashEntryBase * e = First;

        // search for last entry in list
        while (e != NULL)
            {
            // watch for duplicate keys
            if (e->KeyEquals(newe))
                {
                ReportError(HW_DUPEKEY);
                return BOOL_FALSE;
                }
```

```
            if (e->Next == NULL)
                {
                // link entry to end of list
                e->Next = newe;
                newe->Prev = e;

                break;
                }

            e = e->Next;
            }
        }

    return BOOL_TRUE;
    }

Boolean HashBucket::DelEntry(const HashEntryBase * dele)
    {
    if (dele == NULL)
        return BOOL_FALSE;

    HashEntryBase * e = First;

    // search for key in list
    while (e != NULL)
        {
        // if key found, delete it
        if (e->KeyEquals(dele))
            {
            if ((e->Prev == NULL) && (e->Next == NULL))
                First = NULL;
            else
                {
                // remove entry from list
                if (e->Prev == NULL)
                    First = e->Next;
                else
                    e->Prev->Next = e->Next;

                if (e->Next != NULL)
                    e->Next->Prev = e->Prev;
                }

            // delete entry
            delete e;

            // a success!
            return BOOL_TRUE;
```

```
            }

        e = e->Next;
        }

    return BOOL_FALSE;
    }

Boolean HashBucket::IsDupe(const HashEntryBase * dupe)
    {
    if ((dupe == NULL) || (First == NULL))
        return BOOL_FALSE;

    HashEntryBase * e = First;

    // search for key in list
    while (e != NULL)
        {
        // if key found, return it
        if (e->KeyEquals(dupe))
            return BOOL_TRUE;

        e = e->Next;
        }

    return BOOL_FALSE;
    }

const HashEntryBase * HashBucket::FindEntry(const HashEntryBase * finde)
    {
    if ((finde == NULL) || (First == NULL))
        return NULL;

    HashEntryBase * e = First;

    // search for key in list
    while (e != NULL)
        {
        // if key found, return it
        if (e->KeyEquals(finde))
            return e;

        e = e->Next;
        }

    return NULL;
    }
```

```
Boolean HashBucket::Traverse(const HashTableBase & table,
                             HashTravFunc func)
    {
    Boolean result;

    HashEntryBase * e = First;

    while (e != NULL)
        {
        result = (table.*func)(e);

        if (result == BOOL_FALSE)
            break;

        e = e->Next;
        }

    return result;
    }


//————————————————————————————
//   HashTableStrDB
//       Core class for hash tables
//————————————————————————————

Boolean HashTableStrDB::Insert(const KeyString & key,
                               const DataBlock & data)
    {
    // create new HashEntryStrDB
    HashEntryStrDB * entry = new HashEntryStrDB(key,data);

    if (entry == NULL)
        ReportError(HE_ALLOC);

    // insert into table
    return AddEntry(entry);
    }

Boolean HashTableStrDB::Delete(const KeyString & key)
    {
    // create new HashEntryStr
    HashEntryStr * entry = new HashEntryStr(key);

    if (entry == NULL)
        ReportError(HE_ALLOC);

    // insert into table
    Boolean result = DelEntry(entry);
```

```
    delete entry;

    return result;
    }

DataBlock HashTableStrDB::LookUp(const KeyString & key)
    {
    // create new HashEntryStr
    HashEntryStr * entry = new HashEntryStr(key);

    if (entry == NULL)
        ReportError(HE_ALLOC);

    const HashEntryStrDB * e =
            (const HashEntryStrDB *)FindEntry(entry);

    delete entry;

    if (e == NULL)
        return NULL_BLOCK;
    else
        return e->Data;
    }

Boolean HashTableStrDB::Enumerate(HashEnumFuncStrDB func)
    {
    if (func == NULL)
        return BOOL_FALSE;

    EnumCallback = func;

    return Traverse();
    }

Boolean HashTableStrDB::TravCallback(const HashEntryBase * e) const
    {
    if (e == NULL)
        return BOOL_FALSE;
    else
        {
        HashEntryStrDB * e2 = (HashEntryStrDB *)e;

        return EnumCallback(e2->Key, e2->Data);
        }
    }
```

# Chapter 12: Indexing Files with Hash Tables

**Listing 12-1. hashfile.h.**

```
//////////////////////////////////////////////////////////////
//   PERSISTENCE LIBRARY
//      hashfile.h
//
//      Defines a file type for disk-based data files that are
//      indexed via a hash table.
//
//      Copyright 1992 Scott Robert Ladd
//      All rights reserved
//////////////////////////////////////////////////////////////

#ifndef HASHFILE_H
#define HASHFILE_H

#include "hash.h"
#include "datafile.h"


//─────────────────────────────────────
// HashFileEntry
//      An entry in a HashFileBucket
//─────────────────────────────────────

struct HashFileEntry : public HashEntryStr,
                       public Persistent
    {
    DataFilePtr DataPtr;

    HashFileEntry(const KeyString & key,
                       DataFilePtr ptr);

    HashFileEntry(const DataBlock & db);

    virtual operator DataBlock() const;

    private:
        static const Signature Sig;
    };

inline HashFileEntry::HashFileEntry(const KeyString & key,
                                         DataFilePtr ptr)
    : HashEntryStr(key)
    {
    DataPtr = ptr;
    }
```

```
//————————————————————
//   HashFileBucket
//        A bucket for a HashFile
//————————————————————

class HashFileBucket : public HashBucket
    {
    public:
        Boolean WriteEntries(DataFileOutput & file) const;

        Boolean ReadEntries(const DataFileInput & file);

    private:
        static const Signature Sig;
        static const DataBlock EntryEnd;
    };

//————————————————————
//   HashEnumFuncStrDB
//        Function to retrieve all records in table
//————————————————————

typedef Boolean (* HashFileEnumFunc)(const KeyString & k,
                                     DataFilePtr ptr);

//————————————————————
//   HashFileTable
//        The type of HashTable used by HashFile
//————————————————————

class HashFileTable : protected HashTableBase
    {
    public:
        // constructor
        HashFileTable(size_t buckets);

        // insert new object
        Boolean Insert(const KeyString & key, DataFilePtr ptr);

        // delete an object
        Boolean Delete(const KeyString & key);

        // check for duplicate key
        Boolean IsDupeKey(const KeyString & key);

        // look up object
        DataFilePtr LookUp(const KeyString & key);

        // list all objects
        Boolean Enumerate(HashFileEnumFunc func);
```

```
    protected:
        // callback functions for Enumerate
        virtual Boolean TravCallback(const HashEntryBase * e) const;

        HashFileEnumFunc EnumCallback;
    };

inline HashFileTable::HashFileTable(size_t buckets)
    : HashTableBase(buckets)
    {
    // void
    }


//────────────────────────────────
// HashFile
//      A file storing data by key, using a hash table
//────────────────────────────────

typedef KeyString (* ReHashFunc)(const DataBlock & db);

class HashFile : private HashFileTable,
                 private DataFile
    {
    public:
        // constructors
        // existing hash file
        HashFile(const String & basename,
                       size_t    bufsize = 0);

        // new hash file
        HashFile(      size_t    buckets,
                 const String & basename,
                       size_t    bufsize = 0);

        // has file from data file
        HashFile(      size_t     buckets,
                       DataFile & file,
                 const String &   basename,
                       ReHashFunc getKey,
                       size_t     bufsize = 0);

        // copy constructor
        HashFile(const HashFile & hfile);

        // destructor
        ~HashFile();

        // write a record
```

```
        Boolean Write(const KeyString & key,
                      const DataBlock & db);

        // read a record
        DataBlock Read(const KeyString & key);

        // delete a record
        Boolean Delete(const KeyString & key);

        // commit data to disk
        Boolean Commit();

    private:
        // name of hash file
        String HashFileName;

        // extensions for hash file and data file
        static const String HashFileExt;
        static const String DataFileExt;

        static const Signature HashHdrSig;

        // create file name from base and extension
        static String MakeFileName(const String & basename,
                                   const String & ext);

        // get buckets from hash file
        size_t GetBuckets(const String & hashname);
    };

// commit data to disk
inline Boolean HashFile::Commit()
    {
    return DataFile::Commit();
    }

#endif
```

**Listing 12-2. hashfile.h.**
```
/////////////////////////////////////////////////////////////
//   PERSISTENCE LIBRARY
//      hashfile.cxx
//
//      Defines a file type for disk-based data files that are
//      indexed via a hash table.
//
//      Copyright 1992 Scott Robert Ladd
//      All rights reserved
/////////////////////////////////////////////////////////////
```

```
#include "hashfile.h"
#include "string.h"

//————————————————————————————————
//  HashFileEntry
//      An entry in a HashFileBucket
//————————————————————————————————

const Signature HashFileEntry::Sig = SYS_SIG_BASE + 4;

HashFileEntry::HashFileEntry(const DataBlock & db)
    {
    // check sinature
    if (db.GetSignature() != Sig)
        ReportError(HE_BADTYPES);

    // get pointer to data
    const char * ptr = (const char *)db.GetBufferPtr();

    // get file pointer
    DataPtr = *((const DataFilePtr *)ptr);

    // move to beginning of string
    ptr += sizeof(DataFilePtr);

    // create key string
    Key = KeyString(String(ptr));
    }

HashFileEntry::operator DataBlock() const
    {
    // get reference to string
    const String & keystr = Key.GetString();

    // calculate size of block
    size_t sz = sizeof(DataFilePtr) + keystr.Length() + 1;

    // allocate memory
    char * buf = new char [sz];

    if (buf == NULL)
        ReportError(HE_ALLOC);

    // store data ptr
    *((DataFilePtr *)buf) = DataPtr;

    // store string
    strcpy(buf + sizeof(DataFilePtr),(const char *)keystr);
```

```
    // create data block
    DataBlock db(Sig,sz,buf);

    // delete buffer
    delete buf;

    return db;
    }

//————————————————————————————————
//  HashFileBucket
//      A bucket for a HashFile
//————————————————————————————————

const Signature HashFileBucket::Sig = SYS_SIG_BASE + 3;
static const int DummyData = 0;
const DataBlock HashFileBucket::EntryEnd(HashFileBucket::Sig,
                                         sizeof(DummyData),
                                         &DummyData);

Boolean HashFileBucket::WriteEntries(DataFileOutput & file) const
    {
    HashFileEntry * e = (HashFileEntry *)First;

    while (e != NULL)
        {
        if (BOOL_FALSE == file.Write(*e))
            return BOOL_FALSE;

        e = (HashFileEntry *)(e->Next);
        }

    file.Write(EntryEnd);

    return BOOL_TRUE;
    }

Boolean HashFileBucket::ReadEntries(const DataFileInput & file)
    {
    HashFileEntry * e = NULL;
    DataBlock db;

    for (;;)
        {
        db = file.Read();

        if (db.IsNull())
            return BOOL_FALSE;
```

```
        // NOTE: possibly store # of entries in size ?!?
        if ((Sig == db.GetSignature())
        && (sizeof(DummyData) == db.GetSizeOf())))
            break;

        e = new HashFileEntry(db);

        if (BOOL_FALSE == AddEntry(e))
            return BOOL_FALSE;
        }

    return BOOL_TRUE;
    }


//─────────────────────────────
// HashFileTable
//      The type of HashTable used by HashFile
//─────────────────────────────

Boolean HashFileTable::Insert(const KeyString & key, DataFilePtr ptr)
    {
    // create new HashEntryStrDB
    HashFileEntry * entry = new HashFileEntry(key,ptr);

    if (entry == NULL)
        ReportError(HE_ALLOC);

    // insert into table
    return AddEntry(entry);
    }

Boolean HashFileTable::Delete(const KeyString & key)
    {
    // create new HashEntryStr
    HashEntryStr * entry = new HashEntryStr(key);

    if (entry == NULL)
        ReportError(HE_ALLOC);

    // insert into table
    return DelEntry(entry);
    }

Boolean HashFileTable::IsDupeKey(const KeyString & key)
    {
    // create new HashEntryStr
    HashEntryStr * entry = new HashEntryStr(key);
```

```
        if (entry == NULL)
            ReportError(HE_ALLOC);

        // insert into table
        return IsDupe(entry);
        }

DataFilePtr HashFileTable::LookUp(const KeyString & key)
        {
        // create new HashEntryStr
        HashEntryStr * entry = new HashEntryStr(key);

        if (entry == NULL)
            ReportError(HE_ALLOC);

        const HashFileEntry * e = (const HashFileEntry *)FindEntry(entry);

        if (e == NULL)
            return DFP_ERROR;
        else
            return e->DataPtr;
        }

Boolean HashFileTable::Enumerate(HashFileEnumFunc func)
        {
        if (func == NULL)
            return BOOL_FALSE;

        EnumCallback = func;

        return Traverse();
        }

Boolean HashFileTable::TravCallback(const HashEntryBase * e) const
        {
        if (e == NULL)
            return BOOL_FALSE;
        else
            {
            HashFileEntry * e2 = (HashFileEntry *)e;

            return EnumCallback(e2->Key, e2->DataPtr);
            }
        }

//————————————————————————
// HashFile
//      A file storing data by key, using a hash table
//————————————————————————
```

```
const String HashFile::HashFileExt(".HFH");
const String HashFile::DataFileExt(".HFD");

const Signature HashFile::HashHdrSig = SYS_SIG_BASE + 5;

// create file name from base and extension
String HashFile::MakeFileName(const String & basename,
                              const String & ext)
    {
    String name;

    if (basename.Length() < 8)
        name = basename;
    else
        name = basename.CutHead(8);

    name += ext;

    return name;
    }

size_t HashFile::GetBuckets(const String & hashname)
    {
    DataFileInput * file = new DataFileInput(hashname);

    size_t result = 0;

    if (file != NULL)
        {
        DataBlock db = file->Read();

        if ((db.GetSignature() == HashHdrSig)
        && (db.GetSizeOf() == sizeof(size_t)))
            result = *((size_t *)db.GetBufferPtr());
        }
    delete file;

    return result;
    }

// constructors
// existing hash file
HashFile::HashFile(const String & basename,
                   size_t    bufsize)
    : DataFile(MakeFileName(basename,DataFileExt),FM_EXISTING,bufsize),
      HashFileTable(GetBuckets(MakeFileName(basename,HashFileExt))),
      HashFileName(MakeFileName(basename,HashFileExt))
    {
```

```
    // read hash table
    DataFileInput * file = new DataFileInput(HashFileName);

    if (file == NULL)
        DataFileBase::ReportError("can't open input hash file");

    // ignore hash file header
    file->Skip();

    // get hash table entries
    Boolean result;

    for (size_t b = 0; b < NoOfBuckets; ++b)
        {
        // get bucket entries
        result = ((HashFileBucket *)Table[b])->ReadEntries(*file);

        if (result == BOOL_FALSE)
            DataFileBase::ReportError("can't read bucket entries");
        }

    delete file;
    }

// new hash file
HashFile::HashFile(        size_t    buckets,
                    const String & basename,
                          size_t    bufsize)
    : DataFile(MakeFileName(basename,DataFileExt),FM_NEW,bufsize),
      HashFileTable(buckets),
      HashFileName(MakeFileName(basename,HashFileExt))
    {
    // void
    }

// has file from data file
HashFile::HashFile(        size_t      buckets,
                          DataFile & file,
                    const String &    basename,
                          ReHashFunc getKey,
                          size_t     bufsize)
    : DataFile(MakeFileName(basename,DataFileExt),FM_NEW,bufsize),
      HashFileTable(buckets),
      HashFileName(MakeFileName(basename,HashFileExt))
    {
    if (getKey == NULL)
        DataFile::ReportError("invalid rehash function");
```

```
    file.Rewind();

    DataBlock db;

    for (;;)
        {
        // read record from original file
        db = file.Read();

        // assume a NULL block indicates end-of-input
        if (db.IsNull())
            break;

        // write record to HashFile
        Write(getKey(db),db);

        // Note: Duplicate keys will be lost in the conversion!
        //       Also, no error checking is done on Write,
        //       since it returns an error on duplicate keys
        }
    }

// destructor
HashFile::~HashFile()
    {
    // create hash output file
    DataFileOutput * file = new DataFileOutput(HashFileName);

    if (file == NULL)
        DataFileBase::ReportError("can't create output hash file");

    // save hash table
    Boolean result;

    // store # of buckets
    file->Write(DataBlock(HashHdrSig,sizeof(size_t),&NoOfBuckets));

    for (size_t b = 0; b < NoOfBuckets; ++b)
        {
        // write bucket entries
        result = ((HashFileBucket *)Table[b])->WriteEntries(*file);

        if (result == BOOL_FALSE)
            DataFileBase::ReportError("can't write bucket entries");
        }

    delete file;
    }
```

```
// write a record
Boolean HashFile::Write(const KeyString & key,
                        const DataBlock & db)
    {
    // check for (and delete) duplicate key
    if (IsDupeKey(key))
        {
        if (BOOL_FALSE == HashFile::Delete(key))
            return BOOL_FALSE;
        }

    // store data
    DataFilePtr ptr = DataFile::Write(db);

    if (ptr == DFP_ERROR)
        return BOOL_FALSE;

    // add key and pointer to hash table
    Boolean result = Insert(key,ptr);

    return result;
    }

// read a record
DataBlock HashFile::Read(const KeyString & key)
    {
    // get pointer to record via key in hash table
    DataFilePtr ptr = LookUp(key);

    if (ptr == DFP_ERROR)
        return NULL_BLOCK;

    // set file pointer
    if (BOOL_FALSE == DataFile::Seek(ptr))
        return NULL_BLOCK;

    // read record at pointer
    DataBlock db(DataFile::Read());

    return db;
    }

// delete a record
Boolean HashFile::Delete(const KeyString & key)
    {
    // get pointer to record via key lookup in hash table
    DataFilePtr ptr = LookUp(key);
```

```
    if (ptr == DFP_ERROR)
        return BOOL_FALSE;

    // set file pointer
    if (BOOL_FALSE == DataFile::Seek(ptr))
        return BOOL_FALSE;

    // delete record
    Boolean result = DataFile::Delete();

    if (result == BOOL_TRUE)
        {
        // delete key from hash table
        result = HashFileTable::Delete(key);
        }

    // done
    return result;
    }
```

# Chapter 13: Binary Trees

### Listing 13-1. bintree.h.

```
/////////////////////////////////////////////////////////////
//   PERSISTENCE LIBRARY
//       bintree.h
//
//       Binary tree class for Persistent objects
//
//       Copyright 1992 Scott Robert Ladd
//       All rights reserved
/////////////////////////////////////////////////////////////

#ifndef BINTREE_H
#define BINTREE_H

#include "persist.h"

//————————————————————————————————
//   TreeErrorBase
//       Base class providing error handling for Tree classes
//————————————————————————————————

class TreeErrorBase
    {
    public:
        static void SetErrOut(const ErrReporter & er);
```

```
    protected:
        static ErrReporter * ErrOut;

        static void ReportError();
    };

//────────────────────────────────
// TreeNode
//      A node in a binary tree
//────────────────────────────────

struct TreeNode : public TreeErrorBase
    {
    // links
    TreeNode  * Less;
    TreeNode  * Greater;
    TreeNode  * Parent;

    // contents
    KeyString Key;
    DataBlock Data;

    // constructor
    TreeNode(const KeyString & k,
             const DataBlock & db);

    // copy constructor
    TreeNode(const TreeNode & node);

    // assignment operator
    void operator = (const TreeNode & node);
    };

//────────────────────────────────
// BinaryTree
//      A basic binary tree
//────────────────────────────────

typedef Boolean (* TreeEnumFunc)(const KeyString & str,
                                 const DataBlock & db);

class BinaryTree : public TreeErrorBase
    {
    public:
        // constructor
        BinaryTree();

        // copy constructor
```

```
        BinaryTree(const BinaryTree & tree);

        // destructor
        ~BinaryTree();

        // assignment opeartor
        void operator = (const BinaryTree & tree);

        // store an item
        Boolean Insert(const KeyString & key,
                       const DataBlock & db);

        // delete an item
        Boolean Delete(const KeyString & key);

        // retrieve an item
        DataBlock LookUp(const KeyString & key) const;

        // traverse entire tree, calling a function for each node
        void Enumerate(TreeEnumFunc func);

    protected:
        // data members
        TreeNode *   Root;      // root node
        TreeEnumFunc EnumFunc;  // pointer to enumeration function

        // recursive copy function
        void RecursiveCopy(TreeNode * node);

        // recursive traversal function
        void RecurseTraverse(TreeNode * node);

        // recursive deletion function
        void RecursiveDelete(TreeNode * node);
    };

#endif
```

**Listing 13-2. bintree.h.**
```
/////////////////////////////////////////////////////////////
//    PERSISTENCE LIBRARY
//        bintree.cxx
//
//        Binary tree class for Persistent objects
//
//        Copyright 1992 Scott Robert Ladd
//        All rights reserved
/////////////////////////////////////////////////////////////
```

# C++ COMPONENTS AND ALGORITHMS

```cpp
#include "stddef.h"
#include "stdlib.h"
#include "bintree.h"

//————————————————————————————
//  TreeErrorBase
//      Base class providing error handling for Tree classes
//————————————————————————————

ErrReporter * TreeErrorBase::ErrOut = NULL;

void TreeErrorBase::ReportError()
    {
    if (ErrOut != NULL)
        ErrOut->Fatal("memory allocation failure in tree");
    }

void TreeErrorBase::SetErrOut(const ErrReporter & er)
    {
    if (ErrOut != NULL)
        delete ErrOut;

    ErrOut = new ErrReporter(er);
    }


//————————————————————————————
//  TreeNode
//      A node in a binary tree
//————————————————————————————

// constructor
TreeNode::TreeNode(const KeyString & k,
                   const DataBlock & db)
    : Key(k), Data(db)
    {
    Parent  = NULL;
    Less    = NULL;
    Greater = NULL;
    }

// copy constructor
TreeNode::TreeNode(const TreeNode & node)
    : Key(node.Key), Data(node.Data)
    {
    Parent  = node.Parent;
    Less    = node.Less;
    Greater = node.Greater;
    }
```

**736**

```
// assignment operator
void TreeNode::operator = (const TreeNode & node)
    {
    Parent  = node.Parent;
    Less    = node.Less;
    Greater = node.Greater;

    Key     = node.Key;
    Data    = node.Data;
    }


//————————————————————————————
//  BinaryTree
//      A basic binary tree
//————————————————————————————

// constructor
BinaryTree::BinaryTree()
    {
    Root = NULL;
    }

// copy constructor
BinaryTree::BinaryTree(const BinaryTree & tree)
    {
    Root = NULL;

    RecursiveCopy(tree.Root);
    }

// destructor
BinaryTree::~BinaryTree()
    {
    RecursiveDelete(Root);
    }

// assignment opeartor
void BinaryTree::operator = (const BinaryTree & tree)
    {
    RecursiveDelete(Root);

    Root = NULL;

    RecursiveCopy(tree.Root);
    }

// store an item
Boolean BinaryTree::Insert(const KeyString & key,
                           const DataBlock & db)
```

```
    {
Boolean result = BOOL_FALSE;

TreeNode * newnode = new TreeNode(key,db);

if (newnode == NULL)
    ReportError();

if (Root == NULL)
    {
    Root   = newnode;
    result = BOOL_TRUE;
    }
else
    {
    TreeNode * node = Root;

    while (node != NULL)
        {
        // replace a duplicate key
        if (newnode->Key == node->Key)
            {
            // copy links from old node
            newnode->Less    = node->Less;
            newnode->Greater = node->Greater;
            newnode->Parent  = node->Parent;

            // is node the root?
            if (node == Root)
                Root = newnode; // replace root node
            else
                {
                // replace node with newnode in parent
                if (node->Parent->Less == node)
                    node->Parent->Less = newnode;
                else
                    node->Parent->Greater = newnode;
                }

            // delete old node
            delete node;

            result = BOOL_TRUE;

            break;
            }

        if (newnode->Key < node->Key)
```

```
                {
                if (node->Less == NULL)
                    {
                    // insert node
                    node->Less = newnode;
                    newnode->Parent = node;
                    result = BOOL_TRUE;
                    break;
                    }
                else // move to next node
                    node = node->Less;
                }
            else
                {
                if (node->Greater == NULL)
                    {
                    // insert node
                    node->Greater = newnode;
                    newnode->Parent = node;
                    result = BOOL_TRUE;
                    break;
                    }
                else // move to next node
                    node = node->Greater;
                }
            }
        }

    return result;
    }

// delete an item
Boolean BinaryTree::Delete(const KeyString & key)
    {
    TreeNode * node = Root;

    while (node != NULL)
        {
        if (key == node->Key)
            break;

        if (key < node->Key)
            node = node->Less;
        else
            node = node->Greater;
        }

    if (node == NULL)
        return BOOL_FALSE;
```

```
if (node->Greater == NULL)
    {
    if (node->Less == NULL)
        {
        if (node == Root)
            Root = NULL; // tree is now empty!
        else
            {
            // remove leaf node
            if (node->Parent->Less == node)
                node->Parent->Less = NULL;
            else
                node->Parent->Greater = NULL;
            }
        }
    else // node has a "lesser" subtree
        {
        if (node == Root)
            Root = node->Less;
        else
            {
            // splice "less" subtree
            if (node->Parent->Less == node)
                node->Parent->Less = node->Less;
            else
                node->Parent->Greater = node->Less;
            }
        }
    }
else // node has a "greater" subtree
    {
    if (node->Less == NULL)
        {
        if (node == Root)
            Root = node->Greater;  // new root node
        else
            {
            // splice "greater" subtree
            if (node->Parent->Less == node)
                node->Parent->Less = node->Greater;
            else
                node->Parent->Greater = node->Greater;
            }
        }
    else // deleted node has two decendants... ugh!
        {
        // look for immediate successor
        TreeNode * successor = node->Greater;
```

```
            while (successor->Less != NULL)
                successor = successor->Less;

            // unlink successor from tree
            if (successor->Parent->Less == successor)
                successor->Parent->Less = successor->Greater;
            else
                successor->Parent->Greater = successor->Greater;

            // copy data from successor to deleted node
            node->Key  = successor->Key;
            node->Data = successor->Data;

            // update parent links in children
            if (successor->Greater != NULL)
                successor->Greater->Parent = node;

            // set successor to be deleted
            node = successor;
            }
        }

    // delete node that was removed
    delete node;

    return BOOL_TRUE;
    }

// retrieve an item
DataBlock BinaryTree::LookUp(const KeyString & key) const
    {
    TreeNode * node = Root;

    while (node != NULL)
        {
        if (key == node->Key)
            break;

        if (key < node->Key)
            node = node->Less;
        else
            node = node->Greater;
        }

    if (node == NULL)
        return NULL_BLOCK;
    else
        return node->Data;
    }
```

```
// traverse entire tree, calling a function for each node
void BinaryTree::Enumerate(TreeEnumFunc func)
    {
    EnumFunc = func;

    RecurseTraverse(Root);
    }

// recursive copy function
void BinaryTree::RecursiveCopy(TreeNode * node)
    {
    if (node != NULL)
        {
        Insert(node->Key,node->Data);

        RecursiveCopy(node->Less);
        RecursiveCopy(node->Greater);
        }
    }

// recursive traversal method
void BinaryTree::RecurseTraverse(TreeNode * node)
    {
    if (node != NULL)
        {
        RecurseTraverse(node->Less);
        EnumFunc(node->Key,node->Data);
        RecurseTraverse(node->Greater);
        }
    }

// recursive deletion method
void BinaryTree::RecursiveDelete(TreeNode * node)
    {
    if (node != NULL)
        {
        RecursiveDelete(node->Less);
        RecursiveDelete(node->Greater);

        delete node;
        }
    }
```

# Chapter 14: Indexing Files with BTrees

**Listing 14-1. btree.h**

```
///////////////////////////////////////////////////////////
//  PERSISTENCE LIBRARY
//      btree.h
//
//      A btree class for indexing.
//
//      Copyright 1992 by Scott Robert Ladd
//      All rights reserved
///////////////////////////////////////////////////////////

#ifndef BTREE_H
#define BTREE_H

#include "datafile.h"

//———————————————————————————
//  BTreeErrorBase
//      Base class providing error reporting for BTree classes
//———————————————————————————

enum BTreeError
    {
    BTE_ALLOC,      // fatal: memory allocation failure
    BTE_TOOSMALL,   // fatal: created bucket w/ zero buckets
    BTE_CORRUPTED   // fatal: table / list has been corrupted
    };

class BTreeErrorBase
    {
    public:
        static void SetErrOut(const ErrReporter & er);

    protected:
        static ErrReporter * ErrOut;

        static void ReportError(BTreeError err);
    };

//———————————————————————————
//  PageKey
//      A character string optimized for use with BTrees
//———————————————————————————

class PageKey : public BTreeErrorBase
```

**743**

```
    {
    public:
        // constructors
        PageKey();
        PageKey(size_t maxlen, const char * str);
        PageKey(size_t maxlen, const String & str);
        PageKey(const PageKey & pgkey);

        // destructor
        ~PageKey();

        // assignment
        void operator = (const PageKey & pgkey);

        // interrogation
        size_t GetMax() const;
        size_t GetLen() const;

        // get pointer
        operator const char * () const;

        // is this an "empty" key?
        Boolean IsEmpty() const;

        // compare two keys
        int Compare(const PageKey & pgkey);

    private:
        char * Txt; // pointer to buffer containing text
        size_t Len; // number of characters in Txt
        size_t Max; // maximum # of characters in Txt
    };

// interrogation
inline size_t PageKey::GetMax() const
    {
    return Max;
    }

inline size_t PageKey::GetLen() const
    {
    return Len;
    }

// get pointer
inline PageKey::operator const char * () const
    {
    return Txt;
    }
```

```
// is this an "empty" key?
inline Boolean PageKey::IsEmpty() const
    {
    if (Txt == NULL)
        return BOOL_TRUE;
    else
        return BOOL_FALSE;
    }


//————————————————————————————
// Page
//      A page in a BTree
//————————————————————————————

typedef long PageFilePtr;

struct PageHeader
    {
    PageFilePtr FilePtr;   // ptr to location in PageFile
    PageFilePtr ParentPtr; // ptr to parent in PageFile

    size_t      Order;     // maximum # of page links in page
    size_t      MaxKeys;   // maximum # of keys in page
    size_t      MinKeys;   // minimum # of keys in page
    size_t      NoOfKeys;  // actual  # of keys in page
    size_t      KeySize;   // maximum # of characters in a key
    };

struct Page : private BTreeErrorBase
    {
    PageHeader    Hdr; // header information
    PageKey     * Key; // key array [MaxKeys]
    DataFilePtr * Ptr; // rec  index array [MaxKeys]
    PageFilePtr * Lnk; // page index array [Order]

    // construct a new, empty page
    Page(size_t ord, size_t ksize);

    // construct a copy of a page
    Page(const Page & p);

    // destructor
    ~Page();

    // assignment operator
    void operator = (const Page & page);
    };
```

```
//————————————————————
//  PageFile
//      A file that contains btree pages
//————————————————————

extern const PageFilePtr PFP_NULL;

struct PageFileHdr
    {
    size_t KeySize;
    size_t Order;

    PageFilePtr RootPtr;
    PageFilePtr FirstDead;
    };

class PageFile : public DataFileBase
    {
    public:
        // use existing page file
        PageFile(const String & name);

        // create new page file
        PageFile(const String & name,
                    size_t   ord,
                    size_t   ksize);

        // destructor
        ~PageFile();

        // get root page
        Boolean ReadRoot(Page & pg);

        // write a page
        Boolean Write(Page & pg, Boolean root = BOOL_FALSE);

        // read a page
        Boolean Read(PageFilePtr ptr, Page & pg);

        // delete a page
        Boolean Delete(PageFilePtr ptr);

        // commit data & header
        Boolean Flush();

    private:
        // header record
        PageFileHdr Hdr;
    };
```

```
// destructor
inline PageFile::~PageFile()
    {
    Flush();
    }

// get root page
inline Boolean PageFile::ReadRoot(Page & pg)
    {
    return Read(Hdr.RootPtr, pg);
    }

//————————————————————————
// BTreeFile
//      A DataFile that uses a BTree for indexing
//————————————————————————

typedef void (* BTreeEnumFunc)(const   PageKey & str,
                                 const DataBlock & db);

class BTreeFile : private BTreeErrorBase
    {
    public:
        // constructors
        // use existing files
        BTreeFile(const String & basename);

        // create new files
        BTreeFile(const String & basename,
                         size_t ord,
                         size_t ksize);

        // copy constructor
        BTreeFile(const BTreeFile & btfile);

        // destructor
        ~BTreeFile();

        // write a record
        Boolean Write(const PageKey & key,
                    const DataBlock & db);

        // read a record
        DataBlock Read(const PageKey & key);

        // delete a record
        Boolean Delete(const PageKey & key);
```

```
        // enumerate all records
        void InOrder(BTreeEnumFunc func);

    private:
        // data members
        DataFile * Data; // file containing DataBlocks
        PageFile * Tree; // file containing tree pages

        Page        Root; // root page (always in memory)

        String      DataFileName; // name of data file
        String      TreeFileName; // name of tree file

        BTreeEnumFunc EnumFunc; // function called by Traverse

        // search for a node
        Boolean Search(const    Page & pg,
                    const PageKey & searchkey,
                            Page & keypage,
                        size_t & pos);

        // insert node into leaf
        Boolean InsertKey(const PageKey & inskey,
                        DataFilePtr dataptr);

        Boolean PromoteInternal(        Page & pg,
                            const PageKey & inskey,
                                DataFilePtr dataptr,
                                PageFilePtr pagelnk);

        Boolean PromoteRoot(const PageKey & inskey,
                            DataFilePtr dataptr,
                            PageFilePtr lesslnk,
                            PageFilePtr grtrlnk);

        void RecurseTraverse(const Page & pg);

        // extensions for hash file and data file
        static const String TreeFileExt;
        static const String DataFileExt;

        // create file name from base and extension
        static String MakeFileName(const String & basename,
                                const String & ext);
    };

#endif
```

**Listing 14-2. btree.cxx.**

```
//////////////////////////////////////////////////////////
//    PERSISTENCE LIBRARY
//        btree.cxx
//
//        A btree class for indexing.
//
//        Copyright 1992 by Scott Robert Ladd
//        All rights reserved
//////////////////////////////////////////////////////////

#include "btree.h"
#include "stdlib.h"
#include "string.h"


//————————————————————————————
//   BTreeErrorBase
//        Base class providing error reporting for BTree classes
//————————————————————————————

ErrReporter * BTreeErrorBase::ErrOut = NULL;

void BTreeErrorBase::ReportError(BTreeError err)
    {
    if (ErrOut != NULL)
        {
        switch (err)
            {
            case BTE_ALLOC:
                ErrOut->Fatal("memory allocation failure");
                break;

            case BTE_TOOSMALL:
                ErrOut->Fatal("cannot create zero-size table");
                break;

            case BTE_CORRUPTED:
                ErrOut->Fatal("corrupted");
                break;

            default:
                ErrOut->Fatal("unknown");
                break;
            }
        }
    }

void BTreeErrorBase::SetErrOut(const ErrReporter & er)
```

```
    {
    if (ErrOut != NULL)
        delete ErrOut;

    ErrOut = new ErrReporter(er);
    }

//————————————————————————
//  PageKey
//      A character string optimized for use with BTrees
//————————————————————————

// constructors
PageKey::PageKey()
    {
    Max = 0;
    Len = 0;
    Txt = NULL;
    }

PageKey::PageKey(size_t maxlen, const char * str)
    {
    Max = maxlen;

    // allocate buffer
    Txt = new char [Max];

    if (Txt == NULL)
        ReportError(BTE_ALLOC);

    // copy string
    strncpy(Txt,str,Max);

    // make sure there's a terminating NULL
    Txt[Max - 1] = 0;

    Len = strlen(Txt);
    }

PageKey::PageKey(size_t maxlen, const String & str)
    {
    Max = maxlen;

    // allocate buffer
    Txt = new char [Max];

    if (Txt == NULL)
        ReportError(BTE_ALLOC);
```

```
    // copy string
    strncpy(Txt,(const char *)str,Max);

    // make sure there's a terminating NULL
    Txt[Max - 1] = 0;

    Len = strlen(Txt);
    }

PageKey::PageKey(const PageKey & pgkey)
    {
    Max = pgkey.Max;
    Len = pgkey.Len;

    if (pgkey.Txt == NULL)
        Txt = NULL;
    else
        {
        // allocate buffer
        Txt = new char [Max];

        if (Txt == NULL)
            ReportError(BTE_ALLOC);

        // copy string
        strcpy(Txt,pgkey.Txt);
        }
    }

// destructor
PageKey::~PageKey()
    {
    if (Txt != NULL)
        delete [] Txt;
    }

// assignment
void PageKey::operator = (const PageKey & pgkey)
    {
    // delete existing buffer
    if (Txt != NULL)
        delete [] Txt;

    // assign values
    Max = pgkey.Max;
    Len = pgkey.Len;

    if (pgkey.Txt == NULL)
        Txt = NULL;
```

```
    else
        {
        // allocate buffer
        Txt = new char [Max];

        if (Txt == NULL)
            ReportError(BTE_ALLOC);

        // copy string
        strcpy(Txt,pgkey.Txt);
        }
    }

// compare two keys
int PageKey::Compare(const PageKey & pgkey)
    {
    return strcmp(Txt,pgkey.Txt);
    }

//————————————————————————
//  Page
//      A page in a BTree
//————————————————————————

// create a new page
Page::Page(size_t ord, size_t ksize)
    {
    size_t n;

    Hdr.FilePtr   = PFP_NULL;
    Hdr.ParentPtr = PFP_NULL;
    Hdr.Order     = ord;
    Hdr.MaxKeys   = ord - 1;
    Hdr.MinKeys   = ord / 2;
    Hdr.NoOfKeys  = 0;
    Hdr.KeySize   = ksize;

    if (Hdr.Order == 0)
        {
        Key = NULL;
        Ptr = NULL;
        Lnk = NULL;

        return;
        }

    // allocate key array
    Key = new PageKey [Hdr.MaxKeys];
```

```
    if (Key == NULL)
        ReportError(BTE_ALLOC);

    // allocate record pointer array
    Ptr = new DataFilePtr [Hdr.MaxKeys];

    if (Ptr == NULL)
        ReportError(BTE_ALLOC);

    // set pointers to nothing
    for (n = 0; n < Hdr.MaxKeys; ++n)
        Ptr[n] = DFP_ERROR;

    // allocate page pointer array
    Lnk = new PageFilePtr [Hdr.Order];

    if (Lnk == NULL)
        ReportError(BTE_ALLOC);

    /// fill page indexes with "empty" values
    for (n = 0; n < Hdr.Order; ++n)
        Lnk[n] = PFP_NULL;
    }

Page::Page(const Page & pg)
    {
    Hdr = pg.Hdr;

    // allocate key array
    Key = new PageKey [Hdr.MaxKeys];

    if (Key == NULL)
        ReportError(BTE_ALLOC);

    for (size_t n = 0; n < Hdr.MaxKeys; ++n)
        Key[n] = pg.Key[n];

    // allocate record pointer array
    Ptr = new DataFilePtr [Hdr.MaxKeys];

    if (Ptr == NULL)
        ReportError(BTE_ALLOC);

    memcpy(Ptr,pg.Ptr,
            Hdr.MaxKeys * sizeof(DataFilePtr));

    // allocate page pointer array
    Lnk = new PageFilePtr [Hdr.Order];
```

```
    if (Lnk == NULL)
        ReportError(BTE_ALLOC);

    // fill page indexes with source values
    memcpy(Lnk,pg.Lnk,
            Hdr.Order * sizeof(PageFilePtr));
    }

Page::~Page()
    {
    // delete old buffers
    delete [] Key;
    delete [] Ptr;
    delete [] Lnk;
    }

void Page::operator = (const Page & pg)
    {
    Hdr = pg.Hdr;

    // allocate key array
    if (Key != NULL)
        delete [] Key;

    Key = new PageKey [Hdr.MaxKeys];

    if (Key == NULL)
        ReportError(BTE_ALLOC);

    for (size_t n = 0; n < Hdr.MaxKeys; ++n)
        Key[n] = pg.Key[n];

    // allocate record pointer array
    if (Ptr != NULL)
        delete [] Ptr;

    Ptr = new DataFilePtr [Hdr.MaxKeys];

    if (Ptr == NULL)
        ReportError(BTE_ALLOC);

    memcpy(Ptr,pg.Ptr,
            Hdr.MaxKeys * sizeof(DataFilePtr));

    // allocate page pointer array
    if (Lnk != NULL)
        delete [] Lnk;
```

```
    Lnk = new PageFilePtr [Hdr.Order];

    if (Lnk == NULL)
        ReportError(BTE_ALLOC);

    // fill page indexes with source values
    memcpy(Lnk,pg.Lnk,
          Hdr.Order * sizeof(PageFilePtr));
    }

//————————————————————————————
//  PageFile
//      A file that contains btree pages
//————————————————————————————

const PageFilePtr PFP_NULL = -1;

// use existing page file
PageFile::PageFile(const String & name)
    : DataFileBase(name,FM_EXISTING)
    {
    size_t n;

    n = fread(&Hdr,sizeof(PageFileHdr),1,Data);

    if (n == 0)
        ReportError("unable to create header in new page file");
    }

// create new page file
PageFile::PageFile(const String & name,
                        size_t   ord,
                        size_t   ksize)
    : DataFileBase(name,FM_NEW)
    {
    Hdr.Order     = ord;
    Hdr.KeySize   = ksize;
    Hdr.RootPtr   = PFP_NULL;
    Hdr.FirstDead = PFP_NULL;

    size_t n = fwrite(&Hdr,sizeof(PageFileHdr),1,Data);

    if (n == 0)
        ReportError("unable to create header in new page file");

    // create Root page
    Page root(Hdr.Order,Hdr.KeySize);
```

```
    // store root
    Write(root);

    // save root address
    Hdr.RootPtr = root.Hdr.FilePtr;
    }

// write a page
Boolean PageFile::Write(Page & pg, Boolean root)
    {
    size_t n;
    int res;

    // confirm that this page belongs in this file
    if ((Hdr.Order    != pg.Hdr.Order)
    || (Hdr.KeySize != pg.Hdr.KeySize))
        return BOOL_FALSE;

    // if this page has never been written
    // find a spot to write it
    if (pg.Hdr.FilePtr == PFP_NULL)
        {
        if (Hdr.FirstDead != PFP_NULL)
            {
            // write this record to first dead one in list
            pg.Hdr.FilePtr = Hdr.FirstDead;

            // find record where the new page will be written
            res = fseek(Data,Hdr.FirstDead,SEEK_SET);

            if (res)
                return BOOL_FALSE;

            // set first dead to next dead record in list
            n = fread(&Hdr.FirstDead,sizeof(PageFilePtr),1,Data);

            if (n == 0)
                return BOOL_FALSE;
            }
        else // append to end of file!
            {
            // look for end of file
            res = fseek(Data,0,SEEK_END);

            if (res)
                return BOOL_FALSE;

            // and get a pointer to it
            pg.Hdr.FilePtr = ftell(Data);
```

```
        }
    }

// construct block of memory
size_t keysize = (pg.Hdr.MaxKeys * Hdr.KeySize);
size_t ptrsize = (pg.Hdr.MaxKeys * sizeof(DataFilePtr));
size_t lnksize = (pg.Hdr.Order   * sizeof(PageFilePtr));

size_t bufsize = sizeof(PageHeader)
                    + keysize + ptrsize + lnksize;

char * buffer = new char [bufsize];

if (buffer == NULL)
    return BOOL_FALSE;

char * bufptr = buffer;

// copy page header to buffer
memcpy(bufptr,&pg.Hdr,sizeof(PageHeader));

bufptr += sizeof(PageHeader);

memset(bufptr,0,keysize);

// copy keys to buffer
for (n = 0; n < pg.Hdr.MaxKeys; ++n)
    {
    if (!pg.Key[n].IsEmpty())
        strcpy(bufptr,(const char *)(pg.Key[n]));

    bufptr += Hdr.KeySize;
    }

// copy data record pointers
memcpy(bufptr,pg.Ptr,ptrsize);

bufptr += ptrsize;

// copy page links
memcpy(bufptr,pg.Lnk,lnksize);

// write buffer to file
res = fseek(Data,pg.Hdr.FilePtr,SEEK_SET);

if (res)
    return BOOL_FALSE;
```

```
    n = fwrite(buffer,bufsize,1,Data);

    if (n == 0)
        return BOOL_FALSE;

    // delete buffer
    delete [] buffer;

    // update root pointer in header, if this is a new root
    if (root)
        Hdr.RootPtr = pg.Hdr.FilePtr;

    // make sure header is current
    Flush();

    return BOOL_TRUE;
    }

// read a page
Boolean PageFile::Read(PageFilePtr ptr, Page & pg)
    {
    size_t n;
    int    res;

    // locate requested record
    res = fseek(Data,ptr,SEEK_SET);

    if (res)
        return BOOL_FALSE;

    // create a blank page
    Page temp(Hdr.Order,Hdr.KeySize);

    n = fread(&temp.Hdr,sizeof(PageHeader),1,Data);

    // be sure that this header matches the expected values
    if ((n == 0)
    || (temp.Hdr.Order   != Hdr.Order)
    || (temp.Hdr.KeySize != Hdr.KeySize)
    || (temp.Hdr.FilePtr != ptr))
        return BOOL_FALSE;

    // allocate a buffer to hold incoming keys
    size_t bufsize = temp.Hdr.KeySize * temp.Hdr.MaxKeys;

    char * buffer = new char [bufsize];

    if (buffer == NULL)
```

```
        return BOOL_FALSE;

    // read keys from file
    n = fread(buffer,bufsize,1,Data);

    if (n == 0)
        return BOOL_FALSE;

    char * bufptr = buffer;

    // move keys into page
    for (n = 0; n < temp.Hdr.MaxKeys; ++n)
        {
        if (*bufptr == 0)
            temp.Key[n] = PageKey();
        else
            temp.Key[n] = PageKey(temp.Hdr.KeySize,bufptr);

        bufptr += temp.Hdr.KeySize;
        }

    // read data record pointers
    n = fread(temp.Ptr,temp.Hdr.MaxKeys * sizeof(DataFilePtr),1,Data);

    if (n == 0)
        return BOOL_FALSE;

    // read page links
    n = fread(temp.Lnk,temp.Hdr.Order * sizeof(PageFilePtr),1,Data);

    if (n == 0)
        return BOOL_FALSE;

    pg = temp;

    return BOOL_TRUE;
    }

// delete a page
Boolean PageFile::Delete(PageFilePtr ptr)
    {
    // locate record to be deleted
    int res = fseek(Data,ptr,SEEK_SET);

    if (res)
        return BOOL_FALSE;

    // stored the previous head of the deleted list
    size_t n = fwrite(&Hdr.FirstDead,sizeof(PageFilePtr),1,Data);
```

```
        if (n == 0)
            return BOOL_FALSE;

        // update header
        Hdr.FirstDead = ptr;

        Flush();

        return BOOL_TRUE;
        }

// commit data & header
Boolean PageFile::Flush()
        {
        // rewrite header
        rewind(Data);

        size_t n = fwrite(&Hdr,sizeof(PageFileHdr),1,Data);

        if (n == 0)
            return BOOL_FALSE;

        // empty any buffers
        fflush(Data);

        return BOOL_TRUE;
        }

//————————————————————————
//  BTreeFile
//       A DataFile that uses a BTree for indexing
//————————————————————————

// initialization of static class constants
const String BTreeFile::TreeFileExt(".BFT");
const String BTreeFile::DataFileExt(".BFD");

// use existing files
BTreeFile::BTreeFile(const String & basename)
    : DataFileName(MakeFileName(basename,DataFileExt)),
      TreeFileName(MakeFileName(basename,TreeFileExt)),
      Root(0,0)
    {
    // create data file object
    Data = new DataFile(DataFileName,FM_EXISTING);

    if (Data == NULL)
        ReportError(BTE_ALLOC);
```

```
    // create tree file object
    Tree = new PageFile(TreeFileName);

    if (Tree == NULL)
        ReportError(BTE_ALLOC);

    // create root page
    Boolean result = Tree->ReadRoot(Root);

    if (result == NULL)
        ReportError(BTE_ALLOC);
    }

// create new files
BTreeFile::BTreeFile(const String & basename,
                               size_t ord,
                               size_t ksize)
    : DataFileName(MakeFileName(basename,DataFileExt)),
      TreeFileName(MakeFileName(basename,TreeFileExt)),
      Root(0,0)
    {
    // create data file object
    Data = new DataFile(DataFileName,FM_NEW);

    if (Data == NULL)
        ReportError(BTE_ALLOC);

    // create tree file object
    Tree = new PageFile(TreeFileName,ord,ksize);

    if (Tree == NULL)
        ReportError(BTE_ALLOC);

    // create root page
    Boolean result = Tree->ReadRoot(Root);

    if (result == NULL)
        ReportError(BTE_ALLOC);
    }

// copy constructor
BTreeFile::BTreeFile(const BTreeFile & btfile)
    : DataFileName(btfile.DataFileName),
      TreeFileName(btfile.TreeFileName),
      Root(0,0)
    {
    // this is a private function!
    }
```

```cpp
// destructor
BTreeFile::~BTreeFile()
    {
    // delete files
    delete Data;
    delete Tree;
    }

// write a record
Boolean BTreeFile::Write(const PageKey & key,
                         const DataBlock & db)
    {
    // write the data record
    DataFilePtr dataptr = Data->Write(db);

    if (dataptr == DFP_ERROR)
        return BOOL_FALSE;

    // store the key in a page
    return InsertKey(key,dataptr);
    }

// read a record
DataBlock BTreeFile::Read(const PageKey & key)
    {
    Page    inspage(Root.Hdr.Order,Root.Hdr.KeySize);
    size_t inspos;

    Boolean result = Search(Root,key,inspage,inspos);

    if (result == BOOL_TRUE)
        {
        // seek data record
        Data->Seek(inspage.Ptr[inspos]);

        // read data record
        return Data->Read();
        }
    else
        return NULL_BLOCK;
    }

// delete a record
Boolean BTreeFile::Delete(const PageKey & key)
    {
    return BOOL_FALSE;
    }
```

```
// enumerate all records
void BTreeFile::InOrder(BTreeEnumFunc func)
    {
    Tree->ReadRoot(Root);

    EnumFunc = func;

    RecurseTraverse(Root);
    }

// search for a node
Boolean BTreeFile::Search(const    Page & pg,
                          const PageKey & searchkey,
                                 Page & keypage,
                               size_t & pos)
    {
    Boolean result;

    pos = 0;

    int comp;

    for (;;)
        {
        if (pos == pg.Hdr.NoOfKeys)
            {
            result = BOOL_FALSE;
            goto getpage;
            }

        comp = pg.Key[pos].Compare(searchkey);

        if (comp == 0)
            {
            keypage = pg;
            result  = BOOL_TRUE;
            break;
            }
        else
            {
            if (comp < 0)
                {
                ++pos;
                }
            else
                {
                // I know this is a label — so shoot me!
                getpage:
```

```
                    // if we're in a leaf page, key wasn't found
                    if (pg.Lnk[pos] == PFP_NULL)
                        {
                        keypage = pg;
                        result  = BOOL_FALSE;
                        }
                    else
                        {
                        // dynamically allocate to save stack space
                        Page nextpg(pg.Hdr.Order,
                                    pg.Hdr.KeySize);

                        Tree->Read(pg.Lnk[pos],nextpg);

                        // recursively search new page
                        result = Search(nextpg,searchkey,keypage,pos);
                        }

                    break;
                    }
                }
            }

        return result;
        }

Boolean BTreeFile::InsertKey(const PageKey & inskey,
                                DataFilePtr dataptr)
        {
        // refresh root in memory
        Tree->ReadRoot(Root);

        Page    inspage(Root.Hdr.Order,Root.Hdr.KeySize);
        size_t inspos;

        Boolean found = Search(Root,inskey,inspage,inspos);

        if (found)
            {
            // delete old data record
            Data->Seek(inspage.Ptr[inspos]);

            Data->Delete();

            // store new data record pointer
            inspage.Ptr[inspos] = dataptr;

            // rewrite modified page
```

```
        Tree->Write(inspage);
        }
else
    {
    if (inspage.Hdr.NoOfKeys == inspage.Hdr.MaxKeys)
        {
        // temporary arrays
        PageKey     * tempkeys = new PageKey[inspage.Hdr.MaxKeys + 1];
        DataFilePtr * tempptrs = new DataFilePtr[inspage.Hdr.MaxKeys + 1];

        // copy entries from inspage to temporaries
        size_t nt = 0; // index into temporaries
        size_t ni = 0; // index into inspage

        tempkeys[inspos] = PageKey(inskey);
        tempptrs[inspos] = dataptr;

        while (ni < inspage.Hdr.MaxKeys)
            {
            if (ni == inspos)
                ++nt;

            tempkeys[nt] = inspage.Key[ni];
            tempptrs[nt] = inspage.Ptr[ni];

            ++ni;
            ++nt;
            }

        // generate a new leaf node
        Page sibpage(inspage.Hdr.Order,
                    inspage.Hdr.KeySize);

        sibpage.Hdr.ParentPtr = inspage.Hdr.ParentPtr;

        // clear # of keys in pages
        inspage.Hdr.NoOfKeys = 0;
        sibpage.Hdr.NoOfKeys = 0;

        // copy appropriate keys from temp to pages
        for (ni = 0; ni < inspage.Hdr.MinKeys; ++ni)
            {
            inspage.Key[ni] = tempkeys[ni];
            inspage.Ptr[ni] = tempptrs[ni];

            ++inspage.Hdr.NoOfKeys;
            }
```

```
for (ni = inspage.Hdr.MinKeys + 1; ni <= inspage.Hdr.MaxKeys; ++ni)
    {
    sibpage.Key[ni - 1 - inspage.Hdr.MinKeys] = tempkeys[ni];
    sibpage.Ptr[ni - 1 - inspage.Hdr.MinKeys] = tempptrs[ni];

    ++sibpage.Hdr.NoOfKeys;
    }

// Fill any remaining entries in inspage with null.
// Note that sibpage is initialized to null values
// by the constructor.

for (ni = inspage.Hdr.MinKeys; ni < inspage.Hdr.MaxKeys; ++ni)
    {
    inspage.Key[ni] = PageKey();
    inspage.Ptr[ni] = DFP_MARKER;
    }

// write pages
Tree->Write(inspage);
Tree->Write(sibpage);

// promote key and pointer
if (inspage.Hdr.ParentPtr == PFP_NULL)
    {
    // we need to create a new root
    PromoteRoot(tempkeys[inspage.Hdr.MinKeys],
                tempptrs[inspage.Hdr.MinKeys],
                inspage.Hdr.FilePtr,
                sibpage.Hdr.FilePtr);

    inspage.Hdr.ParentPtr = Root.Hdr.FilePtr;
    sibpage.Hdr.ParentPtr = Root.Hdr.FilePtr;

    // rewrite pages
    Tree->Write(inspage);
    Tree->Write(sibpage);
    }
else
    {
    Page parpage(inspage.Hdr.Order,
                 inspage.Hdr.KeySize);

    Tree->Read(inspage.Hdr.ParentPtr,parpage);

    // promote into parent
    PromoteInternal(parpage,
                    tempkeys[inspage.Hdr.MinKeys],
```

```
                              tempptrs[inspage.Hdr.MinKeys],
                              sibpage.Hdr.FilePtr);
                }

            delete [] tempkeys;
            delete [] tempptrs;
            }
        else // simply insert new key and data ptr
            {
            for (size_t n = inspage.Hdr.NoOfKeys; n > inspos; —n)
                {
                inspage.Key[n] = inspage.Key[n - 1];
                inspage.Ptr[n] = inspage.Ptr[n - 1];
                }

            inspage.Key[inspos] = inskey;
            inspage.Ptr[inspos] = dataptr;

            ++inspage.Hdr.NoOfKeys;

            Tree->Write(inspage);
            }
        }

    return BOOL_TRUE;
    }

Boolean BTreeFile::PromoteInternal(          Page & inspage,
                                  const PageKey & inskey,
                                       DataFilePtr dataptr,
                                       PageFilePtr pagelnk)
    {
    if (inspage.Hdr.NoOfKeys == inspage.Hdr.MaxKeys)
        {
        // temporary arrays
        PageKey     * tempkeys = new PageKey[inspage.Hdr.MaxKeys + 1];
        DataFilePtr * tempptrs = new DataFilePtr[inspage.Hdr.MaxKeys + 1];
        PageFilePtr * templnks = new PageFilePtr[inspage.Hdr.Order   + 1];

        // copy entries from inspage to temporaries
        size_t nt = 0; // index into temporaries
        size_t ni = 0; // index into inspage

        templnks[0] = inspage.Lnk[0];

        size_t inspos = 0;

        // find insertion position
```

```
    while ((inspos < inspage.Hdr.MaxKeys)
       && (inspage.Key[inspos].Compare(inskey) < 0))
          {
          ++inspos;
          }

    // store new info
    tempkeys[inspos]     = PageKey(inskey);
    tempptrs[inspos]     = dataptr;
    templnks[inspos + 1] = pagelnk;

    // copy existing keys
    while (ni < inspage.Hdr.MaxKeys)
          {
          if (ni == inspos)
                ++nt;

          tempkeys[nt]     = inspage.Key[ni];
          tempptrs[nt]     = inspage.Ptr[ni];
          templnks[nt + 1] = inspage.Lnk[ni + 1];

          ++ni;
          ++nt;
          }

    // generate a new leaf node
    Page sibpage(inspage.Hdr.Order,
              inspage.Hdr.KeySize);

    sibpage.Hdr.ParentPtr = inspage.Hdr.ParentPtr;

    // clear # of keys in pages
    inspage.Hdr.NoOfKeys = 0;
    sibpage.Hdr.NoOfKeys = 0;

    inspage.Lnk[0] = templnks[0];

    // copy appropriate keys from temp to pages
    for (ni = 0; ni < inspage.Hdr.MinKeys; ++ni)
          {
          inspage.Key[ni]     = tempkeys[ni];
          inspage.Ptr[ni]     = tempptrs[ni];
          inspage.Lnk[ni + 1] = templnks[ni + 1];

          ++inspage.Hdr.NoOfKeys;
          }

    sibpage.Lnk[0] = templnks[inspage.Hdr.MinKeys + 1];
```

```
for (ni = inspage.Hdr.MinKeys + 1; ni <= inspage.Hdr.MaxKeys; ++ni)
    {
    sibpage.Key[ni - 1 - inspage.Hdr.MinKeys] = tempkeys[ni];
    sibpage.Ptr[ni - 1 - inspage.Hdr.MinKeys] = tempptrs[ni];
    sibpage.Lnk[ni - inspage.Hdr.MinKeys]     = templnks[ni + 1];

    ++sibpage.Hdr.NoOfKeys;
    }

// Fill any remaining entries in inspage with null.
// Note that sibpage is initialized to null values
// by the constructor.

for (ni = inspage.Hdr.MinKeys; ni < inspage.Hdr.MaxKeys; ++ni)
    {
    inspage.Key[ni]     = PageKey();
    inspage.Ptr[ni]     = DFP_MARKER;
    inspage.Lnk[ni + 1] = PFP_NULL;
    }

// write pages
Tree->Write(inspage);
Tree->Write(sibpage);

// update child parent links
Page child(sibpage.Hdr.Order,sibpage.Hdr.KeySize);

for (ni = 0; ni <= sibpage.Hdr.NoOfKeys; ++ni)
    {
    Tree->Read(sibpage.Lnk[ni],child);

    child.Hdr.ParentPtr = sibpage.Hdr.FilePtr;

    Tree->Write(child);
    }

// promote key and pointer
if (inspage.Hdr.ParentPtr == PFP_NULL)
    {
    // we need to create a new root
    PromoteRoot(tempkeys[inspage.Hdr.MinKeys],
                tempptrs[inspage.Hdr.MinKeys],
                inspage.Hdr.FilePtr,
                sibpage.Hdr.FilePtr);

    inspage.Hdr.ParentPtr = Root.Hdr.FilePtr;
    sibpage.Hdr.ParentPtr = Root.Hdr.FilePtr;
```

```
            // rewrite pages
            Tree->Write(inspage);
            Tree->Write(sibpage);
            }
        else
            {
            Page parpage(inspage.Hdr.Order,
                         inspage.Hdr.KeySize);

            Tree->Read(inspage.Hdr.ParentPtr,parpage);

            // promote into parent
            PromoteInternal(parpage,
                            tempkeys[inspage.Hdr.MinKeys],
                            tempptrs[inspage.Hdr.MinKeys],
                            sibpage.Hdr.FilePtr);
            }

        delete [] tempkeys;
        delete [] tempptrs;
        delete [] templnks;
        }
    else // simply insert new key and data ptr
        {
        size_t inspos = 0;

        // find insertion position
        while ((inspos < inspage.Hdr.NoOfKeys)
          && (inspage.Key[inspos].Compare(inskey) < 0))
            {
            ++inspos;
            }

        // shift any keys right
        for (size_t n = inspage.Hdr.NoOfKeys; n > inspos; --n)
            {
            inspage.Key[n]     = inspage.Key[n - 1];
            inspage.Ptr[n]     = inspage.Ptr[n - 1];
            inspage.Lnk[n + 1] = inspage.Lnk[n];
            }

        // store new info
        inspage.Key[inspos]     = PageKey(inskey);
        inspage.Ptr[inspos]     = dataptr;
        inspage.Lnk[inspos + 1] = pagelnk;

        ++inspage.Hdr.NoOfKeys;
```

```
    Tree->Write(inspage);
    }

return BOOL_TRUE;
}

Boolean BTreeFile::PromoteRoot(const PageKey & inskey,
                              DataFilePtr dataptr,
                              PageFilePtr lesslnk,
                              PageFilePtr grtrlnk)
{
// create new root page
Page newroot(Root.Hdr.Order,Root.Hdr.KeySize);

// insert key into new root
newroot.Key[0] = inskey;
newroot.Ptr[0] = dataptr;

newroot.Lnk[0] = lesslnk;
newroot.Lnk[1] = grtrlnk;

newroot.Hdr.NoOfKeys = 1;

// write new root to tree file
Boolean result = Tree->Write(newroot,BOOL_TRUE);

// store pointer to new root
Tree->ReadRoot(Root);

return result;
}

void BTreeFile::RecurseTraverse(const Page & pg)
{
size_t n;
Page * p = new Page(pg.Hdr.Order,pg.Hdr.KeySize);
DataBlock * db = new DataBlock;

for (n = 0; n < pg.Hdr.NoOfKeys; ++n)
    {
    if (pg.Lnk[n] != PFP_NULL)
        {
        Tree->Read(pg.Lnk[n],*p);

        RecurseTraverse(*p);
        }

    Data->Seek(pg.Ptr[n]);
```

```
        *db = Data->Read();

        EnumFunc(pg.Key[n],*db);
        }

    if (pg.Lnk[n] != PFP_NULL)
        {
        Tree->Read(pg.Lnk[n],*p);

        RecurseTraverse(*p);
        }

    delete db;
    delete p;
    }

// create file name from base and extension
String BTreeFile::MakeFileName(const String & basename,
                               const String & ext)
    {
    String name;

    if (basename.Length() < 8)
        name = basename;
    else
        name = basename.CutHead(8);

    name += ext;

    return name;
    }
```

# Bibliography

Cormen, Thomas H., Charles E. Leiserson, and Ronald L. Rivest. *Introduction to Algorithms*. McGraw-Hill, 1990.

Ellis, Margaret A., and Bjarne Stroustrup. *The Annotated C++ Reference Manual*. Addison-Wesley, 1990.

Knuth, Donald E. *The Art of Computer Programming, Volume 1: Fundamental Algorithms, 2nd Edition*. Addison-Wesley, 1973.

————*The Art of Computer Programming, Volume 2: Seminumerical Algorithms, 2nd Edition*. Addison-Wesley, 1981.

———— *The Art of Computer Programming, Volume 3: Sorting and Searching*. Addison-Wesley, 1973.

Ladd, Scott Robert. *Turbo C++ Techniques and Applications*. M&T Books, 1990.

Pohl, Ira. *C++ for C Programmers*. Benjamin/Cummings, 1989.

Polk, Michael J., and Bill Zoellick. *File Structures: A Conceptual Toolkit*. Addison-Wesley, 1987.

Press, William A., Brian P. Flannery, Saul A. Teukolsky, and William T Vetterling. *Numerical Recipes in C: The Art of Scientific Computing*. Cambridge, 1988.

Sedgewick, Robert. *Algorithms in C*. Addison-Wesley, 1990.

Stroustrup, Bjarne. *The C++ Programming Language, 2nd Edition*. Addison-Wesley, 1991.

# Index

# A Library of Technical References
## from M&T Books

### Fractal Programming in C
### by Roger T. Stevens

If you are a programmer wanting to learn more about fractals, this book is for you. Learn how to create pictures that have both beauty and an underlying mathematical meaning. Included are over 50 black and white pictures and 32 full-color fractals. All source code to reproduce these pictures is provided on disk in MS-DOS format requiring an IBM PC or clone with an EGA or VGA card, a color monitor, and a Turbo C, Quick C, or Microsoft C compiler. 580 pp.

| | | |
|---|---|---|
| **Book/Disk (MS-DOS)** | **Item #038-9** | **$39.95** |
| **Book only** | **Item #037-0** | **$29.95** |

### Fractal Programming in Turbo Pascal
### by Roger T. Stevens

This book equips Turbo Pascal programmers with the tools needed to program dynamic fractal curves. It is a reference that gives full attention to developing the reader's understanding of various fractal curves. More than 100 black and white and 32 full-color fractals are illustrated throughout the book. All source code to reproduce the fractals is available on disk in MS/PC-DOS format. Requires a PC or clone with EGA or VGA, color monitor, and Turbo Pascal 4.0 or later. 462 pp.

| | | |
|---|---|---|
| **Book/Disk (MS-DOS)** | **Item #107-5** | **$39.95** |
| **Book** | **Item #106-7** | **$29.95** |

### Graphics Programming in C
### by Roger T. Stevens

All the information you need to program graphics in C, including source code, is presented. You'll find complete discussions of ROM BIOS, VGA, EGA, and CGA inherent capabilities; methods of displaying points on a screen; improved, faster algorithms for drawing and filling lines, rectangles, rounded polygons, ovals, circles, and arcs; graphic cursors; and much more! Both Turbo C and Microsoft C are supported. 639 pp.

| | | |
|---|---|---|
| **Book/Disk (MS-DOS)** | **Item #019-2** | **$36.95** |
| **Book only** | **Item #018-4** | **$26.95** |

**Available at bookstores everywhere or call**
**1-800-533-4372 (in CA 1-800-356-2002)**

# A Library of Technical References
from M&T Books

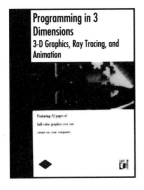

## Programming in 3 Dimensions
## 3-D Graphics, Ray Tracing, and Animation
## by Sandra Bloomberg

*Programming in 3 Dimensions* is a comprehensive, hands-on guide to computer graphics. It contains a detailed look at 3-D graphics plus discussions of popular ray tracing methods and computer animation. Readers will find techniques for creating 3-D graphics and breath-taking ray-traced images as, well as explanations of how animation works and ways computers help produce it more effectively. Packed with examples and C source code, this book is a must for all computer graphics enthusiasts! All source code is available on disk in MS/PC-DOS format. Includes 16 pages of full-color graphics.
500 pp. approx.

| | | |
|---|---|---|
| **Book/Disk (MS-DOS)** | Item #218-7 | $39.95 |
| **Book only** | Item #220-9 | $29.95 |

## Fractal Programming and Ray Tracing with C++
## by Roger T. Stevens

Finally, a book for C and C++ programmers who want to create complex and intriguing graphic designs. By the author of three best-selling graphics books, this new title thoroughly explains ray tracing, discussing how rays are traced, how objects are used to create ray-traced images, and how to create ray tracing programs. A complete ray tracing program, along with all of the source code, is included. Contains 16 pages of full-color graphics. 444 pp.

| | | |
|---|---|---|
| **Book/Disk (MS-DOS)** | Item 118-0 | $39.95 |
| **Book only** | Item 134-2 | $29.95 |

# A Library of Technical References
# from M&T Books

# A Library of Technical References from M&T Books

## Advanced Graphics Programming in C and C++
### by Roger T. Stevens and Christopher D. Watkins

This book is for all C and C++ programmers who want to create impressive graphic designs on their IBM PCs or compatibles. Through in-depth discussions and numerous sample programs, readers will learn how to create advanced 3-D shapes, wireframe graphics, solid images, and more. All source code is available on disk in MS/PC-DOS format. Contains 16 pages of full-color graphics. 500 pp. approx.

| | | |
|---|---|---|
| **Book/Disk (MS-DOS)** | **Item #173-3** | **$39.95** |
| **Book only** | **Item #171-7** | **$29.95** |

## Graphics Programming with Microsoft C 6
### by Mark Mallett

Written for all C programmers, this book explores graphics programming with Microsoft C 6.0, including full coverage of Microsoft C's built-in graphics libraries. Sample programs will help readers learn the techniques needed to create spectacular graphic designs, including 3-D figures, solid images, and more. All source code in the book is available on disk in MS/PC-DOS format. Includes 16 pages of full-color graphics. 500 pp. approx.

| | | |
|---|---|---|
| **Book/Disk (MS-DOS)** | **Item #167-9** | **$39.95** |
| **Book only** | **Item #165-2** | **$29.95** |

## The Verbum Book of PostScript Illustration
### by Michael Gosney, Linnea Dayton, and Janet Ashford

This is the premier instruction book for designers, illustrators, and desktop publishers using Postscript. Each chapter highlights the talents of top illustrators who demonstrate the electronic artmaking process. The narrative keys readers in to the artist's conceptual vision, providing valuable insight into the creative thought processes that go into a real-world PostScript illustration project. 213 pp.

| | | |
|---|---|---|
| **Book only** | **Item #089-3** | **$29.95** |

**Available at bookstores everywhere or call**
**1-800-533-4372 (in CA 1-800-356-2002)**

# A Library of Technical References
# from M&T Books

## The Verbum Book of Electronic Page Design
## by Michael Gosney and Linnea Dayton

This particular volume introduces designers, illustrators, and desktop publishers to the electronic page layout medium and various application programs, such as PageMaker, QuarkXPress, Design Studio, and Ventura Publishing. Each chapter highlights the talents of a top designer who guides readers through the thinking as well as the "mousing" that leads to the creation of various projects. These projects range in complexity from a trifold black and white brochure to a catalog produced with QuarkXPress. More than 100 illustrations, with 32 pages in full-color, are included. 211 pp.

**Book only**              **Item #088-5**              **$29.95**

## The Verbum Book of Digital Painting
## by Michael Gosney, Linnea Dayton, and Paul Goethel

Contained herein are a series of entertaining projects that teach readers how to create compelling designs using the myriad of graphics tools available in commercial painting programs. Presented by professional designers, these projects range from a simple greeting card to a complex street scene. This book also includes portfolios of paintings created by the featured artists, plus an extensive gallery of works from other accomplished artists and 64 pages of full-color paintings. 211 pp.

**Book only**              **Item #090-7**              **$29.95**

# A Library of Technical References
# from M&T Books

# A Library of Technical References from M&T Books

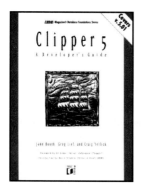

## Clipper 5: A Developer's Guide
## by Joseph D. Booth, Greg Lief, and Craig Yellick

An invaluable guide for all database programmers developing applications for Clipper® 5. Provides a quick introduction to Clipper 5 basics and discusses common programming needs such as designing data files, user interfaces, reports, and more. Advanced topics include networking, debugging, and pop-up programming. Code examples are used throughout the text, providing useful functions that can be applied immediately. All source code is available on disk in MS/PC-DOS format. 1300 pp. approx.

| | | |
|---|---|---|
| **Book & Disk (MS-DOS)** | **Item #242-X** | **$44.95** |
| **Book only** | **Item #240-3** | **$34.95** |

## DOS 5 User's Guide
## A Comprehensive Guide for Every PC User
## by Dan Gookin

Take control of the MS-DOS® operating system with this complete guide to using the world's most popular operating system. *DOS 5 User's Guide* contains clear, concise explanations of every feature, function, and command of DOS 5.0. Novice PC users will gain a quick start on using DOS, while advanced users will learn savvy tricks and techniques to maneuver their way quickly and easily through the system. Practical discussions and helpful examples teach readers how to edit text files, use directories, create batch files, and much more. Advanced topics include using EDLIN, the DOS text editor; configuring the system; and using the DOS shell. 771 pp.

| | | |
|---|---|---|
| **Book only** | **Item #188-1** | **$24.95** |

# A Library of Technical References
## from M&T Books

# ORDER FORM

**To Order:**

Return this form with your payment to M&T books, 501 Galveston Drive, Redwood City, CA 94063 or **call toll-free 1-800-533-4372 (in California, call 1-800-356-2002).**

| ITEM # | DESCRIPTION | DISK | PRICE |
|---|---|---|---|
|  |  |  |  |
|  |  |  |  |
|  |  |  |  |
|  |  |  |  |
|  |  |  |  |
|  |  |  |  |
|  |  |  |  |
|  |  |  |  |
|  |  |  |  |

Subtotal

CA residents add sales tax ____%

Add $3.75 per item for shipping and handling

TOTAL

NOTE: **FREE SHIPPING** ON ORDERS OF THREE OR MORE BOOKS.

**Charge my:**
- ❏ **Visa**
- ❏ **MasterCard**
- ❏ **AmExpress**

- ❏ **Check enclosed, payable to M&T Books.**

CARD NO. _____

SIGNATURE _____ EXP. DATE _____

NAME _____

ADDRESS _____

CITY _____

STATE _____ ZIP _____

**M&T GUARANTEE:** If your are not satisfied with your order for any reason, return it to us within 25 days of receipt for a full refund. Note: Refunds on disks apply only when returned with book within guarantee period. Disks damaged in transit or defective will be promptly replaced, but cannot be exchanged for a disk from a different title.

2276

**1-800-533-4372 (in CA 1-800-356-2002)**

## BUSINESS REPLY MAIL
FIRST CLASS MAIL  PERMIT NO. 1196  BOULDER, CO.

POSTAGE WILL BE PAID BY ADRESSEE

P.O. Box 56187
Boulder, CO 80321-6187

## BUSINESS REPLY MAIL
FIRST CLASS MAIL  PERMIT NO. 1202  BOULDER, CO.

POSTAGE WILL BE PAID BY ADRESSEE

P.O. Box 56623
Boulder, CO 80321-6623

# Tell us what you think and we'll send you a free M&T Books catalog

It is our goal at M&T Books to produce the best technical books available. But you can help us make our books even better by letting us know what you think about this particular title.Please take a moment to fill out this card and mail it to us. Your opinion is appreciated.

## Tell us about yourself

Name_____

Company_____

Address_____

City_____

State/Zip_____

## Title of this book?

_____

## Where did you purchase this book?

☐ Bookstore
☐ Catalog
☐ Direct Mail
☐ Magazine Ad
☐ Postcard Pack
☐ Other

## Why did you choose this book?

☐ Recommended
☐ Read book review
☐ Read ad/catalog copy
☐ Responded to a special offer
☐ M&T Books' reputation
☐ Price
☐ Nice Cover

## How would you rate the overall content of this book?

☐ Excellent
☐ Good
☐ Fair
☐ Poor

## Why?

_____

_____

## What chapters did you find valuable?

_____

_____

_____

## What did you find least useful?

_____

_____

_____

## What topic(s) would you add to future editions of this book?

_____

_____

_____

## What other titles would you like to see M&T Books publish?

_____

_____

_____

## Which format do you prefer for the optional disk?

☐ 5.25"        ☐ 3.5"

## Any other comments?

_____

_____

_____

☐ Check here for M&T Books Catalog

M&T BOOKS

2276